Transactions of the Royal Historical Society

SIXTH SERIES

XXIX

CAMBRIDGE
UNIVERSITY PRESS

Published by the Press Syndicate of the University of Cambridge
University Printing House, Shaftesbury Road, Cambridge CB2 8BS,
United Kingdom
One Liberty Plaza, Floor 20, New York, NY 10006, USA
477 Williamstown Road, Port Melbourne, VIC 3207, Australia
C/Orense, 4, Planta 13, 28020 Madrid, Spain
Lower Ground Floor, Nautica Building, The Water Club,
Beach Road, Granger Bay, 8005 Cape Town, South Africa

First published 2019

A catalogue record for this book is available from the British Library

ISBN 9781108490696 hardback

SUBSCRIPTIONS. The serial publications of the Royal Historical Society, *Royal Historical Society Transactions* (ISSN 0080-4401) and Camden Fifth Series (ISSN 0960-1163) volumes, may be purchased together on annual subscription. The 2019 subscription price, which includes print and electronic access (but not VAT), is £205 (US $342 in the USA, Canada, and Mexico) and includes Camden Fifth Series, volumes 56, 57, 58 and Transactions Sixth Series, volume 29 (published in December). The electronic-only price available to institutional subscribers is £172 (US $286 in the USA, Canada, and Mexico). Japanese prices are available from Kinokuniya Company Ltd, PO Box 55, Chitose, Tokyo 156, Japan. EU subscribers (outside the UK) who are not registered for VAT should add VAT at their country's rate. VAT registered subscribers should provide their VAT registration number. Prices include delivery by air.

Subscription orders, which must be accompanied by payment, may be sent to a bookseller, subscription agent, or direct to the publisher: Cambridge University Press, University Printing House, Shaftesbury Road, Cambridge CB2 8BS, UK; or in the USA, Canada, and Mexico: Cambridge University Press, Journals Fulfillment Department, One Liberty Plaza, Floor 20, New York, NY 10006, USA.

SINGLE VOLUMES AND BACK VOLUMES. A list of Royal Historical Society volumes available from Cambridge University Press may be obtained from the Humanities Marketing Department at the address above.

Printed in the UK by Bell & Bain Ltd, Glasgow

CONTENTS

Transactions of the RHS 29 (2019), pp. 1–25 © Royal Historical Society 2019
doi:10.1017/S008044011900001X

TRANSACTIONS OF THE
ROYAL HISTORICAL SOCIETY
PRESIDENTIAL ADDRESS

By Margot C. Finn

MATERIAL TURNS IN BRITISH HISTORY: II. CORRUPTION: IMPERIAL POWER, PRINCELY POLITICS AND GIFTS GONE ROGUE

READ 23 NOVEMBER 2018

ABSTRACT. This address examines the 'Old Corruption' of Georgian Britain from the perspective of diplomacy and material culture in Delhi in the era of the East India Company. Its focus is the scandal that surrounded the sacking of Sir Edward Colebrooke, the Delhi Resident, during the reign of the penultimate Mughal emperor, Akbar II. Exploring the gendered, highly sexualised material politics of Company diplomacy in north India reveals narratives of agency, negotiation and commensurability that interpretations focused on liberal, Anglicist ideologies obscure. Dynastic politics were integral to both British and Indian elites in the nineteenth century. The Colebrooke scandal illuminates both the tenacity and the dynamic evolution of the family as a base of power in the context of nineteenth-century British imperialism.

In December 1828, a twenty-one-year-old East India Company civil servant, Charles Trevelyan, wrote from Delhi to his mother in England. Trevelyan's letter detailed the steps he had taken to source a pair of Kashmiri shawls intended to serve as gifts back home in Britain.

> When my order for the black shawls ... reached Col[onel] Skinner's agents in Cashmere he forwarded at once to Delhi some shawls of that description which he happened to have by him and as I should have had to wait at least eight months for a fresh supply which after all might not have been handsomer than these are, I have chosen out the two best for yourself & Mrs Halliday & shall send them to you without delay.

Trevelyan reported with evident satisfaction that 'Both the shawls are of the handsomest description procurable in this country & indeed such costly ones are seldom made ... except they are expressly ordered.'[1] His estimate of the time taken to produce Kashmiri shawls was optimistic: woven painstakingly by hand, these material luxuries typically took

---

[1] Charles Trevelyan to Harriet Trevelyan, 18 December 1828, Newcastle University Special Collections (henceforth NUSC), CET 3/12.

well over a year to complete.[2] In precolonial and colonial Mughal princely courts, gifted shawls played vital roles in the production of hierarchical power relations.[3] Shawls were, unsurprisingly, in high demand in Britain among the families of the East India Company, where they circulated as gifts in a complex British patronage market from the later eighteenth century to the early Victorian era.[4] Strategic gifting of Indian luxury goods by the mothers of East India Company civil servants to women who owned Company stock (or were married to influential Company men) was a well-established political and material practice by the 1820s.[5] The fourth of nine children born to genteel but impecunious parents, Charles Trevelyan had connections to East Indian wealth through his mother, Harriet – a daughter of the London merchant, Caribbean plantation- and slave-owner and governor of the Bank of England, Sir Richard Neave.[6] With needy younger brothers in England eager for appointment to the Company service, Trevelyan repeatedly urged his mother to cultivate his 'interest' on their behalf, promising to despatch Indian shawls and 'curiosities' from Delhi as gifts to advance this collective goal.[7]

Charles Trevelyan's letters to his mother from 1828 to 1830 underscored the quality of the items he was sending home, highlighting his immersion in connoisseurial networks that gave him privileged access to the finest Indian luxury goods. The Colonel Skinner from whom Trevelyan had obtained his shawls was James Skinner, a famed military strategist of dual Scottish and Rajput heritage who was also a noted

[2] A fine example dating from the early nineteenth century is preserved in the Victoria and Albert Museum (IS.766A-1883) and can be viewed at http://collections.vam.ac.uk/item/O77019/shawl-unknown/. The accompanying description notes that weaving a large shawl took 'anything from eighteen months to three years to complete'.

[3] Frank Ames, *Woven Masterpieces of Sikh Heritage: The Stylistic Development of the Kashmir Shawl under Maharaja Ranjit Singh 1780–1839* (2010), underscores the shawls' role in royal politics in this era; see more broadly Steven Cohen, Rosemary Crill, Monique Lévi-Strauss and Jeffrey B. Spurr, *Kashmir Shawls: The Tapi Collection* (Surat, 2012).

[4] Michelle Maskiell, 'Consuming Kashmir: Shawls and Empires, 1500–2000', *Journal of World History*, 13 (2002), 35–40; Chitralekha Zutshi, '"Designed for eternity": Kashmiri Shawls, Empire, and Cultures of Production and Consumption in Mid-Victorian Britain', *Journal of British Studies*, 48 (2009), esp. 422–4.

[5] Margot C. Finn, 'Colonial Gifts: Family Politics and the Exchange of Goods in British India, c. 1780–1820', *Modern Asian Studies*, 40 (2006), esp. 204–6, 222.

[6] For the Trevelyans, see Laura Trevelyan, *A Very British Family: The Trevelyans and Their World* (2006). Neave's East India Company connections are noted by Katherine Prior, Lance Brennan and Robin Haines, 'Bad Language: The Role of English, Persian and Other Esoteric Tongues in the Dismissal of Sir Edward Colebrooke as Resident of Delhi in 1829', *Modern Asian Studies*, 35 (2001), 77.

[7] See for example Charles Trevelyan to Harriet Trevelyan, 20 September 1828, NUSC, CET 3/8; Charles Trevelyan to Harriet Trevelyan, 18 December 1828, NUSC, CET 3/12.

patron of north Indian artists and Persian scholarship.[8] At Delhi, Trevelyan and Skinner moved in a trans-imperial world in which warfare, diplomacy, patronage, sociability and the exchange of material objects operated in concert.[9] Vibrant and cross-cultural, imperial politics in late Mughal Delhi and its hinterland linked Indian elites to propertied British families on the subcontinent and in Europe through warfare, courtly politics and material culture. Imbued with emotion, power and artistry, gifted goods operated at multiple social and political levels in this dynamic context – marking hierarchies, eliciting actions and sealing agreements. However, both the contentious imperial context in which these gift exchanges took place and their complexity of function fostered opacity, misunderstanding and mutual recrimination. We scent a whiff of the difficulties that entangled gifted Indian material goods from a later letter Trevelyan, in some embarrassment, despatched to his mother about his Kashmiri shawls. Eighteen months after his original correspondence, he reported that he had sent her new shawls on the ship the *Lord Amherst*, having come to understand that his initial gifts were insufficiently fine. 'The pair of shawls I have now sent you are really handsome and worthy of you and of the affections I bear for you,' he explained. Specially commissioned from Kashmir, they must replace the inferior previous pair, items he now judged were better suited for his mother's housekeeper, 'poor Harrison' as he called her.[10]

Although he did not mention it in this letter, the two new shawls were not the only cargo carried by the *Lord Amherst* from Bengal to Britain at Trevelyan's behest. For among this vessel's passengers were Sir Edward and Lady Colebrooke, sailing home to England against their will. At Trevelyan's instigation in July 1829, the governor general of India, Lord William Bentinck, had suspended Sir Edward from his office as the Resident, or East India Company diplomatic agent, at the court of the king of Delhi. In the ensuing weeks and months, two senior civil servants examined tens of witnesses and pored over thousands of pages of evidence in Delhi. Their task was to determine whether Sir Edward Colebrooke – aided and abetted by Lady Colebrooke, his illegitimate son Edward and his Indian servants – had embezzled vast sums from

[8] For Skinner's military expertise, see Seema Alavi, 'The Makings of Company Power: James Skinner and the Ceded and Conquered Provinces, 1802–1840', in *Warfare and Weaponry in South Asia 1000–1800*, ed. Jos Gommans and D. H. A. Kolff (New Delhi, 2001), 275–308. His entanglement in north Indian artistic and manuscript cultures is detailed in *Princes and Painters in Mughal Delhi, 1707–1857*, ed. William Dalrymple and Yuthika Sharma (New Haven, 2012), esp. 35–8, 43–6.

[9] Mildred Archer and Toby Falk, *India Revealed: Art and Adventures of James and William Fraser, 1815–26* (1989); *Princes and Painters*, ed. Dalrymple and Sharma; Susan Stronge, *Made for Mughal Emperors: Royal Treasures from Hindustan* (2010).

[10] Charles Trevelyan to Harriet Trevelyan, 16 June 1830, NUSC, CET 3/14.

the Company, conducted illicit diplomatic negotiations with nearby Indian states, borrowed money from litigants in a court over which he presided, profited from the private sale of public property and exchanged a plenitude of luxury goods with local Indian princes. In December 1829, following a damning report by the investigators, Bentinck had sacked Colebrooke for corruption.[11]

Aged sixty-seven and with forty years in the Company's service to his credit, Colebrooke was the scion of family with deep links to empire. His father had been both a substantial owner of East India Company stock and an influential chairman of its board of directors; over twenty of Sir Edward's uncles, cousins and nephews had served, or were later to serve, as officers in the Company's armies or in its civil service.[12] His younger brother, H. T. Colebrooke, boasted a distinguished career in the Bengal civil service and retains his reputation as a premier scholar of Oriental law and Sanskrit literature.[13] A bust of H. T. Colebrooke now guards the entrance to the East India Company archive at the British Library; another is prominently displayed at the Royal Asiatic Society, of which he was the founding director. Nested securely within the familial patronage networks that made empire in India both feasible and functional, Sir Edward Colebrooke was nonetheless ousted swiftly and unceremoniously from the Delhi Residency in 1829, at the instance of a twenty-two-year-old upstart with scant administrative experience, abrasive manners and few influential connections in India.[14] In this lecture, I ask what the evidence thrown up by the investigation of Colebrooke for corruption can tell us about the play of imperial power and princely politics as British rule extended from Calcutta, Madras and Bombay to north India. In keeping with the rubric of my four presidential addresses, 'Material Turns in British History', I do so by exploring the narratives that emerge if we attend not only to the world of words, texts and ideologies but also to the material objects that animated cross-cultural diplomacy and imperial rule both in Europe and in Asia. The dominant interpretations of East India Company power in this period focus on discourses of British individualism and Western difference.

[11] The most comprehensive analysis of this scandal is Prior, Brennan and Haines, 'Bad Language'.

[12] Malcolm Sutherland, *Sola Bona Quae Honesta: The Colebrooke Family 1650–1950* (Maidstone, 1998), 23–7, 31–3, 35–48.

[13] Ludo Rocher and Rosane Rocher, *The Making of Western Indology: Henry Thomas Colebrooke and the East India Company* (2012).

[14] His close friend and future brother-in-law, Thomas Babington Macaulay, commented of Trevelyan: 'He is rash and uncompromising in public matters ... His manners are odd, – blunt almost to roughness at times, and at other times awkward even to sheepishness.' Macaulay to Mrs Edward Cropper, 7 December 1834, in *The Letters of Thomas Babington Macaulay: Volume III January 1834–August 1841*, ed. Thomas Pinney (Cambridge, 1976), 101.

Inserting 'things' into interpretative traditions hitherto dominated by language instead reveals common material ground that united (some) British and Indian governing elites. In doing so, it illuminates a contested but shared cultural domain rooted in dynastic forms of politics too often discounted in accounts of empire framed by the concept of 'liberal imperialism'.[15]

I

The Colebrooke saga lends itself readily to two established traditions within British historiography, each of which highlights the triumph of liberal ideologies in imperial contexts. First, we can easily narrate Sir Edward's fall from grace at Delhi by integrating his story into received histories of the rise and fall of political corruption in Georgian Britain. His sacking occurred on the cusp of the 1830s, the decade that historians conventionally see marking a turning point away from so-called 'Old Corruption', the agglomeration of aristocratic privileges identified by radicals and reformers since the 1770s as a fundamental threat to Britain's historic birthright of liberty. Predicated on denunciation of the undemocratic parliamentary franchise, the critique of Old Corruption also attacked the government's ability to purchase supporters and to gain the acquiescence of political adversaries by distributing patronage and pensions.[16] Fiscal and administrative reforms inaugurated by William Pitt in the 1790s, together with legislation that culminated in the expanded franchise of 1832, many historians argue, effectively defanged Old Corruption as a focus of political critique in Britain in the 1830s even as it secured 'the persistence of élite political power well into the Victorian era'.[17] Located within this interpretative paradigm, Colebrooke's removal from Delhi marks a broader nineteenth-century liberal transition away from aristocratic corruption toward a new landscape of democratic and meritocratic politics – a 'revolution

---

[15] Uday Singh Mehta, *Liberalism and Empire: A Study in Nineteenth-Century British Liberal Thought* (Chicago, 1999), offers the most comprehensive analysis of liberal imperialism in the Company era. For a critique of liberal imperialism as an explanatory framework, see Andrew Sartori, 'The British Empire and Its Liberal Mission', *Journal of Modern History*, 78 (2006), 623–42. Sartori suggests the need 'to embed the conceptual structure of liberal thought in the sociohistorical contexts of its articulation' (624), an approach adopted here by focusing on material histories.

[16] W. D. Rubinstein, 'The End of "Old Corruption" in Britain 1780–1860', *Past & Present*, 101 (1983), 55–86, and Philip Harling, 'Rethinking "Old Corruption"', *Past & Present*, 147 (1995), 127–58, anatomise the operation of Old Corruption in Georgian Britain.

[17] Philip Harling, *The Waning of 'Old Corruption': The Politics of Economical Reform in Britain, 1779–1846* (Oxford, 1996), 5. For the wider context of this transformation, see *Rethinking the Age of Reform: Britain 1780–1850*, ed. Arthur Burns and Joanna Innes (Cambridge, 2003).

in government' of which Charles Trevelyan was to become both a key instigator and a key icon.[18] Empire was an essential dimension of the nexus of Old Corruption in Britain. From the 1770s, domestic criticism of the British state and its governing elites escalated as imperial wars placed new burdens on un-enfranchised consumers and taxpayers.[19] That the East India Company's political structures and economic relations were fundamentally corrupt was a commonplace of eighteenth-century British politics. 'Scandal was the crucible in which both imperial and capitalist expansion was forged,' Nicholas Dirks has observed.[20] Gift-giving by and to Indian princely elites was a vital cog in the wheels of this scandalously corrupt system. The emergence of the British as kingmakers in India as the hegemony of the Mughal empire waned rested both on military victory and on the widespread exchange of diplomatic gifts, *douceurs* and bribes. Robert Clive's installation of Mir Jafar as nawab of Bengal after the battle of Plassey in 1757 was accomplished by this Indian prince's distribution of presents reputedly valued at over £1.2 million (perhaps £123 million in present-day purchasing power). The notoriety of Clive's subsequent acceptance of a *jaghir* or land grant from the nawab worth £27,000 per annum (roughly £2.8 million a year today) and Clive's aggressive investment of this Indian fortune in securing votes in both East India Company and parliamentary elections ensured that by the second half of the eighteenth century gifts from Indian princes to East India Company officials epitomised the endemic corruption of politics on the subcontinent and its threat to British liberties at home.[21] In British caricatures, plays, works of fiction and

---

[18] In the 1840s Trevelyan was to administer famine relief in Ireland on the increasingly ascendant principles of liberal laissez-faire; in the 1850s, he instigated and oversaw reform of the British civil service, inaugurating competitive examinations designed to displace established aristocratic elites. For the former, see Robin Haines, *Charles Trevelyan and the Great Irish Famine* (Dublin, 2004); for the latter, Oliver MacDonagh, 'The Nineteenth-Century Revolution in Government: A Reappraisal', *Historical Journal*, 1 (1958), esp. 53, 63–5, and *Studies in the Growth of Nineteenth-Century Government*, ed. Gillian Sutherland (1972).

[19] Paul Seaward, 'Sleaze, Old Corruption and Parliamentary Reform: An Historical Perspective on the Current Crisis', *Political Quarterly*, 81 (2010), 42–3.

[20] Nicholas Dirks, *The Scandal of Empire: India and the Creation of Imperial Britain* (Cambridge, MA, 2006), 8. Anna Clark and Aaron Windel trace the halting transition from this corrupt patronage system to liberal imperialism in their 'The Early Roots of Liberal Imperialism: "The science of a legislator" in Eighteenth-Century India', *Journal of Colonialism and Colonial History*, 14 (2013).

[21] Dirks, *Scandal*, 43–7; H. V. Bowen, 'Clive, Robert, First Baron Clive of Plassey (1725–1774)', *Oxford Dictionary of National Biography* (Oxford, 2004); Bruce Lenman and Philip Lawson, 'Robert Clive, the "Black Jagir", and British Politics', *Historical Journal*, 26 (1983), 801–29, esp. 812. Monetary conversions calculated by comparing 1760 to 2017: http://www.nationalarchives.gov.uk/currency-converter/.

parliamentary debates, orientalised visions of Old Corruption clothed in the fabrics of India signalled both an empire and a gift regime notoriously run rogue.[22] Parliamentary legislation sought to clamp down on this abuse in 1773 and 1784.[23] Within this domestic British political context, Sir Edward Colebrooke's sacking acquires an air of seeming inevitability, standing as the last gasp of an anachronistic system of trans-imperial privilege and corruption destined to give way to modern liberal bureaucracy.

A second historiographical tradition instead interprets the scandal of empire in late Mughal Delhi as a generational shift between so-called 'Orientalist' and 'Anglicist' British governing elites in India. In this analysis, Colebrooke again figures as an anachronism, out of step with the march of liberal modernity, not only because of his association with Old Corruption at home but because his education in India had made him sympathetic to 'Oriental' languages, cultures and princely despotism. Colebrooke was heir to a bankrupt baronet with landed estates in England, Scotland, the Caribbean and North America; his patrimony included sinecures awarded to his male relations for loyal government service, family control of a Tory rotten borough in Surrey and the direct patronage of Warren Hastings – the East India Company governor most notorious for corruption after Clive.[24] Having left school for the subcontinent aged fifteen, Colebrooke studied Indian languages and imbibed Persianate political cultures, acquiring his diplomatic expertise in negotiations with wealthy princes and magnates at the imperial coalface of Bengal revenue and judicial administration. His antagonist, Charles Trevelyan, had City connections with Colebrooke's family through his mother's family; both men's mothers had brought their husbands Caribbean estates on marriage.[25] In socioeconomic background, the two adversaries arguably shared much in common. But Trevelyan's intellectual formation was of a very different order, reflecting the early nineteenth-century turn from Orientalist to Anglicist sympathies within the East India Company's governing elite. Trevelyan's schooling took him from Charterhouse to the Company's administrative college, Haileybury, where Thomas Malthus inspired a

---

[22] Finbarr Barry Flood, 'Correct Delineations and Promiscuous Outlines: Envisioning India at the Trial of Warren Hastings', *Art History*, 21 (2006), 47–78; Tillman Nechtman, 'A Jewel in the Crown? Indian Wealth in Domestic Britain in the Late Eighteenth Century', *Eighteenth-Century Studies*, 41 (2007), 71–86, and idem, *Nabobs: Empire and Identity in Eighteenth-Century Britain* (Cambridge, 2010).

[23] H. V. Bowen, *The Business of Empire: The East India Company and Imperial Britain, 1765–1833* (Cambridge, 2005), ch. 3.

[24] Sutherland, *Sola Bona Quae Honesta*, 20, 24–31.

[25] Prior, Brennan and Haines, 'Bad Language', 77–8; Sutherland, *Sola Bona Quae Honesta*, 33.

new generation of Indian civil servants during his tenure as professor of history and political economy.[26] A Whig by disposition, Trevelyan adopted a hard line in debates that saw younger civil servants in India argue for the Anglicisation, and eventual democratisation, of British rule. Among his pet schemes was a plan not only to replace Persian with English as the language of British statecraft in India, but also to Anglicise regional Indian languages by converting their scripts to Roman characters.[27] It was with pamphlets devoted to schemes such as these that Trevelyan wooed and wed Hannah Macaulay – the sister of the Whig historian Thomas Babington Macaulay – in Calcutta early in the 1830s.[28] Viewed against this backdrop, Sir Edward Colebrooke's disgrace by Charles Trevelyan figures as a logical consequence of the Anglicist triumph over Orientalists within the East India Company's governing elite – a path-determined outcome predicated on discourse that was predestined by the changing intellectual tides of British imperial thought.[29]

My focus on material culture affords a third vantage point for interpreting Colebrooke and Trevelyan's contest. Without rejecting the significance of either the waning of Old Corruption in Britain or the rise of Anglicist administrative ideologies in India, I suggest that we also attend more carefully to the political histories of material goods deployed in cross-cultural diplomatic contexts. As Mark Knights has argued, the chronology of Old Corruption's decline at home in Britain diverged significantly from its colonial trajectory: 'corruption in the imperial sphere persisted, and indeed arguably increased in the nineteenth century, with colonialism itself a form of state-sponsored corruption that systematically exploited imperial assets'.[30] Diplomatic gifting was a vital crucible in which colonial 'corruption' persisted and developed. By surfacing, tracing and contextualising narratives of corrupt gifted and purchased shawls, jewels, ceremonial robes, bedsteads and

---

[26] Trevelyan, *A Very British Family*, 25.

[27] Charles Trevelyan, J. Prinsep, A. D. Tytler and H. T. Prinsep, *The Application of the Roman Alphabet to All the Oriental Languages, Contained in a Series of Papers* ([Calcutta], 1834); *The Great Indian Education Debate: Documents Relating to the Orientalist–Anglicist Controversy, 1781–1843*, ed. Lynn Zastoupil and Martin Moir (Richmond, 1999).

[28] Thomas Babington Macaulay to Mrs Edward Cropper, 7 December 1834, in *Letters*, ed. Pinney, 102. The marriage afforded social cement for Macaulay and Trevelyan's intellectual and political commitment to the Anglicist camp. See esp. Catherine Hall, *Macaulay and Son: Architects of Imperial Britain* (New Haven, 2012), ch. 3.

[29] As Prior, Brennan and Haines, 'Bad Language', 105, argue, the scandal's 'elements of generational conflict were … stark – virtually a parody of the coming battle between the young Anglicists and the old Orientalists'.

[30] Mark Knights, 'Anticorruption in Seventeenth- and Eighteenth-Century Britain', in *Anticorruption in History: From Antiquity to the Modern Era*, ed. Ronald Kroeze, André Vitória and G. Geltner (Oxford, 2018), 182.

elephants, we can discern new voices within this underlying continuity. Object stories capture the intransigence and agency of interlocutors lost to us when we focus only on dominant British political and intellectual traditions. For the traffic in material goods that formed a central part of Trevelyan's charge of corruption against Colebrooke can only be understood if we take cognisance of the beliefs and behaviours of Indian princes – both male and female – and of the problematic presence on the subcontinent in the late Georgian era of East India Company women. I focus here on only two of the many available strands of material culture politics woven into these histories. First is the exchange of robes of honour at the court of the king of Delhi, and second, Lady Colebrooke's elaboration of a material style of diplomacy – including, but also stretching far beyond, gifted robes of honour – newly accessible to Company women. Neither activity sits entirely comfortably within the narrative of the demise of Old Corruption or the rise of Anglicisation because neither was predicated on 'liberal' tenets. Instead, the material politics of Colebrooke's downfall suggest the tenacity of dynastic, family-focused political conflict in the face of liberal imperialism – not least among zealous liberal reformers themselves.

II

Depicted in countless Mughal-era *durbar* paintings, Indian royal courts were prime sites of diplomatic gift exchange.[31] A precolonial practice with ancient and medieval roots extending across Eurasia from China to Iceland, the gifting of garments conferred at investiture ceremonies (to mark changes of status and to incorporate new diplomatic allies) bound princely donors to subordinate recipients through both the human body and material goods. Given by the prince's hand, taken from the prince's person, placed on or around the head, neck, shoulders, torso, arms and legs of the supplicant, robes of honour simultaneously constrained, distinguished and hierarchically ordered donor and recipient.[32] In the Mughal empire's iteration of this pervasive, cross-cultural gifting protocol, the simplest version of the robe of honour or *khil'at* (pl. *khila*) consisted of three items of clothing: a *dastar* (turban), a *jama* (long coat) and a *kamarband* (long scarf). Five- and seven-item ensembles for higher-status recipients included additional items such as turban ornaments, trousers, shawls and girdles. The use of Chinese silks,

---

[31] *Gifts of the Sultan: The Arts of Giving in Islamic Courts*, ed. Linda Komaroff (Los Angeles, 2011).

[32] *Robes of Honour: Khil'at in Pre-colonial and Colonial India*, ed. Stewart Gordon (Oxford, 2003), and *Robes and Honor: The Medieval World of Investiture*, ed. Stewart Gordon (New York, 2001).

velvets, brocades, gold-threaded fabrics and textiles embellished with jewels registered increasingly higher levels of status, which could be further augmented by gifts of jewellery, swords, horses, harnesses, howdahs and elephants.[33] In return for receiving ceremonial robes and their associated honour, the supplicant gave the prince a *nazr*, a financial offering in the coin of the ruler's realm. *Peshkash*, valuables that included fine textiles, precious stones, horses or elephants, often accompanied *nazr* payments to princes.[34] The conferring of *khila* by the Mughal emperor represented the apex of a pervasive system of honorific exchange that was replicated, with regional distinctions, throughout the Maratha, Rajput, Sikh and Deccani successor states that established an uneasy and partial independence from Delhi – seat of the royal family – in the eighteenth and early nineteenth centuries.

Colonialism complicated the presentation of *khila*. In Bernard Cohn's influential analysis, the first half of the nineteenth century was marked by a conflict between an 'indigenous theory of rulership in India' and British ideologies of rule based instead on contract, which equated princely gifting with corruption.[35] Yet we should be wary of 'indigeneity' as a concept. As Balkrishan Shivram has observed, South Asian robing cere-monies were the product of centuries of syncretic cross-cultural fusion. In precolonial India, Mughal ceremonial 'reflected an amalgam of Persian, Turkish, Central Asian, Indian, and specifically dynastic traditions'.[36] Already hybrid, 'indigenous' Indian diplomatic gifting was, moreover, integrated into wider circuits of exchange between South Asian and European princes, states and diplomatic representatives that dated from the sixteenth century. Working at the intersection between material culture studies and the 'new diplomatic history', Zoltán Biedermann, Anne Gerritsen and Giorgio Riello have argued that early modern gifts exchanged between Asian and European princes and states 'were key agents of social cohesion and transcultural systems of value in the emergence of a global political community'.[37] Serving as 'social glue' in an 'open-ended, fast-evolving system' of war, invasion and trade, they argue, these 'global gifts afford us a glimpse

[33] Balkrishan Shivram, 'From Court Dress to the Symbol of Authority: Robing and "Robes of Honour" in Pre-colonial India', 6: http://iias.ac.in/sites/default/files/article/Balkrishan%20Shivram.pdf.
[34] Bernard S. Cohn, 'Representing Authority in Victorian India', in *The Invention of Tradition*, ed. E. J. Hobsbawm and T. O. Ranger (Cambridge, 2012), 168.
[35] *Ibid.*, 171.
[36] Shivram, 'From Court Dress', 4–5.
[37] Zoltán Biedermann, Anne Gerritson and Giorgio Riello, 'Introduction: Global Gifts and the Material Culture of Diplomacy in Early Modern Eurasia', in *Global Gifts: The Material Culture of Diplomacy in Early Modern Eurasia*, ed. Zoltán Biedermann, Anne Gerritson and Giorgio Riello (Cambridge, 2018), 1.

into the "commensurability" of shared diplomatic practices across large parts of Eurasia'.[38] As the East India Company's military treaties with the Mughal emperor and with lesser rajas, sultans and nawabs proliferated, their attendance at royal courts or *durbars* became increasingly visible. Ornate, conspicuous and conferred in public, gifts received from Indian princes were material signs at once of British subservience and of Company corruption. Efforts to bar Company men from accepting gifts from Indians date from the same period as British reformers' attempts to bring Old Corruption to heel at home. The Regulating Act of 1773 prohibited Company employees from accepting gifts from Indian princes of the sort made notorious by Robert Clive; Pitt's India Act of 1784 extended these prohibitions further.[39] From the time of Marquess Cornwallis's governorship of 1786–93, both Company servants and their dependants, whilst allowed to accept Indian gifts at public princely ceremonies, were required to deposit them immediately thereafter in the Company's local *toshkhana* (or treasury). Here they were available for individuals to purchase at a price set by an auctioneer, cleansed of their taint of corruption through a market transaction, whilst conveniently swelling the Company's coffers.[40]

Diplomatic gifting thus straddled a labile and opaque boundary between licit and illicit exchange. Formally prohibited from retaining or profiting privately from gifts offered to them by 'native' princes, Company men were nonetheless repeatedly seen, heard and recorded publicly accepting these gifts at the hands of Indian elites. As the British extended their territorial control from Bengal to south India, the Deccan and (in 1803) Delhi and its hinterland, moreover, they initiated their own gift-giving rituals to strengthen their fragile military grip with symbolic power. The Company's highest officials – the governor general, the commander-in-chief and the Residents or diplomatic agents at princely courts such as Delhi – now took to conferring *khila* on Indian rulers and notables, as a visual and material statement of waxing British power on the subcontinent.[41] By the 1800s, high-ranking British officials were thus both givers and receivers of *nazr*, both donors and recipients of *khila*. Running directly counter to the intentions of the Regulating Act, Pitt's India Act and Cornwallis's reforms (which had sought to contain and ultimately suppress gifting regimes), the increasing

[38] *Ibid.*, 24.
[39] Prior, Brennan and Haines, 'Bad Language', 80; Natasha Eaton, 'Between Mimesis and Alterity: Art, Gift, and Diplomacy in Colonial India, 1770–1800', *Comparative Studies in Society and History*, 46 (2004), 819–20.
[40] Cohn, 'Representing Authority', 172.
[41] *Ibid.*, 171–2.

prominence of Company officials as givers of Indian princely presents caused mounting disquiet in the upper reaches of the Company administration.

North India in the early nineteenth century was a hotbed of political intrigue, not only between the East India Company and the Mughal emperor (whom the British insisted on denominating merely the king of Delhi), but also within the royal family, between the emperor and the princes who ruled over the sixty-ish successor states in Delhi's political ambit and between the Company and these many rulers.[42] Akbar II (r. 1806–37), the penultimate Mughal emperor, is conventionally described as a political cipher. 'The Mughal emperor, recognised by the British as the King of Delhi, retained nominal power, but he was in actuality a British pensioner, eking out a tawdry, tinselled existence in the diminished splendour of the Red Fort,' Katherine Prior, Lance Brennan and Robin Haines (for example) argue.[43] William Dalrymple and Yuthika Sharma have, however, modified this overwhelmingly pessimistic assessment, highlighting the emperor's continued symbolic power, and the use by successive 'kings' of Delhi of artistic patronage to shore up their ceremonial status.[44]

Scrutiny of the Company's diplomatic correspondence and gift-giving practices in the decades immediately before Sir Edward Colebrooke's appointment as the Delhi Resident further reinforces this image of Akbar II as a man of considerable political ambition and nous. For, notwithstanding their insistent belittlement of him, the acts and claims of the king of Delhi necessarily mattered to the British. As Akbar insistently reminded them, the Company's territorial presence, revenue functions and judicial legitimacy in India ultimately derived from Clive's treaty of 1765 with his ancestor, Emperor Shah Allam II (r. 1760–1806). In return for the right to administer Bengal, the Company had agreed to pay Shah Allam twenty-six lacs of rupees per annum. It suspended this payment in 1772, after the emperor, in the words of one Company memo, had 'thrown himself into the hands of the Mahrattas', and thereby 'withdrawn himself from the Company's protection, and abandoned the Countries assigned to him'.[45] British victories in the Second Anglo-Maratha War had, however, brought the emperor back into the

[42] K. N. Panikkar, *British Diplomacy in North India: A Study in the Delhi Residency, 1803–57* (Delhi, 1968).

[43] Prior, Brennan and Haines, 'Bad Language', 78.

[44] *Princes and Painters*, ed. Dalrymple and Sharma; Yuthika Sharma, 'Mughal Delhi on My Lapel: The Charmed Life of the Painted Ivory Miniature in Delhi, 1827–1880', in *Commodities and Culture in the Colonial World*, ed. Supriya Chaudhuri, Josephine McDonagh, Brian H. Murray and Rajeswari Sunder Rajan (2017), 15–31.

[45] Chairman to Mr Grant, 24 October 1831, British Library (henceforth BL), IOR/H/708/Part 1, f. 50.

British fold in 1803, with Sir David Ochterlony appointed as the first of the Company's diplomatic Residents at Delhi. In heritage, sociability, cultural attributes and political behaviour, Ochterlony embodied trans-imperial hybridity. English and Welsh on his mother's side, a Scot by his paternal line, he was born in Boston, Massachusetts, and served in the Bengal army from 1777. Rumoured to have multiple Indian *bibis* or concubines, he took as his favourite companion or wife a Hindu dancing girl known to the British (after her conversion to Islam) as Mubaruck ul Nissa Begum.[46] Their country house, north of Delhi, was Mubaruck Bagh (or 'happy garden').[47] Here and in Delhi at the official Residency, Ochterlony laid the groundwork for diplomatic conventions and gifting regimes that his successors would elaborate, in dialogue and collusion with, as well as in opposition to, the successive kings of Delhi and rulers of lesser princely states.

The return of the Mughal emperor to British protection saw the Company, the king of Delhi and the plethora of princes who ruled over north Indian successor states elaborate a congeries of mutual but unequal diplomatic ceremonies. The arrival in Delhi of a new Resident or of the British commander-in-chief was, for most of Akbar II's reign, marked by the conferral of a *khil'at* to the senior British officer – and to many of his subordinates – by the king, seated on the Peacock Throne at his *durbar*. In return, British military officers and civil officials offered multiple *nazrs* and *peshkash* to the Mughal potentate. This ceremony was followed, typically on the next day, by counter-visits from the king and/or his sons to the British Residency. Ochterlony spent lavishly on the palatial structure and furnishing of the Residency, where the Resident in turn conferred gifts upon the male representatives of the royal family.[48] These episodic rituals were augmented throughout the year by visits to the Red Fort on seven annual Muslim festival days, on which the Resident by agreement again presented *nazr* to the king. Vast processions through the streets of Delhi accompanied these ceremonies. Many rulers of north Indian successor states attended these royal *durbars* or sent their diplomatic envoys to them; in their own courts, they too elaborated reciprocal ceremonials that enmeshed the British in elaborate gift-giving.[49]

[46] A. P. Coleman, 'Ochterlony, Sir David, First Baronet (1758–1825)', *Oxford Dictionary of National Biography* (Oxford, 2004).

[47] For an image and brief history of this country house, see www.bl.uk/onlinegallery/onlineex/apac/addorimss/t/019addor0005475u00067vrb.html.

[48] David Ochterlony to Charles Metcalfe, 2 April 1820, BL, IOR/H/Misc/738, f. 773.

[49] *Princes and Painters*, ed. Dalrymple and Sharma, provides the most detailed analysis of these visits and their visual and material culture.

The rich visual and material record of these events conveys their scale, splendour and importance, and reflects the time, money and strategic thinking Akbar II expended on projecting his image as a powerful emperor. Elephants and their appurtenances loomed large in these cere-monies, fulfilling multiple symbolic and pragmatic functions.[50] As Sujit Sivasundaram has argued, British understandings of the meaning and use of elephants rested on centuries of Indian precedent. In the Hindu Vedas, elephant 'anthropomorphism worked alongside religious ador-ation', while Mughal royal literature both invested elephants with 'mystic and divine qualities' and interpreted the emperor's control over wild elephants 'as a sign of his ability to bring order to his kingdom and also as proof of divine rule'.[51] Elephants were highly valued by the Mughals for their use in warfare, and emperors often exacted them as annual tribute.[52] By the later eighteenth century, them-selves now mired in Indian warfare, the British too had come to under-stand the elephant's importance.[53] Replete with meaning and utility, the elephant was the perfect gift.[54] The evolution of diplomatic ceremonial in north India heightened their strategic and symbolic value. At festivals and investiture ceremonies, riding atop these magnificently caparisoned beasts ensured that power was visually manifest on a vertical hierarchical axis. Propinquity to the ruler was also coveted as a sign of high status, projecting this power grid onto a horizontal plane. Convention moreover decreed that the procession's senior potentate would be joined in his ornate howdah by subordinate princes or Company officials.[55] At the Mughal court, this process entailed a further show of subordination to the king as the lesser visitor dismounted his own elephant and ascended to join his superior in the latter's howdah. A shortage of howdah ladders not infrequently resulted in an unseemly scrambling at the feet of the monarch's elephant.[56]

The indignity of scrambling up onto princely elephants in public, offering *nazrs*, accepting a *khil'at* (which was conferred by the king's hand and worn over their European dress) and being subjected to a

[50] See for example the 'Panorama of a Durbar Procession of Akbar II', *c.* 1815, BL, Add. Or.888.

[51] Sujit Sivasundaram, 'Trading Knowledge: The East India Company's Elephants in India and Britain', *Historical Journal*, 48 (2005), 47, 48.

[52] *Ibid.*, 32, 33, 37.

[53] *Ibid.*, 32–6.

[54] As Sivasundaram observes, 'This made the elephant a perfect present. Under Mughal rule … the exchange of elephants served as both a symbol of friendship and subservience.' *Ibid.*, 36.

[55] See for example Major Archer, *Tours in Upper India, and in the Parts of the Himalaya Mountains: With an Account of the Courts of the Native Princes, &c.* (2 vols., 1833), 1: 4, 14.

[56] *Ibid.*, 1: 14, 16.

seemingly endless flow of suspect gifts irked reform-minded Company officials. Akbar II exacerbated this hostility by using these opportunities to insist upon his superior status, to bargain for an increased pension, and to assert his claim to choose his own successor. In royal letters, and through diplomatic envoys and royal ceremonial, he repeatedly proclaimed his paramount power to a succession of increasingly exasperated governor generals, condescendingly denominating them 'my son' and conferring titles upon them and their subordinate officers that implied or explicitly asserted a relation of feudal vassalage. Already in 1807 (a year after his succession), engaged in bitter disputes with the governor general on these subjects, the king had flexed his muscles by informing the Company that he would confer *khila* not only on all the princes in Delhi's hinterland but also upon the British, including the governor general himself. The British clearly understood what was at stake in this assertion: the *khil'at* for the governor general was 'a public acknowledgement of vassalage and submission to the throne of Delhi' and must be refused.[57] The following years saw ongoing hostilities between the king and his Company captors along these lines. The British exiled his favoured third son to Allahabad, infuriated by Akbar's refusal to honour British rules of primogeniture by naming his eldest son as his natural heir.[58] In 1819, this rumbling dispute came to a head. Buoyed up by his victories in the Third Anglo-Maratha War, Governor General Hastings refused to honour long-standing British diplomatic epistolary forms. The royal seal with which Akbar II signed diplomatic letters to him, Hastings expostulated, had 'inscribed on it the humiliating designation of *Favee Acber Shah* or vassal of the King Acbar'. So offended was Hastings by this received formulation of sovereignty, that he cut off all official communication between the governor general and the king, a relationship that would be resumed at this level only in 1826, by Lord Amherst.[59]

Amherst's negotiations to resume diplomatic relations with the king of Delhi in 1826 provide an essential context for Colebrooke's diplomatic behaviour from 1827 to 1829. Planning a tour of the Upper Provinces of north India, Amherst was cognisant of Akbar II's desire to restore official communications with the governor general. Suffering from sharply diminished Company confidence in the aftermath of a disastrous war in Burma, he now took steps to restore communication with the king.

[57] Memorandum Concerning the Claims of the King of Delhi [1831], BL, IOR/H/708/Part 1, ff. 76–7, 90.

[58] The harem and dynastic politics of Akbar's reign are detailed in Major General George Cunningham to Mr Ellis, 24 September 1831, BL, IOR/H/708/Part 1, ff. 13–36.

[59] Memorandum Concerning the Claims of the King of Delhi [1831], BL, IOR/H/708/Part 1, ff. 141–2. See also Sharma, 'Mughal Delhi', 17–19.

Sir Charles Metcalfe, the Delhi Resident, had written to Amherst underlining the king's discontent at the break in diplomatic relations: 'the King
complained lately of the neglect with which he has been treated, particularly in not receiving any communication for the Governor General's
intended journey', he observed. Himself keen to effect a reconciliation,
Metcalfe was nonetheless adamant that 'any thing derogatory' to
British power must be avoided. 'Any Nuzzur on the part of His
Lordship, I suppose to be out of the question,' he advised.[60] A month
later, indeed, Metcalfe urged Amherst to insist on his political parity
with the king if any visit were agreed, and proposed informing Akbar
II 'that the Governor General did not intend to visit Delhi, as he
could only meet the King on a footing of equality, which might not be
agreeable to his Majesty'. Negotiations broke down when the king
indeed insisted on inducing 'some acknowledgement of [his] superiority'
to Amherst.[61] When talks resumed a few weeks later, however, both sides
made concessions. The king proposed ten points of etiquette for
Amherst's visit. Among them, he agreed to forgo payment of *nazr* by
the governor general, to accept a salaam from him 'in the English
fashion by taking off the Hat', and to permit Amherst to be seated on
a chair. In return, he stipulated, Amherst must accept a gift of 'whatever
may be deemed proper … from the Royal neck, some article of
Jewellery', must receive *paan* from the king – 'to be given by the Royal
Hand' – and must subsequently invite the king to visit him at the
Delhi Residency. Here Akbar expected to receive 'a suitable Peshkush
and reception: not the same as that given by his Majesty to the
Governor General'.[62]

Two weeks later, Amherst made major concessions to these demands,
accepting the king's restoration of rank, to a status higher than that of the
governor general of India. He was now, his secretary reported, 'fully prepared to admit a superiority of rank on the part of the King of Delhi, as
the titular representative of a long established and renowned Dynasty of
Emperors; whose accession to the Throne and dignities of his ancestors,
has been formally recognized, during many years by the British
Government'.[63] Accepting that 'At Delhi in his own dominions, the
King must rank above all others, and in that sense his Majesty's superiority to his visitor, was admitted beyond questions,' Amherst still refused to
accept a *khil'at* or to offer a *nazr*. But he laid essential groundwork for the
later Colebrooke scandal by agreeing that the Delhi Resident could
accept a *khil'at* without detracting from the important message that

[60] Metcalfe to Stirling, 17 September 1826, BL, IOR/F/4/1179/30741, ff. 14–15.
[61] Metcalfe to Stirling, 12 November 1826, *ibid.*, 15–17.
[62] Metcalfe to Stirling, 17 November 1826, *ibid.*, ff. 18–19.
[63] Stirling to Metcalfe, 6 December 1826, *ibid.*, ff. 23–4.

'the relation of a sovereign and vassal has ceased to exist, even in name, between his Majesty and the head of the British Government in India'.[64] Having conceded this major point, Amherst then negotiated hard to ensure that he would be carried in a tonjon, not forced to walk, from his elephant to the king's presence, and that the chair on which he would sit would be his own chair of state.[65] Its height, he acknowledged, 'is scarcely greater than that of a common chair, but as its appearance is rich and handsome … its admission should … be urged'.[66] This uneasy ceasefire saw vassalage displaced from the governor general to the Resident, but left Amherst's body caught between two competing regimes of material politics. In one, the king's hand would drape the governor general's neck with Indian jewellery, signalling political hierarchy through received conventions of royal touch and royal gifting. In the other, Amherst – sitting in European dress on his own 'throne chair', of Indian manufacture but British design – would project the hybrid rule of Indian and British elites on the north Indian frontier of Company power. It proved a fragile reconciliation. Before Amherst left Delhi, the king had sent him 'a paper of demands', reasserted his authority to confer *khila* and receive *nazzr* and *peshkash* from all subordinates and insisted that the Company had 'violated its engagements with the royal family'. By February 1829, rejecting established diplomatic protocols, he had bypassed the new governor general, Lord Bentinck, and despatched a letter directly to the king of Great Britain.[67] Bentinck, a proponent of reform and Anglicisation, responded to this challenge by issuing orders to his subordinates prohibiting all exchanges of gifts with Indian princes.[68]

III

It was in this context of resumed but fractious royal relations and diplomatic gifting regimes that the Colebrookes arrived in Delhi in 1827, and enthusiastically threw themselves into the material politics of Mughal diplomacy. Lady Colebrooke, like her husband – who was her first cousin once removed – had lived most of her life in India, having been born (out of wedlock) to a Colebrooke military officer in Madras.

[64] *Ibid.*, ff. 25–6.
[65] Crafted in Lucknow and now in the Victoria and Albert Museum (IS.6-1991), Amherst's 'throne chair' can be viewed at https://collections.vam.ac.uk/item/O39550/throne-chair/.
[66] Stirling to Metcalfe, 6 December 1826, BL, IOR/F/4/1179/30741, ff. 29–30, 32–3.
[67] Memorandum Concerning the Claims, BL, IOR/H/708/Part I, ff. 142, 144–5, 146.
[68] Archer, *Tours of Upper India*, 1: 7–10. Notwithstanding this directive, Archer – like the commander-in-chief – continued to accept gifts at state ceremonies. See for example *ibid.*, 109–15.

Sir Edward's son Edward, twenty when the couple arrived in Delhi, had been born to one of the Resident's pre-marital Indian concubines.[69] Neither his illegitimacy nor his mixed heritage marked him out in Delhi's hybrid European community: James Skinner's mother was Rajput, and William Fraser (who presided over Delhi's criminal court) had several children by his Indian companion, Amiban.[70] Like the Residents at other princely courts, Colebrooke daily entertained both his nuclear kin and an extended 'family' or household of Company men at his table, enjoying an official allowance of 5,000 rupees per month to do so. His young revenue assistant, Samuel Sneade Brown, having excitedly reported his acceptance of a khil'at from the king of Delhi in May 1828, wrote home to his mother in June to commend Colebrooke's hospitality. 'I find it rather a pleasant change to dine with Sir Edward every evening after business is over; he is a frank and pleasant old gentleman; I like him much.' His opinion of Lady Colebrooke was less sanguine. 'We call his lady the *Bore* Constrictor,' he commented, without elaboration.[71]

Also dining together with the Colebrookes at the Residency table but in mounting distress was Charles Trevelyan, whose sensibilities were outraged by the Colebrooke family's acquisitive behaviours, and by Lady Colebrooke in particular. Among the twenty-nine main charges and seventy-six sub-charges of corruption Trevelyan levelled against Sir Edward in the summer of 1829 were myriad accusations of gifts accepted from Indian princes or their agents, and reputedly retained by the Colebrookes for private profit.[72] The new Resident, Trevelyan claimed in his first charge, had accepted 'various sums of money in nuzzurs from every native above the lowest rank who has been introduced to him with hardly any exception, none of which he has brought to the public account'.[73] By denominating these accepted gifts *nazrs*, Trevelyan effectively named Colebrooke as an Indian prince, corrupt by nature, despotic by culture. His next charges enumerated the Resident's acceptance of (for example) a horse and trappings gifted illicitly by the raja of Bikaner, Colebrooke's subsequent presentation to the raja of three unauthorised *khila*, his receipt of an elephant from the raja of Ulwur and his presentation to another prince of 'a large bed on which [his predecessor as Resident] Sir C. Metcalfe used to sleep'.[74]

[69] Sutherland, *Sola Bona Quae Honesta*, 38–40.
[70] *Princes and Painters*, ed. Dalrymple and Sharma, 126–9.
[71] Samuel Sneade Brown, *Home Letters, Written from India between the Years 1828 and 1841* (printed for private circulation, 1878), 8, 11.
[72] For the enumeration of charges, see [Sir Edward Colebrooke], *Papers Relative to the Case at Issue between Sir Edward Colebrooke, Bt., and the Bengal Government* (1833), 18.
[73] [Charles Trevelyan], *Papers Transmitted from India by C.E. Trevelyan, Esq.* (1830), 108.
[74] *Ibid.*, 116, 117, 119; BL, IOR/F/4/1200/30914A, f. 274.

With Metcalfe's bed, Trevelyan signalled the familial and dynastic character of the Colebrookes' corruption: rooted in the domestic objects of their official home, their material diplomacy refused to register the proper, gendered demarcation between private and public spheres.

Many of the charges Trevelyan laid against Lady Colebrooke highlighted her refusal to remain within a private sphere and her insistence on participating in Sir Edward's diplomatic dealings with Indian princes. At stake was not simply her venality but also her familiarity with and propinquity to material objects – *khila*, elephants and shawls, for example – endowed with royal meanings and princely power. Lady Colebrooke's collusive diplomatic acts were especially objectionable to Trevelyan: in exercising political power she had adopted and adapted the insistent, material diplomacy that so frustrated British liberal reformers. Again and again Trevelyan described the corrupt payments Lady Colebrooke accepted from Indian rulers as *nazrs* and specified that they were paid – as were all *nazrs* – in gold *mohurs*.[75] Not content to accept these monetary tokens of submission to her, Lady Colebrooke had arrogated to herself the power to confer not only gifts – the double-barrelled gun, for example, she gave to the raja of Patiala – but also *khila* to north Indian princes.[76] Adding insult to injury, her meetings with Indian rulers in the Delhi Residency were known as *durbars* – it was with this term that not only Trevelyan but also the senior officials in Calcutta (to whom his streams of accusations flowed) described them.[77] The very elephant upon which one raja had ridden to the Residency on a visit, he claimed, had been extracted from under this dignitary by Lady Colebrooke, as a coerced gift.[78] To Trevelyan, the elephant represented an obvious invasion of the masculine world of diplomacy by a woman who belonged in the private home. Colebrooke's defence of his wife, in sharp contrast, highlighted her right to engage in market transactions in the public sphere. The elephant was in fact a 'purchase', not a gift, from the raja, he insisted. Moreover, Lady Colebrooke had 'never once mounted it; and it was therefore sent among the rest of the public elephants in the public Feel Khana [Company elephant enclosure], where it has been ever since'.[79]

The histrionic tone of Trevelyan's charges against Lady Colebrooke was highly sexualised. His accusations dwelt at length upon the 'native gentlemen' who gained access to her private chambers and there laid

---

[75] [Trevelyan], *Papers Transmitted*, 129, 132.
[76] For the gun, BL, IOR/F/4/1200/30914A, ff. 261, 265, 272–4, 279.
[77] For example, [Colebrooke], *Papers Relative*, 79.
[78] *Ibid.*, 26–7.
[79] *Ibid.*

hands on her material goods.[80] Elite Indian men, Trevelyan fumed, were 'in daily attendance at the residency, and ... admitted to the most familiar intercourse with Lady Colebrooke'.[81] These claims suggest that her violation of the increasingly rigid sexual norms of late Georgian domestic ideology was an essential component of his case against her husband.[82] Trevelyan's sexualised focus on Lady Colebrooke enraged her husband. Jealousy, coloured by sexual deprivation, had driven the claims of his upstart assistant, Colebrooke suggested. 'Mr. Trevelyan, who, like the Turk, can bear no brother near the throne ... became jealous of Lady Colebrooke,' he asserted.[83] As a bachelor whose relations with women were confined to illicit sex coerced from natives, Colebrooke claimed, Trevelyan was poorly placed to interpret Lady Colebrooke's behaviour as the Resident's wife.[84] In sharp contrast, he (as a married man of the world) trusted his wife not only with European men at the Residency but with Indian princes and their subordinates. 'My permission to the native gentlemen, to visit Lady Colebooke, in her private apartment, is the origin of the rancour, hatred, and malice, which are driving this man to seek the gratification of his revenge by every violence and outrage, by every disgraceful and underhand means, which a fiend could devise, and a scoundrel put in practice,' he argued.[85] Lady Colebrooke herself vigorously defended her right to inhabit the public sphere, both in her home and in those of the Indian men she visited, and – like her husband – projected sexual dishonour back on her antagonist. When Trevelyan's accusations began to circulate in Delhi, she issued a circular 'appealing to the public' in which she observed 'that *liar* and *villain* are the mildest terms which can be applied to such an act of depravity in so young a man'.[86]

Antagonism to elite British women's unbridled behaviour – at once politically and sexually corrupt – in the public sphere was well established in British reformers' critiques of Old Corruption.[87] But it is also essential to recognise the extent to which the regional dynamics of princely politics in north India shaped both Lady Colebrooke's actions

[80] In examining witnesses to Lady Colebrooke's sale of a necklace to a nawab for use in his investiture ceremony, Trevelyan made a point of confirming that she gave the necklace 'with her own hand'. 'Deposition of Khaja Qasim', 5 November 1829, BL, IOR/F/4/1203/30914E, f. 1699.

[81] [Trevelyan], *Papers Transmitted*, 14.

[82] For the broader parameters of British moral reform in this period, see M. J. D. Roberts, *Making English Morals: Voluntary Association and Moral Reform in England, 1787–1886* (Cambridge, 2004).

[83] [Colebrooke], *Papers Relative*, 4.

[84] *Ibid.*, 93–4, 188.

[85] *Ibid.*, 20.

[86] [Trevelyan], *Papers Transmitted*, 13.

[87] See esp. Anna Clark, *Scandal: The Sexual Politics of the British Constitution* (Princeton, 2004).

and the character and force of Trevelyan's invective. Like Trevelyan, Indian princes clearly recognised that Lady Colebrooke's gifts were freighted with political potential. They accordingly actively incorporated this European woman into their diplomatic dealings. When she sent the nawab of Tonk gifts to mark the birth of a grandchild, the nawab specified that the items be brought to him 'in state' so that 'high and low' would learn of their conferral. According to this princely state's newsletter, dancing girls and music accompanied the presentation of Lady Colebrooke's gift.[88]

Reading the sources thrown up by the Colebrooke case provides abundant evidence not only that Lady Colebrooke acted as an unabashed political agent in Delhi, but also that her gender allowed her and Sir Edward to recognise (and take advantage of) the political agency of Indian princely women behind the purdah curtain. Among the elite women in their circle was Farzana, 'Begum Sombre', well known for her active, visible roles in north Indian diplomacy and warfare.[89] But the archives of the Colebrooke controversy identify many more Mughal, Maratha and Rajput princely women with whom Sir Edward and his wife engaged in the business of politics. Pre-eminent among them was the rani and ex-regent of Bharatpur, a Rajput princely state. Bharatpur had gained iconic status in the Company imagination in an infamous siege of 1805, when its impregnable fort failed to fall to the otherwise victorious British forces at the end of the Second Anglo-Maratha War. Between 1825 and 1826, a succession crisis afforded the British an opportunity to rectify this anomaly; in victory, they razed the fort and installed a council of regency to rule for the infant raja.[90] Lord Amherst's son was among the military officers who sent looted objects from the Bharatpur palace to the governor general's family in Calcutta in 1826.[91] Among Trevelyan's charges in 1829 was the accusation that, on a visit together with her husband to Bharatpur in that year, Lady Colebrooke had gifted a watch to Imrut Koar, the widowed rani ousted in 1828 as the regent – a status she was determined to renegotiate. For Trevelyan, the illicit gift of a watch encapsulated a much wider field of corruption. Lady Colebrooke had also presented the rani's *vakil* (or diplomatic agent) with two Indian

---

[88] 'Proceedings Relating to the Removal of Sir Edward Colebrooke', BL, IOR/F/4/1200/30914B, ff. 338–9.

[89] Michael H. Fisher, *The Inordinately Strange Life of Dyce Sombre: Victorian Anglo-Indian MP and Chancery 'Lunatic'* (2010), chs. 1–3.

[90] Hiralal Gupta, 'British Policy towards Successions in Bharatpur State, 1823–1826, and Its Repercussions', *Itihas: Journal of the Andhra Pradesh Archives*, 14 (1988), 65–75.

[91] The looted items included 'the magnificent State Palanquin & five hunting Tygers' as well as 'some curiosities from the Palace' for Lady and Miss Amherst. Combermere to Amherst, 19 December 1825, BL, MSS Eur F140/80(a), f. 19.

shawls, and the *vakil* had prepared a formal petition addressed to Lady Colebrooke for restitution of her lost rights as regent.[92] To Trevelyan, Lady Colebrooke's gifting was of a piece with the statement (he alleged) she had repeatedly made at the Residency table, that in return for Indian gifts she would influence her husband on the behalf of Indian princes.[93] Colebrooke flatly rejected these claims, dismissing the status of the rani's *vakil* as that of a mere 'messenger' and pointedly underlining that unlike the 'Hindoostanee kept mistresses' with whom he accused Trevelyan of cohabiting, British wives must be considered as 'entitled to partake of the privileges attached to the stations of their husbands'.[94]

British wives, sisters and daughters of senior Company men were increasingly conspicuous on the subcontinent in this period, residing with them in European settlements and accompanying them on tours of newly conquered territories.[95] Governor General Amherst's wife was at the forefront of this trend in Delhi, entering actively into her husband's plans to restore diplomatic relations with the king in 1827. She visited the king's senior wife and the spouse of his presumed heir in February of that year, presenting them with necklaces and earrings from the Company *toshkhana*, and receiving jewels in return 'which were all placed in the Public Stores'.[96] Lady Colebrooke's dealings extended far beyond Lady Amherst's 'public' gifts, forcing open discussion of the problematic status of diplomatic wives' transactions. As a woman, Lady Colebrooke had no formal place in the Company's service. For Trevelyan, her ability to be 'in constant communication with every official character about the residency' was on a par with Colebrooke's subversion of authority by depending unduly on his Hindu man of business.[97] Legally, her only binding contract in Delhi was her marriage to her husband. Under the common law principle of coverture, the gifts and money she obtained from Indian princes were not her own, but (if indeed they were licit private property) her husband's. Her lack of standing notwithstanding, Lady Colebrooke had allegedly entered into negotiations with independent Indian states – an action that, even had she been a man and the Resident, was prohibited by Company regulations. In the context of the king of Delhi's refusal to acknowledge British paramount power, Lady Colebrooke's rogue

[92] [Trevelyan], *Papers Transmitted*, 126.
[93] *Ibid.*, 111.
[94] [Colebrooke], *Papers Relative*, 35–6.
[95] Joan Mickelson Gaughan, *The 'Incumberances': British Women in India, 1615–1856* (Oxford, 2013), chs. 12–16.
[96] A. Stirling to G. Swinton, 3 March 1827, BL, IOR/F/4/1179/30741, ff. 47–8.
[97] [Trevelyan], *Papers Transmitted*, 84.

behaviour represented a new political threat to an already unstable, corrupt imperial regime.

IV

What can we conclude from the Colebrooke corruption case if we read it from the perspective of material culture? Taken as a whole, Trevelyan's accusations smack of hysteria: of his twenty-nine main charges against Colebrooke, only twelve were taken seriously by the investigators, and many of even these they dismissed.[98] Trevelyan was avowedly a 'liberal' reformer who rejected the corrupt practices of the Company's Orientalist camp. But his one request to Bentinck – as a reward for the success of his campaign against Colebrooke – was patronage to promote his brother within the Company's ranks, their mother's influence at home having failed to meet the family's needs.[99] The governor general, citing Trevelyan's 'manly conduct' in rescuing 'your Country' from Colebrooke's 'foul deeds', happily complied with this request, appointing Trevelyan's brother assistant at Ajmer.[100]

The gender politics of this scandal are also vitally important, for in scrutinising the record of the Colebrookes' gifting we see both the assertion and the denial of female agency exercised by British and Indian women. Lady Colebrooke's active collusion with Indian ranis and rajas who offered her gifts is evident throughout the records of her husband's prosecution. Charles Trevelyan recognised these gifts as acts of political corruption. This was, however, a charge that her husband and the Company's most senior officials were desperate to deny. Acknowledging that her husband 'permitted Lady Colebrooke to receive the agents of many … independent states', the investigations concluded that 'a corrupt understanding with any of them is not established'. Refusing to intrude on 'the private conversations of Sir Edward's family' even when they took place at his public table, they insisted that 'such conversations, if proved, could establish no corrupt act'.[101] To accept that Lady Colebrooke was a political agent was to fly in the face of her status as a British wife, a female whose gender and marital condition subsumed her person under her husband's legal aegis and consigned her to a private sphere outside Company politics. The public role of British women in India in the 1820s – their presence at Company dinners attended by

---

[98] One of the two principal investigators, moreover, had an obvious vested interest in finding Colebrooke guilty, having been engaged since 1823 in a protracted attack on 'the Delhi system' of revenue and government. See 'Embezzlement at Delhi', IOR/F/4/ 1279/51299.

[99] Charles Trevelyan to Harriet Trevelyan, 30 December 1829, NUSC, CET/3.

[100] Charles Trevelyan to Harriet Trevelyan, 1 December 1832, NUSC, CET21/11.

[101] [Trevelyan], *Papers Transmitted*, 110–11.

Indian men, their willingness to speak out, their proclivity for drink – all came under increasing scrutiny in this period. 'Asiatic notions of female delicacy and decorum are so vitally assailed in the very public manner in which European ladies display themselves at these parties, that if they knew ... that contempt is the least offensive feeling their presence excites, they would refrain from going into the company of natives,' Major Archer, aide-de-camp to Lord Bentinck's commander-in-chief, expostulated in his memoirs.[102] This assessment conveniently effaced the evidence that punctuated his own autobiographical account of north Indian politics in the late 1820s: his memoir records dinners with (and hosted by) Begum Sombre, as well as occasions on which ranis insisted on articulating their claims to Company officials from behind purdah screens.[103] Recovering these lost female voices is enabled if we attend to records that trace their entanglement in the exchange of material things.

Gender was not, however, the only elephant in the room – or rather, in the Residency stables – in late Mughal Delhi. Viewed from the vantage point of material diplomacy, the Colebrookes' conspicuous and undoubted venality appears not simply as one episode in the extended history of Old Corruption nor as an example of anachronistic, entrenched Orientalist convictions succumbing to the Anglicist challenge. To be sure, both Old Corruption and Anglicising ideology left deep marks on this controversy. But it is also essential to locate the Colebrookes' behaviours and their reception within specific places, cultures and temporalities on the subcontinent, and thereby to recognise the diplomatic levers being pulled in late Mughal Delhi by Indian princes (including princely women). From his accession in 1806 until his death in 1837, Akbar II fought against British interpretations of his status as merely the king of Delhi, deploying not only artwork but furniture, jewels, elephants, *khila* and a cornucopia of other Indian goods to assert and reinforce his claims to paramount power. Lesser princes in north India echoed and elaborated these forms of resistance. Diplomacy exercised on the fragile border between licit and illicit gifting established by Company regulations was fraught with many temptations, and with many opportunities for British and Indian agents to develop new diplomatic practices, expectations and norms. The narrative arc traced by parliamentary and Company regulations against gifting by and to Indian princes, from the Regulating Act of 1773 to Bentinck's orders of 1828, marked a trajectory away from material culture politics and toward a monetised bureaucratic order. But the grand narrative of Indian power relations under British rule repeatedly

---

[102] Archer, *Tours in Upper India*, 2: 90.
[103] *Ibid.*, 1: 136–44, 2: 44, 50.

failed to adhere to this teleological arc.[104] Bentinck's successors were to enter enthusiastically into gifting regimes in north India, sealing their relations with Ranjit Singh's Sikh kingdom in the 1830s, for example, through the exchange of elaborate gifts and counter-gifts at his court in Lahore.[105] In the aftermath of the Indian Uprising of 1857, it was to this ceremonial regime of *durbar* politics that the crown increasingly turned to stabilise its regime.[106] Far from fading away with the demise of the Company state in 1858, princely politics of this ilk was shored up and reanimated. Scholars such as Ranajit Guha and James C. Scott remind us of the power of the wily forms of resistance exercised by peasant populations under imperial rule.[107] The Colebrooke corruption case reminds us that these so-called weapons of the weak had their counterparts among imperialised elites. In India, the persistent refusal of ranis, rajas, nawabs and the Mughal emperor himself to adhere to British diplomatic forms made this resistance palpably evident through material objects to the British.

In the twenty-first century, it is easy to dismiss Georgian-era princely politics as an atavistic form of power, incompatible with modern states and their diplomacy. We do so at our peril. Resilient, adaptable, effective and yes – like democracies – vulnerable to corruption, the family- and clan-based politics of the princely state are a postcolonial, no less than a colonial, a Western, no less than an Eastern, problem for contemporary politics and global order.[108]

---

[104] See esp. Jonathan Saha, *Law, Disorder and the Colonial State: Corruption in Burma c.1900* (Basingstoke, 2013).

[105] Emily Eden, *'Up the Country': Letters Written to Her Sister from the Upper Provinces* (1867).

[106] Miles Taylor, *Empress: Queen Victoria and India* (New Haven, 2018).

[107] Ranajit Guha, 'The Prose of Counter-Insurgency', in *Subaltern Studies: Writings on South Asian History and Society*, ed. Ranajit Guha (Delhi, 1983); James C. Scott, *Weapons of the Weak: Everyday Forms of Peasant Resistance* (New Haven, 1985).

[108] For the earlier period, see Jeroen Duindam, *Dynasties: A Global History* (Cambridge, 2016); for contemporary regimes, Robert Lacey, *Inside the Kingdom: Kings, Clerics, Modernists, Terrorists and the Struggle for Saudi Arabia* (New York, 2009) and Vicky Ward, *Kushner, Inc.: Greed. Ambition. Corruption. The Extraordinary Story of Jared Kushner and Ivanka Trump* (New York, 2019).

within larger modern entities.[11] 'The Türks' or 'the Kitan' no longer exist as groups, and in our sources they are broad etic names that conflate considerable diversity under a convenient label.[12] We may achieve greater precision by speaking of dynasties and regimes named in our sources, such as the Tang 唐, 618–907 (not 'the Chinese'), the Uyghur Khaghanate, 740–844 or Qocho 高昌, 850–1209 (not 'the Uyghurs'), Liao (not 'the Kitan'), Goguryeo 高句麗, 37 BCE–668 CE or Balhae 渤海, 698–926 (not 'the Koreans'), Heian 平安, 794–1185 (not 'the Japanese'). Regimes are more clearly definable in time, including appearance, disappearance and sometimes reappearance, and we can track their changing geographical compositions. These overtly political labels also open necessary questions about who was included in these units.[13]

We also need more clarity about where was included. Using the names of political units to refer to geography implies fixed territorial extent when in fact borders changed continually, and may suggest an unlikely uniformity of circumstances (one favourite concept among historians is 'control') across everywhere claimed by a given regime. Focusing on geographical regions encourages greater precision and further helps to break the link with presentist habits. Thus, for example: the Japanese archipelago (not 'Japan') and the Korean peninsula (not 'Korea'). These geographical features (see Figure 1) give us a contrasting mainland, considered as regions of different sizes for different purposes and periods: the Tarim basin, the Mongolian or eastern steppe, the Gobi region, Manchuria, Sichuan, the Gansu corridor, Guanzhong, the Ordos, the Yellow River valley, the Huai–Yangzi region, the middle and lower Yangzi, Lingnan, and so on.[14] We get a sharper focus, more precision, a more human scale. It becomes easier to remember the local, which reminds us to keep relating the global back to it.

Thirdly: East Asia historians habitually refer to chronological periods in terms of dynasties, which could be several centuries long, like Tang 唐

---

[11] The relationship between the pre-modern Uyghurs and the modern Uyghurs of Xinjiang is a subject of considerable debate, inflected by the opposing political goals of the PRC government and Uyghur desires for greater autonomy.

[12] Some claims have been made to 'Kitan' ethnicity in the PRC, but with little visible impact. Gwen Bennett, personal communication.

[13] So far these questions have been insufficiently discussed in a historiography that has focused heavily on Sinitic literati elites. On one large literature see Hilde De Weerdt, 'Recent Trends in American Research in Song Dynasty History: Local Religion and Political Culture', in Taiwan Song shi yanjiu wang 臺灣宋史研究網, 1 February 2006: www.ihp.sinica.edu.tw/~twsung/breview/subpage/02/files/Recent_Trends_in_American_Research_in_Song_Dynasty_History.pdf.

[14] The names include terms derived from different historical periods, deployed for their descriptive convenience. Use of regional names is already happening among Koreanists, Japanologists and local historians of the Song, among others, but the theoretical advantages have not been emphasised.

(618–907) or Goryeo 高麗 (918–1392). Of course, some developments spanned areas larger than one political unit – which dynastic chronology should take priority? – and did not automatically respect dynastic changes. Referring to centuries instead offers neutrality and greater precision.

Technologies

This approach to a pre-modern global eastern Eurasia requires an organising principle that maintains an analytical rejection of the nation-state and instead frames discussion using other groupings and combinations. The structuring possibilities are limited only by the historian's imagination, and here I have chosen the concept of technologies, broadly understood. While my topics have a strongly material inclination, the concern is not so much with specific techniques, such as building watertight bulkheads or rammed-earth construction – although some of these do feature – as with sets of practices that solve particular problems such as how to build an oceangoing ship or a city wall, or indeed how to convey religious ideas, get an heir or train an effective bureaucracy. It is these sets of practices that constitute technologies in this usage.[15] Here I draw from the section of my project on 'Technologies of everyday life', which includes discussion of cities.

Technologies suit my purpose because they place human agency front and centre. People do not adopt ways of doing things just because they are or become available, or because they are the best solution for a given problem. New situations require methods for addressing new challenges. Where a method is already in place, people need reasons to change from what they already do. The adoption, modification, rejection or abandonment of any given technology always involves agency, and often on the part of anonymous ordinary people in everyday life.[16] Technologies thus assist in the quest to extend the scope of pre-modern studies beyond the elites, often genealogically associated with modern nation-states, who have dominated both textual and material sources. I would emphasise, however, that technologies are simply one among many potentially useful approaches to global history, and as the field expands, I would hope to see many analytical structures coexisting.

If I am to avoid a history consisting of merely a set of descriptions of Things People Did, then I must reassemble my discussion of technologies into some kind of larger pattern or set of patterns. Having rejected the

---

[15] My inspiration here has been Francesca Bray, *Technology and Gender: Fabrics of Power in Late Imperial China* (Berkeley, 1997), esp. 12–21.

[16] Kevin Greene, 'Historiography and Theoretical Approaches', in *The Oxford Handbook of Engineering and Technology in the Classical World*, ed. John Oleson (Oxford, 2009), 73–84. In fact, I learned most about this from various conversations with Kevin over lunch: testament to the value of not eating at one's desk.

blocks represented by ostensibly ethnopolitical units, I have opted instead for *layers*, which allow us to pursue specific technologies wherever they may be found, without regard for extraneous barriers.

A relatively small number of technologies become embedded as practices that undergird the everyday life of all or virtually all the people in all social strata in a given region, such that removal or abandonment of those practices would fundamentally alter the substance of life in those areas. I call such foundational technologies *substrates*, and we may think of other everyday practices as being rooted in them. Considering religions as technologies, for example, we see that Mahayana Buddhism was by 600 a substrate across the whole of eastern Eurasia, having been embraced in the guise of one sect or another by at least a large proportion of all levels of society in almost every region from the Tarim to the Japanese archipelago, and making indelible material impacts through rock carving, proliferation of the new architectural form of the pagoda, and treatment of the dead, as well as permanent incorporation of concepts such as *nirvana* and merit-making into beliefs and everyday practices. The absence of this layer would have made eastern Eurasia a very different place.[17] As we shall see, basic construction techniques formed another substrate that spanned the whole region, though the geographical range of these methods was not completely coterminous with the extent of Buddhism. The limits attained by each layer of technology cannot be presumed to align, but must be traced separately.

Most technologies do not form substrates. Textiles, for example, were essential to the functioning of societies but did not structure those societies as Buddhism did. Textiles were indispensable for clothing, but had many other uses that they shared with other items. Silk was produced in very large quantities, and was used as tax payment, money, religious offering and status marker, among other things, in each of which uses it could be joined or substituted by other items such as grain, silver, votive objects, or tallies marking rank. Unlike Buddhism, if silk had disappeared its place could have been taken by other options without generating permanent rearrangement of the fundamentals of life.[18] Analytically, each use for each item forms its own layer.

Technologies may occur in specific locations or among specific groups that form discrete *nodes*, a more familiar concept, including examples such

---

[17] Scholars have sometimes written about parts of the region as if Buddhism did not exist, which has had a powerful distorting effect; see Tansen Sen, 'The "Decline" of Buddhism in China', in *Demystifying China: New Understandings of Chinese History*, ed. Naomi Standen (Lanham, 2013), 51–8.

[18] Textiles more generally, together with their production methods, could potentially form a substrate, since clothing is an essential of human life. With thanks to Josh Wright, personal communication.

as silk workshops or storehouses, specific urban sites such as those discussed below, or indeed, individual Buddhist temples, rock-carving sites or pagodas. Each set of nodes of a particular type creates a layer that overlays the broader substrate. And each individual node is usually a place where a number of different layers interact with greater intensity.

Those interacting layers may also include *networks* created by specific technologies, which often have nodes but do not require them. While we may sometimes wish to consider nodes of silk production and storage, scholarship thus far has paid more attention to flows of silk through economic, political and religious links, emphasising the connecting role of these textiles rather than the nodes between which the silk travelled.[19] By contrast, in a chain of fortifications the individual nodes may well be deemed of crucial importance, since the overall effect depends on the presence of each element. In cases like this the nodes and the network are interdependent. Many technologies will be amenable to both nodal and networked analysis, with each forming its own layer, though one may be emphasised over the other in any given project or discussion.

The three types of layer – substrates, nodes and networks – coexist and interact. As noted above, different substrates are not automatically coterminous either spatially or chronologically. Each of many networks underwent numerous changes, which included appearing, intensifying, thinning, moving, evolving, reconfiguring and disappearing, among others. We may trace different shapes and extents depending on the technology in question and the timing. Nodes each have their own chronology too, and may be stationary but do not have to be; examples of moving nodes include armies on campaign, peripatetic courts or cities rebuilt near but not on top of an earlier site, or transferring the name and functions of an administrative unit to a new geographical location. If we imagine a set of layers, with each technology often providing more than one stratum of different types, then the connections between different technologies are made by looking down vertically through the filo sheets, where the everyday life of a city is shaped by, for example, its Buddhist temples, the activities of its clergy and the worship by its citizens, by the activities of officials met with compliance or resistance, by flows of trade goods that are produced, pass through or are consumed there, and by the armies defending or besieging its walls.[20]

[19] For example, flows of silk are a focus of works including Liu Xinru, *Silk and Religion: An Exploration of Material Life and the Thought of People, AD 600–1200* (Delhi, 1996); Frances Wood, *The Silk Road: Two Thousand Years in the Heart of Asia* (2002). By contrast, Valerie Hansen, *The Silk Road: A New History* (Oxford, 2012), emphasises nodes of production, exchange and consumption.

[20] Approaches of this kind are in the air at the moment. See, for instance, David Ambaras and Kate McDonald, 'Bodies and Structures', https://scalar.chass.ncsu.edu/bodies-and-structures/index (accessed 10 January 2019), among a diverse and rapidly growing

In its concern for interlocking specificities this is fundamentally a microhistorical approach that accordingly does not lend itself to the kind of generalisation usual in short regional histories spanning many centuries. Instead I undertake case studies of specific technologies in specific subregions in specified sub-periods, seeking spatialised patterns but mostly not attempting to provide narrative arcs. This may lead to a weak sense of change over time, although I do address this within certain topics. Instead the focus is on a selection of longer or shorter historical moments, which may deny the reader the satisfaction of the overall story expected from a historian, but finds an analogue in the methods of archaeologists, who tend to see themselves as providing snapshots of general moments in the past as pieces towards an incomplete and ever evolving jigsaw. The absence of a unifying narrative staves off overgeneralisation but does not obviate arguments or conclusions.

The most necessary outcome of this approach is that political units become a function of interactions between a number of layers of activity, rather than the pre-existing containers for everything else. By separating out political units from technologies – that is, seeing political units as a manifestation of technologies of politics, or as results arising from intersections of several technologies – we may disrupt the 'methodological nationalism'[21] that all too easily assumes political units as the basic building blocks; that cultural, social, economic and other boundaries all align to a significant degree with political borders; and that this is as it should be. When we see culture, social entities and economics, along with politics, religion, gender and the rest, as technologies or the manifestations of technologies, we have a framework that can take us beyond the merely *trans*national – where the national remains fundamental to the conceptualisation – to possibilities for presenting not only specific but also more general histories without reliance on the framework provided by political units.

II Eastern Eurasian urban centres

This is all very well, but our ability to globalise eastern Eurasia in this way may be deflected before we even start by the predominance of materials about 'China' in the surviving sources, and in the resulting modern scholarship, which is only now beginning, sometimes, to locate analysis in global context.[22] Explicitly or implicitly, researchers have all too often

collection of projects. With thanks to Gwen Bennett for the link. The mapping of thematic spatial information in the form of a separate layer for each variable (for example, rivers, contours, settlements, roof tiles, glazed potsherds, unglazed potsherds, least-cost routes, viewsheds) is the prime function of GIS (Geographical Information Systems), which enables sophisticated analysis of interactions between any selection of layers.

[21] I have borrowed the term from Pomeranz, 'Histories for a Less National Age', 2.

[22] See, for example, the Amsterdam University Press series on 'Global Chinese Histories, 250–1650', www.aup.nl/en/series/global-chinese-histories-250-1650 (accessed 11 January 2019).

followed the sinocentrism of their sources to narrate the inexorable pro-
gression of pre-modern 'Chinese' dynasties towards the modern nation-
state of China, both of which shower civilisation on the surrounding bar-
barians in a colonisation of historiography visible then and now.[23] I
believe it is important to disrupt the normativity and dominance of
'China' in the region both in historical study and in the present day,
and to that end my project seeks its case studies from specific locations
scattered across the whole of the broader region. Thus, for instance, I
consider padi rice production in the Japanese archipelago and the examination system in the Korean peninsula, and here I explore city forms in
the Liao dynasty based in present-day Inner Mongolia. The approach
through technologies, often evidenced to a significant degree by material
remains, offers a fine opportunity to grant agency to people deemed 'peripheral' in the usual sinocentric approach, and thereby to make them
central in their own story. In the case of the Liao, this work hopes to
diversify perceptions of both 'nomads' and 'cities' in eastern Eurasia
beyond the assumptions that nomads did not have cities and – since
that assumption is clearly false – that those they did have followed
models borrowed from 'China'. I will use primarily archaeological evidence for a topic for which there are few textual sources.[24]

The Liao were a northern dynasty founded by two intermarrying clans
of agropastoralists based in the Shira Muren valley in what is now south-
eastern Inner Mongolia.[25] Commonly labelled as 'pastoral nomads'
defined by their mobility, and sharply contrasted with the sedentary agricultural 'Chinese' and their network of cities, the Liao have not received
enough attention for their own rather extensive use of urban centres:
some 200 at a recent count.[26] Here I offer three comparisons, each
pairing a Liao site with one from a neighbouring area, each of which
is typically taken to represent a different cultural zone, although I shall
not be discussing them in these terms but rather to counter this conceptualisation (Figure 2). The goal here is not to try to trace linear

[23] The continuation of the attitude that non-Han people are in need of civilisation may be
seen starkly at time of writing in the treatment of Uyghurs by the Chinese state. See, for
instance, Joanne Smith Finley, www.chinafile.com/reporting-opinion/viewpoint/now-
we-dont-talk-anymore (accessed 29 December 2018).

[24] For the regions north of the line of the Great Wall – or as the texts more often put it,
'north of the mountains' – city forms and especially functions are only beginning to be
examined in depth. A first comparative effort was the Bonn workshop on 'Cities in the
Eurasian Steppe 10–14th Century', noted above.

[25] The standard works in English are Denis Twitchett and Klaus-Peter Tietze, 'The
Liao', in *The Cambridge History of China*, vol. 6: *Alien Regimes and Border States, 907–1368*, ed.
Herbert Franke and Denis Twitchett (New York, 1994), 43–153; and Karl Wittfogel and
Feng Chia-sheng, *History of Chinese Society: Liao (907–1125)* (Philadelphia, 1949).

[26] Hu Lin, 'Perceptions of Liao Urban Landscapes: Political Practices and Nomadic
Empires', *Archaeological Dialogues*, 18 (2011), 227.

connections or 'influence' (a deeply problematical term), but to explore the Liao uses in their cities of specific elements that we may conceive as having been drawn from a pool of available possibilities.[27] The resulting accumulation of diversity sets in question the habitual quasi-national conceptualisation of the Liao.

For the whole of eastern Eurasia, from the eastern Tarim to the Japanese archipelago and from Mongolia to Lingnan, scholarship has posited a model form of the city which, like so many other things, has been said to stem from the Yellow River empires. Within this model, the key diagnostic feature of a city was its wall, or rather its walls, to the extent that the same character, *cheng* 城, was used for both the city and at least the outer and main dividing walls.[28] Within those divisions there were further walls around wards, and walls around residential compounds and major buildings. All of these walls were typically built of rammed earth dug from the surrounding land. This method produced a surprisingly hard and strong structure, which after centuries of weathering may survive to several metres in height. Stone or fired brick were generally used only in specific locations: gates, defences, paving for roads or major buildings, column bases, and certain types of building such as pagodas. Important buildings had roofs of heavy ceramic tiles, glazed for structures of the highest status. Columns, beams, thresholds, complex *dougong* bracketing systems to bear the weight of the roof, non-structural infill between columns, temporary forms for making rammed-earth buildings, and internal strengthening lattices for city walls were all made of wood.[29] All of these features may be found at one Liao urban site or another, but these are not the only elements visible.

Turning to the texts, capital sites form the top layer described in Sinitic[30] administrative geographies – for the Liao as for other dynasties – that commonly present a neatly hierarchical system of capitals controlling prefectures controlling counties, each governed from an administrative seat

---

[27] Greene, 'Historiography and Theoretical Approaches', 75, on the 'technology shelf'.

[28] See, for instance, Nancy Steinhardt, *Chinese Imperial City Planning* (Honolulu, 1990), 29–36; Paul Wheatley, *Pivot of the Four Quarters* (Edinburgh, 1971), 411 and references.

[29] Survival of organic material is of course rare, but there are multiple earlier examples in the Tarim basin, notably at Niya (introduced in Susan Whitfield, *The Silk Road: Trade, Travel, War and Faith* (2004), 170–3), and occasional other finds such as a door sill at Chintolgoi Balgas: *Chintorugoi jōseki no kenkyū 2010 toshi chōsa hōkoku: Nara daigaku tokubetsu kenkyū 'Mongoru Ryōdai jōkakutoshi no kōzo to kankyō hendō'* チントルゴイ城跡の研究2010年調査報告: 奈良大学特別研究「モンゴル遼代城郭都市の構造と環境変動」 [Research report of Liao Dynasty's castle town site Chintolgoi, Mongolia], comp. Senda Yoshihiro 千田嘉博 and Altangerel Enkhtur (Nara, 2011), 12–13, 31.

[30] This term is increasingly used for the logographic written language used by literate elites from the Tarim to the Japanese archipelago and what is now Vietnam. This coexisted with numerous other scripts, written vernaculars and spoken languages.

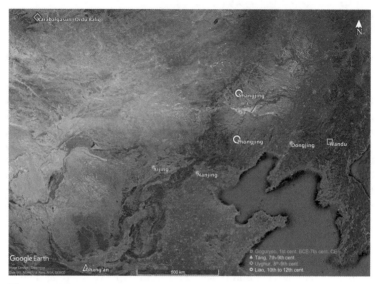

Figure 2 Map showing the five Liao capitals and three comparator capitals. Image: Standen, based on Google Earth.

that was a smaller version of the one at the level above.[31] Similarity of form easily implies similarity of function across different regimes and geographies and centuries, but in fact there was a much wider range of both form and function.[32] Here I will take the Liao as my focus, placing urban settlements associated with the dynasty within their broader landscapes, to seek a more expansive and plural view.

III Tang Chang'an 長安 (618–904) and Liao Zhongjing 中京 (1007–c. 14th cent.)

In the Sinitic tradition the classic city was imaginary: a capital planned as a walled square orientated to the north, with orthogonal streets running to multiple gates. The ruler's palace complex 宮城 (gongcheng), also walled, was positioned centrally and there were markets to the north

---

[31] A useful critical analysis of the Song administrative system in theory and practice is Ruth Mostern, 'Dividing the Realm in Order to Govern': The Spatial Organization of the Song State (960–1276 CE) (Cambridge, MA, 2011), 35–56.

[32] This is a general problem: 'diversity of cities is neglected because only a few cases fit the prevailing models': Making Ancient Cities: Space and Place in Early Urban Societies, ed. Andrew Creekmore and Kevin Fisher (Cambridge, 2014), 15.

and altars to the east and west.[33] The city plan reflected the cosmological ideal of order, and building according to this model contributed to a ruler's legitimation. But in fact, no real city actually looked like this, even though they were often drawn as if they did, as illustrated in Figure 3a.[34] Tang Chang'an is commonly taken as representative of the classic model in practice. The Tang capital was planned and constructed as a square facing north, divided by a central avenue 155 m wide and other orthogonal main streets running to numerous gates (Figure 4). Tang ideology and practice conceived cities at all levels primarily as administrative centres, established by imperial fiat to house government offices, ritual locations, permanent markets, and troops, in buildings that, except for the gates and bell or drum towers, rarely exceeded two levels. Commoner dwellings and workshops, largely single-storey, occupied the grid of wards in the Outer City 外城 (waicheng).

These practical developments still fitted the classic model, but in several areas supposedly archetypal Chang'an strayed from the ideal. The classic model placed the ruler at the very centre both physically and cosmologically.[35] At Chang'an the officials' Inner City 內城 (neicheng) and the court's Imperial City 皇城 (huangcheng) instead formed two halves of a square on the northern outer wall, their enclosures neither square nor central, while the emperor's palace complex formed an extension protruding to the north, and surrounded by a huge hunting park. Most visibly, there were a number of tall pagodas scattered around the city in conjunction with Buddhist temples, following no particular pattern.[36] The pagodas towering above an overwhelmingly low-level built environment were a constant physical reminder that Buddhism stood outside the orthodox cosmology.[37] If not Chang'an, then where could possibly conform to the model? So rather than speaking of 'variations' from a classic plan,[38] I invite you instead to take pleasure in diversity, through the lens offered by the material analysis of three Liao cities and three comparators.[39]

---

[33] Nancy Steinhardt, 'China', in *The Oxford Handbook of Cities in World History*, ed. Peter Clark (Oxford, 2013), 111.

[34] Examples courtesy of my Ph.D. student, Lance Pursey.

[35] Steinhardt, *Chinese Imperial City Planning*, 30–5.

[36] Vividly described in Heng Chye Kiang, *Cities of Aristocrats and Bureaucrats: The Development of Medieval Chinese Cityscapes* (Honolulu, 1999), 8–16.

[37] Buddhism was sometimes seen or used as a challenge to orthodox 'Confucian' ideology. These relationships have attracted a huge literature, but are not my concern here.

[38] Steinhardt, *Chinese Imperial City Planning, passim*.

[39] Material analysis of what is clearly considerable diversity in city plans in the Yellow River valley, the Yangzi valley and the southern ports, among other places, is frequently hindered by the difficulty of retrieving historical ground plans from beneath modern urban centres.

(a)

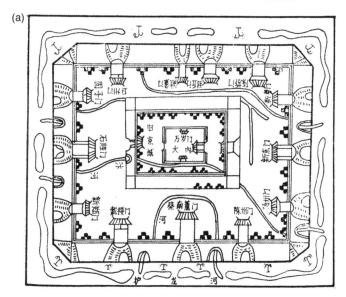

(b)

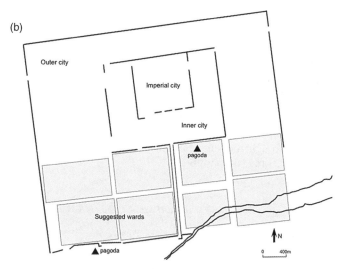

Figure 3 (a) Idealised plan of Bianliang (Kaifeng) alongside (b) archaeological plan of Liao Zhongjing. Images: (a) From Dong Jianhong 董鑒泓 *et al.*, *Zhongguo chengshi jianshe shi* 中國城市建設史 (Beijing: Zhongguo jianzhu gongye chubanshe, 1982), p. 42. With thanks to Nancy Steinhardt. (b) Standen after Gwen Bennett, based on Google Earth. Original composite courtesy of Lance Pursey.

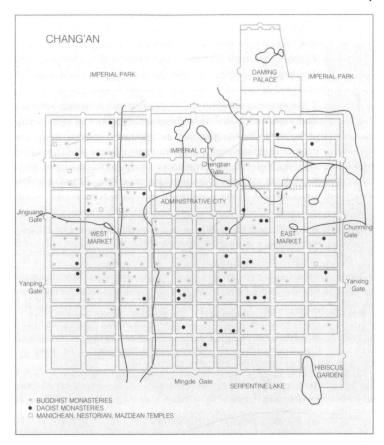

Figure 4 Plan of Tang Chang'an. Image: from Patricia Ebrey, *Cambridge Illustrated History of China* (Cambridge, Cambridge University Press, 1996), p. 117. With kind permission of Cambridge University Press.

Tang emperors used two capitals for much of the dynasty,[40] while the Liao by the mid-eleventh century had five (see Figure 2).[41] The Liao

[40] The other was the Eastern Capital, Luoyang 洛陽, some 325 km downstream where the Luo and the Yellow Rivers meet.

[41] Simultaneous multiple capitals were commonplace in polities across eastern Eurasia, including Goguryeo, Sui 隋 (581–618), Balhae, Uyghur Qocho, Later Liang 後梁 (907–923), Later Tang 後唐 (923–936), Goryeo, Jin 金 (1126–1234) and Yuan 元 (1260–1368). In the Japanese archipelago sequential transfer of a single capital to new locations was more usual.

Central Capital, Zhongjing, was founded late, in 1007, on the flat northern bank of the Laoha River 老哈河 'where of old the imperial tent of the kings of Xi 系 stood', and which had been used for both pasturage and agriculture.[42] As at Chang'an, the ground plan does not follow the concentric ideal. Zhongjing was a nearly square walled site more than 15 km around (Figure 3b),[43] with a central avenue 64 m wide, lined with stone channels for water and pillared corridors typical of markets.[44] Unlike at Chang'an, the inner and imperial cities are nested and do not abut the outer wall, which would bring them closer to the ideal but for their location in the north-central part of the plan. A founding story claims that the city was planned and constructed as a single coherent project.[45] However, excavation revealed several stages of building and rebuilding.[46] While Tang Chang'an was filled with walled wards

[42] For an account of different uses in different periods see Han Maoli 韩茂莉, *Caoyuan yu tianyuan: Liao Jin shiqi Xi Liao he liuyu nongmuye yu huanjing* 草原与田园 — 辽金时期西辽河流域农牧业与环境 [Pastureland and farmland: agriculture and pastoralism and the environment in the basin of the West Liao River in Liao and Jin times] (Beijing, 2006), 56–9. For location see *Nei Menggu dongnanbu hangkong sheying kaogu baogao* 内蒙古东南部航空摄影考古报告 [Report of aerial photographic archaeology in south-eastern Inner Mongolia], ed. Zhongguo lishi bowuguan yaogan yu hangkong sheying kaogu zhongxin 中国历史博物馆遥感与航空摄影考古中心 [National History Museum Archaeological Centre for Remote Sensing and Aerial Photography] and Nei Menggu Zizhiqu wenwu kaogu yanjiusuo 内蒙古自治区文物考古研究所 [Inner Mongolia Autonomous Region Cultural Relics and Archaeology Research Institute] (Beijing, 2002) [hereafter *Aerial Photographic Archaeology*], 96. For quotation reference see n. 45.

[43] Different lengths have been recorded for the walls. See Steinhardt, *Chinese Imperial City Planning*, 126–7 and n. 12, and Conrad Leyser, Naomi Standen and Stephanie Wynne-Jones, 'Settlement, Landscape and Narrative: What Really Happened in History', in *The Global Middle Ages*, ed. Holmes and Standen, 251 n. 77.

[44] Liao Zhongjing fajue weiyuanhui 辽中京发掘委员会 [Liao Zhongjing Excavation Committee], 'Liao Zhongjing chengzhi fajue de zhongyao shouhuo' 辽中京城址发掘的重要收获 [Important outcomes from the excavations of the site of the Liao Central Capital], *Wenwu* 文物 [Cultural Relics] (1961: 9) [hereafter 'Important outcomes'], 35; Li Yiyou 李逸友, 'Liaodai chengshi he minyong jianzhu' 辽代城市和民用建筑 [Liao cities and commoner buildings], *Zhongguo kaogu jicheng (dongbei juan)* 中国考古集成 (东北卷) [Collected archaeology of China (North-east)], ed. Sun Jinyi 孙进己, Feng Yongqian 冯永谦 and Su Tianjue 苏天钧 (Beijing, 1997), repr. *Dongbei Liaodai gucheng yanjiu huibian* 东北辽代古城研究汇编 [Compilation of research on Liao cities in the North-east], ed. Wang Yulang 王禹浪, Xue Zhiqiang 薛志强, Wang Hongbei 王宏北 and Wang Wenyi 王文轶 (Harbin, 2007), 87.

[45] *Liao shi* 辽史 [History of the Liao Dynasty], comp. Toghto 脱脱 *et al.* (Beijing, 1974), 39: 481–2, trans. Wittfogel and Feng, *History of Chinese Society*, 371. The transliteration of Chinese has been changed to *pinyin* and the capitalisation regularised. In preparing this paper I have not had access to the new edition of the text: Zhonghua shuju, 2016.

[46] *Aerial Photographic Archaeology*, 96–113; 'Important outcomes'; Liao Zhongjing fajue weiyuanhui, 'Neimenggu fajue Liao Zhongjing "Zijincheng" faxian xuduo zhongyao yiji yiwu' 内蒙古发掘辽中京"紫金[sic]城"发现许多重要遗迹遗物 [Excavations of the 'Forbidden City' of the Liao Central Capital in Inner Mongolia discover much of archaeological importance], *Wenwu* (1960: 2), 77.

that survive well archaeologically, within the walls of Zhongjing there are some fairly regular wards but also large areas that lack building foundations, which may have been for horticulture or may reflect textual accounts of seasonal occupation by the 'tent cities' of the emperor's entourage.[47] At the other extreme, Zhongjing contains the largest extant Liao pagoda.[48]

The classic model features markets but not the production sites that feature heavily in the archaeology at Zhongjing and other urban sites. At Zhongjing, buildings for boneworking reflect the ready access to animals from nearby pastures, while deposits of metal – probably slag or other production debris – 1–2 m thick may suggest weapons manufacturing, and agricultural tools have been found. The texts place a granary in the south-west corner, where a half-metre layer of burned grain was found.[49] In the hills to the west are brick and tile kilns ranging over a kilometre, which was probably just one of the extramural production centres needed for everyday goods.[50] If we want to suppose that the plans for parts of the city were derived from a Central Plains model, the extensive modifications suggest that, as we have seen at Chang'an, this design did not fulfil all the needs of the Liao rulers, and certainly not of the commoners without whom the city could not function. As we shall see, Liao city-builders may also have appropriated – and diverged from – other sources of inspiration, and the resulting variety makes it difficult to identify any standard city form that might be labelled as 'Liao'.

IV Liao Shangjing 上京 (918–*c.* 12th cent.) and Ordu Baliq (744–840)

It is important to place urban sites within their broader landscapes. The first Liao capital was the Supreme Capital or Shangjing, built in 918 with rivers on three sides in the heartland of the Liao imperial clan, just 270 km north of Zhongjing, but in a quite different environment, and with a dissimilar plan. The region around Shangjing contained the ruling elite's best pastureland, and would have been grazed regularly by the flocks and

[47] *Liao shi*, j. 32, with selected translations in Wittfogel and Feng, *History of Chinese Society*, 131–4.

[48] The relative political status of Buddhism for the Tang and Liao emperors has yet to be systematically explored, but some issues have been set out for the subsequent period by Jesse Sloane, 'Contending States and Religious Orders in North China and in East Asian Context, 906–1260' (Ph.D. thesis, Princeton University, 2010), esp. chs. 3–4.

[49] Gu Zhoujie 贾洲杰, 'Liao Jin Yuan shidai Nei Menggu diqu de chengshi he chengshi jingji' 辽金元时代内蒙古地区的城市和城市经济 [Cities and their economies in the Inner Mongolia region in the Liao, Jin and Yuan], *Nei Menggu daxue xuebao* 内蒙古大学学报 [Journal of Inner Mongolia University] (1991: 4), repr. *Dongbei Liaodai gucheng*, ed. Wang *et al.*, 370.

[50] *Ibid.*, 369.

herds of clan members. The initial building of the capital was managed, and possibly designed, by a notable migrant who came to Liao from an autonomous borderland province just before the end of the Tang, whose education and early administrative–military postings would have made him familiar with ideal city plans and practical building methods. The work was apparently completed in 100 days, and the walls were extended and palace buildings constructed in 926.[51]

Shangjing appears to have been built in conjunction with the settlement nearby of tens of thousands of people captured in Liao raids and warfare, as part of a wider process that involved 'causing each one to have a spouse, and to bring wasteland and abandoned fields under cultivation' to supply additional grain, fruit and vegetables to supplement the meat, fish and gathered plants typical of pastoralist diets; and to provide tax revenue.[52] The supply needs of capitals must have been a known concern, especially to officials, highlighted by the increasingly desperate and expensive responses generated by the degradation of Tang Chang'an's hinterland from the seventh century, and its abandonment as a metropolitan centre in the late ninth century.[53] For their part, Liao rulers had been transporting huge populations to farm in the northern borderlands for two decades before Shangjing was begun, and latterly receiving refugees from collapsing regimes,[54] so it is hard to know whether the capital was built to manage the people or the populations were transported to supply the capital. Most likely there was a useful and necessary conjunction. We do not know exactly where these imported farmers lived, but both their communities and the city itself would have reduced the pastureland available, and we must therefore reflect on the impact of new urban sites on the wealth of imperial clan members and probably the livelihoods of the actual herders.

Shangjing was designed as a dual city (see Figure 5), comprising what is usually described as an Imperial City to the north, and to the south a *hancheng* 漢城, usually translated as 'Chinese City', although the archaeology does not allow us to ascribe the inhabitants' ethnicity, and they are

---

[51] *Liao shi*, j. 1: 12, 37: 437–42, partly trans. Wittfogel and Feng, *History of Chinese Society*, 367–70. The official in charge, Kang Moji 康默記, has a biography at *Liao shi*, 74: 1230.

[52] Han Yanhui 韓延徽 is given general credit for these developments without association with any named place: *Liao shi*, 74: 1231 and others, see Standen, *Unbounded Loyalty: Frontier Crossings in Liao China* (Honolulu, 2007), 110 and references. *Aerial Photographic Archaeology*, 82, makes him responsible for the 926 expansion, but there is no evidence for this. Han Maoli offers extensive analysis of the population transfer in *Caoyuan yu tianyuan*, 8–55.

[53] The story may be pieced together: *The Cambridge History of China*, vol. 3: *Sui and T'ang China, 589–906*, ed. Denis Twitchett and John Fairbank (Cambridge, 1979), 174–7, 186–95, 258, 277, 356–8, 392, 395, 399–400, 420, 475, 479; Ling Zhang, *The River, the Plain, and the State: An Environmental Drama in Northern Song China, 1048–1128* (Cambridge, 2016), 31–3, 37, 46–7, 73–90, 93–6, 110–11, 127–41, 167–71.

[54] Standen, *Unbounded Loyalty*, appendix: Frontier crossings arranged by date, #1–22.

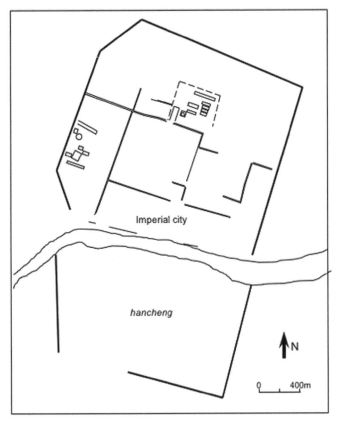

Figure 5 Plan of Liao Shangjing. Image: Standen, based on Google Earth, with thanks to Gwen Bennett and Lin Hu.

better defined as commoners.[55] A *hancheng* was a feature of a good pro-portion of known Liao urban centres, but was not found in Tang cities. Shangjing is orientated towards the north-east, and both parts are irregular polygons within an outer wall totalling nearly 9 km long. The two sections are divided by the river that would have watered the city and surrounding lands, but may have been prone to flooding then as it has been since.[56] The walls are of rammed earth and include defen-sive features such as *mamian* 馬面 bastions, which are common on fortified

[55] To avoid reinforcing ethnic assumptions for an anglophone audience, I will retain the transliteration for this feature rather than using a translation.

[56] *Aerial Photographic Archaeology*, 84.

walls across eastern Eurasia. The Imperial City had many streets, but no central avenue or systematic grid of wards.[57] There are 3.5 m of cultural layers, including tiled floors, rammed-earth foundation platforms, stone tortoises which supported stelae, and stone column bases, all of which indicate high-status buildings and long occupation in the many places where they are found across our region.[58] A palace complex lies centrally in the Imperial City,[59] which also includes a large area probably for a 'tent city'.[60] The *hancheng* contains concentrations of bricks and tiles, suggesting large buildings, as well as a dense scatter of potsherds and other artefacts that indicate intensive habitation, although there is no other evidence, such as flues for stoves, of large-scale residential occupation.[61] In the *hancheng* there were workshops for oil, iron and harnesses,[62] and kilns inside the city and in the mountains outside produced bricks, tiles, everyday pottery and high-quality wares to supply the city and perhaps beyond. Many stone grindstones and mortars indicate that a lot of wheat and other grains was being ground for flour-based foodstuffs.[63] There were pagodas within and outside the walls.

Rather than seeing the central location of the palace complex and the familiar building methods at Liao Shangjing as necessarily imitating a Tang-style capital, we might instead pay more heed to what was being produced and consumed within and around the walls, identify the networks to which the city contributed and consider why this city might have been built at all. Shangjing was established by a new emperor from a primarily pastoralist background who had long experience, both among his group and personally, of the neighbouring Tang world and its ubiquitous urban centres. The new capital was built under the direction of lowly non-aristocratic officials from that world,

---

[57] Hu Lin, 'Urban Landscape and Politics: The Making of Liao Cities in Southeast Inner Mongolia', 2 vols. (Ph.D. thesis, University of Chicago, 2009), 157.

[58] *Aerial Photographic Archaeology*, 88.

[59] Zhongguo Shehuikexueyuan kaogu yanjiusuo Nei Menggu di er gongzuodui 中国社会科学院考古研究所内蒙古第二工作队 [The Inner Mongolia Second Work Team of the Institute or Archaeology, Chinese Academy of Social Sciences] and Nei Menggu Wenwu kaogu yanjiusuo 内蒙古文物考古研究所 [Inner Mongolia Archaeology and Cultural Relics Research Institute], 'Nei Mengguo Balinzuoqi Liao Shangjing gongcheng chengqiang 2014 nian fajue jianbao' 内蒙古巴林左旗辽上京宫城城墙2014年发掘简报 [Brief report on the 2014 excavations of the walls of the Palace City at Liao Shangjing in Balinzuoqi, Inner Mongolia], Kaogu 考古 [Archaeology] (2015: 12), 78.

[60] Neimenggu zizhiqu wenwuju 内蒙古自治区文物局 [Inner Mongolia Cultural Relics Bureau], *Neimenggu wenwu gailan* 内蒙古文物概览 [Overview of Inner Mongolian Cultural Relics] (Hohhot: Neimenggu zizhiqu wenwuju, 2007) [hereafter *Neimenggu wenwu gailan*], 53.

[61] *Aerial Photographic Archaeology*, 94.

[62] Lin, 'Urban Landscape and Politics', 224 and reference, noting that details are yet to be published.

[63] Gu, 'Liao Jin Yuan shidai Nei Menggu de chengshi', 367–8.

one of whom was still in his thirties when he gave general encouragement to the building of city walls.[64] The central roles of these officials in city-building reflect flows of know-how that readily crossed eastern Eurasian borders and boundaries formed by politics, language, social status and ethnicity. Departures and returns, fresh arrivals, and evidence for continuing cross-border contact suggest that the movements of those with expertise in governance were not one-offs, but passed through and helped to constitute ongoing networks of knowledge and personnel.[65] These networks of interactions and relationships between individuals shared some elements – nodes formed by specific urban centres – with the formal networks of cities created by the administrative geographies of more than one political unit. But cities were just one element in intangible networks, which were also of different shapes than the pattern of administrative centres, and extended where they would regardless of jurisdiction. The knowledge and connections present in these networks could be drawn upon by anyone with the capacity and desire to employ network members.

Despite the Tang models familiar to the Liao founder and Shangjing's designers, the urban settlement that resulted from interactions within these intangible networks did not follow the plan of a Tang city such as Chang'an, even though Shangjing's functions appear to have included the same administrative and ritual activities. Shangjing's wider landscape included both agricultural and pastoral producers, as well as additional manufacturing for everyday needs, all presumably governed by authorities based in the city.[66] For each of these activities the city formed one node in a distinctive network variously involving production, supply of raw materials, transportation, taxation, imports and exports, any of which could extend a specific network well beyond the city's hinterland. Such networks required skills and knowledge that may have been confined to a particular category of worker – notably but by no means exclusively officials – but were not restricted to any one political or cultural group. The capital also seems to have had an important role as a place for periodic gatherings by people who brought their accommodation with them, implying that it was a political centre too, and it may have had some kind of legitimating function with those people and with envoys visiting from other realms.[67] Each different set of political actors placed Shangjing in yet another network that involved a distinctive set of elements and reached its own extent. Shangjing consisted of

---

[64] See nn. 51–2.

[65] Standen, *Unbounded Loyalty*, is one example, but this is a growing field of enquiry.

[66] The structure of authority over the surrounding districts is set out conveniently in Wittfogel and Feng, *History of Chinese Society*, 62–5.

[67] Lin, 'Urban Landscape and Politics'.

many aspects, many of them beyond the walls, reflecting a larger range of functions than the classic city represented – though no more embodied – by Tang Chang'an.[68] Each city was constructed to meet a particular set of needs.

The rulers of the Uyghur Khaghanate (744–840)[69] built numerous walled settlements in Mongolia, but before the advent of aerial photography, remote sensing, and the money to deploy these methods, these sites were hard to locate.[70] By contrast, the palace at the Khaghanate's capital of Ordu Baliq, begun in the later 750s and also known at times as Karabalgasun or Kharbalgas, has surviving walls at heights that make it easy to see from far away across the broad valley bottom around the Orkhon, in which numerous other cities were also built at different times over many centuries.[71] The palace complex is orientated almost east–west and outside each of the longer walls is a line of stupa mounds – a rare feature (see Figure 6). The complex includes a square inner wall, outside the eastern gate of which is a broad avenue flanked by a grid of compounds and buildings. However, this is only a fraction of the area covered by the ruins which, at 7×2.5 km, form the largest pre-modern urban settlement in Mongolia.[72] The designers are said to have been Sogdians,[73] but their role seems to have been limited to the palace complex, which is the one regular rectangle, located in the north-east corner alongside generally organic clusters of small buildings and walled spaces. The largest of the walled clusters, about three times the size of the palace, is an irregular square containing densely packed buildings.[74] Stone column bases and heavy fired bricks are among the common building methods that help to distinguish administrative from residential and manufacturing areas, there is plenty of space for the markets mentioned in the texts, and some of the ceramics feature distinctive decorations.[75]

---

[68] See also Peregrine Hordern and Nicholas Purcell, *The Corrupting Sea: A Study of Mediterranean History* (Oxford, 2000), 89–122.

[69] Not 'the Uyghurs', see above, p. 31. The Khaghanate was a multi-ethnic political formation like any other imperial polity.

[70] Daniel C. Waugh, 'Nomads and Settlement: New Perspectives in the Archaeology of Mongolia', *The Silk Road*, 8 (2010), 103, and references cited there.

[71] *Ibid.*, 100–11 *passim*.

[72] J. Daniel Rogers, Erdenebat Ulambayar and Mathew Gallon, 'Urban Centres and the Emergence of Empires in Eastern Inner Asia', *Antiquity*, 79 (2005), 804.

[73] Lucie Šmahelová, 'Kül-Tegin Monument: Turkic Khaganate and Research of the First Czechoslovak–Mongolian Expedition in Khöshöö Tsaidam 1958' (Ph.D. thesis, Charles University, Prague, 2014), 25.

[74] See LiDAR in Helmut Roth, Ulambaâr Èrdènèbat, Ernst Pohl and Eva Nagel, *Qara Qorum-City (Mongolia) I, Preliminary Report of the Excavations 2000/2001* (Bonn, 2002), plate XXII; and plan in Rogers *et al.*, 'Urban Centres', 804.

[75] Burkart Dähne and Erdenebat Ulambayar, 'Archaeological Excavations in Karabalgasun by K. Maskov during Kotwicz's Expedition of 1912: A New Contribution

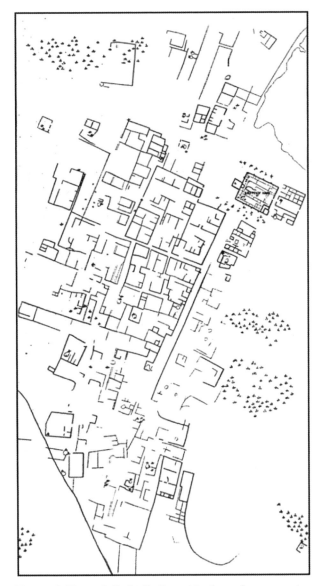

Figure 6 Plan of Ordu Baliq, with the palace complex towards the top right corner. Image: from V. V. Radlov, *Atlas drevnostei Mongolii*, vyp. 2. Trudy Orkhonskoi ekspeditsii. Sanktpeterburg: Tipografiia Imperatorskoi akademii nauk, 1893, plate XXVII/1, with deep thanks to Daniel C. Waugh.

The city lay in a predominantly pastoralist landscape, but an envoy of the Abbasid caliph in 821 described 'a great town, rich in agriculture and surrounded by districts full of cultivation and villages lying close together'.[76] Recent archaeology confirms the envoy's report, adding that these districts were all enclosed, in a mixture of square and oval shapes (see Figure 7).[77] The squares contain potsherds, and roof tiles with the semicircular section found from the Korean peninsula to the Tarim basin, suggesting farming households of men, women and children, dating between the end of the seventh and the mid-ninth century. Biomarkers imply that domesticated animals like pigs or dogs were kept inside the square walls, and an abundance of butchered and burnt bones were found in one surrounding ditch, together with ceramics. A surface-collection survey of one of the ovals found no artefacts, while biomarkers for herbivore faeces were uniformly abundant both within and outside the walls, indicating that herds were not restricted inside them. The biomarkers show that this oval was not an animal corral but probably for horticulture.[78] The archaeology gives us a view of primary producers providing meat, vegetables and related products, allowing herbivores into their oval horticulture enclosures for fertilisation but then shutting them out during the growing season, when herds would

to the Research History of the Capital of the Eastern Uighur Khaganate', in *In the Heart of Mongolia: 100th Anniversary of W. Kotwicz's Expedition to Mongolia in 1912, Studies and Selected Source Materials*, ed. Jerzy Tulisow, Osamu Inoue, Agata Bareja-Starzynska and Ewa Dziurzynska (Cracow, 2012) (column bases); Waugh, 'Nomads and Settlement', 103 (bricks); Jan Bemmann, Eva Lehndorff, Riccardo Klinger, Sven Linzen, Lkhagvardorj Munkhbayar, Martin Oczipka, Henny Piezonka and Susanne Reichert, 'Biomarkers in Archaeology: Land Use around the Uyghur Capital Karabalgasun, Orkhon Valley, Mongolia', *Praehistorische Zeitschrift*, 89 (2014), 348–9 (ceramics).

[76] Vladimir Minorsky, 'Tamīm ibn Bahr's Journey to the Uyghurs', *Bulletin of the School of Oriental and African Studies*, 12 (1948), esp. 283; Bemmann *et al.*, 'Biomarkers'.

[77] Earlier archaeology confirmed cereal agriculture in places such as Tuva in northwestern Mongolia, together with the corollary millstones, pestles and irrigation canals: Colin Mackerras, 'The Uighurs', in *The Cambridge History of Early Inner Asia*, ed. Denis Sinor (Cambridge, 1990), 337, citing Russian archaeological work. The inhabitants of ninth-century Qocho practised the oasis agriculture suited to their environment (Peter B. Golden, *An Introduction to the History of the Turkic Peoples: Ethnogenesis and State-Formation in Medieval and Early Modern Eurasia and the Middle East* (Wiesbaden, 1992), 171 and references in note), but those at Ordu Baliq did not, being in a different environment again.

[78] Bemmann *et al.*, 'Biomarkers'. Bemmann notes (340) that two significant instances of cereal pollen from the Orkhon lowlands south of Karakorum give some support to textual claims of good harvests along the Orkhon, referring to Frank Lehmkuhl, Alexandra Hilgers, Susanne Fries, Daniela Hülle, Frank Schlütz, Lyudmila Shumilovskikh, Thomas Felauer and Jens Protze, 'Holocene Geomorphological Processes and Soil Development as Indicator for Environmental Change around Karakorum, Upper Orkhon Valley (Central Mongolia)', *Catena*, 87 (2011), 31–44; and to Wittfogel and Feng, *History of Chinese Society*, 556. The translation states that the relevant section speaks of 982–1013, but the original passage sits between incidents dated to 1006 and the reign era 1032–55: *Liao shi*, 91: 1362.

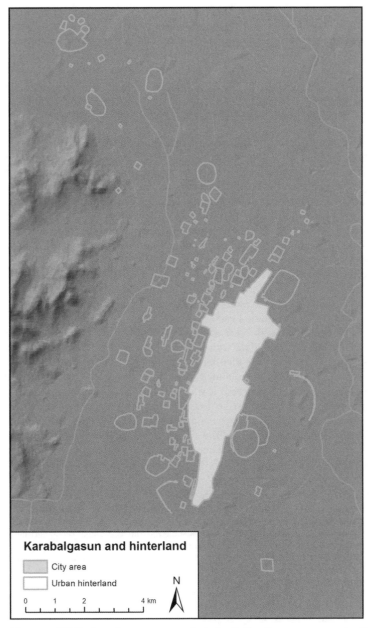

Figure 7 Walled enclosures around Ordu Baliq. Image: courtesy of Susanne Reichert.

move to summer pastures. Whereas for the time of Shangjing's construction we have abundant textual evidence that the Liao emperors' revenue was at least coming to rely on agricultural taxation requiring a city-based bureaucracy, at Ordu Baliq we lack any such surviving evidence, so we may be a little more confident that for the Uyghur khaghans the capital came first and its farmers were moved into or settled upon this landscape for the purpose of supporting the city.[79] Certainly we cannot be sure that the settlements around each of these cities were for wholly the same purposes.

Elements of the urban landscape of Ordu Baliq, including the hinterland together with the concentration of buildings around the palace, bore family resemblances to parts of another Uyghur town that seems to have begun in the seventh century and was reused by the Liao, probably in the tenth or eleventh century, with few changes.[80] We may therefore suppose that members of the Liao ruling group were familiar with these options too. The same archaeological techniques used at Ordu Baliq would be needed to test whether Liao Shangjing, 1400 km away, had similar provisioning arrangements, but we should not be surprised at the Liao appropriating different elements from their diverse predecessors in different locations, any more than we should be surprised by the much wider prevalence of relatively simple and quick construction methods such as rammed earth.

The cities discussed so far were in reasonably flat sites in river valleys and, except for Chang'an, with little or no prior permanent habitation. Such environments lent themselves to fulfilling any desire there might have been for building planned cities to a cosmologically significant design, but as we have seen, it was rare for Liao, other 'steppe cities', and even Tang Chang'an, to follow ritual prescriptions in preference to building according to their needs, which included different combinations of administration, politics, display, subsistence, manufacturing, exchange and legitimation. The result was cities that shared little but the basic building techniques of rammed-earth walls within walls,

---

[79] The scanty evidence gives no indication of an administration focused on taxing farmers. Administrative experience and models came mainly from Sogdians, accustomed to organising trade networks rather than pursuing the Sinitic view that cereal agriculture was the moral and fiscal basis of the state. The Khaghanate's main revenue streams appear to have been tariffs on the oasis trade in the Tarim, and annual Tang payments in the shape of the purchase of tens of thousands of overpriced horses, some suitable for military use but also many nags. Mackerras, 'The Uighurs', 338 and references; Golden, *Introduction*, 159–61, who notes that the early empire already controlled Ferghana.

[80] We cannot tell if there was a break in usage or not. Khermen Denzh: Nikolay N. Kradin, Aleksandr L. Ivliev, Ayudai Ochir, Lkhagvasuren Erdenebold, Sergei Vasiutin, Svetlana Satantseva and Evgenii V. Kovychev, 'Khermen Denzh Town in Mongolia', *The Silk Road*, 13 (2015), 97.

usually polygonal shapes, gates, and pillared major buildings placed in clusters, constructed to an intial plan but subject to later modification. These broadest of similarities formed a substrate of construction methods that spanned eastern Eurasia, and no meaningful claim can be made that they 'belonged' to any one group rather than another or that they could accordingly 'influence' others. They were simply how you did construction across this whole region, and were subject to pretty much infinite local variation; diversity was the norm.

V Zuzhou 祖州 (bef. 926–12th cent.) and Wandu[81] 丸都 (209–c. 7th cent?)

Scholars of pre-modern urbanism in the Korean peninsula often categorise their cities into mountain and flatland types, and the Liao and others also made use of 'mountain cities' 山城 (*shancheng*). Here we find that although some activities overlap with those of urban centres in broad valleys, a distinctive function of some mountain cities, in different locations and under different governing regimes, was burial and memorialisation. The Liao founder's tomb, Zuling 祖陵, was built after his death and is concealed inside one spur running down from a horseshoe of steep-sided, wooded mountains 20 km south-west of Liao Shangjing.[82] The accompanying city of Zuzhou does not lie in the flat valley bottom that opens out below the mountain defile, but clings to the first sufficiently flat spot on the lower slopes of the eastern side (Figure 8). Although the outer wall of the main city is nearly rectangular (approx. 600 × 300 m), conforming to the landscape has created a pentagon orientated towards the north-west, housing the officials who performed the regular rituals for the imperial dead, and a dense crowd of households, probably attached to a military unit.[83] As usual, all the walls are of rammed earth, including a narrow rectangular enclosure at the west end, opening onto a wide avenue.[84] This inner city contains buildings identified by their column bases as ritual halls, some of which are named in the *Liao shi* 遼史.[85] Zuzhou itself is named as the autumn location of the emperor's travelling court, but any space for a 'tent city' appears to be small, and there is little space to camp outside the walls either.

Most curiously, on a rise in the north-western corner of the main city is a structure known simply as the Stone House 石室 (*shishi*) (Figure 9), built

---

[81] Korean: Hwando.

[82] *Neimenggu wenwu gailan*, 60.

[83] Lin, 'Urban Landscape and Politics', 156 and references (dense housing); Wittfogel and Feng, *History of Chinese Society*, 63.

[84] *Neimenggu wenwu gailan*, 60.

[85] *Liao shi*, 37: 442.

Figure 8 Aerial photograph of Zuzhou, showing location and plan. Image: Google Earth.

of seven massive stone slabs with the corners originally connected by iron brackets, leaving a T-shaped opening that looks south-east along the same line as the city.[86] The function of this structure remains a mystery.[87] If it was already there when the city was constructed then the walls were built around it, and in the unlikely event that it was built by the Liao, we have no idea what it was for. There was nothing else like it in Liao, but it bears an obvious resemblance to dolmens seen especially in Manchuria, while we find the use of large stone slabs most obviously in some of the Goguryeo tombs above Wandu on the Yalu, to which we shall shortly return.[88] Whatever the Stone House's date and function, the textual evidence for a ritual city combined with

[86] Nancy Steinhardt, 'Shishi: A Stone Structure Associated with Abaoji in Zuzhou', Asia Major, 3rd series, 19 (2006), 241–66, with plan at 242. Scholarship thus far does not seem to have made much of this shared alignment.

[87] Josh Wright has developed a strong opinion that this is the tomb chamber for an unbuilt royal tomb, due to the way its interior is smoothed and polished like other tomb chambers (personal communication). On the basis of the available neighbouring tomb traditions, this hypothesis implies that a huge mound of earth or possibly stone (see below) would have been planned to be constructed over the chamber.

[88] Steinhardt, 'Shishi', 246–8.

Figure 9 The 'Stone House'. Photo: Standen.

the formal layout of the inner walled section may suggest a primarily monumental site, which may readily have incorporated the Stone House, although it remains odd that this structure is mentioned in no surviving text.

At a more quotidian level, an extramural suburb that follows the landscape abuts the main city, and has a central main street flanked by what are thought to be markets and artisanal workshops, possibly including one for imperial textiles. Aside from Zuzhou, evidence for extensive workshops of this kind is found in Liao only at Shangjing and three other grassland cities.[89] Although the urban structures share in the east Eurasian substrate of basic building methods, they also present several unique or unusual features compared to other Liao cities.

The mountain defile containing the tomb has a spring and a single entrance where there are remains of a wall and gate to guard access. On the hill beside the gate and further into the defile are three halls which may have housed eulogistic stelae mentioned in texts.[90] Figure 10 shows how the low points in the encircling ridge are filled in with drystone walls to create a more even profile, and similar infill walls are found, once again, at Wandu, which at the start of Deguang's reign was part of Balhae, a city-building regime which governed the northern Korean peninsula and southern Manchuria from

[89] Gu, 'Liao Jin Yuan shidai Nei Menggu de chengshi', 371; Lin, 'Urban Landscape and Politics', 224–5 and *Liao shi*, 37: 442.
[90] *Aerial Photographic Archaeology*, 122.

Figure 10 Infill walls at Zuling. Photo: Standen.

the seventh century.[91] The Zuling tomb was built by the second Liao emperor, Deguang 德光 (r. 926–47), and he or his officials had opportunities to see such infill walls during the Liao conquest of the Balhae in 926 and in the process of taking over and governing the region.[92] The combination of Zuzhou and Zuling makes a landscape that includes mountains with a river running down to flatland – and ultimately to Shangjing – a burial ground, and ritual, residential, production and market areas. Zuzhou's walls were intended to be defensible, and indeed the city held out against attackers for long enough in 1119 to suffer extensive fire damage.[93]

We also find this pairing of imperial burial grounds with defensible urban settlements in neighbouring mountain and flatter land in the Korean peninsula, with somewhat different purposes and arrangement. The urban landscape at Wandu mountain city near the North Korean border includes a city in the Changbai mountains 長白山 and another

[91] Personal observation, 1991–2014; *Neimenggu wenwu gailan*, 60.
[92] For urban sites in this period see *Zhongguo lishi ditu ji 6 – Song, Liao, Jin* 中国历史地图集 6—宋辽金时期, ed. Tan Qixiang 谭其骧 *et al.* (Shanghai: Ditu chubanshe, 1982), pp. 8–9 (Liao Dongjing, the Eastern Capital).
[93] *Aerial Photographic Archaeology*, 114.

downstream nestled near a confluence on the Yalu (Figure 11). Wandu was the Goguryeo capital from 209 to 427, after which its associated 'flatland city', Guoneicheng 國內成, remained a secondary capital.[94] As just noted, the area was taken over by the Balhae, then conquered by the Liao in 926. There were many mountain cities; one scholar has tabulated the characteristics of sixty-seven, largely strung out along both banks of the Yalu and paired with a 'flatland city'.[95] As is common in the northern Korean peninsula and southern Manchuria, most of these cities were built of stone, although a significant minority were of rammed earth.[96] Mountain cities made up 28 per cent of the 260 known urban sites in the region along the modern border, including nearly all of the largest. Most of these urban settlements seem to fall into eight regions, in each of which cities formed chains of fortifications along the six main routes in and out of Balhae. The Liao reused such sites as they did some cities used by the Uyghur Khaghanate, adding to the variety of forms in their urban portfolio.[97]

The plans of the mountain cities followed the often severe terrain, while the flatland cities could be closer to rectangular.[98] Wandu's outer walls form a strongly distorted diamond, while below it Guoneicheng is orientated to the north-east and is roughly square, with a broad transverse main street and two loosely orthogonal cross streets.[99] The walls of Wandu feature extensive surviving drystone walls using well-dressed blocks of regular size, surviving best at the lower edge where they include a gated wall that closes off access from the valley below, as at Zuling.[100] The mountain cities, Wandu among

---

[94] Li Dianfu 李殿福, 'Gaogouli Wandu shancheng' 高句丽丸都山城 [Wandu mountain city in Goguryeo], *Wenwu* (1982: 6), 84; Wei Cuncheng 魏存成, 'Gaogouli chuzhongqi de ducheng' 高句丽初中期的都城 [Capital cities of early and middle Goguryeo], *Beifang wenwu* 北方文物 [Northern Cultural Relics] (1985: 2), 33. There is some debate about which of the mountain or downstream sites was referred to by this name: Sun Weiran 孙炜冉, 'Gaogouli "Weina yancheng" kaobian' 高句丽'尉那岩城'考辨 [The identification of the 'Weina cliff city' in Goguryeo], *Beifang wenwu* (2017: 1), 77–81.

[95] Chen Dawei 陈大为, 'Liaoning Gaogouli shancheng zai tan' 辽宁高句丽山城再探 [Further discussion of the Goguryeo mountain cities in Liaoning], *Beifang wenwu* (1995: 3), table 60–3.

[96] *Ibid.*

[97] Liu Xiaoxi 刘晓溪, Jiang Ming 姜铭 and Pauline Sebillaud, 'Yanbian zhou Liao Jin shiqi chengzhi ji qi fenbu qingkuang gaishu' 延边州辽金时期城址及其分布情况概述 [An overview of Yanbian region Liao and Jin cities and their distribution], *Kaogu yu wenwu* 考古与文物 [Archaeology and Cultural Relics] (2015: 2), esp. appended map.

[98] Chen, 'Liaoning Gaogouli shancheng', 60–3; Wang Mianhou 王綿厚, *Gaogouli gucheng yanjiu* 高句麗古城研究 [Research on ancient Goguryeo cities] (Beijing: Wenwu chubanshe, 2002), ch. 5, 67ff. (mountain); 138ff. (plain).

[99] Wang, *Gaogouli gucheng*, pp. 54, 49ff.

[100] Li, 'Gaogouli Wandu shancheng', 83. *Mamian* appear to be a later feature: Wang, *Gaogouli gucheng*, 165.

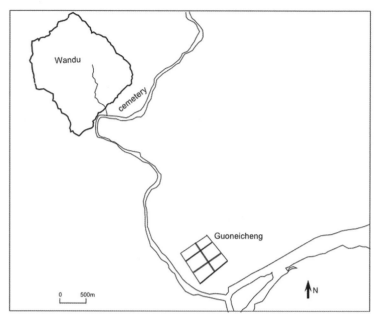

Figure 11 Plan of Wandu mountain city and Guoneicheng. Image: Standen, based on Google Earth, with thanks to Gwen Bennett.

them, likewise feature infill walls of stone at the peaks of the surrounding mountains.[101] Wandu is also typical in having good access to springs for water, and like other mountain cities it has a reservoir too. The city contains a large 'palace' building set on two narrower hillside terraces flanking a wider one, where rows of column bases suggest two 'corridor' halls around a larger space.[102] This is a design also found at other Balhae sites such as Balhae Shangjing.[103] As often in northern settlements, *kang*s (sleeping or living platforms heated from beneath) are commonly found, and roof decorations are distinctive.[104]

---

[101] Chen, 'Liaoning Gaogouli shancheng', 60–3.

[102] Li, 'Gaogouli Wandu shancheng', 84.

[103] Heilongjiang sheng Wenwu kaogu yanjiusuo 黑龙江省文物考古研究所 [Heilongjiang Provincial Cultural Relics and Archaeology Research Institute], *Bohai Shangjing cheng: 1998–2007 niandu kaogu fajue diaocha baogao* 渤海上京城: 1998–2007 年度考古发掘调查报告 [Balhae Shangjing: Report on Archaeological Excavation and Survey, 1999–2007], (3 vols., Beijing, 2009), 634.

[104] Wang, *Gaogouli gucheng*, 168, 170.

Despite serving as a capital, Wandu is not described in the twelfth-century history of Goguryeo, which provides only the barest indication of the administrative structure within which cities like Wandu and Guoneicheng were presumably situated.[105] Given the locations and fortifications of the mountain cities, scholars have naturally argued that they were primarily for defence in the context of a highly fragmented political situation including attacks from the west, and especially from the Tang.[106] This is convincing enough for the paired mountain and flatland cities in general, but at Wandu there is a remarkable additional element, for the mountain city presides over a large extramural cemetery on the riverbank 3 km upstream of Guoneicheng, containing dozens of tombs of which some use stone slabs and many use blocks (Figures 12 and 13).[107] The extensive use of stone both for tombs and for some city walls makes sense in the rocky environment of the region, and may be taken to mark one geographical limit of the substrate created by the overwhelming predominance of rammed-earth surrounding walls down to at least the eleventh century.

Comparison of Wandu and Guoneicheng with Zuzhou and Zuling, each pair located in its own landscape, is not a simple matter. As at the other sites discussed here, the substrate elements of rammed-earth construction, regular shapes where landscape allows, nested enclosures, pillared buildings, and planning are all present, and both paired cities were imbricated in their respective networks of administrative hierarchy. Both pairs would have been nodes of activity in trade, religion, production and supply, but we lack the evidence to comment on what connections may have existed, so their involvement in these networks can only be by inference. We see, however, that Zuzhou or its vicinity are claimed textually as part of the Liao court's political network, while spatial analysis identifies Wandu/Guoneicheng as part of a chain or network of defences. We note that several of the elements specific to these city pairs are similar: associated mountain and flatland sites, a relatively regular design for the lower city, a burial ground, infill walls between the surrounding mountain peaks, and at least one stone slab structure. The politics of death were also key elements of both locations, but were manifested in markedly different ways: dozens of highly visible

[105] The geographical treatise in the twelfth-century *Samguk sagi*, j. 37 essentially lists only place names, with almost no discursive text. Kim Pu-shik 金富軾, *Samguk sagi* 三國史記 [History of the Three Kingdoms] (Seŏul, 1977).

[106] Wang, *Gaogouli gucheng*, 38ff.; Wei, 'Gaogouli chuzhongqi de ducheng', 35. On Tang: Chen, 'Liaoning Gaogouli shancheng', 60; Huang K'uan-chung and David Wright, 'Mountain Fortress Defence: The Experience of the Southern Song and Korea in Resisting the Mongol Invasions', *Warfare in Chinese History*, ed. Hans Van de Ven (Leiden, 2000), 222–51.

[107] The best known of the slab tombs is Accompanying Burial #1 of the 'General's Tomb'.

Figure 12 The Goguryeo tombs at Ji'an, Jilin. Image: Google Earth.

Figure 13 A slab tomb: accompanying burial #1 of the 'General's tomb',
Ji'an. Photo: Standen.

riverside stone tombs as against a single hidden mountain tomb, which
was located separately from a solitary enigmatic slab building; two
walled enclosures or one; concealment in the mountains or defence.
We do not (yet) know if any of these features drew these cities into a
necropolitan network.[108] What we can say is that if Liao emperors or

---

[108] This term comes from Ph.D. work by Lance Pursey.

city designers sometimes appropriated elements from landscapes they saw in Balhae, they made their own creative and distinctive use of them, in some places combining that with what they selected from sites constructed by others such as Uyghur khaghans or Tang emperors, while also at times deploying features of their own such as concealed imperial burials. From such a mixture, or set of mixtures, it is impossible to identify a specifically 'Liao' urban style.

VI Conclusions

It is unhelpful to continue to frame the Liao – or indeed any eastern Eurasian polity – in terms of their relationship to Sinitic culture and its hegemonic source base.[109] Once other sources of inspiration are taken seriously, the idea that 'Liao' cities are unified by anything but their use by the Liao dynasty falls apart. Zhongjing was not a poor imitation of an idealised model that was not even followed by Tang Chang'an, but – why should we be surprised? – was built to fulfil specific needs and then evolved further by both accident and design. Liao Shangjing and khaghanal Ordu Baliq, both 'steppe cities', each featured large identifiable hinterlands of production and supply, and the extramural habitation that these required. Shangjing's planners had access to khaghanal models but it did not necessarily require direct appropriation to come up with similar solutions to a similar question: how to sustain a population concentration in one spot within an environment that did not lend itself to intensive exploitation. In the third comparison, Liao Zuzhou and Zuling exhibit some similar uses and features of Goguryeo paired mountain and flatland cities such as Wandu and Guoneicheng, complete with the latter pair's royal cemetery. Most of the shared elements of both pairs could be independent responses to specific and partly similar circumstances, and certainly generated diverse results that make the idea of borrowing as reductive as it is undemonstrable. The one exception may be the construction of infill walls between mountain peaks, a choice that has defied explanation and accordingly is hard to imagine arising independently in two places just a few hundred kilometres apart. If this one element was indeed an appropriation from Goguryeo to Liao, then it highlights the importance of considering each element separately rather than assuming the adoption of an entire package.

---

[109] Since the textual sources for eastern Eurasia are overwhelmingly in Sinitic, which was produced very largely by literate elites educated in the associated ideological, conceptual and literary tradition, and since those sources have been interpreted predominantly from perspectives similar or sympathetic to the concerns of those literate elites, the term 'hegemonic' appears to be justified.

If we accept that it stretches the urban evidence to continue to see the Liao – to a greater or lesser exent – as simply imitators of the Tang, another option would be to regard the Liao as appropriating from multiple sources in a merely eclectic fashion; indecisive, incoherent, lacking clear identity, without direction. As much World History would have it, these are also the failings of pre-modernity more generally, before centralisation, systematisation, clear boundaries, and – a word that has been attempting a comeback lately – progress. Confident identifications of the Tang model in Liao forms might give way to a careful teasing out of what came from where in linear – or even complex – flows of transmission, but even the most generous interpretation of eclecticism only upends the paradigm; it does not replace it. In this view there is still something called '*Liao* urbanisation' and the Liao still 'borrow' from their neighbours, just from many instead of one. However, the evidence presented here provides no features that clearly link Liao cities that do not also link many non-Liao cities. There is nothing distinctively 'Liao' about the cities used by that dynasty.

Instead of seeking common elements that might give these cities a discrete shared identity, we could hold the diversity as we meet it, and see different elements working at different levels and different scales. It is more instructive to reconsider cities such as Tang Chang'an and Liao Zhongjing as the urban elements within broader landscapes, and furthermore, from global perspectives that allow us to locate any given city within patterns created by substrates, networks and nodes. We might see a substrate of common techniques underpinning urban construction across the whole of eastern Eurasia, its origins effectively untraceable to contemporaries and at best hazy to us; belonging to none and used by all. The urban sites themselves may then be nodes of specific expression of itemised aspects more widely found, such as types of ground plan or methods for provisioning the city. Sets of those nodes might become linked into networks of varying density, shape, pattern, depth – such as a set of political relationships, an administrative hierarchy or a defensive chain. With a different set of cases or fresh evidence, commercial, religious, production, fiscal or other networks might be more prominent.

What makes a history global is precisely its refusal to sit within conventional bounds of nation-states, being prepared instead to follow the topic wherever it leads, which might be a chain of connections – or not – from Karabalgasun to Wandu or Chang'an, or might be a much shorter distance from the farmhouse to the urban centre. Either way, what we are choosing to see is the contemporary working of assumptions about how things were done that were shared with a constellation of other people who spoke different languages, ate different food, were under different jurisdictions, and so on. Thus our analyses should not be distracted by texts that arrange cities into hierarchies as a contribution towards imperial legibility both historical and historiographical; it may be hard to think without state boundaries, but it is worth the effort. We must also remember that while it may have been states that established urban centres, it was people who lived in them; many cities later lost their administrative status but not their inhabitants. The more useful unit of study is *landscapes*, which leads us to very different questions from what the sources want to tell us, and may speak better to our needs in the present.

It is a matter of importance that global histories of this kind and others offer some purchase on a key task for the present day: to denaturalise the idea of the nation-state. As I write, we are seeing only too clearly that where scholars present pre-modern histories in quasi-national terms then – wittingly or otherwise – they assist present-day nationalists. Historians can help by writing firmly non-national histories – global histories – in which medieval periods have a particularly valuable role, precisely because this age can more readily stand outside the trajectories towards nationalism that seem impossible for modernists to avoid.

Presentist politics aside, global approaches to the pre-modern may also help us to escape from historical writing that is too often competitive, and even triumphalist. Books concerned with some Big Picture are frequently underpinned by concern to find the biggest, earliest, strongest, greatest, longest, richest and so on. This kind of macho history not only becomes tiresome, but its emphasis on competition and expansion, power and money, centralisation and integration, misses out huge and crucial areas of human activity, to do with praxis, women (and children), and generally people who were not the ruling elite.

That is not a new observation, and I do not pretend to have all the answers, but I do believe it is important to apply to global history some of the approaches developed in other fields of history, and especially to emphasise the everyday: how people got their food, how politics and religion and power happened on the daily level, how children were acquired, how things moved around, and the painful realities of conflict. That means, of course, that we must read against the power-focused textual sources, and against the tendency to focus on the shinier parts of material culture, which are also focused on power, and we must seek out new sources as well. We cannot do it by ourselves. My current project strains at, if it does not overstep, my own capabilities – I do not read Korean, for example. We have to collaborate, cooperate and listen to each other. In the present state of the world, that in itself is a radical move.

Transactions of the RHS 29 (2019), pp. 65–77 © Royal Historical Society 2019
doi:10.1017/S0080440119000033

SALADIN'S 'SPIN DOCTORS'

Prothero Lecture

By Carole Hillenbrand

READ 6 JULY 2018

ABSTRACT. We might flatter ourselves that the idea of a spin doctor is rather a
modern one, but I wonder. Obviously enough, powerful rulers have always had
their coterie of close advisers. But in the medieval Muslim world there is one outstanding example of something rather more than this: the team of three counsellors
that Saladin assembled who watched over his interests and, crucially, his reputation,
with unflagging devotion for decades. Two of them were, by any standard, intellectual stars who could have turned their multifarious talents in many directions but
who chose rather to dedicate them to a man whom they not only admired but
also loved. One of them, the poet 'Imad al-Din al-Isfahani, was a Persian with a
truly awesome command of Arabic, a gift which he delighted to exhibit in and
out of season. His pyrotechnic performances, solid with metaphor, saturated with
puns, wordplay, alliteration, assonance and verbal acrobatics, are such a nightmare
to understand that generations of Western Orientalists – and indeed Arab scholars
too, for that matter – have recoiled from the task of editing certain of his works.
Sometimes in his writings manner eclipses matter, but he is also capable of reaching
heights of solemn eloquence, as in his paean of triumph at the recapture of
Jerusalem, or his threnody on the death of Saladin. The other, the Qadi al-Fadil –
his title means 'The Excellent Judge' – though only a somewhat pedestrian poet,
was an acknowledged master of the epistolary prose that was de rigueur in
Islamic chanceries, and for centuries his letters were regarded as models of their
genre. His appearance, hunchbacked and skeletal, made him the butt of the
court's satirical poets, but his political skills were beyond reproach, and indeed in
his master's absence he governed Egypt for a time. It has been said that biography
adds an extra terror to death, but in that respect Saladin need not have worried. For
Ibn Shaddad, the third member of this distinguished triumvirate, who joined the
team after the fall of Jerusalem but thereafter never left Saladin's side and therefore
saw him in good times and bad, was a plain man with a plain style. But he rose to the
occasion and crafted a biography of his hero Saladin that lets the facts speak for
themselves. He has no time for stale panegyric; instead, his admiration for
Saladin shines through his account at every turn, and it is he who laid the foundations for his master's posthumous celebrity. The lecture will explore the impact of
these three men on the Saladin legend, which transformed a minor Kurdish
warlord into an emblem of chivalry, piety and military glory which captured the
hearts and the imaginations of Muslims for centuries to come – and still does.

I Introduction

Saladin was the third, and easily the most famous, of the Muslim military commanders of the twelfth century who turned the tide and began to recapture the lands seized by the Crusaders from 1098 onwards. Saladin grew up in a Kurdish military family that served the Turkish barons who controlled the Middle East, and more especially Syria and the Holy Land. From the early eleventh century the nomadic Turks had swept from Central Asia right across the eastern Islamic world, and by the 1060s their military strength had pushed aside all opposition from the Persians and Arabs, whose lands they now ruled.

Severe religious and political disunity had made the Muslim world unable to withstand the onslaught of the First Crusade. Or to put it another way, the spirit of jihad had become forgotten. As a result, the Muslims saw with pain the rapid creation of four Crusader states on Middle Eastern soil. In 1099, the loss of Jerusalem, the third most holy city in Islam, with its two Muslim sacred monuments, the Aqsa Mosque and the Dome of the Rock, in particular caused great anguish. But it took the Muslims well over half a century to find the kind of military leadership they needed to begin to defeat the Crusaders and regain their lands.

The first two Muslim military commanders who achieved major successes against the Crusaders were father and son, the Turks Zengi and Nur al-Din. Those names, incidentally, tell a story. Zengi did indeed have a title – 'Imad al-Din, 'Support of Religion' – but was commonly referred to by his given personal name, Zengi, whereas his son Mahmud was universally known by his title Nur al-Din, 'Light of Religion'. That difference spells the sea-change between the warlord and the wager of holy war, the *mujahid*. Saladin himself, raised in a Muslim Turkish military environment and serving Nur al-Din, was a Kurd whose family had originated from the Caucasus.[1] The way forward for Kurds in the twelfth century lay in service as mercenary soldiers, and that was Saladin's background. From 1171 onwards Saladin seized the territories of his Turkish predecessor and master, Nur al-Din – Egypt, Syria and Palestine. Saladin then built on the achievements of Nur al-Din. He acquired a power base with the help of his vast family network, won a famous victory against the Crusaders at the battle of Hattin in 1187 and that same year attained his crowning achievement – the reconquest of Jerusalem for Islam. He failed, however, to defeat the forces of Richard the Lionheart in the Third Crusade which immediately followed the Muslim reconquest of Jerusalem. Saladin died in 1193. But he had not finished the task. He had scotched the snake, not

[1] Vladimir Minorsky, *Studies in Caucasian History* (1953), 107–57.

killed it. Indeed, the Crusaders were to remain in the Middle East for almost another century before the Mamluks of Egypt finally expelled them in 1291.[2]

The combination of Saladin and Richard has entranced western Europe ever since. Popular legend has linked them together and both have enjoyed heroic status until modern times. Saladin's reputation in medieval Europe was extremely high; he was praised for his magnanimity, and most unusually a portrait of him hangs in the Uffizi in Florence.[3]

Many people, then, have heard of Saladin, but why is he the best-known medieval Muslim in the West apart from Muhammad himself? The prosaic reality, underlined by scholars such as Ehrenkreutz and Holt in their writings about Saladin, is that in his time Saladin was no more than a regional warlord, certainly not a figure of pan-Islamic significance.[4] They would argue that had Saladin died just a year or two before his conquest of Jerusalem he would have been remembered as simply yet another military baron. It could also be pointed out that the Muslim success against the Crusaders was more the achievement of Nur al-Din (in sole power for twenty-eight years) rather than Saladin (in sole power for nineteen years), who built on the foundations of conquest that Nur al-Din had left him.[5] And unlike his illustrious predecessor, Nur al-Din, Saladin did not leave a significant number of religious monuments in the Levant which testified to his commitment to Islam and the prosecution of jihad. Saladin is celebrated for just one outstanding achievement, his reconquest of Jerusalem for Islam.

In wider Islamic terms, moreover, Saladin had no great legacy to speak of; his nephew, al-Kamil, the Ayyubid sultan, surrendered Jerusalem to Frederick II of Sicily in 1229, and his own family dynasty foundered after fifty-seven years. The territories that he ruled were substantial but not vast. His reign was relatively short; he captured Jerusalem but not Outremer. So, his achievements were not colossal. Saladin has had his detractors,[6] and his key successes should indeed be placed alongside his reverses, the less savoury aspects of his career in Egypt and his harsh treatment of certain Crusader leaders and the Knightly Orders.

[2] See Anne-Marie Eddé, *Saladin* (Paris, 2008); Anne-Marie Eddé, *Saladin*, trans. Jane Marie Todd (Cambridge, MA, 2011).

[3] See Jonathan Phillips, *The Life and Legend of the Sultan Saladin* (2019).

[4] Andrew Ehrenkreutz, *Saladin* (Albany, 1972); Peter Holt, *The Age of the Crusades: The Near East from the Eleventh Century to 1517* (1986).

[5] Nikita Elisséeff, *Un grand prince musulman de Syrie au temps des Croisades* (2 vols., Damascus, 1967).

[6] The great medieval Muslim historian Ibn al-Athir (d. 1233), who wrote in detail about the Crusading period, was clearly biased in favour of Nur al-Din and his Zengid dynasty and he was discreetly critical of Saladin; Ibn al-Athir, *Tar'ikh al-dawla al-atabakiyya*, ed. 'Abdul Kader Tulaymat (Cairo, 1963).

So, with this curriculum vitae, how did Saladin garner such fame east and west? How did it happen? The answer in the Muslim east (the Christian west, from Crusader times onwards, is a different matter) lies with his three major advisers, his 'spin doctors'. So how did he attract these brilliant men? And how did they manage to burnish his reputation so successfully that the whole Sunni Muslim world subsequently accepted their story, and a number of twentieth-century Muslim leaders vied for the title of 'the Second Saladin'?

II Short biographies of Saladin's three spin doctors

Firstly, al-Qadi al-Fadil (1135–1200).[7] Abu 'Ali 'Abd al-Rahim al-Baysani al-'Asqalani, al-Qadi al-Fadil – his title means 'the excellent judge' – was one of the most famous political and literary figures in medieval Islamic history. Born in Ascalon in 1135, he came from a family of judges (qadis). His father sent him to Cairo in 1148 to study epistolary prose (insha') and he worked as a trainee in the chanceries of Fatimid Alexandria and Cairo. He survived there precariously in the unstable decade which preceded the downfall of the Fatimid Isma'ili Shi'ite caliphate in 1171. Like many Fatimid officials and courtiers, the Qadi al-Fadil had been imprisoned for a while before being released by Saladin's uncle, Shirkuh, who had taken power in Egypt in 1169 on behalf of Nur al-Din, who was a devout Sunni.

After Shirkuh's death, Saladin took over the role of ruling Egypt as the vizier of the Fatimid caliph al-'Adid, and the Qadi al-Fadil gained favour with Saladin when he composed a grand diploma of investiture in this new role for him.[8] After he had assisted Saladin in abolishing the Fatimid caliphate and restoring Egypt to Sunni Islam in 1171, the Qadi al-Fadil accompanied Saladin in his expeditions to Syria and he remained Saladin's most valued adviser for the rest of Saladin's life.

The medieval Muslim biographer Ibn Khallikan (d. 1282) writes that the Qadi al-Fadil was 'one of the ornaments of the age' who was 'always treated with the very highest favour' by Saladin.[9] For him, the years when he had to carry the heaviest responsibilities were 1188–91, when Saladin charged him with the management of the financial administration and the reorganisation of his army and his fleet. After Saladin's death in 1193, the Qadi al-Fadil lived in Cairo until his death in 1200. His tenure of the office of vizier – twenty-two years – was the longest of any

[7] Hadia Raghib Dajani-Shakeel, 'Al-Qadi al-Fadil. His Life and Political Career' (Ph.D. thesis, University of Michigan, 1972).

[8] The Arabic text of this document is given in Adolph H. Helbig, Al-Qadi al-Fadil, der Wezir Saladins (Leipzig, 1908), 53–64.

[9] Ibn Khallikan, Wafayat al-a'yan, trans. W. M. de Slane as Ibn Khallikan's Biographical Dictionary (4 vols., Paris, 1843–71), II, 112.

vizier in the twelfth and thirteenth centuries in the Levant. Most viziers found their high office to be a poisoned chalice.

Little is known of the early life of Saladin's second spin doctor, the Persian 'Imad al-Din al-Isfahani (1125–1201). He was born in Isfahan in 1125 and studied Islamic religious sciences in Baghdad and Basra. He became secretary, first to Nur al-Din and then to Saladin himself. He was treated with great respect by both these men. 'Imad al-Din drew up letters equally well in Persian and Arabic. He tried to win the favour of Saladin by reciting eulogies to him. He wrote several books on history, including *Al-fath al-qussi fi'l-fath al-qudsi*,[10] which covers the fall of Jerusalem until Saladin's death, and *Al-barq al-shami* (The Syrian Bolt of Lightning), which describes Saladin's life and deeds from 1175 onwards.[11] He also wrote hundreds of poems and collected those of other writers in anthologies which filled ten volumes. He eventually became Saladin's secretary and enjoyed high favour. Thereafter he rarely left Saladin's side.

Saladin's third spin doctor, Baha' al-Din Ibn Shaddad (1145–1234), was born in Mosul.[12] His early career was the customary one of an aspiring young scholar of the Islamic sciences; he memorised the Qur'an in his youth and studied Islamic law, first in Mosul and then in Baghdad. In 1174 he returned home to Mosul where he was appointed professor in a madrasa there. In 1188, the year after Saladin's victory at the battle of Hattin and his reconquest of Jerusalem, Ibn Shaddad went on the pilgrimage to Mecca and he then visited Jerusalem and Hebron. Saladin had admired a work written by Ibn Shaddad called *Fada'il jihad* (The Merits of Jihad), and when he learned of Ibn Shaddad's arrival in the Holy Land, he sent for him and invited him to join his entourage of specialist advisers.[13] Ibn Shaddad was soon given the important posts of *Qadi al-'askar* (judge of the army) and governor of Jerusalem. He also accompanied Saladin on his later campaigns to reconquer the Crusader-held ports on the Levantine coast. Saladin left Ibn Shaddad in charge of Jerusalem whenever he went to take a rest in Damascus, his favourite city.[14] When Saladin became very ill in 1192, he summoned Ibn

[10] *Kitab al-fath al-qussi fi'l fath al-qudsi*, ed. C. Landberg (Leiden, 1888). Note the rhyming and punning title of this work. See also 'Imad al-Din al-Isfahani, *Conquête de la Syrie*, trans. H. Massé (Paris, 1972).

[11] Gabrieli comments that this is an important author for Saladin's life but he adds that concrete details are lost in a complicated mass of verbiage; Francesco Gabrieli, *Arab Historians of the Crusades* (1969), xxx.

[12] For a detailed biography of Baha' al-Din Ibn Shaddad, see *Ibn Khallikan's Biographical Dictionary*, trans. de Slane, IV, 417–35.

[13] Baha' al-Din Ibn Shaddad, *The Rare and Excellent History of Saladin or al-Nawadir al-Sultaniyya wa'l-Mahasin-al-Yusufiyya*, trans. D. S. Richards (Aldershot, 2001), 81.

[14] *Ibn Khallikan's Biographical Dictionary*, trans. de Slane, IV, 541.

Shaddad to come to him there and Ibn Shaddad was with him during his last illness.[15] After Saladin's death in 1193 Ibn Shaddad moved to Aleppo where he worked for one of Saladin's sons. He died in 1234.

It is important to note that Ibn Shaddad worked for Saladin for a much shorter time than the Qadi al-Fadil and 'Imad al-Din – a mere five years. But during that period he was most of the time in contact with Saladin, wherever he went. Ibn Shaddad's book about Saladin is called *Al-nawadir al-sultaniyya wa'l mahasin Yusufiyya* (The Sultan's Rare Deeds and Joseph-like Merits).[16] This laudatory title contains a pun on the personal name of Saladin, i.e. Joseph, who is highly praised in both the Old Testament and the Qur'an.

III The relationships of the three spin doctors with Saladin

All three men have left copious written personal evidence of their roles in Saladin's life and work. There is no doubt that they treasured their privileged intimacy with him, and that they also had a clear sense of his historical significance. Details of their relationships with Saladin are also recorded at length in contemporary and later medieval primary Arabic chronicles.

The Qadi al-Fadil

It will be convenient to begin with the Qadi al-Fadil. Whatever the primary and contingent purpose of the official letters, diplomas and other government documents that he prepared, another crucial motive was ever-present, namely to build up Saladin's political profile. In this respect, although 'Imad al-Din's written output was enormous, it was the work of al-Qadi al-Fadil which was without doubt continuously more important in matters of state. Al-Qadi al-Fadil is said to have kept a diary for thirty-six years (from 1164 to 1199). Moreover, the complete collection of the letters of the Qadi al-Fadil, of which all were considered technical masterpieces of elevated chancery prose, is said to have comprised not less than 100 volumes. Whilst this statement may be a rhetorical exaggeration, it is important to note that even today there survive literally hundreds of official letters, diplomas and decrees which bear the name of al-Qadi al-Fadil and which are still preserved in unedited manuscripts in London, Beirut, Paris and Tübingen. Already in his own lifetime, the epistolary style of al-Qadi al-Fadil gained him an extraordinary reputation. As Saladin's counsellor and secretary, and as the head of his chancellery, he was the sultan's right-hand man. Saladin very soon found in al-Qadi al-Fadil a man of diverse

---

[15] Ibn Shaddad, *The Rare and Excellent History of Saladin*, 243–4.
[16] Baha' al-Din Ibn Shaddad, *Al-nawadir al-sultaniyya*, ed. J. El-Shayyal (Cairo, 1964).

capabilities and immense energy who became indispensable to him. According to his friend and colleague, 'Imad al-Din al-Isfahani:

> Under the administration of al-Qadi al-Fadil things were stable ... Saladin was afraid that some mishap might happen in al-Qadi al-Fadil's absence, and whenever they were parted for a long time, Saladin was apprehensive about dealing with matters alone.[17]

Once Saladin had seized full independent power in Egypt and broken away from his master Nur al-Din in Syria, there was a pressing need for him to gain legitimacy quickly. In the early years of his independent rule, after the death of Nur al-Din in 1174, his regime, under the skilful hand of the Qadi al-Fadil, relied heavily on many official letters written by him and sent in many directions, and especially to the Sunni caliph in Baghdad, to spread his jihad propaganda and to communicate with the different areas of his growing empire in Syria, which he seized from the family of Nur al-Din. The letters of the Qadi al-Fadil would be read out to the individuals to whom they were addressed but they were also read out in public places, such as in the mosques, as well as in the camps and citadels of the minor Turkish military barons who gradually allied themselves with Saladin. Again, the evidence of 'Imad al-Din is valuable here; he writes that the Qadi al-Fadil

> conducted the empire by his counsels, and fastened the pearls (of style) on the thread (of discourse); when he pleased, he could compose in a day, nay, in a single hour, documents which, were they preserved, would be considered by masters of the epistolary art as the most precious materials they could possess.[18]

The Qadi al-Fadil wrote decrees after towns were conquered; a typical example is the one he sent on Saladin's behalf to Aleppo in 1183. This document allowed protection and fair treatment for the Jews and Christians living there and permitted them to keep their jobs in the administration.

So much for the superb administrative work of the Qadi al-Fadil in support of Saladin. It is perhaps surprising that he also found time to write poetry. But it should be noted too that Saladin himself is reported to have listened regularly to recitations of poetry.[19] The Qadi al-Fadil's poetic output is mentioned in the primary Arabic sources as being spectacularly large;[20] according to one Arabic chronicler,[21] Sibt b. al-Jawzi, the Qadi al-Fadil composed 100,000 verses of poetry. Such an

---

[17] Hadia Dajani-Shakeel, *Al-Qadi al-Fadil 'Abd al-Rahim al-'Asqalani* (Beirut, 1993), 54.

[18] *Ibn Khallikan's Biographical Dictionary*, trans. de Slane, II, 112; Ibrahim Hafsi, 'Correspondance officielle et privée d'al-Qadi al-Fadil' (4 vols., Thèse Université de Paris 3, 1980).

[19] Al-Bundari, *Sana' al-barq al-shami*, ed. R. Seşsen (Beirut, 1971), 233–7.

[20] *Diwan al-Qadi al-Fadil*, ed. A. Badawi and I. al-Ibyari (Cairo, 1961).

[21] Dajani-Shakeel, *Al-Qadi al-Fadil*, 17.

exaggerated number as this is clearly implausible but it is evident from a range of sources that the Qadi al-Fadil did indeed write a large amount of poetry, and in various genres, such as panegyrics, satires and religious odes. When young, he had memorised quantities of early Arabic poetry, and this knowledge enriched his own poetic style.

Moreover, in the often poisonous atmosphere at court, full of competitors and rivals for power, the Qadi al-Fadil wrote satirical poems taunting those who cruelly mocked his physical disability. He was portrayed by his contemporaries as ugly. He had a hunchback which he used to conceal in a shawl-like garment worn over his head and shoulders.[22] A Syrian poet, Ibn Unayn, did not hesitate to mock al-Qadi al-Fadil's physical appearance, saying: 'Our sultan is lame, his secretary ['Imad al-Din] is bleary-eyed and his vizier [al-Qadi al-Fadil] is a *hunchback.*'[23] Another rival poet, this time a Moroccan called al-Wahrani, also wrote light verse of a sharply malicious kind, referring to al-Qadi al-Fadil, though not by name, as 'strange-looking with neither a head or a neck. His face is sunk in his chest and his beard in his stomach.'[24]

After 1184, when Saladin finally focused intensively on fighting the Crusaders and expelling them from the Holy City, the Qadi al-Fadil, not surprisingly at this crucial time, concentrated on spreading the message of Saladin's jihad ideology in his letters. And after Jerusalem had been reconquered, he wrote joyful, passionate and triumphant lines to the Sunni caliph in Baghdad, glorifying Saladin's achievements, vigorously emphasising his removal of the Christian defilement of the Holy City and attacking the Christian doctrine of the Trinity.

Ibn Khallikan cites a letter of the Qadi al-Fadil to the Sunni caliph, al-Nasir, in Baghdad about the conquest of Jerusalem.[25] It is extremely long, enriched with Qur'anic references covering nine pages. It is full of jubilation, not only because Saladin has conquered but also because Islam has triumphed. Its phrasing, though lofty, is not too baroque or overblown:

> The affairs of Islam have taken an excellent turn, and the faith of its followers is now fixed by the most evident proofs ... In this country, the true faith was like a stranger in a foreign land, but now, it finds itself at home ... The order of God has been executed in despite of the infidels ... God's promise of making his religion triumph over all the others received its fulfilment ... The Holy Land has become the pure one, after being in a state of impurity; there the only God is now one, He being one who, according to them, was the third. The temples of infidelity have been overturned and the fangs of polytheism are now plucked out.

[22] *Ibid.*, 26.
[23] Malcolm C. Lyons and David E. P. Jackson, *Saladin. The Politics of the Holy War* (Cambridge, 1982), 118.
[24] Al-'Wahrani, *Manamat al-Wahrani*, quoted by Dajani-Shakeel, *Al-Qadi al-Fadil*, 27.
[25] *Ibn Khallikan's Biographical Dictionary*, trans. de Slane, IV, 515ff.

'Imad al-Din al-Isfahani

It is now time to move to 'Imad al-Din al-Isfahani.[26] He was one of those authors who would never use three words when 300 would do. As the French historian, Claude Cahen, writes: ''Imad al-Din is an embarrassing author. A stylistic virtuoso ... It is often impossible to distinguish in his writings between what comes from history and what is stylistic acrobatics.'[27] Henri Massé, who translated *Al-fath al-qussi* into French, speaks of the florid rhetoric of 'Imad al-Din's state documents and set pieces of eulogy, but he also adds that 'Imad al-Din writes other passages which are striking in their sober vigour.[28]

However, the rhetorical literary style in medieval Arabic and Persian prose-writing has received very little true appreciation from Western scholars, partly because it is so difficult to read and partly because it sacrifices content to form. For example, Francesco Gabrieli, who courageously translated excerpts from one of the books of 'Imad al-Din about Saladin, spoke of his 'wearisome obscurities'. [29]

'Imad al-Din has gained a certain notoriety for the prurient piece of baroque pornography[30] which he wrote about the arrival of 300 Crusader women in the Levant; his tone is one of gleeful outrage:

> There arrived by ship three hundred lovely Frankish women, full of youth and beauty, assembled from beyond the sea and offering themselves for sin ... They glowed with ardour for carnal intercourse. They were all licentious harlots, proud and scornful, who took and gave, foul-fleshed and sinful, singers and coquettes ... ardent and inflamed, tinted and untinted, desirable and appetising.[31]

And this high-flown licentious rhyming prose continues for two more pages in similar vein. Even in English translation the virtuosity of this passage, saturated in metaphor and simile, compels astonishment. But in Arabic it attains a different level altogether, for the puns, the alliterations, the assonances, come thick and fast and their cumulative impact is simply overwhelming. The whole passage is one long anti-Crusader propagandistic, lascivious coloratura aria delivered at full throttle. It reveals to the full 'Imad al-Din showing off his egotism and pride.

---

[26] For a detailed analysis of the writing of 'Imad al-Din al-Isfahani, see Lutz Richter-Bernburg, *Der Syrische Blitz. Saladins Sekretär zwischen Selbstdarstellung und Geschichtsschreibung* (Beirut, 1990), esp. 257–382, where passages of the text are translated.

[27] Claude Cahen, 'Review of 'Imad al-Din al-Isfahani. tr. Henri Massé, *Conquête de la Syrie et de la Palestine par Saladin*', *Arabica*, 21 (1974), 213–14.

[28] See P. M. Holt's review of Henri Massé's translation of *Al-fath al-qussi*, *Bulletin of the School of Oriental and African Studies*, 37 (1974), 691–3.

[29] For a balanced account of 'Imad al-Din al-Isfahani, see Donald S. Richards, ''Imad al-Din al-Isfahani: Administrator, Littérateur and Historian', in *Crusaders and Muslims in Twelfth-Century Syria*, ed. Maya Shatzmiller (Leiden, 1993), 133–46.

[30] This phrase is Gabrieli's in *Arab Historians*, 204, n. 2.

[31] Trans. Gabrieli, *Arab Historians*, 204.

Other aspects of 'Imad al-Din's brilliant mind concern his portrayal of Saladin. Straightforward narratives of events in his career are found in the Muslim chronicles of the late twelfth and thirteenth centuries. But 'Imad al-Din's accounts are contemporary. He lived through the heights of Saladin's successes against the Crusaders; he was there with Saladin or heard about the events from eyewitnesses. He then presented them in his own inimitable fashion, in poetic prose which was meant to be recited aloud to a scholarly elite at court or in the mosques.

'Imad al-Din mentions that he worked with Saladin every evening, discussing matters of state:

> Saladin was very fond of sitting with his particular friends from amongst men of intelligence ... If he needed a letter written ... he would dictate what he wanted to me to write and I would remain awake that night and bring it to him in the morning.[32]

'Imad al-Din's book about Saladin's life from the fall of Jerusalem in 1187 until his death in 1193 is an elaborate eulogy. In it, Saladin is depicted as an ideal Muslim ruler, pious, just, generous, a fighter for the faith. This work begins in March 1187. 'Imad al-Din writes that he will deal only with the period which he knows and which he has seen with his own eyes. For example, only a few hours after Saladin's victory at Hattin, 'Imad al-Din went to survey the battlefield. He mentions explicitly Saladin's ruthless treatment of the Templars and the Hospitallers who had fought at Hattin. Nor does 'Imad al-Din gloss over Saladin's involvement in the killing of his arch-enemy, Reynald of Chatillon. He writes that after the victory at Hattin, Saladin summoned Reynald. He went straight up to him, struck his shoulder with his sword and then ordered his head to be cut off.[33]

'Imad al-Din is at his most eloquent when he writes about Saladin's death. Indeed, his obituary notice is a linguistic tour de force; it is extremely long; it contains many pages of heavy, highly elaborate, fullblown, florid rhetorical prose, piled high, as usual, but imbued with feelings of grief and deep affection.

Baha' al-Din Ibn Shaddad

Finally, let us turn to the third member of this distinguished triumvirate of Saladin's devoted advisers, Baha' al-Din Ibn Shaddad. He wrote a very moving and detailed personal biography of Saladin in a style which is simpler than the writings of the Qadi al-Fadil or 'Imad al-Din. The work is in two parts: the first discusses in detail Saladin's

---

[32] Al-Bundari, *Sana' al-barq al-shami*, 244.
[33] Gabrieli, *Arab Historians*, 134.

qualities and especially his devotion to Islam, and the second is a history of his conquests.[34]

Part 1 of the book is a romanticised idealistic view of Saladin's personal commitment to Islam; his piety, his love of justice (every Monday and Thursday he sat in public to administer justice), his generosity (when he died his treasury was almost empty), his courage in battle, his endurance of frequent ill-health and other virtues. Part 2 is a very detailed account of the history of Saladin's conquests. Ibn Shaddad describes the battle of Hattin in much milder panegyric than that used by the Qadi al-Fadil and 'Imad al-Din. He does not elaborate on Saladin's killing of the Hospitallers and Templars. He just notes soberly that he spared none of them. As for the reconquest of Jerusalem, Ibn Shaddad is overjoyed. He provides ample details of this momentous event, but without the fanfare given to it by the Qadi al-Fadil or 'Imad al-Din, or indeed by many of the Arab chroniclers.

How did Ibn Shaddad write about Saladin's death? After his account of the last time that he and the Qadi al-Fadil had been with Saladin, he ends with the following simple but profoundly moving words: 'We left the citadel, each longing to give his own life to ransom the sultan's.'[35] His intense, deeply felt and eloquent elegy on the death of Saladin comes right from the heart rather than from conventional flowery panegyric:

> Never since Islam and the Muslims lost the first caliphs, never from that time, had the faith and the faithful suffered a blow such as that they received on the day of the Sultan's death. The castle, the city, the whole world, were thereby plunged into grief, of which God alone could fathom the intensity.[36]

What light do Saladin's closest associates shed on his personality and how he lived when he was not campaigning? For all their intense and thorough focus on Saladin's military achievements and his prosecution of jihad, the three spin doctors do also on occasion discuss more personal aspects of Saladin's life. Ibn Shaddad reports that Saladin was very fond of his children but that he bore parting with them manfully. Saladin also wept bitter tears when he heard the news of the death of one of his nephews. He is described as being hospitable to guests, even the occasional Crusader one.

It is highly likely that when Saladin went back to his favourite city, Damascus, to rest in between his military campaigns, he would enjoy the usual court pursuits of a medieval Muslim ruler: giving banquets; falconry; hunting; listening to music and to poetry. On the other hand,

---

[34] In the detailed introduction to his translation of Baha' al-Din Ibn Shaddad, Richards explains the structure of the book; see *The Rare and Excellent History of Saladin*, 1–9.

[35] *Ibid.*, 243.

[36] Quoted by Lyons and Jackson, *Saladin*, 374.

Saladin disapproved of ostentation. On one occasion, seeing 'Imad al-Din writing from an inkwell embellished with silver, he condemned its usage. The inkwell was never seen in public again.

But it seems likely that in general Saladin and his entourage of close advisers had very little spare time for the pursuit of pleasure. In modern parlance, they may be labelled 'workaholics'. 'Imad al-Din reports that Saladin dictated letters to him at night. He then turned Saladin's words – it is not clear in which language Saladin used to dictate to him – into the flowery prose for which 'Imad al-Din is celebrated.

IV Conclusions

Saladin is unusual in medieval Islamic history in that he had the benefit, so to speak, of three court biographers, three 'spin doctors', if you like: the Qadi al-Fadil, 'Imad al-Din al-Isfahani and Baha' al-Din Ibn Shaddad. They have all three left glowing accounts of their master. These provide more information for him than we have for previous Muslim rulers of the twelfth century, and what is much more, they have an unmistakable personal touch. On occasion, their devotion to him seems to transcend the customary panegyric and clichéd phrases familiar from court titulature on inscriptions and coins, so much so that it does seem that in Saladin we are dealing with an exceptional person.

The Qadi al-Fadil and 'Imad al-Din al-Isfahani, one an Arab and one a Persian, were clearly what we might now call public intellectuals. They had, furthermore, been in Saladin's service for a very long time, without losing his favour. Both were deeply committed to promoting Saladin's image as a pious Muslim ruler and a fervent jihad warrior, a man who could show pity and dispense justice. As already mentioned, the Qadi al-Fadil was the rock on which Saladin leaned at all times. Al-'Umari (d. 1343) writes of him:

> The Qadi al-Fadil was the state of Saladin. He was its secretary, its vizier, its master, its adviser, and the supplier of its army. He carried all its burdens, ruled over all its regions … He was invested with full authority in the state of Saladin and was the one who decided on the fate of people and on matters of life and death.[37]

What of 'Imad al-Din al-Isfahani? It is likely that he spent more time with Saladin than the Qadi al-Fadil, who for lengthy periods had to look after Egypt on Saladin's behalf, let alone Ibn Shaddad who joined Saladin's service much later. It is probable that alongside his superb literary versatility 'Imad al-Din must have been an entertaining companion for

---

[37] Dajani-Shakeel, *Al-Qadi al-Fadil*, 1.

Saladin. Ibn Shaddad, on the other hand, joined Saladin's entourage in 1188, spending only five years with him at the very end of his life. Nevertheless, their daily relationship, at a time when Saladin was tired and unwell, was intense and very meaningful at a religious level.

Despite some differences of approach, Saladin is thus seen by his three spin doctors as the greatest Muslim opponent of the Crusaders. His rule forms the precise focus of these three men's writings and they are unanimous in their laudatory view of him. Of course, these three major advisers of Saladin were not the only people who contributed to the 'spin' around him. Famous Arab poets wrote long panegyrics about him and declaimed them in Saladin's court. Moreover, contemporary Arab chroniclers praised Saladin's achievements, and later Muslim historians and biographers in the thirteenth and fourteenth centuries eulogised him in hindsight, helping to create in the Muslim world a highly favourable image of Saladin, the victor over the Crusaders at Hattin, the Kurdish military leader and jihad warrior, who reconquered Jerusalem for Islam.

In modern times Saladin has been not just an inspirational model for military success but also for the political unification of the Arab world against the infidel and the external aggressor. Saddam Husayn, Hafez Asad and Mu'ammar al-Qaddafi each promoted themselves publicly as the second Saladin. And yet others, like President Sadat of Egypt in the 1970s, have invoked him as one worthy of emulation by heads of state for his fabled qualities of generosity, compassion and tolerance towards those of other faiths. And that formidable and fragrant legacy rests most of all on the devotion of his spin doctors, which shines across the centuries.

Transactions of the RHS 29 (2019), pp. 79–103 © Royal Historical Society 2019
doi:10.1017/S0080440119000045

MUSICALISING HISTORY

By Matthew S. Champion

Gladstone Prize Winner

and

Miranda Stanyon

ABSTRACT. While there have been growing calls for historians to listen to the past, there are also significant barriers to integrating music in particular into broader historical practice. This article reflects on both the gains and difficulties of this integration, moving from an interrogation of the category of music to three case studies. These concern musical terms, compositional practices and cultures from the fifteenth to eighteenth centuries, revisiting some key debates in musicology: first, the highly charged language of sweetness deployed in the fifteenth century; second, connections discerned in nineteenth-century music history between medieval polyphony and contemporary attitudes towards time and authority; and, third, debate over the anti-Jewish implications of Handel's music, which we approach through his *Dixit Dominus* and a history of psalm interpretation stretching back to late antiquity. Through these case studies, we suggest the contribution of music to necessarily interdisciplinary fields including the study of temporality and emotions, but also explore how a historical hermeneutic with a long pedigree – 'diversity of times' (*diversitas temporum*) – might help to reframe arguments about musical interpretation. The article concludes by arguing that the very difficulty and slipperiness of music as a source can encourage properly reflective historical practice.

Historians need to listen to the past. This is the charge of recent developments in the history of the senses, the cultural history of music, and the burgeoning field of sound studies.[1] Why is it, then, that historians,

---

[1] A number of general works now address these trends, including Charles Burnett, Michael Fend and Penelope Gouk (eds.), *The Second Sense: Studies in Hearing and Musical Judgement from Antiquity to the Seventeenth Century* (1991); Veit Erlmann (ed.), *Hearing Cultures: Essays on Sound, Listening, and Modernity* (Oxford, 2004); Mark M. Smith (ed.), *Hearing History: A Reader* (Athens, GA, 2004); Jane F. Fulcher (ed.), *The Oxford Handbook of the New Cultural History of Music* (New York, 2011); Trevor J. Pinch and Karin Bijsterveld (eds.), *The Oxford Handbook of Sound Studies* (New York, 2012); Michael Bull and Les Back (eds.), *The Auditory Culture Reader*, 2nd rev. edn (Oxford, 2015). Important individual studies include Alain Corbin, *Village Bells: Sound and Meaning in the Nineteenth-Century French Countryside* (New York, 1998); Emily Ann Thompson, *The Soundscape of Modernity: Architectural Acoustics and the Culture of Listening in America, 1900–1933* (Cambridge, MA,

despite the substantial and growing body of literature in these fields, still find it hard to integrate music into their interpretations of past worlds?[2]

One reason for music's relative absence from scholarly work outside musicology is obvious: music demands specific skills to access and evaluate its notations, its harmonic traditions, and music-specific analytical models – Renaissance modal theory, say, or Schenkerian analysis. Then there is the drama of translation (or 'transduction') within the study of sound.[3] The representation of sound in both notation and words confronts in complicated ways the problems of representation faced by any academic discipline. How can we mediate experiences of phenomena like music in ways that pay attention to the visual and textual media of its transmission, its sounds and performances, and to the material, social and cultural worlds within which it appears?

This problem is intensified by the difficulty of locating 'music' – in a score, an historically 'informed' or 'uninformed' performance, a thickly reconstructed event, a memory, or that elusive concept, the 'work'. The category of music is neither transtemporal nor transcultural (does it include Qur'an recitations, keening rituals, or postmodern noise installations?). In other words, music's 'presence' or 'existence' seems particularly unstable – although it might better be said that sound foregrounds epistemological and ontological difficulties endemic to any historical object of study.

To compound difficulties, a strong strand in nineteenth-century thought made music a paradigm of the aesthetic. In the process, music was often constructed as escaping articulable meaning, instrumental reason and historical mediation; music is imagined as underdetermined and resistant to the verbal and hermeneutic procedures underpinning the humanities and social sciences. Paradoxically, these developments secured enormous cultural value for music, but made its study vulnerable to marginalisation and trivialisation within the academy. Historians sometimes persist in caricaturing musicologists as arcane specialists, closed formalists, or technicians who do not wish to contribute to a wider scholarly programme of integration. And we, of course, risk perpetuating another caricature by inventing a realm of 'historians' as opposed to 'musicologists', musicologists who are not already historians

---

2002); Jonathan Sterne, *The Audible Past: Cultural Origins of Sound Reproduction* (Durham, NC, 2003); Veit Erlmann, *Reason and Resonance: A History of Modern Aurality* (New York, 2010); Emma Dillon, *The Sense of Sound: Musical Meaning in France, 1260–1330* (New York, 2012).

[2] For a recent reflection, see Beth Williamson, 'Sensory Experience in Medieval Devotion: Sound and Vision, Invisibility and Silence', *Speculum*, 88 (2013), 1–43.

[3] In sound studies, transduction describes the transformations of sound, and of its meanings, as it moves between media and different 'energetic substrate[s] (from electrical to mechanical, for example)'. Stefan Helmreich, 'Transduction', in *Keywords in Sound* (Durham, NC, 2015), ed. David Novak and Matt Sakakeeny, 222.

of sound, art, performance, politics, economics, devotion, liturgy and more.[4]

A final observation: the knowledge required to understand music notations, and traditions of elite conoisseurship associated particularly with Western art music, has meant that many historians have found the languages of sound and soundscape more congenial to analysing experiences of the world as heard across the social spectrum. We absolutely agree that the study of sound is critical to rich historical practice. But sound includes music, and we can miss critical aspects of social and cultural life if we do not analyse all facets of the sonic world.

What does this mean for our arguments here about music and history? Firstly, we will not use a language of novelty: current generations are not the first to think historically about music. Rather, a language of amplification and interaction between disciplines and methodologies will help us continue the task of understanding music's roles within integrative interpretations of the past. Secondly, engagements with particular compositions and techniques (like the ones discussed in the following) should be located within broader thinking about how 'music' is positioned as 'music'. This will involve considering music's changing others and its partners: from sound itself, noise, silence, chant, language and emotion, to ratio, astronomy, geometry, mathematics and magic.[5] Thirdly, we need to think about how our histories can be musicalised, to consider how music might contribute to and modify histories which seek to unite the study of culture with its material and social settings. In what follows, we fail to perform these tasks adequately. But we hope the failure is productive and will contribute to wider attempts to musicalise history.

Our argument is divided into three parts. We begin with some forms of fifteenth-century music and the language used to describe them. This section gives in miniature some of the problems in approaching music as a subject of historical investigation. More pointedly, it suggests how fifteenth-century theories of diversity might offer resources for creative

[4] For a survey of integrative moves within musicology, see Jane F. Fulcher, 'Introduction: Defining the New Cultural History of Music, Its Origins, Methodologies, and Lines of Inquiry', in *The Oxford Handbook of the New Cultural History of Music*, ed. Jane F. Fulcher (New York, 2011), 1–14.

[5] See, for example, Gary Tomlinson, *Music in Renaissance Magic: Towards a Historiography of Others* (Chicago, 1993); Penelope Gouk, *Music, Science and Natural Magic in Seventeenth-Century England* (New Haven, 1999); Elizabeth Eva Leach, *Sung Birds: Music, Nature, and Poetry in the Later Middle Ages* (Ithaca, 2007); Nicky Losseff and Jennifer R. Doctor, *Silence, Music, Silent Music* (Aldershot, 2007); Karin Bijsterveld, *Mechanical Sound: Technology, Culture, and Public Problems of Noise in the Twentieth Century* (Cambridge, MA, 2008); Georgina Born, 'For a Relational Musicology: Music and Interdisciplinarity, beyond the Practice Turn', *Journal of the Royal Musical Association*, 135 (2010), 205–43.

historicising responses to music, then and now. The second section continues to interrogate fifteenth-century music, widening to imagine a
musicalisation of the history of time, and a history of music informed
by research on temporality. We then turn, by means of an interpretive
tradition strong in fifteenth-century culture, to the musicalisation of
psalm interpretation, taking as our case study a single verse of Psalm
109/110. Uniting a hermeneutic of diversity with a long history of this
psalm, this final section continues to explore how reflection on past
sounds can contribute to other areas of history, in this case histories of
emotions, religions and temporalities.

I

In fifteenth-century Europe, polyphonic music was changing. Historians
of music have somewhat obsessively turned to a passage from Martin le
Franc's *Le Champion des Dames* to discuss the possible influence of an
English polyphonic style (associated with composers such as John
Dunstaple (*c.* 1390–1453) on Burgundian composers like Gilles Binchois
(*c.* 1400–1460) and Guillaume Du Fay (*c.* 1397–1474):[6]

> For they have a new way
> of making lively concord,
> in loud and soft music,
> in *fainte*, in *pause*, and in *muance*.
> And they have taken up something of the
> English style [or manner], and followed Dunstable;
> This is why wonderful pleasure makes
> Their song joyful and noteworthy [or memorable].[7]

---

[6] See, recently, David Fallows, *Henry V and the Earliest English Carols: 1413–1440* (Abingdon
and New York, 2018), 237–49; Lisa Colton, *Angel Song: Medieval English Music in History*
(Abingdon and New York, 2017), 190–210; also Margaret Bent, 'The Musical Stanzas in
Martin Le Franc's *Le Champion des Dames*', in *Music in Medieval Manuscripts: Paleography and
Performance*, ed. John Haines and Randall Rosenfeld (Aldershot, 2004), 91–127; Rob
C. Wegman, 'New Music for a World Grown Old: Martin Le Franc and the
"Contenance Angloise"', *Acta Musicologica*, 75 (2003), 201–41; Reinhard Strohm, 'Music,
Humanism and the Idea of a "Rebirth" of the Arts', in *Music as Concept and Practice in the
Late Middle Ages*, ed. Reinhard Strohm and Bonnie J. Blackburn (Oxford, 2001), 368–85;
Christopher Page, 'Reading and Reminiscence: Tinctoris on the Beauty of Music',
Journal of the American Musicological Society, 49 (1996), 2–4; Philip R. Kaye, *The "Contenance
Angloise" in Perspective: A Study of Consonance and Dissonance in Continental Music, c. 1380–1440*
(New York, 1989); David Fallows, 'The *Contenance Angloise*: English Influence on
Continental Composers of the Fifteenth Century', *Renaissance Studies*, 1 (1987), 189–208;
Sylvia W. Kenney, *Walter Frye and the Contenance Angloise* (New Haven, 1964).

[7] Lines 16265–72, translation from Bent, 'Musical Stanzas'. Note, however, the English
style or manner might also be translated as the 'countenance of angels/Angles' as in
Colton, *Angel Song*, 204.

What might have been meant by describing consonance as 'lively' (*frisque*) or music as 'joyous' (*joieux*)? How do we historicise terms like this? The history of musicological discussions of this passage shows just how vexed such questions can be. One contested explanation is that Dunstaple allowed 'imperfect' thirds and sixths into the range of acceptable consonances, thus marking a change from earlier 'perfect' harmonies. Others dispute the passage's reference to harmonic change, and see it evoking performance style, or as not necessarily reflecting any 'real' change in practice at all. Whatever we make of these debates, the passage does deploy a range of words to describe experiences of music – but the sounds described seem to slip beyond our grasp.

If we turn from the *Champion des Dames* to the evidence of musical notation, we face similar problems. The famous fifteenth-century composer associated with Cambrai Cathedral, Guillaume Du Fay, seems to have set texts relating to peace and unity using a technique known as *faux bourdon*, where (usually) two notated voices moving in parallel sixths were supplemented by an improvised third voice.[8] This might suggest that Du Fay linked such sonorities with order, harmony and stability.[9] *Faux bourdon* is known to have been used frequently in Cambrai's liturgy, but how might listeners have experienced it? One contemporary who gives some indication of his reception of choral music at Cambrai is the cathedral's dean, Gilles Carlier (*c.* 1400–1472). In the 1450s, Carlier reflected on the role of liturgical music in a short treatise, the *Tractatus de duplici ritu cantus ecclesiastici in divinis officiis* (Treatise on the Twofold Practice of Church Music in the Divine Offices).[10] The treatise repeatedly refers to 'sweet' (*dulcis*) and 'jubilant' music. Its opening specifically describes the 'sweet jubilation (*iubilatio*) of harmoniously blended voices', clearly referring to a variety of elaborate ecclesiastical music celebrating divine blessings.[11]

Carlier's theorisation of 'sweet jubilation' enlarges, and goes beyond, the connotations of unity and brightness possibly associated with Du

---

[8] For technical debates, see Fallows, *Henry V and the Earliest English Carols*, 72–83.

[9] Willem Elders, 'Guillaume Dufay's Concept of Faux-Bourdon', *Revue Belge de Musicologie/Belgisch Tijdschrift voor Muziekwetenschap*, 43 (1989), 179, 183. Craig M. Wright, 'Performance Practices at the Cathedral of Cambrai 1475–1550', *Musical Quarterly*, 64 (1978), 295–328.

[10] Reproduced in J. Donald Cullington and Reinhard Strohm, *'That Liberal and Virtuous Art': Three Humanist Treatises on Music* (Newtownabbey, 2001), 31–57 (hereafter Carlier, *Tractatus*). See further Matthew S. Champion, *The Fullness of Time: Temporalities of the Fifteenth-Century Low Countries* (Chicago, 2017), 90–106.

[11] On varieties of elaborate music and debates over its worth, see Ulrike Hascher-Burger, *Gesungene Innigkeit. Studien zu einer Musikhandschrift der Devotio moderna (Utrecht, Universiteitsbibliotheek, Ms. 16 H 34, olim B i 13)* (Leiden, 2002), 185–205; Cullington and Strohm, *'That Liberal and Virtuous Art'*, 13–14; Rob C. Wegman, *The Crisis of Music in Early Modern Europe, 1470–1530* (New York, 2005), esp. 49–51.

Fay's *faux bourdon*. Sometimes referred to in fifteenth- and sixteenth-century sources as a quality of English singing, jubilation here more broadly relates to a theological tradition found in Augustine's (354–430) *Enarrationes in Psalmos* and elsewhere.[12] Augustine's use of the term *iubilatio* is connected with a joyous response to God characterised by both 'sighing' and 'singing'. Sweet jubilation and longing for God commingle. The relationship of the sweet music of jubilation to wider Augustinian emotional vocabularies becomes clearer as Carlier goes on to quote directly from Augustine's *Confessions* (Book 9.6). Augustine confesses that he 'wept at [God's] hymns and canticles, pierced to the quick by the voices of thy sweet-sounding church'. While for Augustine the sweet sound of the church was marked not by polyphony but by plainchant hymnody, we might say that for both writers *dulcis* is a polyphonic concept. For the 'voices of Thy sweet-sounding church' effect both jubilation and tears. All this indicates something of the semantic complexity of musical sweetness, which in medieval traditions could often link joy and sorrow through the 'sweetness' of Christ's passion and the taste of the Eucharist, events which combined suffering and sorrow with redemption and joy.[13]

The rich, allusive and imprecise language used to describe music within medieval liturgical and theological discourses draws attention to the crucial observation that responses to music are framed by the situation in which it is heard. Augustine's emotional response to hymnody is framed by his narrative setting, grounded in his discussion of sin and God's graciousness. Augustine was, of course, also aware of music's potential for different effects, arguing that music could direct the heart towards God or ensnare the soul in sensual distraction. Carlier similarly indicated that responses to music could not be essentialised. Following his citation of Augustine, he immediately acknowledged that responses to music would differ according to 'rank, person, time and place'.[14]

This potentially radical language of diversity has recently been traced by Carlo Ginzburg to origins in the writings of Paul and Augustine.[15] In *On Christian Doctrine*, Augustine argued that differences in time, place and

---

[12] See Bonnie J. Blackburn, 'Music and Festivities at the Court of Leo X: A Venetian View', *Early Music History*, 11 (1992), 14–17; Ulrike Hascher-Burger, 'Music and Meditation: Songs in Johannes Mauburnus's *Rosetum exercitiorum spiritualium*', *Church History and Religious Culture*, 88 (2008), 361–4.

[13] See Mary Carruthers, 'Sweetness', *Speculum*, 81 (2006), 999–1013; Friedrich Ohly, *Süsse Nägel der Passion. Ein Beitrag zur theologischen Semantik* (Baden-Baden, 1989).

[14] Carlier, *Tractatus*, 23.

[15] Carlo Ginzburg, 'The Letter Kills: On Some of the Implications of 2 Corinthians 3:6', *History and Theory*, 49 (2010), 71–7. Compare Mary Curruthers, '*Varietas*: A Word of Many Colours', *Poetica* (2009), 45–9.

person should shape the interpretation of texts and acts.[16] As Klaus
Schreiner has shown, this hermeneutic became increasingly important
in the later Middle Ages.[17] It was applied to music by Carlier's uncle,
the influential theologian and reformer Jean Gerson (1363–1429).[18] For
Gerson, the value of music depended on the relationship of the soul
with God.[19] In this way, the 'same' song might be the old song of a
sinful soul for one singer, and in the mouth of another the song of the
new creation and a soul properly directed to God.[20] Music's meaning
is not fixed, but varies according to person, time and setting.[21]

If we return to the implications of this excursus for the modern historian, we can see that understanding fifteenth-century polyphony requires
not only knowledge of particular sounds (e.g. intervals of thirds and
sixths), but also a sense of their aural quality in relation other sounds
(e.g. fourths and fifths), and, further, the history of their use in earlier polyphony – we need something like a 'period ear', attuned to earlier sonic
horizons of expectation.[22] Understanding, then, requires interpretation
of these aural qualities alongside the cultural structures which helped
give these sounds meaning. We have drawn attention to only some of
the linguistic and theological possibilities here; visual culture, social networks and spatial and performative dimensions remain unexamined.[23]
From the inherently slippery figurative representation of aural qualities,
to more specific but less evocative technical designations ('third' or
'sixth'), the discussion of fifteenth-century music is fraught with theoretical and practical complexity.[24]

A specific question for historians dealing with music is how we relate to
these vocabularies, both the technical (sixth, fifth, etc.) and the qualitative

[16] Augustine, *De Doctrina Christiana*, ed. Roger P. H. Green (Oxford, 1995), III.35–78.

[17] Klaus Schreiner, "'Diversitas temporum'' – Zeiterfahrung und Epochengliederung im
späten Mittelalter', in *Epochenschwelle und Epochenbewusstsein*, ed. Reinhart Herzog and
Reinhart Koselleck (Munich, 1987), 381–428.

[18] See Isabelle Fabre, *La Doctrine du chant du cœur de Jean Gerson: édition critique, traduction et
commentaire du 'Tractatus de canticis' et du 'Canticordum au pélerin'* (Geneva, 2005).

[19] For the following, see Joyce L. Irwin, 'The Mystical Music of Jean Gerson', *Early Music
History*, 1 (1981), 194–7.

[20] *Tractatus secundis de canticis* (Second Treatise on Songs), section 23, reproduced in Fabre,
La Doctrine, 309–476, here 383.

[21] *Ibid.*, 395–6. Also, see Irwin, 'Mystical Music', 199.

[22] Compare Shai Burstyn, 'In Quest of the Period Ear', *Early Music*, 25 (1997), 692–701; in
relation to sound, Jan Missfelder, 'Period Ear: Perspektiven einer Klanggeschichte der
Neuzeit', *Geschichte und Gesellschaft*, 38 (2012), 21–47.

[23] For fuller attempts to situate music in a fifteenth-century context, see Andrew
Kirkman, *The Cultural Life of the Early Polyphonic Mass* (Cambridge, 2010).

[24] Even the 'technical language' of thirds and sixths must be modified by historicisations
of temperament. See, for example, Rogers Covey-Crump, 'Pythagoras at the Forge:
Tuning in Early Music,' in *Companion to Medieval and Renaissance Music*, ed. Tess Knighton
and David Fallows (1992), 317–26.

(sweetness, joy, etc.). Trained musicians within the humanities have a set of skills not available to many historians. They can (typically) hear internally a melodic leap like a sixth with a variety of timbres, and (perhaps) hear sixths internally as a concurrent sonority. A choral singer might know how it *feels* when sixths and thirds are absent from the harmonic structure. For modern singers, this might feel 'bare' or 'raw'. But such apparently immediate feelings, of course, grow from particular experiences, including habituation to an harmonic tradition that values major and minor triads, with their mediating or sweetening third.[25] A historian trained in music might well internally hear individual lines of a score, although hearing these concurrently becomes increasingly difficult the more parts or lines are present. This 'internal hearing', however, is itself a fraught process with historical baggage, linked with idealising mental performance over and above the physical impermanence of external performance.[26]

Even armed with these (perhaps dubious) resources, we still face a problem of how to be convinced, or unconvinced, by a musical interpretation – how can we evaluate descriptions of sonority? This is partly a problem of expertise, but also of intellectual process. We cannot normally press a book's page to hear a recording of the score in front of us, although new technologies can help us here. Still, in the main, the author who discusses music relies either on readers conjuring up an internally heard performance, or remembering a work already heard; or presupposes that the reader has an instrument, recording or YouTube to hand to consult mid-argument. In all of these cases difficulties multiply. To take only an obvious example: sounding out fifteenth- or sixteenth-century vocal music on a twenty-first-century keyboard will bring 'anachronisms' in timbre and tuning, and technical impediments when it comes to music with, say, forty vocal lines. So the difficulties of accessing and evaluating the ephemeral physical sound of music are a barrier to scholarly conversation in their own right.

This terminology – 'physical sound' – should itself ring methodological alarm bells. Even if we can hear a choir singing a mass by a fifteenth-century composer like Du Fay, it is impossible for the performance to create the same sets of harmonic, rhythmic and textural relations

---

[25] See, for example, E. T. A. Hoffmann's depiction of the sweet-voiced youth 'Third' in his *Ritter Gluck* (1809/14), *Sämtliche Werke in sechs Bänden*, ed. Hartmut Steinecke et al. (Frankfurt, 1993), vol. 2.1, 24. See Miranda Stanyon "'Rastrierte Blätter, aber mit keiner Note beschrieben": The Musical Sublime and Aporias of Inscription in Hoffmann's *Ritter Gluck*', *German Quarterly*, 83 (2010), 412–30.

[26] Gary Tomlinson, 'Musicology, Anthropology, History', in *The Cultural Study of Music. A Critical Introduction*, ed. Martin Clayton, Trevor Herbert and Richard Middleton (New York and London, 2003), 39–40. On performance, see Carolyn Abbate, 'Music – Drastic or Gnostic?', *Critical Inquiry*, 30 (2004), 505–36.

created and heard in the fifteenth century by particular voices and instruments in particular listening environments.[27] Nor can one recreate the
situations and communities of hearing in the particular places and
times when music was heard. These difficulties do not, however, bar
the historian and musicologist from reconstructing a diversity of interpretations of musical practices, nor bar musicians from reinterpreting works
in ways not entirely divorced from the sounds of the past.[28] These
attempts must be made in the knowledge that the musical past cannot
be recaptured, any more than other alterities.

II

How then might we integrate musical analysis into the understanding of
the past? In the following, we pursue one possible answer, through a particular case study: we consider what music might bring to the history of
time. We begin with a hoary old musicological chestnut: the relationship
between music and scholasticism. In his *Geschichte der Musik* (1864–8),
the musicologist August Wilhelm Ambros (1816–1876) drew analogies
between structures of fifteenth-century liturgical music and the
methods of scholasticism.[29]

> In these [composers], though, here and there, something can still be sensed which has a
> kind of analogy with scholasticism – at that time already being overcome by an altered
> world view – and its 'nit-picking, word-rummaging method' (Schopenhauer). Some
> lengthy passages of music above a motive in the tenor consisting of just a few notes
> taken from Gregorian chant, constantly repeated or returning under changing time sig-
> natures, upon which motive the most artful canonic imitations and every possible
> contrapuntal subtlety are then built in the contrapuntal voices, can recall quite directly
> the intellectual edifices that the scholastic philosopher piled up over some thesis taken
> from the dogma of the church.[30]

While we would dissent from Ambros's Hegelian schematisation of
history, with its negative appraisal of scholasticism, his structural

---

[27] On listening environments, see Dillon, *Sense of Sound*, 6–7. For recent studies engaging
with acoustics and historical space, see Deborah Howard and Laura Moretti, *Sound and Space
in Renaissance Venice: Architecture, Music, Acoustics* (New Haven, 2009); Bissera V. Pentcheva and
Jonathan S. Abel, 'Icons of Sound: Auralizing the Lost Voice of Hagia Sophia', *Speculum*, 92
(2017), 336–60. See also the Edinburgh College of Art project 'Space, Place, Sound and
Memory', www.eca.ed.ac.uk/research/space-place-sound-and-memory (accessed 19 April
2019).

[28] This is an attempt to navigate between historicist 'authenticity' and fatalistic diagnoses
of history's impossibility. On this debate in relation to 'historically informed' performance,
see Richard Taruskin, *Text and Act: Essays on Music and Performance* (Oxford, 1995); Peter Kivy,
Authenticities: Philosophical Reflections on Musical Performance (Ithaca, 1995); John Butt, *Playing with
History: The Historical Approach to Musical Performance* (Cambridge, 2002).

[29] August Wilhelm Ambros, *Geschichte der Musik* (Leipzig, 1868), III, 8. Compare Kirkman,
Cultural Life, 9–20.

[30] Ambros, *Geschichte der Musik*, III, 8.

observation is significant. The method of composition from a tenor does have intriguing similarities with scholastic argument. But what are the temporal characteristics of this similarity? To answer the question, we first review the structure of a basic scholastic argument. Our example is the article from Aquinas's *Summa Theologiae*: 'should songs be used in praising God?' (2.2.91.2), a text Carlier also deploys in the opening to his *Tractatus*.

The article begins with a question ('whether God should be praised with song'?). It then moves to five objections. The first opens with the negative proposition that 'it would seem that God should not be praised with song' and then cites an authority (Colossians 3:16), from which is derived the argument that humans should 'employ not corporeal but spiritual canticles'. This structure is common to the first four objections: each derives its authority from a variety of pre-existing texts. The fifth objection, however, purports to derive from experience: if singers pay too much attention to the process of chanting, and chanting makes the words less comprehensible, then the music presents a barrier to the heart's true praise of God. Then follows the *sed contra*: 'Blessed Ambrose established singing in the Church of Milan, as Augustine relates (*Confessions*, ix)'. From this authoritative statement, Aquinas moves to his answer, that music is necessary 'to arouse man's devotion towards God'. He substantiates his answer by referring to his response to the previous question (Whether God should be praised with the lips?) and drawing on the authority of Aristotle, Boethius and, finally, Augustine. The argument then replies individually to each of the five objections.

The temporal structure involved in reading scholastic argument is highly discursive; it runs to and fro (*discurrere*) between different positions. From the initial objections, the reader familiar with the method can derive the form of the positive proposition, projecting the argument's future shape. The turning point of the argument is the invocation of an authoritative text, followed by an explication and elaboration in the answer which the reader, again, already expects. The replies to the objections that conclude each section demand a mode of reading where the negative and positive arguments are held in tension, despite their temporal position at either end of the argument, and where the reader's mind oscillates between objection and reply.

Guillaume Du Fay certainly made use of argumentative principles similar to those of the scholastic tradition in a short work, *Iuvenis qui puellam*, composed in Italy around 1436/7.[31] *Iuvenis qui puellam* sets sections

---

[31] Alejandro Enrique Planchart, *Guillaume Du Fay: The Life and Works* (2 vols., Cambridge, 2018), I, 143–4, II, 407–8. David Fallows, *The Songs of Guillaume Dufay: Critical Commentary to the Revision of Corpus Mensurabilis Musicae, ser. 1, vol. VI* (Neuhausen–Stuttgart, 1995). For a score,

of a letter from Pope Eugenius III (r. 1145–53) that had been incorporated into Gratian's authoritative twelfth-century collection of canon law, the *Decretum*. The sole and damaged surviving manuscript of the piece has the title 'William Du Fay's Decretal' (*Decretalis Guillermus dufay*).[32] After the legal text is stated, the piece turns to a sterile academic disputation on the subject:

> A young man, who married a girl not yet seven years old, was tempted perhaps, however, on account of human weakness, to complete that which he was not able to, although her age should have repelled him.
>
> Since therefore in doubtful matters we ought to hold to the safer course, and because she is said to have been his wife, both for the honour of the church and because of the aforesaid doubt, we order that the cousin of the girl, whom the young man married later, be separated from him.
>
> *The first argument.* It is argued against you where it is suggested by you that the attempt will be punished and not take effect; which would be clearly proved, but brevity does not permit.
>
> *Solution to the first argument.* To this I reply briefly thus: in not reciting the case which you have made against me in due form, that which is maintained by you is not open to the justice of public honour.
>
> *The second argument.* Although you have spoken well, nevertheless I argue against you. For you conclude by saying that she should be separated from him, and yet you can see the opposite in the single chapter which you cited elsewhere, under the sixth heading.
>
> *Solution to the second argument* … [manuscript incomplete][33]

Several attempts have been made to clarify the text's meaning. The least helpful attempt quasi-allegorical readings of the girl as the Council of Basel, the young man as the Duke of Savoy. Far more persuasive is the interpretation of the piece as a parody legal dispute in the tradition of satirical quodlibetal questions.[34]

In following the conventions of the law, the arrangement of Du Fay's text resembles, rather than precisely follows, scholastic argument. But, significantly, there is a stark musical contrast between the legal order *Mandamus* ('We order') and those sections of argument articulated by the objector. Du Fay set the authoritative text with breves topped with fermata marks, which have the effect of slowing the harmonic rhythm (Figure 1). The meaning of these fermatae or *cantus coronatus* (crowned song) is, again, a matter of disagreement among musicologists. Whether we take these marks to signal slow and reverent performance or as a trigger for rhythmically and melodically complex improvisation above sustained chords, the wider point remains clear: the structure of meaning effected by the sonority and fermatae at this point links

see Heinrich Besseler and David Fallows (eds.), Guillaume Dufay, *Opera Omnia*, vol. 6 (Neuhausen, 1995), 15–18.

[32] Munich, Bayerische Staatsbibliothek, Mus. ms. 3224.

[33] Translation adapted from Leofranc Holford-Strevens, 'Du Fay the Poet? Problems in the Texts of His Motets', *Early Music History*, 16 (1997), 151–2.

[34] *Ibid.*, 150–7.

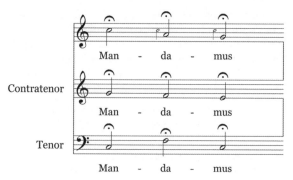

Figure 1 Measure 52, Guillaume Du Fay, *Iuvenis qui puellam.*

authority with harmonic and temporal stability (perhaps with emphatic decoration).[35]

In contrast, the first objection is set to rhythmically intricate and highly imitative polyphony between the upper voice (*cantus*) and the lower voice (*tenor*). The listener might notice the academic sophistication (and potential for sophistry) of this dense imitation. As well as having a strong implication of forward motion, created amongst other things by the numerous scalar passages and through their imitation (in modern score, measures 76ff, 85ff), the parts create a highly discursive mode of listening (Figure 2). The ear is drawn, entry by entry, to switch backwards and forwards between the initial statement and its imitation.

The appearance of such imitation and its accompanying sense of oscillation mirrors the temporal structure embedded in the typical arrangement of objection and reply in traditional medieval legal and scholastic argumentation. By contrast, those sections in which the harmonic rhythm slows and points of authority are specifically marked resemble forms of textual authority and their direct and emphatic

---

[35] For improvisation on *cantus coronatus*, see Charles W. Warren, '*Punctus Organi* and *Cantus Coronatus* in the Music of Dufay,' in *Dufay Quincentenary Conference*, ed. Allan W. Atlas (Brooklyn, 1976), 128–43. For wider revision and debate, see Timothy Brothers, *Chromatic Beauty in the Late Medieval Chanson: An Interpretation of Manuscript Accidentals* (Cambridge, 1997), esp. 3–5, 76, 84; Timothy J. McGee, *The Sound of Medieval Song: Ornamentation and Vocal Style* (Oxford, 1998), 104–10; Bonnie J. Blackburn, 'The Dispute about Harmony *c.* 1500 and the Creation of a New Style', in *Théorie et analyse musicales 1450–1650/Music Theory and Analysis 1450–1650*, ed. Anne Emmanuelle Ceulemans and Bonnie J. Blackburn (Louvain-la-Neuve, 2001). Some theorists associated the fermata mark with a cardinal's hat, suggesting again the mark's signalling of authority. See, for example, Anonymous, *Tractatus et compendium cantus figurati (mss London British Libr., Add. 34200; Regensburg, Proskesche Musikbibl., 98 th. 4°)*, ed. Jill M. Palmer (Stuttgart, 1990), 64.

Figure 2 Measures 72–88 (*Primum argumentum*), Guillaume Du Fay, *Iuvenis qui puellam*.

statement at the heart of each question. The fermatae can even be read as analogous to citations within brackets. They not only slow the process of reading, but are also crucial markers of textual authority.

This relationship between musical and verbal structures is underscored by the form of *Iuvenis qui puellam*'s manuscript. Like almost all fifteenth-century polyphony, the song is notated in parts. Unlike score notation, where imitative parts are synchronised and surveyable at a glance, the separation of parts (for example the *cantus* and *tenor* in the first objections) requires forms of composition and transcription which mirror the discursive process of reading scholastic objections and replies. Consonances between voices must be verified and maintained across physical manuscript space, just as argumentative consonance must be maintained across scholastic argument.

The performance of the motet complicates this temporal arrangement, as various areas of the manuscript page are brought together into a single moment. The discursive patterns of listening described above curiously coincide with a synchronisation of musical parts within the flow of time. This is the same kind of temporal process which must occur as a result of scholastic reasoning: arguments made at different times in the process of the argument (objection, reply) must be placed together with the answer to form a coherent sense of the argumentative 'whole'. This movement between part and whole is a characteristic both of writing and reading scholastic logic, on the one hand, and of singing and listening to fifteenth-century polyphony, on the other.

Similar temporal structures are created by Du Fay's four-voice *Missa Ecce ancilla Domini*. The mass, written in 1464 in Cambrai, is a *cantus firmus* mass, based on the plainchants *Ecce ancilla Domini* (Behold the handmaiden of the Lord) and *Beata es Maria* (Blessed art thou, Mary).[36] It was this process of building music around earlier authoritative melodies which led Ambros to associate 'Netherlandish' composers like Du Fay with 'gothic' scholasticism.

The temporal persistence of chant's authority is embedded in musical works like *Ecce ancilla*. In the Gloria, for example, temporal persistence or permanence is signalled by the length and slow movement of the first statement of the chant (the *cantus firmus*). Against an intricate duet between cantus and contra, it enters in the tenor in slow and stable breves (measure 21, Figure 3). This entry is striking. The texture thickens from two to four voices, and rich sonorities contrast starkly with the intricate and discursive movement of the upper parts which precedes and follows. This *cantus firmus* functions in a way particularly similar to Aquinas's citation of Augustine in the section of the *Summa* analysed

---

[36] Planchart, *Guillaume Du Fay*, II, 603–10.

Figure 3 Measures 1–38, *Gloria*, Guillaume Du Fay, *Missa Ecce ancilla Domini*.

above. The authoritative citation appears near the centre both of the mass's four voices (in the tenor) and of the *Summa* article (in the *sed contra*). Its placement within the discursive structures of polyphony mirrors the placement of authoritative proof texts within the *Summa*'s discursive oscillation between objection and reply.

The temporalities of reading, listening and citation implied by scholastic argument and by Du Fay's music also resonate with explicit arguments about time propounded within scholasticism and widely accepted in fifteenth-century learned culture. These arguments contrast synchronic and diachronic knowledge. For Aquinas, God's intellective knowledge in eternity encompasses all time, enfolding past, present and future into a single 'intellective' glance (*Summa contra gentiles* 1.66.7).[37] God's vision of time can be formulated as the relationship between a circle's central point (God's eternity) and its circumference (time). This image resonates strongly with the musical structures of *Missa Ecce ancilla*. The chant *Ecce ancilla* sits within the arc of the surrounding counterpoint. This repeated *cantus firmus* melody provides the points which harmonically define and underpin the diachronic arcs of the surrounding parts.[38]

As opposed to God's eternal intellective knowledge of time, human knowledge for Aquinas is always temporally bound: 'we see what is future because it is future with respect to our seeing, since our seeing is itself measured by time' (*De veritate* 2.12). This means that human thinking always involves 'a kind of motion, running from one thing to another' (*Summa Theologiae* 1.1.79.9; 1.1.58.3). For Aquinas, imperfect human thought involves 'partial views' from different moments being resolved into some form of 'intelligible unity'. Following this logic, we might make the case that the diversity of partial comprehensions of music makes it a human art par excellence. Yet by its modes of representing the comprehension of complex wholes, those ways of comprehending many voices in a single ear-glance (for want of a better word), music might also model ways of ascending from human discursivity, approaching an intellective understanding of the ratios of the created order. The waning of this kind of metaphysical understanding of music and harmony separates much modern musical thought from its classical and medieval forebears, and is a reminder that music is a cultural resource that extends beyond often more limited modern definitions, crossing artificial boundaries of human knowledge and praxis.

---

[37] See *Summa Theologiae* 1.1.10, 1.10.2.4, 1.14.13; *Compendium Theologiae*, ch. 133. For further discussion, see Champion, *Fullness of Time*, 71–2.

[38] A speculative extension of this argument could be made to *Iuvenis qui puellam*. Charles Warren has argued that the fermata originally had a referential function: the dot signifies the notated note; the arc signified the improvisatory material elaborated around it (on debates surrounding this interpretation, see n. 37 above). The fermata, then, could be seen as embodying visually the same temporal schemas which are heard in the music: the fermata is a diagram of diachronic improvisation around points of authoritative and rich harmonic stasis. Warren, '*Punctus Organi* and *Cantus Coronatus*', 132, 135–6.

The preceding discussion is only one way of approaching a history of time and music. We have suggested resonances between the temporalities of verbal texts and music, set with wider cultural structures of time; we have not properly considered, however, the difficult question of how to interpret – or even identify – conceptual 'dissonances' and lack of synchronisation between music and words. What might music tell us about the history of time that differs from that which words can tell us, and how would we articulate and maintain this 'musical' knowledge without citing authoritative (because more explicit) verbal texts?[39] (Ambros's progress-oriented discussion in fact alludes to this problem: he criticised 'scholastic' fifteenth-century polyphony for seeming old-fashioned and out-of-synch with the rest of culture, which was in the process of 'overcoming' medieval scholasticism.) And we have not touched on the performance contexts of Du Fay's music, its social production, its possible roles in forming and maintaining identity, or its possible functions as (bad) comedy in elite cultures of masculine learning. But this partial analysis nonetheless suggests one way of drawing Du Fay's piece into a wider, intermedial history of tensions between discursivity and synchronicity, dispute and authority, time and eternity in late medieval culture.

III

As numerous scholars have noted, questions of eternity and time are deeply bound up with textual interpretation in the Christian tradition. Central to this tradition are ways of reading the Hebrew scriptures as figural announcements of Christ – his advent, crucifixion, resurrection and ascension.[40] In this final section, we explore how this tradition functions in relation to the long and intermedial history of the psalm *Dixit Dominus* (Psalm 109/110). Our hope is that threads from the previous two reflections – vocabularies of affect, hermeneutics of diversity, synchrony and diachrony, eternity and time – might tie into some thoughts on the roles of music and of Jews in this story (bringing us as far as eighteenth-century music and its performances in the present).

In early Christianity, Psalm 110 became a prominent proof text for the claim that Jesus was the prophesied Messiah.[41] In the words of Augustine's influential interpretation: 'Our psalm deals with these

---

[39] Andrew Bowie, *Music, Philosophy, and Modernity* (Cambridge, 2007), advocates approaching music as way of thinking, rather than simply an object (and problem) for verbal thought.

[40] The classic discussion is Eric Auerbach, 'Figura', in *Scenes from the Drama of European Literature* (Manchester, 1984), 11–76.

[41] See Michel Gourges, *À la droite de Dieu. Résurrection de Jésus et actualisation du Psaume 110:1 dans le Nouveau Testament* (Paris, 1978); Ulli Roth, *Die Grundparadigmen christlicher Schriftauslegung – im Spiegel der Auslegungsgeschichte von Psalm 110* (Münster, 2010); Miriam von Nordheim, *Geboren von der Morgenröte? Psalm 110 in Tradition, Redaktion und Rezeption* (Neukirchen–Vluyn, 2008).

promises [of the coming of Christ]. It speaks prophetically of our Lord and Savior Jesus Christ with such certainty and clarity that we cannot doubt that it is he who is proclaimed here.'[42]

For Augustine, the psalm's first verse, 'The Lord said to my Lord: sit at my right hand until I make thine enemies thy footstool,' unequivocally showed David acknowledging that God the Father ('the Lord') had decreed that Jesus ('my Lord') should sit at his right hand. Asked who Jesus was, the Jews 'should have found the answer in the scriptures which they read but did not understand'; '[t]hey did not seek after [Jesus] as the Lord, for they did not recognize him as David's descendant'.[43] This failure justifies Augustine's inclusion of the Jews among Christ's enemies:

> Now you reign amid your enemies, Lord: now in this transient age while the centuries roll on, while mortal humanity propagates itself and the generations succeed each other, while the torrent of time (*torrens temporum*) slips by, now is the scepter of your power sent forth from Zion that you may hold sway in the midst of your enemies. Be Lord of them: be Lord, you son of David who are also David's Lord, be Lord amid pagans, Jews, heretics and false brethren. *Have dominion in the midst of your foes.*[44]

A particular language of time appears here: time as a torrent. For Augustine, it was this torrent that washes away the Old, allowing the new age of Christian knowledge and social order to emerge. This appearance of the torrent of time foreshadows Augustine's discussion of the psalm's enigmatic final verse, *de torrente in via bibet, propterea exaltabit caput* ('He will drink from the torrent beside the way, and therefore he will raise his head'):[45]

> Let us also contemplate him drinking from the torrent on his journey. But first, what torrent is this? The cascade of human mortality. A stream is formed by rainwater; it swells, roars, rolls swiftly, and as it surges forward it is running downward to the end of its course. The course of mortal life is like this …
>
> The torrent is the stream of birth and death, and Christ accepted it. He was born and he died; thus he *drank from the torrent beside the way*, for *he leapt up like a giant to run his course with joy* (Ps. 19:5). Because he refused to stand still and linger *in the way of the sinner* (Ps.1:1) he *drank from the torrent beside the way*, and therefore *he will raise his head*. Because he *humbled himself and was made obedient to the point of death, even death on a cross, God raised him high and gave him a name above every other name, that at the name of Jesus every knee should bow, in heaven, on earth or in the underworld, and every tongue confess that Jesus Christ is Lord, in the glory of God the Father.* (Phil. 2:8–11)[46]

---

[42] Maria Boulding and Boniface Ramsey (eds.), *The Works of Saint Augustine. A Translation for the 21st Century*, vol. III.19: *Expositions of the Psalms 99–120* (Hyde Park, NY, 2003), 263.

[43] *Ibid.*, 266, 264.

[44] *Ibid.*, 272.

[45] All translations in the *Vetus Latina* database use *torrens*. Modern translations often use 'brook' instead of 'torrent' here – 'brook' originally denoting a strongly rushing stream.

[46] Augustine, *Psalms 99–120*, 284. See also Augustine's commentary on Psalm 123/124: 'As long as this world flows on, with its succession of births and deaths, it is a torrent, and from it

Read this way, the final verse of *Dixit Dominus* becomes the moment both of God's intense temporalisation – his incarnation, passion and death – and an affirmation of his eternity – his exultation, ascension and immortality.

This interpretation was dominant until historicist readings emerged in the nineteenth century. Even before then, its inflections changed – as Augustine himself would have it – according to time, person and place. In thirteenth-century Paris, following the famous arrival of the relic of the crown of thorns, a new liturgy was composed that featured *De torrente* as a responsory.[47] Now the exulted head was not Augustine's risen and ascended Christ, but the bloodied head of Christ on the cross, crowned, as another antiphon for the Feast has it, by Jewish men: 'Drinking of the torrent (*De torrente bibens*) of misery, the king of glory lifted up his head (*exultavit caput*), crowned with thorns of agony.'[48]

Christ suffering at Jewish hands became the keynote of the *de torrente* motif in the later Middle Ages. As others have shown, the psalm episode became attached to increasingly elaborate descriptions of Christ's passion.[49] There was precedent for this. The Jews' role in Christ's suffering was explicit in the early commentary of Cassiodorus (*c.* 485–*c.* 583), where the psalm's torrent was 'the turbulent persecution of the Jews, of which the Lord Christ drank on the way'.[50] The narrative of Jews as Christ-killers was combined with Jerome's reading of the torrent as the brook Cedron over which Christ was led to his crucifixion. This was elaborated in texts and images portraying Christ falling into, or being dragged through, the brook. Here is one account from a fifteenth-century vernacular Dutch version:

And the cursed Jews led Jesus through the valley of Josaphat, and when they came to the bridge over the stream or brook of Cedron, they ... dragged Jesus through the water so

---

arise persecutions. Our head drank from it first, he of whom it is said in another psalm, *He drank from the torrent beside the way.*' Jerome (*c.* 340–420) had earlier related drinking from the torrent to Christ's passion. 'Commentarioli in Psalmum CVIIII', in *S. Hieronymi Presbyteri Opera* 1.1 [CCSL 72] (Turnhout, 1959), 232; 'Tractatus de Psalmo CVIIII', in *S. Hieronymi Presbyteri Opera* 2 [CCSL 78] (Turnhout, 1958), 227–30. Hereafter Jerome, *Tractatus*. See also James H. Marrow, *Passion Iconography in Northern European Art of the Late Middle Ages and Early Renaissance* (Kortrijk, 1979), 104; Rudolf Berliner, 'Die Cedronbrücke als Station des Passionsweges Christi', in *Rudolph Berliner (1886–1967): 'The Freedom of Medieval Art' und andere Studien zum christlichen Bild*, ed. Robert Suckale (Berlin, 2003), 24.

[47] Judith Blezzard, Stephen Ryle and Jonathan Alexander, 'New Perspectives on the Feast of the Crown of Thorns', *Journal of the Plainsong and Mediaeval Music Society*, 10 (1987), 23–53.

[48] Cambrai Mediathèque Municipale, Ms. 38, f. 428v; Paris, Bibliothèque nationale de France, Ms lat. 15182, f. 291r, f. 293r.

[49] Marrow, *Passion Iconography*; Berliner, 'Die Cedronbrücke'.

[50] 'Expositio in Psalmum CIX', in *Magni Aurelii Cassiodori Senatoris Opera* 2.2 [CCSL 98] (Turnhout, 1958), 1012.

that the prophesy spoken by David, He shall drink of the brook in the way, would be fulfilled.[51]

The survival of this trope in the Catholic Low Countries into the seventeenth century is shown in three images by the Antwerp artist Frans Francken II (1581–1642).[52] Here, Christ's passage through Cedron is framed by the deformed faces of his Jewish and Roman persecutors (Figure 4).[53] The darkness of this scene amplifies Jerome's early gloss on the meaning of the brook's name – 'Cedron in the Hebrew tongue means shadows … All who hate the light, love shadows.'[54]

Which brings us to the best-known musical interpretation of *De torrente*: George Frideric Handel's (1685–1759) setting of *Dixit Dominus* (1707). Handel's *De torrente* is an intricate, chromatic and affective duet for two sopranos (Figure 5). The intertwined soprano duet, comprised of plangent suspensions and dissonant leaps, presents the text *de torrente in via bibet* ('he will drink from the torrent beside the way') until almost the movement's close. In the sopranos' oscillating semiquaver exchanges, we might hear a kind of dialogue. The melismatic duet is punctuated by syllabic, unison interjections from a lower chorus singing *propterea exaltabit caput* ('therefore he shall lift up his head'). After the first entry, each choral interjection commences with one octave leap and closes with another.[55] Apart from these leaps, each phrase sung by the men remains fixed on a single note. By contrast, the soprano duet weaves a plaintive, thorny path to its final resolution.

In this description we are, of course, suggesting an interpretation, a reading of Handel's music in relation to the textual tradition of interpreting Psalm 110. This typological tradition helps understand the intense pathos of Handel's setting – something even a listener attuned to eighteenth-century harmonic culture might recognise with puzzlement on a first hearing. (It must be recognised, however, that trained listeners will not be unanimous: John Eliot Gardiner recently noted *De torrente*'s

[51] *Fasciculus Mirre*, Leiden, Bibliotheek der Rijksuniversiteit, Ms. Lett. 357, f. 113*v*, cited in Marrow, *Passion Iconography*, 106–7.

[52] *Ibid.*, 106. To Marrow's example – Bob Jones University Gallery, Greenville (inv. no. P64.336) – should be added Musée des Beaux-Arts, Tourcoing (inv. no. D335, dated 1630), and an example in a private collection (1639). The scene also appears in a betrayal image. See Ursula Härting, *Frans Francken der Jüngere (1581–1642): Die Gemälde mit kritischem Oeuvrekatalog* (Freren, 1989), 281–2.

[53] On such crowds, see Sara Lipton, *Dark Mirror: Jews, Vision, and Witness in Medieval Christian Art, 1000–1500* (New York, 2014).

[54] Jerome, *Tractatus*, 229.

[55] Except at measures 23–25 for the tenors, for tessitura reasons; the first entry is a leap of a fourth.

Figure 4 Frans Francken the Younger, Christ being dragged through the brook of Cedron. Private Collection. © Christie's Images/ Bridgeman Images.

'grinding harmony clashes', yet summed up its mood as 'gentle and soothing'.[56])

We could enrich this interpretation by examining other musical settings of the psalm, or by comparing Handelian instances of word-painting which explicitly portray the Passion, Resurrection, darkness, torrents and so on. Or we could cite early modern commentaries on the psalms from Handel's lifetime: the reading of the psalm text as a prophecy of Christ's suffering and final victory by the Lutheran professor of Hebrew and court preacher Martin Geier (1614–1680);[57] the commentary of the eminent Catholic theologian Joseph Maria Thomasius (1649–1713), published in Rome in 1697, that draws on Cassiodorus, Jerome and Augustine to speak of the torrent 'of great and heavy afflictions' which Christ drank in his sufferings;[58] or we could turn to the English traditions so relevant to Handel's later career, and find Symon

[56] John Eliot Gardiner, sleeve notes to Gardiner, Monteverdi Choir and English Baroque Soloists, *Live at Milton Court: Handel, Bach, Scarlatti* (Monteverdi Productions, 2014), 7.

[57] Martin Geier, *D. Martini Geieri opera omnia* etc. (Amsterdam: Rembertus Goethals, 1696), I, cols. 1740–2.

[58] Joseph Maria Thomasius, *Psalterium cum canticis versibus prisco more distinctum argumentis et orationibus vetustis* etc. (Rome: Joseph Vannaccius, 1697), 488–90.

Figure 5 Measures 12–16, *De torrente*, George Frideric Handel, *Dixit Dominus*.

Patrick (1626–1707), the latitudinarian bishop first of Chichester and then of Ely, defending figural interpretations of the psalm against

> the Jews [who] have taken a great deal of pains, to wrest this Psalm to another sense; yet they are so divided in their opinions about it, (speaking inconsistent things, like drunken men, as Saint Chrysostom's words are, or rather, says he, like men in the dark, running against one another) that from thence alone we may be satisfied they are in the wrong, and have their eyes blinded.[59]

Alongside interrogating the affective range of the movement, we might also interpret Handel's setting as playing with the long musical tradition in which a *cantus firmus* might be aligned with a synchronic apprehension of time, and an interwoven imitation might emulate the diachronic, discursive flow of time (time's torrent). The flow of sorrowful time in the upper voices contrasts with the stable male synchrony of the exulted Lordship of Christ over creation. We could work this interpretation into a series of reflections on the gendering of time and creation, the weeping women at the foot of the cross, or the women who weep because they know not where the Lord has been taken – those very women who are comforted in the Gospel by an angelic (and male) voice speaking of Christ's resurrection and freedom from the bonds of mortality.

But we want to return to the untied threads of our discussion, to consider other historical ways of hearing Handel's music. It is possible that *Dixit Dominus* was first performed within an elaborate liturgy for the Feast of Our Lady of Mount Carmel for Rome's Carmelite church, S. Maria di Montesanto, in 1707.[60] These feasts became a remarkable spectacle in early eighteenth-century Rome, with illuminations,

---

[59] Symon Patrick, *The Book of Psalms Paraphras'd; with Arguments to Each Psalm* (London: J.H., [2]1691), 546.

[60] See Graham Dixon, 'Handel's Vesper Music: Towards a Liturgical Reconstruction', *Musical Times*, 126 (1985), 393, 395–7; *idem*, 'Handel's Music for the Carmelites: A Study in Liturgy and Some Observations on Performance', *Early Music*, 15 (1987), 16–30. Other occasions are possible, but less likely. Handel certainly directed music for the Feast on 15 July 1707. See recently Juliane Riepe, *Händel vor dem Fernrohr. Die Italienreise* (Beeskow, 2013), 207n, 236, 237n, 447. Donald Burrows observes that the context of *Dixit*'s first performance has 'generated strong disagreements, rival performances and recordings, and bizarre situations that would make good material for an extended comedy film'. Burrows, 'What We Know – and What We Don't Know – about Handel's Career in Rome', in *Georg Friedrich Händel in Rom: Beiträge der Internationalen Tagung am Deutschen Historischen Institut in Rom, 17–20 Oktober 2007*, ed. Sabine Ehrmann-Herfort and Matthias Schnettger (Kassel, 2010), 103. The work's composition history is also debated. Intriguingly, John H. Roberts has recently (and persuasively) argued that Handel probably completed a version of *Dixit Dominus* in Venice, but 'later revised it in Rome, discarding the original last two sections [including *De torrente*] in favor of new versions'. Roberts, '"Souvenirs de Florence": Additions to the Handel Canon', *Handel Jahrbuch*, 57 (2011), 205–7.

fireworks, elaborate newly commissioned music for orchestral and choral forces, and large crowds of spectators and participants. A learned Carmelite, or visiting cleric, might indeed have perceived in this music something of the arcs of interpretation we have traced here.

Beyond this possibility, how did the work's liturgical placement frame its reception as sacred object, as entertainment, or object of incomprehension? Would the music be the same for a devout Catholic spectator as for, say, a curious Protestant attracted by the immense scenery erected on the processional *via* leading to the church?[61] One such Protestant visitor to the Carmelite festivities was Prince Anton Ulrich of Saxe-Meiningen. He noted in his diary the 'lovely music' directed by 'the German Handel from Halle', but was seemingly less concerned with devotion to Our Lady of Mount Carmel – whose church he records as '*la Madonna dell Clementini*', before correcting this to '*Carmi*' – than with seeing and being seen ('Cardinal Ottoboni himself spoke to me as he passed by'; 'I spoke … with a certain French *Marquis*').[62] Or how might Handel have heard his own music, or his music have been heard by a fellow composer? Would perceptions have changed with the memory of previous liturgies with different settings of *Dixit Dominus*; might there be some element of 'emulation, competition, and homage' in operation?[63] What roles did the power of Handel's music play in exalting the Carmelite Order, or constructing the power of the festival's patron, Cardinal Colonna, and his family? Could a listener possibly be transported to a vision of Christ's passion, seeing the bleeding crown of thorns and a crowd of persecuting Jews? Or, indeed, might one hear Handel's work as the violent appropriation of a Jewish psalm in the service of the false cult of a false Messiah? Might an equally historicised account imagine the work's vigorous energy and 'sublimity' overwhelming a visiting music lover – anticipating the response to *Dixit Dominus* of a later Jewish and Christian reader of the work, Felix Mendelssohn?[64] How is the gendered interpretation of the psalm

---

[61] *Idem*, 'Handel's Music for the Carmelites', 18. On Protestants in Handel's Rome and interconfessional relations, see Sabine Ehrmann-Herfort and Matthias Schnettger (eds.), *Georg Friedrich Händel in Rom: Beiträge der Internationalen Tagung am Deutschen Historischen Institut in Rom, 17–20 Oktober 2007* (Kassel, 2010).

[62] See Riepe, *Händel vor dem Fernrohr*, 143.

[63] Howard Mayer Brown, 'Emulation, Competition, and Homage: Imitation and Theories of Imitation in the Renaissance', *Journal of the American Musicological Society*, 35 (1982). Relationships between Handel's *Dixit* and other settings are debated. See Hans Joachim Marx, 'Händels lateinische Kirchenmusik und ihr gattungsgeschichtlicher Kontext', *Göttinger Händel Beiträge*, 5 (1993), esp. 118–19, 142; Riepe, *Händel vor dem Fernrohr*, 160–1.

[64] Ralf Wehner, 'Mendelssohn and the Performance of Handel's Vocal Works', in *Mendelssohn in Performance*, ed. Siegwart Reichwald (Bloomington, 2008), 165. Published soon after Handel's death, John Mainwaring's *Memoirs of the Life of the Late George Frederic*

altered if we recall that the soprano parts would have been sung by cas-
trati in Rome?[65] We are returned to the question of *diversitas*. Handel's
Dixit is part of time, of space, of people, and its 'is-ness' is therefore
full of diverse receptions and constructions of meaning, embedded in a
rich historical sediment, in the limitations and possibilities of this
musical setting as it was and is appropriated, re-inscribed, re-performed
and re-heard according to a variety of times, places and persons.

An emphasis on diversity does not lend itself to a simple summary of
the difficulties and gains of incorporating music into historical practice.
Still, the argument on one level should be clear from the cases sketched
here: histories of sweetness should consider sweet sonorities; histories of
temporality should include compositional techniques; histories of
liturgy, biblical interpretation, and of anti-Jewish thought, should be
alert to musical word-painting, as well as to musical perception and
unperceptiveness; histories of emotion should incorporate musical
genres and discourses of diverse kinds.[66] Sonic sources belong in
general historical practice, just as we increasingly accept as the case for
visual sources. (Indeed, one fertile direction for methodology is to consider the parallel between 'high' art/visual culture and 'classical'
music/sonic culture.) This is true despite the need for particular kinds
of expertise, and despite music's ability to generate a tide of methodological and interpretive questions. Why? Not least because these questions also make music a model among our sources. Take the plunge
into the torrent: this is musicalised history – to realise that musical
sounds, musical works, musical texts and images, exist in their genesis
and performances, in their receptions and interpretations, and that
these ephemeral presences can both be touched and flow out of our
reach, even as we attempt to hold them fast.

Handel (1760) already claimed that Handel had left Italian audiences 'thunderstruck with the
grandeur and sublimity of his stile' and eminent musicians 'puzzled how to execute' his
secular music's 'amazing fulness, force, and energy' (53, 56, 62).

[65] On musicians for the Carmelite Feasts, see Riepe, *Händel vor dem Fernrohr*, 237–8.

[66] Detailed grapplings with music and anti-Jewish traditions include John H. Roberts,
'False *Messiah*', *Journal of the American Musicological Society*, 63 (2010), 45–97; Ruth
HaCohen, *The Music Libel against the Jews* (New Haven, 2012); Michael Marissen, *Tainted
Glory in Handel's 'Messiah'* (New Haven, 2014).

Transactions of the RHS 29 (2019), pp. 105–125 © Royal Historical Society 2019
doi:10.1017/S0080440119000057

LOVE, CARE AND THE ILLEGITIMATE CHILD IN EIGHTEENTH-CENTURY SCOTLAND*

By Katie Barclay

David Berry Prize Winner

ABSTRACT. This article uses a combination of court and Kirk (Church of Scotland) session records, and several sets of letters written by the mothers of illegitimate children to explore how such children were loved and cared for in eighteenth-century Scotland. It argues that legitimacy, as well as class and gender, mattered in the love and care that children received. Illegitimacy also had an impact on who mothered, fracturing the bond between the biological mother and child, for a mothering given by other mothers, including wet-nurses, grandparents and, later, employers. Its conclusion is that how a child was mothered, the love and care they received, were products of a child's positioning – gender, class, legitimacy, parentage – in the world. Love was a social product, framed and shaped by and through the social, economic and legal networks in which the child was positioned. Whilst the legitimate child, both in law and social practice, might have expected its care to be framed primarily through the nuclear family, the bastard child belonged, as the law suggested, to the community, requiring its mothering to be dispersed.

In 1742, George Innes was thirty-nine and still unmarried when Elizabeth Graham became pregnant.[1] George was the son of an Aberdeenshire merchant, and part of a rapidly upwardly mobile family. He would eventually rise to the position of cashier in the Royal Bank of Scotland and purchase a local estate. Elizabeth was a maid within the household of Lady Whiteford of Blairquahan when she met George, at that time a clerk for Allan Whiteford, Lady Whiteford's brother-in-law. Elizabeth was the daughter of William Graham, a schoolmaster in Ratho, a small village west of Edinburgh. She was likely around twenty-eight

* I would like to thank the anonymous reviewers for their comments and Jean McBain for her research assistance on this project. This research was funded by the Australian Research Council DE140100111.

[1] This case study is developed from a series of letters between the children's mothers and other caregivers and George Innes of Stowe, as well as his accounts of their expenditure. They are found at National Records of Scotland (hereafter NRS), Papers of George Innes, c.1742–1762, GD113/4/165/999–1094.

years old, and clearly expected George to marry her.[2] Her pregnancy was made public when the Reverend David Fordyce joked about it over dinner one evening, and it was overheard by the footman and circulated downstairs.[3] She was dismissed from her job; George apologised to his employer and offered to resign, but was forgiven. A daughter was born in September 1742 and named Jean, probably after George's mother.

Unfortunately, for Elizabeth, she was not the only woman George impregnated that year. Another mistress, with the surname Hamilton, gave birth to a daughter who was named George. George senior had a healthy fear of his own father's wrath and, recognising that he would 'urge' marriage, immediately proposed to a third woman whose family could more readily enable his ambition of social mobility, and they married in November. Elizabeth was angry, as were her parents. However, it was too late. George continued to support Elizabeth Graham and both his illegitimate children, as well as the five children he had with his wife. Elizabeth initially moved into the countryside outside Edinburgh to give birth and lived there in the succeeding months whilst her daughter was sent out to nurse. She spent her time avoiding questions about whether she was married; visiting her child; and taking in laundry for work, including George's, which supplemented her allowance.

In August 1743, when Jean was almost a year old, she was reintroduced into her mother's house over several weeks, an experience that was not without difficulty. 'Your daughter came to me Tuesday Last,' Elizabeth wrote to George. 'I belive she will break her heart and mine both before that time for she niver gos to bed nor creddel with out alarming the wholl nightbours in the Land with Craying and sobbing that I think her heart shall burst for want of her nurse.'[4] Despite this, when Jean returned to her nurse, Elizabeth found that: 'I think my self much Lonlyer since she is gone then I was before she came being used with her these 2–3 days and she beginning to know me I desin if you please to see her again the end of this week in her owne quarters that her aquentances and mine may not wier out again.'[5] In October 1743,

---

[2] The birth of an Elizabeth Graham, the daughter of William Graham and Margaret Savage, was registered in Mid-Calder (five miles from Ratho) in 1715. They also had a son, John, born in 1720. However these are common names so this identification is not confirmed. Twenty-eight was a fairly typical age for a servant to have their first illegitimate child: Alice Reid, Ros Davies, Eilidh Garrett and Andrew Blaikie, 'Vulnerability among Illegitimate Children in Nineteenth-Century Scotland', *Annales de Démographie Historique*, 1.189 (2006), 89–113.

[3] This appears to be David Fordyce (1711–1751), moral philosopher, and brother of James, the advice book writer.

[4] Elizabeth Graham to George Innes, 11 August 1743, NRS, GD113/4/165/1087.

[5] Elizabeth Graham to George Innes, 15 August 1743, NRS, GD113/4/165/1086.

Elizabeth and Jean moved to her parents' home in Ratho and Elizabeth actively sought a position in service.

In 1747, Elizabeth Graham died whilst still living in Ratho. Jean's care and education was supervised by her maternal uncle John and her grandfather William. In 1754, her writing was poor, but she had a genius for arithmetic and was learning Latin. She also attended a sewing school, before being apprenticed for three years as a mantua-maker in 1755, when she was thirteen. Jean died in January 1762 in her uncle's house at age twenty, after an illness of several months. Her step-sibling George, known as Joan, had died of consumption in 1752 at her mother's home in Edinburgh at age eight. We know less about her, but that she was 'comely lookt, genteel of station' with bad eyes and loved 'truth & her books, had no bad habits ever I heard of & many of her expression might have well become more advanced years'.[6]

Jean and Joan were relatively fortunate illegitimate children. They had a father, who does not appear to have seen them regularly, but who consistently financially provided during childhood. His provisioning purchased Jean a high-quality wet-nurse that ensured she survived her infancy; it paid for an education that included instruction in Latin, despite her gender, and an apprenticeship as a mantua-maker, a training that marked her status as a daughter of the Scottish gentry.[7] Importantly, her maternal family's decision to provide this education was not simply about economics. She was raised and personally educated by her grandfather and uncle, who were the local schoolmasters, and they could have provided this education without an external income – yet they had not done so for her mother. Rather, the desire to educate her as a member of her father's class and, in doing so, mark her of that social group, informed their decision-making around her education. They took pride in this act of care, reporting their actions and her successes to her father. It could be argued that it was an act of care that evidenced their love for her. That this family chose to claim this status for this illegitimate child, despite the impact of her birth on the reputation of her mother, their sister and daughter, is suggestive of an affective commitment to her success that could be described as love.

Questions of love also arise in her other caring relationships. Jean spent the first year of her life with another mother, who fed and parented her – a mother whom she was distressed to leave when reintegrated into

[6] Note by George Innes re death of George Innes Hamilton, 28 April 1752, NRS, GD113/4/165/1000.

[7] Deborah Simonton, 'Milliners and *Marchandes de Modes*: Gender, Creativity and Skill in the Workplace', in *Luxury and Gender in the European Town, 1700–1914*, ed. Deborah Simonton, Marjo Kaartinen and Anne Montenach (2015), 19–38; Katherine Glover, *Elite Women and Polite Society in Eighteenth-Century Scotland* (Woodbridge, 2011).

her biological mother's home. This was a woman for whom there is no record of a continuing relationship in later years, although this was possible in some families.[8] As a teenager, she was also parented by the woman who gave her a trade, moving into a new household for this stage of her life.[9] Had Elizabeth Graham found employment after her pregnancy, as was typical, Jean might have had limited access to her biological mother across her life. As it was, her mother died. Was Jean loved in these relationships or only cared for, and whose experience matters here – a toddler's distress may evidence its love for a caring nurse but does it also suggest that the nurse loved in return?

Jean's story is an account that raises questions about the relationship between practices of caring and those of love. When does economic provision or the intimate labours of child-rearing become love? When does caring *for* become caring *about*? as the feminist philosopher Nel Noddings famously asked.[10] For the historian, these questions are inflected through a new history of emotions that highlights the historical contingency of ideas about what love is, how it is practised and how it is related to concepts of care.[11] This article uses a case study of how illegitimate children were cared for in eighteenth-century Scotland to explore how practices of love and care were inflected by their social status. Many accounts of love in the historiography have interpreted it as something that was applied or not, that was found or absent. Thus, the mother that abandoned her child but enquired into its health has been viewed as 'loving', and those that have walked away were not. Yet, perhaps it might be more fruitful to think of love as something offered in degrees, as a social and cultural practice that was highly contextual and situational, and that its situatedness meant that the experience of love could vary enormously across individuals, shaped by their social, cultural and temporal positioning.

---

[8] For example Sir Robert Montgomerie of Skelmorlie to John Todd, his gardener, 25 June 1665, NRS, GD3/5/646; for discussion Katie Barclay, 'Emotional Lineages: Blood, Property, Family and Affection in Early Modern Scotland', in *A History of Heritage: Emotions in Blood, Stone and Land*, ed. Alicia Marchant (2019), 84–98.

[9] Ilana Krausman Ben-Amos, *Adolescence and Youth in Early Modern England* (New Haven, 1994).

[10] Nel Noddings, *Caring: A Relational Approach to Ethics and Moral Education* (Berkeley, 1986); J. Tronto, *Moral Boundaries: A Political Argument for an Ethic of Care* (1994).

[11] This is a huge literature: William Reddy, *The Making of Romantic Love: Longing and Sexuality in Europe, South Asia, and Japan, 900–1200 CE* (Chicago, 2012); Theodore Zeldin, *An Intimate History of Humanity* (1998); Claudia Jarzebowski, 'The Meaning of Love: Emotion and Kinship in Sixteenth-Century Incest Discourses', in *Mixed Marriages: Transgressive Unions in Germany from the Reformation to the Enlightenment*, ed. David Luebke and Mary Lindemann (Oxford, 2014), 166–83; Clare Langhamer, 'Love, Selfhood and Authenticity in Post-War Britain', *Cultural and Social History*, 9 (2012), 277–97; Katie Barclay, *Love, Intimacy and Power: Marriage and Patriarchy in Scotland, 1650–1850* (Manchester, 2011).

Maternal love has not been ignored by historians. If early social historians argued that maternal love was a product of modernity, enabled by
material conditions, a reduced child mortality rate and a softening of attitudes towards 'bastard-bearers', others have countered with a long
history of evidences of parental affection towards children.[12] A more
recent historiography has sought to complicate maternal love, evidencing
its different forms at particular moments. Joanne Begiato has highlighted
how the cult of sensibility worked to romanticise the parent–child bond,
informing social practice.[13] I and others have highlighted the significance
across the seventeenth and eighteenth centuries of the concept of 'natural
affection', parental love as an innate human instinct, but one that was
practised as a form of duty displayed in provisioning, education and
physical care of the child.[14] As Emma Griffin recently highlighted in
her work on Victorian motherhood however, women conforming to gendered expectations of material care for children were not always seen as
loving by children, within a context where ideas about loving behaviour
were rapidly changing.[15] The relationship between love and care thus
not only evolves over time and place, but across generations, something
particularly critical for histories of the parent–child relationship. It can
also extend beyond the mother into other relationships, as Jean's experience suggests. Several historians in recent years, typically informed by

[12] Edward Shorter, *The Making of the Modern Family* (1976); Lawrence Stone, *The Family, Sex and Marriage in England 1500–1800* (1977); Randolph Trumbach, *The Rise of the Egalitarian Family* (Oxford, 1978); Albrecht Classen, 'Philippe Aries and the Consequences. History of Childhood, Family Relations and Personal Emotions. Where Do We Stand Today?', in *Childhood in the Middle Ages and the Renaissance: The Results of a Paradigm Shift in the History of Mentality*, ed. Albrecht Classen (Hawthorne, NY, 2011), 1–65; Stephanie Miller, 'Parenting in the Palazzo: Images and Artefacts of Children in the Italian Renaissance Home', in *The Early Modern Italian Domestic Interior, 1400–1700*, ed. Erin Campbell, Stephanie R. Miller, Elizabeth Carroll Consavari and Allison Levy (2013), 67–88; Mathew Knox Averett (ed.), *The Early Modern Child in Art and History* (2015); Simon Schama, *The Embarrassment of Riches: An Interpretation of Dutch Culture in the Golden Age* (Berkeley, 1988).

[13] Joanne Begiato (Bailey), *Parenting in Early Modern England, 1760–1830: Emotion, Identity and Generation* (Oxford, 2012).

[14] Katie Barclay, 'Natural Affection, Children and Family Inheritance Practices in the Long-Eighteenth-Century', in *Children and Youth in Medieval and Early Modern Scotland*, ed. Elizabeth Ewan and Janey Nugent (Woodbridge, 2015), 136–54; *idem*, 'Natural Affection, the Patriarchal Family and the "Strict Settlement" Debate: A Response from the History of Emotions', *Eighteenth Century Theory and Interpretation*, 58 (2017), 309–20; Sherrin Marshall, '"Dutiful Love and Natural Affection": Parent–Child Relationships in the Early Modern Netherlands', in *Early Modern Europe: Issues and Interpretation*, ed. James B. Collins and Karen L. Taylor (Oxford, 2006), 138–52.

[15] Emma Griffin, 'The Emotions of Motherhood: Love, Culture, and Poverty in Victorian Britain', *American Historical Review*, 123 (2018), 60–85; Joanne Bailey, 'The History of Mum and Dad: Recent Historical Research on Parenting in England from the 16th to 20th Centuries', *History Compass*, 12 (2014), 489–507.

gender and feminist theory, have directed us to the love offered by fathers and wider society, as methods of decentring the mother in caring practices.[16] This work has highlighted the significance of the shared and 'social' parenting offered by both parents, wider kin, servants and broader society.

Such dispersed parenting was particularly significant for illegitimate and poor children, due to their social and economic precariousness. The experience of love and care in many cultures was shaped by social group. As Kate Gibson has also shown for England, the care received by illegitimate children with at least one middle- or upper-class parent was often of a higher quality – better clothing, food, standard of education – than that of the poor. Yet, such care was often still differentiated from that of their legitimate siblings, who may have received more investment in their upbringing again, as well as being more likely to be raised by their own parents.[17] More widely, child-rearing practices have been shaped by gender, class and race. That the child of the same man might end up in slavery or of high status, depending on the position of their mother, has drawn attention to how experiences of childhood are inflected by the circumstances of birth.[18] Individual experiences also mattered. Some parents had 'favourites', something associated with sons in the early modern period and daughters in the nineteenth century; conversely, others subjected a particular child to

---

[16] Megan Doolittle, 'Fatherhood and Family Shame: Masculinity, Welfare and the Workhouse in Late-Nineteenth-Century England', in *The Politics of Domestic Authority in Britain since 1800*, ed. L. Delap, B. Griffin and Abigail Wills (2008), 84–108; Julie-Marie Strange, *Fatherhood and the British Working Class, 1865–1914* (Cambridge, 2015); Bianca Premo, '"Misunderstood Love": Children and Wet Nurses, Creoles and Kings in Lima's Enlightenment', *Colonial Latin American Review*, 14 (2005), 231–61; Susan Broomhall and Jacqueline Van Ghent, 'In the Name of the Father: Conceptualising Pater Familias in the Letters of William the Silent's Children', *Renaissance Quarterly*, 62 (2009), 1130–66; Alison Cathcart, *Kinship and Clientage: Highland Clanship 1451–1609* (Leiden, 2006); Joel Harrington, *The Unwanted Child: The Fate of Foundlings, Orphans and Juvenile Criminals in Early Modern Germany* (Chicago, 2009), 278–86; Stephanie Tarbin, 'Caring for Poor and Fatherless Children in London, c. 1350–1550', *Journal of the History of Childhood and Youth*, 3 (2010), 391–410.

[17] Kate Gibson, 'Experiences of Illegitimacy in England, 1660–1834' (Ph.D. thesis, University of Sheffield, 2018); Jana Byars, 'From Illegitimate Son to Legal Citizen: Noble Bastards in Early Modern Venice', *Sixteenth-Century Journal*, 42 (2011), 643–63.

[18] Kathryn A. Sloan, *Women's Roles in Latin America and the Caribbean* (Santa Barbara, 2011), 8; Sasha Turner, *Contested Bodies: Pregnancy, Childrearing and Slavery in Jamaica* (Philadelphia, 2017); Elizabeth Anne Kuznesof, 'Slavery and Childhood in Brazil, 1550–1888', in *Raising an Empire: Children in Early Modern Iberia and Colonial Latin America*, ed. Ondina E. González and Bianca Premo (Albuquerque, 2007), 194; Susan Staves, 'Resentment or Resignation? Dividing the Spoils among Daughters and Younger Sons', in *Early Modern Conceptions of Property*, ed. John Brewer and Susan Staves (1995), 194–218.

abuse.[19] Yet, if we recognise that how children were cared *for* is shaped by their circumstances, how that relates to caring *about* has been less interrogated. That love itself might take different forms for particular categories of children has received little attention from historians, particularly given an earlier historiography that sought to calculate the economic value of parental investments in children in the early modern period.[20]

This is not to say there is not a historiography of love and the illegitimate child. Indeed, love overshadows the three key historiographies that surround such children in this period. The first is that of the infanticidal mother – the woman driven by shame, and by a desire to protect her reputation, to kill.[21] If this mother loved her child, it was perhaps a love stifled by the humiliation and risk associated with the loss of sexual reputation. As Garthine Walker suggests, it might nonetheless be a love hinted at in the care offered to the deceased child, its burial in places of personal or cultural significance, in statements of contrition or confession after arrest.[22] Care and love of the infanticide victim might also be marked by early modern communities, in their enactment of legislation designed to protect such children; in their horror at the crime; and in the care they took when uncovering, moving and reinterring the dead.[23]

A similar mother is presented in the historiography of child abandonment, where women driven by a desire to protect reputations, or by economic necessity in a context where single motherhood was stigmatised or difficult to manage, left their child to the kindness of strangers or to institutions. These histories measure the practical and emotional care offered by foster parents, foundling hospitals, residential care, and religious and state organisations.[24] They have found continued expressions of caring

[19] Barbara Harris, 'Property, Power and Personal Relations: Elite Mothers and Sons in Yorkist and Early Tudor England', *Signs*, 15 (1990), 606–32; Caroline Castiglione, *Accounting for Affection: Mothering and Politics in Early Modern Rome* (Basingstoke, 2015); Katie Barclay, 'Narrative, Law and Emotion: Husband Killers in Early Nineteenth-Century Ireland', *Journal of Legal History*, 38 (2017), 203–27.

[20] Stone, *The Family, Sex and Marriage*.

[21] Margaret Brannan Lewis, *Infanticide and Illegitimacy in Early Modern Germany* (2016); Anne-Marie Kilday, *A History of Infanticide in Britain, c. 1600 to the Present* (Basingstoke, 2013).

[22] Garthine Walker, 'Child-Killing and Emotion in Early Modern England and Wales', in *Death, Emotion and Childhood in Premodern Europe*, ed. Katie Barclay, Kim Reynolds with Ciara Rawnsley (Houndmills, 2016), 151–72.

[23] Katie Barclay with Kim Reynolds, 'Small Graves: Histories of Death, Childhood and Emotion', in *Death, Emotion and Childhood*, ed. Barclay *et al.*, 1–24.

[24] Alysa Levene, *The Childhood of the Poor: Welfare in Eighteenth-Century London* (Basingstoke, 2012); Alysa Levene, *Childcare, Health and Mortality at the London Foundling Hospital, 1741–1800* (Manchester, 2007); Sally Holloway, 'Materialising Maternal Emotions: Birth, Celebration and Renunciation in England c. 1688–1830', in *Feeling Things: Objects and Emotions through History*, ed. Stephanie Downes, Sally Holloway and Sarah Randles (Oxford, 2018), 154–74; Susan Broomhall, 'Beholding Suffering and Providing Care: Emotional Performances

from mothers who sought to monitor their children's well-being from a distance, or to reclaim children to their care when circumstances permitted. As a strategy of caring used by many pauper families, legitimate or otherwise, such histories also highlight the ways that care for poor children could be fragmented across families and institutions, wet-nurses, different types of kin, employers and more.[25] This is a history that stresses that many, probably most, illegitimate children were not abandoned or murdered, but incorporated into families if not necessarily in the same way as those born within wedlock. However, the histories of those children and their experiences of love and care are much harder to find.

A final historiography of illegitimate children focuses less on their practical care than on their legal status. This scholarship highlights how the stigma of illegitimacy was enshrined in law, with such children having limited rights to parental property and care, to inheritance, and even to bequeath their own property forward.[26] At particular times, bastardy could also restrict the rights and obligations of an individual within society, limiting their occupational and political choices. If love arises in such history, it is usually assumed that this legal framing reduced the capacity of society to offer love towards the illegitimate child. Yet, it sits alongside those above that are suggestive that care and affection may have multiple forms. A key question for this article is how this legal status – the locating of illegitimate children as second-class citizens, as stigmas that drove some women to murder – informs their care, their experience of love.

To answer this, this article uses a combination of justiciary and sheriff court records, where illegitimate children arise incidentally in criminal cases and in the civil suits fought to determine their legitimacy or right to alimony, as well as several sets of letters written by the mothers and other relatives of illegitimate children, typically to their fathers.[27] Most of the latter capture cross-class relationships, but some like George

---

on the Death of Poor Children in Sixteenth-Century French Institutions', in *Death, Emotion and Childhood*, ed. Barclay *et al.*, 65–86; Lola Valverde, 'Illegitimacy and the Abandonment of Children in the Basque Country, 1550–1800', in *Poor Women and Children in the European Past*, ed. John Henderson and Richard Wall (1994), 52–3.

[25] Harrington, *The Unwanted Child*; Philippa Maddern, 'Between Households: Children in Blended and Transitional Households in Late-Medieval England'. *Journal of the History of Childhood and Youth*, 3 (2010), 65–86; Valerie Fildes, *Wet-Nursing: A History from Antiquity to the Present* (Oxford, 1988).

[26] Alysa Levene, 'The Mortality Penalty of Illegitimate Children: Foundlings and Poor Children in Eighteenth-Century London', in *Illegitimacy in Britain, 1700–1920*, ed. Alysa Levene, Timothy Nutt and Samantha Williams (Basingstoke, 2005), 34–49; Matthew Gerber, *Bastards: Politics, Family, and the Law in Early Modern France* (Oxford, 2012); Susan Marshall, 'Illegitimacy in Medieval Scotland, 1165–1500' (Ph.D. thesis, University of Aberdeen, 2013).

[27] These records are predominantly found in the NRS, although some sheriff and Kirk session records are held in local archives. Their abbreviations are Justiciary Court – JC;

Innes and Elizabeth Graham, or Dorothy Salisbury and Alexander Inglis, reflect connections between servants of similar status (at least when the relationship began).[28] The article begins by situating the Scottish illegitimate child within its broader affective context, before moving to explore their experience of care. It argues that love was a social product, framed and shaped by and through the social, economic and legal networks in which the child was positioned. Whilst the legitimate child, both in law and social practice, might have expected its care to be primarily through the nuclear family, the bastard child belonged, as the law suggested, to the community, requiring its mothering to be dispersed.

I The affective contexts of the illegitimate child

The experience of the illegitimate child in Scotland was shaped by the broader cultural, social, economic and legal context into which it was born. Illegitimacy was never rare in Scotland; between the 1660s and 1760s, 3 to 5 per cent of all births happened outwith marriage.[29] As elsewhere in Europe, the latter part of the century saw a rapid increase in the illegitimacy rate to around 10 per cent across the nineteenth century.[30] These figures hid remarkable regional diversity however, with the north-east and south-west of Scotland known for very high illegitimacy rates, perhaps reflecting the prominence of tenant farmers – and their large numbers of unmarried servants who generally predominate amongst the parents of illegitimate children – in these areas. In contrast, other locations had very few illegitimate births. By the eighteenth century in Scotland, there were few legal impediments placed upon an illegitimate person. Early Church law, following Roman tradition, had separated illegitimate children into categories by the circumstances of their birth: the child of two unwed parents was less problematic than those born in incest or adultery. These categories informed both a person's

Sheriff Court – SC; Kirk Sessions – CH2. The letters have mainly survived as part of collections associated with elite families, again many in the NRS.

[28] For more on Dorothy Salisbury and Alexander Inglis, see Katie Barclay, 'Gossip, Intimacy and the Early Modern Scottish Household', in *Fama and Her Sisters: Gossip in Early Modern Europe*, ed. Claire Walker and Heather Kerr (Turnhout, 2015), 187–207. The Innes family have several sets of illegitimate children associated with them: see Katie Barclay, 'Marginal Households and their Emotions: The "Kept Mistress" in Enlightenment Edinburgh', in *Spaces for Feeling: Emotions and Sociabilities in Britain, 1650–1850*, ed. Sue Broomhall (2015), 95–111; Katie Barclay, 'Illicit Intimacies: The Many Families of Gilbert Innes of Stow (1751–1832)', *Gender & History*, 27 (2015), 576–90.

[29] Rosalind Mitchison and Leah Leneman, *Girls in Trouble: Sexuality and Social Control in Rural Scotland* (Edinburgh, 1998), 74–8; Andrew Blaikie, *Illegitimacy, Sex and Society: North-East Scotland, 1750–1900* (Oxford, 1993).

[30] Blaikie, *Illegitimacy, Sex and Society*; Peter Laslett, 'Introduction', in *Bastardy and its Comparative History*, ed. Peter Laslett, Karla Oosterveen and R. M. Smith (1980), 1–68.

rights – such as their capacity to enter the Church – and their social standing; illegitimacy was a form of moral corruption and the degree of their parent's immorality shaped the character of the child in the cultural imagination.[31] If Church and secular courts had largely lost these distinctions by the eighteenth century, they were subtly retained by the Kirk (the Church of Scotland), which issued punishments of differing levels of severity to the parents of such children, largely following a similar moral framework.[32]

The idea of the illegitimate child as a site of moral corruption also continued in Scottish popular culture, which drew heavily on texts from wider Britain, Europe and increasingly the Americas. Older tales that located the illegitimate son – illegitimate women were relatively rare in early modern popular culture – as evil, corrupt or tainted in character continued to circulate, but increasingly competed with newer texts where a person's – both male and female – circumstance of birth was less significant to their character.[33] Rather their dislocation from traditional familial structures offered them an 'independence' that offered narrative opportunities for writers.[34] The illegitimate child was one that discomforted traditional structures of patriarchal authority, challenged definitions of family, and had the capacity for social mobility or transformation. Native literary productions in Scotland were equally part of this conversation, from the handsome illegitimate sons that appear to trouble marriages in ballads like *Child Maurice*, and its spin-off play *The Douglas Tragedy*, to Lucy Sindall in Henry Mackenzie's *Man of the World* (1773) and the deceased infant of Effie Dean in Walter Scott's *Heart of Midlothian* (1819).[35]

---

[31] Marshall, 'Illegitimacy in Medieval Scotland'; Gerber, *Bastards*.

[32] *Acts of the General Assembly of the Church of Scotland, 1638–1842* (Edinburgh, 1843).

[33] Michael Neill, '"In Everything Illegitimate": Imagining the Bastard in Renaissance Drama', *The Yearbook of English Studies*, 23 (1993), 270–92.

[34] Katie Pritchard, 'Legitimacy, Illegitimacy and Sovereignty in Shakespeare's British Plays' (Ph.D. thesis, University of Manchester, 2011); Gibson, 'Experiences of Illegitimacy in England'; Katie Barclay, 'Illegitimacy', in *Early Modern Childhood: An Introduction*, ed. Anne French (2020), 217–34; Lisa Zunshine, *Bastards and Foundlings: Illegitimacy in Eighteenth-Century England* (Columbus, OH, 2005). For a discussion of 'independence' Matthew McCormack, *The Independent Man: Citizenship and Gender Politics in Georgian England* (Manchester, 2012); and in relation to illegitimate children: Katie Barclay, 'Family, Mobility and Emotion in Eighteenth-Century Scotland', in *Keeping Family in an Age of Long Distance Trade, Discovery and Settlement, 1450–1850*, ed. Heather Dalton (Amsterdam, forthcoming).

[35] Deborah Symonds, *Weep Not for Me: Women, Ballads and Infanticide in Early Modern Scotland* (University Park, PA, 1997); Svetla Baloutzova, 'When a Lass Goes "So Round", with Her "Tua Sides High": Oral Culture and Women's Views on Illegitimacy', in *Women in Eighteenth-Century Scotland: Intimate, Intellectual and Public Lives*, ed. Katie Barclay and Deborah Simonton (Farnham, 2013), 55–74.

As important, however, was a body of work that located the illegitimate child as victim of the circumstances of its birth. Children, especially
infants, who were murdered by desperate mothers returned to haunt
these unfortunate women, or left marks of their existence behind,
calling to the world for justice. These children were clearly marked as
innocents through their deaths as young children or when older due to
their handsome appearances, which signified good character.[36] It was
a representation that coalesced with the Scottish legal protections for
illegitimate children in the 1690 'Act Anent Murthering of Children',
which required women to declare their illegitimate pregnancies or risk
being prosecuted for murder if the child died. Within the law and its
articulation in indictments, illegitimate children were deemed as
worthy of life and protection from the community, their deaths 'cruell
and barbarous'.[37]

This is not to suggest that illegitimate children were uniformly welcomed. The shame of undergoing public discipline in the Kirk clearly
shaped responses to out-of-wedlock pregnancy, marked in attempts to
avoid the sessions or in reluctant fathers denying paternity.[38] The 480
cases of infanticide that came before the courts in Scotland between
1700 and 1820 are evidence of the reputational and practical challenges
that illegitimate births brought to parents, families and communities –
perhaps especially for mothers, who often found themselves unemployed
as a result.[39] Given that this number was considerably higher than in
England and even Ireland (where infanticide rates would be exception-
ally high in the following century), as well as much of Europe, it is suggestive that the stigma of illegitimacy remained more significant in
Scotland than elsewhere.[40] Yet, stigma that attached to parents only
complexly informed the treatment of illegitimate children, particularly
once parents and family had made a commitment to raise them.

Illegitimate children were entitled to provision from their parents.
Indeed, Scots law was generous in this regard. Stair's *Institutions of the
Laws of Scotland* (1681), the key text that consolidated Scots law at the
end of the seventeenth century, argued that amongst the 'natural obligations' of mankind, were the natural affection, education and provision
owed by parents to children. He defined provision as including
aliment and entertainment in meat, clothes, medicine and burial, obligations due before and after the parent's death (thus enabling provision to

---

[36] Symonds, *Weep Not for Me*.
[37] Barclay with Reynolds, 'Small Graves'.
[38] Blaikie, *Illegitimacy, Sex and Society*.
[39] Kilday, *A History of Infanticide*, 30.
[40] *Ibid.*, 27–31; see also Elaine Farrell, '*A most diabolical deed*': *Infanticide and Irish Society, 1850–
1900* (Manchester, 2013).

be drawn from the parental estate). Drawing heavily on natural law theory, he included illegitimate children under this umbrella, noting that nature did not distinguish between children in regard to parental obligations. As a result of this, illegitimate children were considered to be in the power of their parents throughout their minority, their labour available to the common good of the family.[41]

The key difference between natural and legitimate children was that the former were not entitled to inherit property from their fathers. This was phrased in multiple legal texts as 'having no father in law', yet as the former provisions suggested, this was quite particular to inheritance. Illegitimate children could be left property by parents and could succeed to their mother's property if legitimate heirs failed, but could only receive paternal property if explicitly provided for. As they were not formally part of their paternal family, they also suffered restrictions on their own property ownership. Unless they married and had legitimate offspring (or they were legitimated), their property returned to the crown on their decease. This was partly because Scottish succession law followed the paternal line, before it returned to the maternal (so a child with no father had no paternal kin to inherit).[42] Why a bastard could not leave his property by testament is unclear, but it may reflect that even legitimate individuals had restricted testamentary rights.

As I have argued elsewhere, this legal framework for family relationships and inheritance was underpinned by the concept of natural affection, thought to be an instinctual emotion that family members had towards their kin, particularly children, designed to ensure the survival of the lineage.[43] Natural affection was said to motivate the fulfilment of parental duties towards their offspring, but also underpinned the obligations of obedience and care from children to parents, and the (positively construed) desire to favour and support siblings over wider mankind. It was associated with charity, and thus can be understood as unselfish or outward-looking sentiment, tied to practical action.[44] It could also be connected to jealousy – 'suspicion arising from love' – such as a husband may have towards his wife, a jealousy that arose from his property in her and particularly her chastity.[45] As this suggests,

[41] James Dalrymple, Viscount of Stair, *The Institutions of the Law of Scotland* (2 vols., Edinburgh, 1693), I, 37–41; for an extended discussion see Barclay, 'Natural Affection, Children'.

[42] Dalrymple, *The Institutions*, I, 424–8; Andrew MacDowall, Lord Bankton, *An Institute of the Laws of Scotland in Civil Rights* (2 vols., Edinburgh, 1751), I, 280.

[43] Barclay, 'Natural Affection, Children'; Barclay, 'Natural Affection, the Patriarchal Family'.

[44] Dalrymple, *The Institutions*, I, 431.

[45] *Ibid.*, I, 24; Samuel Johnson, *A Dictionary of the English Language …* (Dublin, 1768), s.v. jealousy.

natural affection was suggestive of an emotion that extended the self through family members, providing a vested interest in their lives, behaviours and bodies (something that can be directly seen in the right to a child's labour that arose from fulfilling parental duties). If natural affection can be understood as a form of parental love, which I would suggest it is for eighteenth-century Scots as other Europeans, then it was an emotion that both promoted and arose from the fulfilment of practical duties of care; a love that was outward-looking and benevolent in its concern for another.[46] Like other types of love, it also reinforced patriarchal power and both shaped and was shaped by the economic basis of the early modern household.[47]

This was particularly critical for illegitimate children. If their right to affection, education and provisioning arose 'naturally', their property rights were curtailed by their status. The law of the succession was explicitly understood as the imagined 'will of the defunct', the expected emotional hierarchies of the ordinary citizen when distributing property. It prioritised children, then siblings, then parents, before moving to wider kin, as natural law suggested this is who they would 'naturally' preference.[48] In refusing bastards this right, so too did the law suggest that their affective connections to their paternal family were reduced or uncertain. This was particularly critical for an imagining of love or affection where economic provisioning – money – was an evidence of love in action. The illegitimate child was prohibited from expressing her or his love through a distribution of property, marking him or her as distinct from the family group. Natural affection was therefore relative; it had different limits for different types of children. It was a logic apparent not just in theory, but applied during legitimacy suits, where the level of provisioning and standard of education offered to a child became central evidences of a child's status.[49] The love and care offered to an illegitimate child was thus shaped by a larger framework that recognised them as entitled to both physical care and affection and which may have viewed them as relative innocents worthy of

[46] Marshall, '"Dutiful Love and Natural Affection"'; it can be fruitfully compared here to the parent–child reciprocity and filial piety found in England: Begiato, *Parenting*; Illana Krausman Ben-Amos, 'Reciprocal Bonding: Parents and Their Offspring in Early Modern England', *Journal of Family History*, 25 (2000), 291–312.

[47] Katie Barclay, 'The Emotions of Household Economics', in *The Routledge Companion to Emotions in Europe: 1100–1700*, ed. Susan Broomhall and Andrew Lynch (2019), 185–99; Barclay, *Love, Intimacy and Power*.

[48] Siblings are prioritised before parents not because sibling love was greater than a child's love for a parent, but because it was thought the siblings' shared parents would prefer this distribution to receiving the property. This is likely an example of trying to make old law fit new natural law theory.

[49] Barclay, 'Natural Affection, Children'.

family protection, but where they continued to trouble the family through their independent legal status. It was a context that shaped how they were cared for in practice.

II Providing love for the illegitimate child

The close association between caring *for* and caring *about* in Scots law ensured that negotiations about how, when and where children should be cared for inflected both the understanding and experience of love during the period. Given Stair's contention that parents owed an obligation of natural affection, education and provision to their children, there was little legal debate during the eighteenth century around whether illegitimate children should receive support. Rather the alimony suits that provide a key evidence of social practices of caring highlight that what was under contest was paternity, where responsibility for physical care lay (with the mother or father) and, if money was owed, how much. Paternity cases were, in some senses, relatively straightforward; men denied fatherhood and the court either took them on oath or heard evidence to prove the mother's claims. If filiation was proved, fathers became responsible for their part of child support. In law, both parents owed their children a duty of care, including financial provisioning. Elite mothers could therefore find themselves obligated to support minor children, and many suits refer to mothers being liable for half of their children's upkeep.[50] In practice, the ordinary servant women who produced the majority of alimony suits were generally not expected to provide financial support to their children, a claim one lawyer based on a Court of Session (high court) decision but which was certainly commonly accepted by courts.[51] Mothers who gave their children to their fathers were therefore not liable for costs. Rather it was generally expected that men would pay alimony to mothers to nurse and in many cases support them in subsequent years.

Alimony suits are not especially common, and would have been relatively expensive (although legal aid was available to the very poor), suggestive that most couples came to an agreement out of court. From 1778, this was encouraged by a Court of Session decision that created for the children of labourers a standard baseline of alimony of £3 sterling per annum paid quarterly (a number that followed common practice in

---

[50] Several cases affirm this decision, e.g. Finnie against Oliphant (1631); Children of the Earl of Buchan against Lady Buchan (1666); Simon Ramsay against Rigg (1687); Hay against his grandfather and mother (1729); The younger children of Bissett of Leffendrum against their brother (1748). See William Morrison, *The Decisions of the Court of Session ...* (Edinburgh, 1811), vol. 2.

[51] The lawyer dates this decision to the 1 March 1755, but I cannot identify such a case, Aberdeen Sheriff Court, Ann Hay against William Allardyce (1761), NRS, SC1/11/30.

earlier decades).[52] In practice, the amount rose slightly over the next few decades before declining again in the early nineteenth century, reflecting inflation and shifts in the economy – 'the price of almost every necessary of life is increased to an enormous rate', one defendant argued in 1800.[53] Most women coming to court only requested the 'going rate'.[54]

Despite this, especially at times of economic downturn, fathers were willing to dispute the affordability of payments. Based on the (alleged) earnings of these men, alimony was often around 50 per cent of their cash income – typically around £4 out of £8 sterling, a number that would align with wage estimates for the poorest workers.[55] As most servants received food, board and some clothing as part of their wage, this request was not considered unreasonable during the period. However, it could cause challenges for men who had more than one child to support, as well as limiting their opportunities for marriage and an independent household.[56] Many resisted it on the basis that it was too high a claim on their small income. Within a context where economic provisioning was so closely associated with parental love, these were disputes that not only angered mothers but were suggestive of a lack of care, both practical and affective, something that men tried to counter through the frame of affordability.

Mothers replied that the costs of a child did not reduce because the father was poor. Clothing seems to have been a particular issue here, with at least one mother dismissing a defence from the father that he had given some clothing with the remark that his contribution had been negligible, and she was happy to take payment in clothes, the implication being the value would exceed the cash.[57] In addition to alimony, fathers were expected to pay for lying-in costs and any nurse. Some agreements provided women with a higher alimony rate for the first year of birth. This seems to reflect a broad agreement that nursing was a form of labour that could be recompensed, and which certainly restricted nursing mothers from gaining further employment. In 1763, Clementina Durrand specifically observed in her petition that she should receive her lying-in costs because 'the mother is above the rank

[52] Scott against Oliver (1778): see William Morrison, *The Decisions of the Court of Session …* (Edinburgh, 1811), vol. 5.

[53] Dumfries Sheriff Court Goodfellow against Elliot (1800), NRS, SC15/10/233.

[54] For example, NRS SC15/10/233; Dumfries Sheriff Court Burnet v Johnston (1801), NRS, SC15/10/233.

[55] A. J. S. Gibson and T. C. Smout, *Prices, Food and Wages in Scotland, 1550–1780* (Cambridge, 1995).

[56] Aberdeen Sheriff Court Wallace against Wilson (1811), NRS, SC1/11/318.

[57] Murray against Galation (1829), NRS, Aberdeen Sheriff Court, SC1/11/476; see also Crosbie against Raddick (1801), NRS, Dumfries Sheriff Court, SC15/10/233; Moffat against Stephens (1808), NRS, Edinburgh, SC39/17/539.

of common servants and nursed the child her self and was detained from doing or gaining any thing to herself during all the eighteen months and for a full month took care of & sat up with the child when bad of a fever'.[58] Whilst no mothers made a direct claim of payment for nursing, a rebuttal in suits where fathers desired to take custody was that they should instead pay the nursing fee to the mother, a sum that would generally be larger than alimony.[59] As this suggests, a mother's contribution to the care of the child was also imagined in economic terms, if paid in bodily labour and practical care, rather than money. Love and provisioning intertwined for women, as it did for men.

Mothers were considered the appropriate custodians of illegitimate children by the court. Fathers were typically expected to pay alimony until the child was at least seven or could support itself. Many mothers requested orders that stretched to twelve or fourteen years of age. The cases that reached the higher courts generally ordered alimony until the later age, believing that it was unrealistic to expect children to maintain themselves before that date.[60] Lower courts were more conservative, limiting provision to age seven, nine or ten.[61] Some fathers requested custody of their illegitimate children, but generally were refused. In Aberdeen in the 1760s, the erroneous idea that if a father asked for custody and was declined he was no longer liable for alimony appears to have circulated in the community. The responses of mothers suggest a certain dry humour as they reply by asking men to demonstrate their capacity to provide either a nurse or place for a child to stay.[62] Following common practice for both legitimate and illegitimate children, it was generally agreed children should be raised by mothers until aged seven. But even for older children, mothers were often viewed as the most appropriate carer. This was affirmed by the Court of Session in 1765, a case that highlighted the ambiguity of a father's rights over the person of his illegitimate child. It was a decision that the court made on the grounds of affection: 'his little connection with the child during its infancy, it is not to be expected he will be very tenderly attached to

[58] Durrand against Fry (1763), NRS, Aberdeen Sheriff Court, SC1/11/30.

[59] Elite wet-nurses were typically being paid around £10 sterling per annum in the second half of the eighteenth century. See Barclay, 'Gossip, Intimacy'. One example of a nurse to an ordinary family still saw a claim around £1 per quarter plus food and clothing, a number higher than alimony. Farras against Elmslie and Gray (1752), NRS, SC1/11/5.

[60] Graham against Kay (1740); Short against Donald (1765). See William Morrison, *The Decisions of the Court of Session*, vol. 2.

[61] For example: Hay against Allardyce (1761), NRS, Aberdeen Sheriff Court, SC1/11/30; Gordon against Cruickshank (1802), NRS, Aberdeen Sheriff Court, SC1/11/252; Burnet against Johnston (1801), NRS, Dumfries Sheriff Court, SC15/10/233.

[62] See Hay against Allardyce (1761), NRS, Aberdeen Sheriff Court, SC1/11/30; Young against Anachie (1761), NRS, Aberdeen Sheriff Court, SC1/11/30; but see also Smith & Williamson against Fordyce (1811), NRS, Aberdeen Sheriff Court, SC1/11/318.

it. As to the mother there is no uncertainty. The connection with her is strongest.'[63] There was no reason to think this would change at age seven, observed the mother's counsel.

Despite such rulings, mothers were at lengths to display their competent care when fathers contested custody, framing their mothering in legal terms. As well as nursing, clothing and managing health and well-being (such as through purchasing medicines), mothers of older children often noted their commitment to educating children. Charlotte Keith strenuously denied in 1821 that 'the boy is at present quite neglected in his education, cloathing and maintenance', arguing he was as well cared for 'as any one in his station can be'.[64] As this suggests, the legal framework of care expected of parents played a significant role in shaping narratives, and presumably practices, of care of children by parents, and so how parental love was articulated within this community. It was a framework that at times encompassed and downplayed caring practices that were considerably more complex.

If mothers brought suits for alimony from their children's father, they often did so as the legal parent who had claim to support. They were not always the primary carer, but rather contributed to the upkeep of the child through their own earnings. Many women returned to work after the birth of their child, leaving her or him in the care of others. Margaret Halcrow was awarded the exceptional sum of £12 yearly to pay the nurse to care for her child with William Halcrow in 1781; William Elliot provided Isobel Goodfellow with 'a good and sufficient nurse' in 1801, but (having initially agreed to this arrangement) Goodfellow refused to hand the child over after its birth.[65] Margaret Young lived with her mother Margaret Baird whilst her child was young; the grandmother cared for the child whilst Young worked and was active in pursuing alimony payments from William Anachie.[66] Mary Crosbie left her first child with her mother when she returned to service, only to become pregnant a second time to John Raddick in 1801. Ann Hay refused to ask her father for financial support, in lieu of alimony, he having been generous in the past.[67] Fathers too claimed support of kin. Several men wished to place their children with their mothers, whilst Helen Smith's daughter resided for a time with her paternal grandfather, where she was 'in such a miserable state both with

[63] Short against Donald (1765), William Morrison, *The Decisions of the Court of Session*, vol. 2.
[64] Keith against Sellar (1821), NRS, Aberdeen Sheriff Court, SC1/11/406.
[65] Halcrow denied paternity as the child was born eight days early, Halcrow against Halcrow (1781), Shetland Museum and Archives (hereafter SMA), Shetland Sheriff Court, SC12/6/1781/11; Goodfellow against Elliot (1800), NRS, Dumfries Sheriff Court, SC15/10/233.
[66] Young against Anachie (1761), NRS, Aberdeen Sheriff Court, SC1/11/30.
[67] Crosbie against Raddick (1801), NRS, Dumfries Sheriff Court, SC15/10/233.

respect to cloathing and also to its cleanliness that it became absolutely necessary for the pursuer herself to look after her'.[68]

As this suggests, children moved between parental homes, and a number of alimony disputes appear to have arisen because the division of care had not been straightforward. Helen Smith, above, had nursed her own child, but lived and took meat in the paternal grandfather's home. Some time later, she moved with her daughter to lodgings with John Bettie, but as the father, James Fordyce, would not pay alimony, she had to return to work. She therefore gave custody to Fordyce, who lived with his parents. The latter 'tired of it' and the child was sent to lodge with Bettie, but again financial support was not forthcoming. Bettie returned the child to the grandparents, who – alleged Smith – treated her poorly. Smith, having married, rescued her and brought her to live with her husband who was 'very humanely disposed towards the child'. Fordyce disputed that the child was poorly treated, and wished to have her returned to his custody. By the time of the lawsuit, the child was four.

A similar case was presented by Jean Wallace in the same year. Jean lived with her aunt and uncle in the house next door to James Wilson, the father of her daughter Ann.[69] The properties shared a common yard. The child regularly spent time in her father's house, on the holding he held with his brother. Wilson claimed that after many disputes about alimony payments (between the couple and between her uncle and Wilson) Wallace had given Ann into his custody. The uncle had stolen her back several days later. Wallace claimed this was not the case, but rather on one occasion the child had been late at the house and was asleep. Rather than wake her to return home, Wallace agreed to collect Ann the next day, which she did. Whichever version was true, the case highlighted the often fluid nature of custody arrangements, situated across homes and caregivers, a picture suggested also in the life of Elizabeth Graham and many other accounts of illegitimate and legitimate children during the period where nurses and grandparents feature prominently.[70] As acts of practical care given by a range of caregivers, the love received by these children was thus distributed across a wider range of 'parents', which may have acted to counterbalance absences of affection or physical care in other parts of their lives.

Family was not the only group that took an interest in caring for the illegitimate child. That the court not only heard alimony cases, but provided legal counsel for the poor (in some cases taking suits to the high courts through appeal), is suggestive of a legal system that recognised

---

[68] Smith & Williamson against Fordyce (1811), NRS, Aberdeen Sheriff Court, SC1/11/318.

[69] Wallace against Wilson (1811), NRS, Aberdeen Sheriff Court, SC1/11/318.

[70] Blaikie, *Illegitimacy, Sex and Society*; Begiato, *Parenting*.

its role in ensuring at least their well-being. Similarly, the Kirk supported alimony cases; in some instances, they pursued them on their own behalf when children fell on the coffers of the parish. Reverend McNeveson, on behalf of the Session of Penpont, sued Thomas Kirkpatrick in 1801 for refusing to take custody of his child.[71] His daughter Margaret had initially lived with her mother, but on the latter's death was given to Kirkpatrick. His wife treated her cruelly and Margaret moved in with Kirkpatrick's sister, her aunt. When the aunt left the country on marrying, the father refused to accept her home. Margaret became homeless, living on the streets of Penpont and begging. Several parishioners had given her charity, including clothing. But they all agreed she was filthy and starving, and refused to do further for her while her father was 'going about like a gentleman'. The Reverend emphasised that if she had been an orphan the villagers were willing to take responsibility. One difficulty that arose was that Margaret was eleven and, her father believed, able to earn her own meat. However, she was also disabled, unable to use a leg and an arm. The Reverend reported she was also the size of a seven-year-old; it was broadly agreed she was not capable of earning for herself. Kirkpatrick eventually took the child into his care, so proceedings ceased. A similar case of the community taking responsibility for an illegitimate child can be seen in the case of John Fee, who at age eight was either abandoned or ran away from his father who used him to beg on the street. He was eventually taken in by a travelling merchant and her husband, a chimney sweep, but not without some reluctance (they claimed at least).[72] When Fee's father tried to regain custody, the family all attested to affective connections that had developed between them, as the basis of their custody arrangement.

The picture that emerges from this evidence presents a complex model of love and care for illegitimate children, as a particularly precarious category of poor children.[73] The existence of the suits, as well as the many denials of paternity that appear in them, is suggestive of a refusal of care, usually by fathers; yet, this should not be overstated. If some men rejected their obligations entirely, many others wished to negotiate the terms – particularly financial – of their commitment. For some, this was in a context where they had intermittently held or desired custody. A cynical reading – often taken by their ex-partners – was that a desire for custody was simply a cost-cutting exercise. But both

---

[71] McNeveson against Thomas Kirkpatrick (1801), NRS, Dumfries Sheriff Court, SC15/10/233.

[72] Thomas Hastings and Ann Anderson for plagium, 1813, NRS, AD14/13/64; Katie Barclay, 'Family, Mobility'.

[73] Social parenting can be observed for other categories of poor children too: Doolittle, 'Fatherhood and Family Shame'; Begiato, *Parenting*; Harrington, *The Unwanted Child*.

men and women drew heavily on a legal rhetoric of natural affection, maintenance and education that was suggestive that they understood the practical and affective nature of the obligation of parenting. Everyone agreed that these children deserved a baseline of care, a baseline that the court conveniently put a legal financial minimum upon.

Women may have claimed for alimony as mothers, but they too did not always offer care directly. Many returned to service, leaving children with nurses or grandparents. If children died under these arrangements, it was not necessarily due to a lack of parental interest. After returning to service, Dorothy Salisbury regularly reminded the father of her child to visit the nurse where it was placed and to provide her accounts of its well-being.[74] And this concern mattered to the community. Fathers were quick to point to mothers who had not shown any interest when away from their children. Despite this, some children did fall out of care, becoming homeless or suffering abuse. That so many were part of poor families, were shuffled between carers, and often ended up on the outskirts of the new conjugal unit of their parents, perhaps made this more liable to happen. Yet, at least for those who appear in the historical record, when it happened the community, especially the parish, stepped in to provide care. The question remains as to how many illegitimate children went unnoticed by the authorities when their family arrangements failed. Within this context, love was dispersed across the different dimensions of care – across caregivers, types of care, levels of affection and so forth – produced through their combination and so with differential impacts on individuals.

The significance of money to understanding care should not be ignored. This is a product of the court record, which was trying to place a financial value on care, and which can also be seen in legitimacy suits where the value of care parents provided marked their social status. But it also reflected that children cost money, particularly when very young, and that some people thought pursuing an income to enable them to survive was worth doing. Alimony generally ceased for the poor when children became economically active. This could be interpreted as suggesting that such children could care for themselves, but it was underpinned by a logic that care was less burdensome to provide for older children and so caring for them more desirable. Such articulations of care tightly bound it to household economies, and through them to hierarchies built on land and wealth. Poor illegitimate children could be offered 'less' care, in a literal economic sense, because they were deemed to be worth less. If the care offered by parents and grandparents was more generous, more giving of time,

[74] Barclay, 'Gossip, Intimacy'.

concern, anxiety and love than money allowed, if poor families too sought to fill their natural obligations as parents, nevertheless this was a care inflected by the social value placed on these children. Material conditions informed not just how children were cared for, but the extent to which they were cared about.

III Conclusion

What then of parental love? For eighteenth-century Scots, the close association between natural affection and the practical fulfilment of duty – in the case of parents through providing maintenance and education – tied practices of caring into a wider affective regime of love. Yet, if love arose from and motivated care, natural affection was a distinct obligation of its own. That this was regarded as 'natural' might suggest that it was an emotion that parents expected to feel, and so most accordingly did. But as Griffin argues and John Fee and Margaret Kirkpatrick's refusals to return to their parents suggest, not all children felt loved by their biological parents or wider kin. This was an experience likely exacerbated by their social positioning, where both the law and popular culture situated such children as somewhat outside or independent of the structures of family. Yet, it would be incorrect to say these children experienced no love or care, and it is particularly problematic to deny the intimate bonds produced even within families which were abusive or cruel. Rather it is perhaps more useful to reflect on parental love as an emotion that involved both affection and various practices of care, where its different dimensions contributed in degrees to its whole.

The economics of poverty thus became significant in offering a framework for how and whether care should and could be offered, with implications for the experience of love. As a multi-dimensional experience, love came to refract broader social and economic beliefs and hierarchies, disadvantaging illegitimate children who had little social status. Some families may have compensated through their own emotional or economic generosity; others may not. Thus, how illegitimate children experienced love varied by situation, by wealth, by the commitment of others to love and care for them, and by the social discourses that taught them how to interpret such practices. Theirs was also a love that could be dispersed across caregivers, an experience not distinct to them, but which was perhaps more common given the circumstances of their birth and more significant due to their dislocation from traditional family structures. Within such a context, a feeling of parental love – a thing that much scholarship has interpreted as present or absent – only plays one part in the experience of love, and may be less significant than the caring practices that may or may not accompany it. Loving the illegitimate child was an ongoing social practice.

Transactions of the RHS 29 (2019), pp. 127–151 © Royal Historical Society 2019
doi:10.1017/S0080440119000069

PROPORTIONATE MAIMING: THE ORIGINS OF THOMAS JEFFERSON'S PROVISIONS FOR FACIAL DISFIGUREMENT IN BILL 64*

By Emily Cock

READ 14 APRIL 2018
AT THE UNIVERSITY OF SOUTH WALES CARDIFF

ABSTRACT. In 1779, Thomas Jefferson proposed the use of nose-cutting to punish women convicted of specific offences, and the use of retaliation (*lex talionis*) for anyone who deliberately disfigured another person. These punishments were intended to replace the death penalty for these crimes, and as such formed part of Jefferson's attempt to rationalise the Virginian law code in line with eighteenth-century reform principles. Jefferson drew on British laws from the Anglo-Saxon period to the Coventry Act for his bill, but his proposals contrast strikingly with British movements away from corporal marking as punishment used against their own citizens. This article examines the origins and fates of equivalent crimes and punishments in the law codes Jefferson examined, and compares the legal and wider connotations of facial appearance and disfigurement that made these proposals coherent in Virginia when they had long ceased elsewhere. Tracing examples and discussion of these intersecting cases will greatly increase our understanding of Jefferson's proposals, and the relationships between facial difference, stigma and disability in eighteenth-century America.

CRYNODEB. Ym 1779, cynigiodd Thomas Jefferson y dylid cosbi menywod a oedd yn euog o droseddau penodol drwy dorri eu trwynau, a defnyddio dial (*lex talionis*) ar gyfer unrhyw un a anffurfiodd berson arall yn fwriadol. Bwriad y cosbau hyn oedd disodli'r gosb eithaf ar gyfer y troseddau hyn, ac felly roeddent yn rhan o ymgais Jefferson i resymoli cod cyfreithiol Virginia yn unol ag egwyddorion diwygio'r ddeunawfed ganrif. Cynlluniodd Jefferson fesur ar sail cyfreithiau Prydeinig o'r cyfnod Eingl-Sacsonaidd hyd at Ddeddf Coventry, ond roedd ei gynigion yn cyferbynnu'n drawiadol â symudiadau Prydain oddi wrth gosbi ei dinasyddion yn gorfforol. Mae'r erthygl hon yn edrych ar darddiad a thynged troseddau a chosbau cyfatebol y cyfreithiau roedd Jefferson yn eu harchwilio. Mae'n cymharu'r arwyddocâd cyfreithiol ac ehangach o ymddangosiad y wyneb ac anffurfio'r wyneb, a olygodd bod y cynigion hyn yn rhesymegol yn Virginia pan oeddent wedi dod i ben

*I would like to thank the audiences at Diverse Histories and the Cardiff Early Modern History seminar, and the reviewers at the *Transactions*, for their valuable feedback and suggestions on this article. I would also like to acknowledge a fellowship granted by the Robert H. Smith International Centre for Jefferson Studies at Monticello, and the warm support of their staff.

mewn mannau eraill ers amser maith. Byddwn yn cynyddu'n dealltwriaeth o gyni-gion Jefferson wrth olrhain enghreifftiau a thrafod yr achosion croestoriadol hyn, a'r berthynas rhwng anffurfio'r wyneb, stigma, ac anabledd yn America yn y ddeu-nawfed ganrif.

I Introduction

Announcing that Thomas Jefferson (1743–1826) proposed boring a hole in the noses of women convicted of certain moral offences, and introducing an eye-for-an-eye system of retaliation (*lex talionis*) for anyone who disfigured any other person, tends to provoke a strong reaction. Even among those who see paradox in the author of the Declaration of Independence promot-ing equality of humanity while owning slaves, the punishments put forward by Jefferson in his proposed overhaul of capital offences in Virginian crim-inal law seem strange and anachronistic for a man thought preoccupied with eighteenth-century tastes for civility and legal reform.

Jefferson's proposals were the result of impressive research on common and statutory laws, preserved in his ample manuscript annota-tions in modern and Old English, Latin and French. They never became law: thus, while frequently acknowledged as anomalous to Jefferson's broader humanitarian principles, they have received less attention from Jefferson scholars.[1] Markus Dirk Dubber judged the bill a 'remark-able failure' in comparison to Jefferson's other reforms, symptomatic of the Early Republic's widespread inability to grapple with the philosophy and extent of legitimate punishment, and the relationships between legal persons and authority.[2] Maurizio Valsania has recently offered fascinat-ing close scrutiny of Jefferson's corporeality and attitudes towards others' bodies, but omits discussion about these proposals for punitive mutila-tion.[3] Yet Kathryn Preyer argued that the bill, along with Jefferson's pro-posals for religious freedom, property reform and free education, formed 'part of a single broad and energetic program of reform', and further scholars have traced the revolutionary effects of many of his proposals.[4]

---

[1] See e.g. Merrill D. Peterson, *Thomas Jefferson and the New Nation: A Biography* (New York, 1970); John D. Bessler, *Cruel & Unusual: The American Death Penalty and the Founders' Eighth Amendment* (Boston, MA, 2012), 143–51.

[2] Markus D. Dubber, '"An Extraordinarily Beautiful Document": Jefferson's Bill for Proportioning Crimes and Punishments and the Challenge of Republican Punishment', in *Modern Histories of Crime and Punishment*, ed. Markus D. Dubber and Lindsay Farmer (Stanford, 2007), n.p. (Kindle edition).

[3] Maurizio Valsania, *Jefferson's Body: A Corporeal Biography* (Charlottesville, 2017).

[4] Kathryn Preyer, 'Two Enlightened Reformers of the Criminal Law: Thomas Jefferson in Virginia and Peter Leopold, Grand Duke of Tuscany', in *Blackstone in America: Selected Essays of Kathryn Preyer*, ed. Mary Sarah Bilder, Maeva Marcus and R. Kent Newmyer (Cambridge and New York, 2009), 252–76, at 271. Further Preyer, 'Crime, the Criminal Law and Reform in Post-Revolutionary Virginia', *Law and History Review*, 1 (1983), 53–85;

Jefferson also included the provisions in *Notes on the State of Virginia* (1787), thus giving them a much wider, international circulation. To understand Jefferson's proposals it is necessary to examine the fate of equivalent crimes and punishments in the law codes he examined, especially Britain's, and to compare the legal and wider connotations of facial disfigurement that made these proposals coherent in Virginia when they had long ceased elsewhere.

Prior to American independence, the common law of England was imported into the colonial courts, its decisions widely available in printed proceedings, and the Privy Council remained the highest appellate court. Jefferson's 'A Bill for Proportioning Crimes and Punishments in Cases Heretofore Capital' was Bill 64 of the 126 bills prepared by himself, Edmund Pendleton and George Wythe for the revision of Virginia's laws. The criminal laws were initially assigned to George Mason, but Jefferson soon took over after Mason's retirement.[5] The committee submitted the bills to the legislature in 1779. Bill 64 restricted execution to first degree murder and treason (more narrowly defined), and predominantly prescribed hard labour in the public works, and transplantation for slaves. The lack of a prison in the commonwealth precluded extensive incarceration.

The two provisions that deal with facial disfigurement, as written in Jefferson's fair manuscript copy, are as follows:

> Whosoever shall be guilty of rape, polygamy, or sodomy with man or woman shall be punished, if a man, by castration, if a woman, by cutting thro' the cartilage of her nose a hole of one half inch diameter at the least.

and

> Whosoever on purpose and of malice forethought shall maim another, or shall disfigure him, by cutting out or disabling the tongue, slitting or cutting off a nose, lip or ear, branding, or otherwise, shall be maimed or disfigured in like sort: or if that cannot be for want of the same part, then as nearly as may be in some other part of at least equal value and estimation in the opinion of a jury, and moreover shall forfeit one half of his lands and goods to the sufferer.[6]

Holly Brewer, 'Entailing Aristocracy in Colonial Virginia: "Ancient Feudal Restraints" and Revolutionary Reform', *The William and Mary Quarterly* 54 (1997), 307–46; Matthew Crow, *Thomas Jefferson, Legal History, and the Art of Recollection* (Cambridge, 2017).

[5] The original committee also included Thomas Lightfoot Lee, but he died soon after: Preyer, 'Crime', 56.

[6] '64. A Bill for Proportioning Crimes and Punishments in Cases Heretofore Capital, 18 June 1779', *Founders Online*, National Archives (USA), last modified 13 June 2018, http://founders.archives.gov/documents/Jefferson/01-02-02-0132-0004-0064 (original source: *The Papers of Thomas Jefferson*, vol. 2, *1777–18 June 1779*, ed. Julian P. Boyd (Princeton, 1950), 492–507); hereafter Bill 64 Online.

The collection was put to the Assembly in the sessions of 1785–6, but only fifty-six bills were enacted into law.[7] James Madison suggested to Jefferson (by then in Paris) that desire to retain horse stealing as a capital offence had contributed significantly to the defeat of the entire bill.[8] The offences subsequently remained capital.

II Eighteenth-century law: death and violence

The committee had agreed that the revisions to the criminal law should significantly reduce use of the death penalty, and Jefferson desired them 'strict and inflexible but proportioned to the crime'.[9] He was influenced by writers like Cesare Beccaria, William Eden, Jean-Jacques Rousseau and Montesquieu, who emphasised proportionality of punishment and restriction of the death penalty as guarantors of individual rights and a check on state abuse.[10] The spectacle, ritual and vigour of corporal and capital punishments played a key role in performances of power by developing states in early modern Europe, and would arguably continue to do so in the fragile Early Republic.[11] Judicial wounds to the face allowed for the ongoing stigmatisation of the individual alongside perpetual testimony to the power of authority.

The rise of a progressive penology from the late eighteenth century, emphasising reform rather than retribution, and especially the turn toward imprisonment, would significantly decrease or remove corporal and capital punishments from most European and American jurisdictions. Scholars have highlighted a decreasing acceptance of violence in Britain over the course of the eighteenth century, which accompanied the decline in public corporal punishments and eventually the death penalty.[12] As Randall McGowen notes, scholarship on early modern punishments has nevertheless substantially complicated understanding of the move from bodily punishments to the mind (as Michel Foucault

---

[7] Jefferson, *Autobiography*, in *The Works of Thomas Jefferson*, Federal Edition, ed. Paul Leicester Ford (12 vols., New York, 1904), II, 385.

[8] James Madison to Jefferson, 15 February 1787. All letters are taken from the National Archives (USA), *Founders Online*, https://founders.archives.gov/.

[9] Jefferson to Pendleton, 26 August 1776.

[10] Frank McLynn, *Crime and Punishment in Eighteenth-Century England*, 1989 (Oxford, 1991), 253; Leon Radzinowicz, *A History of English Criminal Law and Its Administration from 1750* (5 vols., 1948), I, 369–70.

[11] David Garland, 'Modes of Capital Punishment: The Death Penalty in Historical Perspective', in *America's Death Penalty: Between Past and Present*, ed. David Garland, Randall McGowen and Michael Meranze (New York, 2011), 30–71.

[12] Peter King, 'Punishing Assault: The Transformation of Attitudes in the English Courts', *Journal of Interdisciplinary History*, 27 (1996), 43–74; Robert Shoemaker, 'Male Honour and the Decline of Public Violence in Eighteenth-Century London', *Social History*, 26 (2001), 190–208.

famously framed it), highlighting the role of shame, pain, sympathy and salvation within the symbolic universe in which these punishments operated.[13] Medievalists have also highlighted the legitimation required for the infliction of disfiguring violence by rulers in that period.[14] Violence did not disappear from the British Atlantic: one facet of the tense distinction between not only Britons and colonised peoples, but Britons living in Britain against those in the colonies, was acceptance of violence in peripheral zones, combined with emphasis on legal and customary niceties, which concealed contests of authority and justice.[15] Scholars of colonialism have complicated the modernising narrative of crime and punishment by highlighting ways in which penal practices followed different paths in colonies and regions within them, the fact that these subsequently affected the metropoles, and that violence toward subjugated groups and individuals was integral to Enlightenment philosophies.[16] Within a colony, infliction of 'English' punishments, even on settlers, was a means of reiterating authorities' and the community's adherence to ideals of civilisation.[17] The American South remained rooted in codes of honour, including expectations of violence to defend it – whether eye-gouging, the duel or nose-pulling – and militarily active.[18]

---

[13] Randall McGowen, 'Through the Wrong End of the Telescope: History, the Death Penalty and the American Experience', in *America's Death Penalty*, ed. Garland, McGowen and Meranze, 106–28, at 111–12; Garland, 'Modes of Capital Punishment', 49; Michel Foucault, *Discipline and Punish: The Birth of the Prison*, 1975, trans. Alan Sheridan (1977); Robert Shoemaker, 'Streets of Shame? The Crowd and Public Punishments in London, 1700–1820', in *Penal Practice and Culture, 1500–1900*, ed. Simon Devereuaux and Paul Griffiths (Houndmills, 2004), 232–57; Pieter Spierenberg, *The Spectacle of Suffering: Executions and the Evolution of Repression: From a Preindustrial Metropolis to the European Experience* (Cambridge, 1984).

[14] Patricia Skinner, 'Visible Prowess?: Reading Men's Head and Face Wounds in Early Medieval Europe to 1000 CE', in *Wounds and Wound Repair in Medieval Culture*, ed. Larissa Tracy and Kelly DeVries (Leiden, 2015), 81–101.

[15] Eliga H. Gould, 'Zones of Law, Zones of Violence: The Legal Geography of the British Atlantic, circa 1772', *The William and Mary Quarterly*, 60 (2003), 471–510, at 473, 500; and *Among the Powers of the Earth: The American Revolution and the Making of a New World Empire* (Cambridge, MA, 2012), 59–63.

[16] Kerry Ward, 'Defining and Defiling the Criminal Body at the Cape of Good Hope: Punishing the Crime of Suicide under Dutch East India Company Rule, circa 1652–1795', in *Discipline and the Other Body: Correction, Corporeality, Colonialism*, ed. Steven Pierce and Anupama Rao (Durham, NC, 2006), 35–60, at 38; Lauren Benton, *Law and Colonial Cultures: Legal Regimes in World History, 1400–1900* (Cambridge, 2002).

[17] Michael Meranze, *Laboratories of Virtue: Punishment, Revolution, and Authority in Philadelphia, 1760–1835* (Chapel Hill, 1996), 188.

[18] Edward L. Ayers, *Vengeance and Justice: Crime and Punishment in the 19th-Century American South* (New York, 1984), 21; Kenneth S. Greenberg, 'The Nose, the Lie, and the Duel in the Antebellum South', *American Historical Review*, 95 (1990), 57–74; Elliott J. Gorn, '"Gouge and Bite, Pull Hair and Scratch": The Social Significance of Fighting in the Southern Backcountry', *American Historical Review*, 90 (1985), 18–43.

Studies of Jefferson's attitude toward physical punishments have focused on his reticence to use physical violence on his own slaves: he has been considered a 'better' sort of slave-owner in this respect, preferring to sell off troublemakers.[19] However, Jefferson's relation to violence has come under revision in light of insights into the manner in which violence was entrenched and strategically manoeuvred in the period. There is also vital and growing scholarship on the disabling of enslaved communities.[20] As Tristan Stubbs notes, Enlightenment patriarchs like Jefferson in many cases displaced blame for violence onto figures such as overseers, while their own force was 'subsumed into gentler rhetoric'.[21] Jefferson's strategic use of supervision at Monticello also introduced what scholars have recognised as principles of the panopticon to his plantation.[22]

Jefferson argued that writers like Beccaria 'had satisfied the reasonable world of the unrighteousness and inefficacy of the punishment of crimes by death'.[23] Jefferson's legal commonplace book demonstrates his extensive engagement with Beccaria's views.[24] He stopped short of following Beccaria's call for abolition of the death penalty, nor does Stuart Banner find much evidence for disapproval of the punishment across colonial America.[25] Beccaria also objected to differentiation of punishments for repeat offenders, which was a major source of mutilation punishments in the American context, including the benefit of clergy that Jefferson removed.[26] Text added to the final bill suggests he was not alone in the opinion that 'a hope of impunity' encouraged offenders, and therefore the best thing for a strong law was the image of fair inflexibility.[27] Jefferson argued that restriction of the death penalty would be more humane, but also that 'cruel and sanguinary laws' accompanied by too much judicial discretion discouraged prosecutions, and induced

[19] Joseph J. Ellis, *American Sphinx: The Character of Thomas Jefferson* (New York, 1997), 149; Valsania, *Jefferson's Body*, 127.

[20] E.g. Dea H. Boster, *African American Slavery and Disability: Bodies, Property, and Power in the Antebellum South, 1800–1860* (2013).

[21] Tristan Stubbs, *Masters of Violence: The Plantation Overseers of Eighteenth-Century Virginia, South Carolina, and Georgia* (Columbia, 2018), 4.

[22] Valsania, *Jefferson's Body*, 123–8; Terrence W. Epperson, 'Panoptic Plantations: The Garden Sights of Thomas Jefferson and George Mason', in *Lines That Divide: Historical Archaeologies of Race, Class, and Gender*, ed. James A. Delle, Stephen A. Mrozowski and Robert Paynter (Knoxville, 2000), 58–77.

[23] Jefferson, in *Works of Thomas Jefferson*, ed. Ford, I, 71.

[24] Jefferson, *Jefferson's Legal Commonplace Book*, ed. David Thomas Konig and Michael P. Zuckert (Princeton, 2019), 491–524. Further Preyer, 'Cesare Beccaria and the Founding Fathers', in *Blackstone in America*, ed. Bilder, Marcus and Kent, ch. 8.

[25] Stuart Banner, *The Death Penalty: An American History* (Cambridge, MA, 2002), 23.

[26] Cesare Beccaria, *On Crimes and Punishments*, ed. Richard Bellamy, trans. Richard Davies (Cambridge, 1995), ch. 4.

[27] The Bill as presented to the Assembly: *Works of Thomas Jefferson*, ed. Ford, II, 395.

local judges to listen to evidence with 'bias', and 'smother testimony'.[28] The same publicness and deep ingratiation within local communities that made the application of the law, and especially shaming punishments such as the pillory, so effective, also threatened its impartial application.

Jefferson demonstrates a volte-face around the efficacy of shaming for criminal reform. Even when sending a draft of Bill 64 to Wythe, he expressed concern that the punishments would 'exhibit spectacles in execution whose moral effect would be questionable'.[29] Nevertheless, the opening of the bill referred hopefully to the 'reformed' individuals serving as 'living and long continued spectacles to deter others from committing the like offences'.[30] He also retained shaming punishments like the pillory, and ducking for pretensions to witchcraft. Nevertheless, in his autobiography Jefferson expressed dissatisfaction with the way humiliating public labour in Pennsylvania 'with shaved heads and mean clothing ... produced in the criminals such a prostration of character, such an abandonment of self-respect, as, instead of reforming, plunged them into the most desperate and hardened depravity of morals and character'.[31] His inclination was thereafter toward imprisonment, in which he coincided with the general shift across the country.[32]

III Jefferson's sources

Jefferson covered Bill 64 in neat annotations. The key legal authorities he cites are Fleta, Bracton and Britton. 'Fleta' (*fl.* 1290–1300) is the name used for the author of a Latin treatise on English law (*Fleta*) that updated and reorganised Henry of Bratton's (d. 1268) slightly earlier *De legibus et consentudinibus Angliae*. The text only survives in one manuscript, but the later Anglo-Norman *Britton*, based on *Fleta*, enjoyed much greater circulation in the fourteenth century. *Fleta* was then revitalised as a legal authority in the early seventeenth century by Sir Edward Coke.[33] Jefferson owned the first printed edition of *Fleta* in Latin (1647), a 1640 edition of *Britton* (also Latin) and Edmund Wingate's 1640 English translation of Bracton. He also draws on his copies of Coke's *Institutes*

[28] Bill 64 Online.

[29] Jefferson to Whythe, 1 November 1778.

[30] Bill 64 Online. See also Jefferson to Pendleton, 26 August 1776. Jefferson expands on public labour in Bill 68.

[31] Jefferson, in *Works of Thomas Jefferson*, ed. Ford, I, 72.

[32] Adam Jay Hirsch, *The Rise of the Penitentiary: Prisons and Punishment in Early America* (New Haven, 1992); Meranze, *Laboratories of Virtue*.

[33] David J. Seipp, 'Fleta (*fl.* 1290–1300)', *Oxford Dictionary of National Biography*, Oxford University Press, 2004, www.oxforddnb.com/view/article/9716 (accessed 11 November 2016).

of the Laws of England (1628), the 1759 translation of Sir Henry Finch's legal digest (*Law, or, a Discourse thereof*) and Sir William Blackstone's *Commentaries on the Laws of England* (1765–9).[34] Coke and Blackstone were the most widely read legal authorities in Virginia, making them sensible sources to highlight, although Jefferson always preferred what he considered Coke's Whig mentality over Blackstone's Toryism.[35]

Jefferson framed his use of medieval law codes very carefully. He professed his role in the criminal law revisions as being 'in general … to reduce the law to its antient Saxon condition, stripping it of all the innovations & rigorisms of subsequent times, to make it what it should be'.[36] The revision of the laws played an important part in the negotiation of independent American identity. Europe and especially Britain continued to be the benchmark against which American elites measured civility and rule of law, and this inferiority anxiety was a major driver of legal reforms.[37] While all states addressed the status of laws inherited from England, some were content to distinguish American legal identity by retaining common law unless 'repugnant' to the constitution.[38] One of the ways in which Jefferson negotiated a break between 'English' and 'American' was to return to the world of the pre-Norman-conquest Anglo-Saxon, positioning America as the inheritor of this tradition, and encouraging study of the laws, language and culture. He considered his own Whig politics, grounded in the rights of Parliament and the people, to be based ultimately in Anglo-Saxon codes, while the Tory focus on hereditary rule and arbitrary authority found its roots in the Norman influence.[39]

This positioning also accounts for notable omissions from Virginian law. The most significant are *The Lawes Divine, Morall and Martiall* (Dale's laws), active in Virginia from 1611–18 but shaping Virginia's

[34] Confirmed through Thomas Jefferson's library catalogues: http://tjlibraries.monticello.org/search/search.html (accessed 2 September 2018).

[35] W. Hamilton Bryson, 'Legal Education', in *Virginia Law Books: Essays and Bibliographies*, ed. W. Hamilton Bryson (Philadelphia, 2000), 316–96, at 322, 332; Dubber, '"An Extraordinarily Beautiful Document"'.

[36] Jefferson to Skelton Jones, 28 July 1809.

[37] Kariann Akemi Yokota, *Unbecoming British: How Revolutionary America Became a Postcolonial Nation, 2011* (New York, 2014); Ellen Holmes Pearson, 'Revising Custom, Embracing Choice: Early American Legal Scholars and the Republicanization of the Common Law', in *Empire and Nation: The American Revolution in the Atlantic World*, ed. Eliga H. Gould and Peter Onuf (Baltimore, 2005), 93–111.

[38] Mary Sarah Bilder, *The Transatlantic Constitution: Colonial Legal Culture and the Empire* (Cambridge, MA, 2004), 187.

[39] John D. Niles, *The Idea of Anglo-Saxon England 1066–1901: Remembering, Forgetting, Deciphering and Renewing the Past* (Chichester, 2015), 268; María José Mora and María José Gómez-Calderón, 'The Study of Old English in America (1776–1850): National Uses of the Saxon Past', *Journal of English and Germanic Philology*, 97 (1998), 322–36.

authoritarian legal style through the seventeenth century.[40] The *Lawes* followed contemporary models from the Star Chamber in prescribing ear-cutting for accessories to the destruction of livestock (article 21), or perpetrators of a range of food adulterations and thefts (article 37), among other mutilations (there were no provisions for boring the nose).[41] They had been published in London to reassure English investors that Virginia was being run strictly and efficiently, and in close alignment with English law, thus representing a deviation from Jefferson's desired Anglo-Saxon models.[42]

IV The face in Virginia

Jefferson's provisions to both prevent and enforce forms of disfigurement attest to the importance of appearance. There has been increasing attention paid to Jefferson's own face and body – health, decorum, dress and the construction of what biographers following Merrill D. Peterson have assessed as his 'impenetrable' image.[43] The circulation of political portraiture, including Jefferson's, was a valuable tool for the embodiment of 'abstract ideals of civic virtue' in post-revolutionary America.[44] At the same time, portraits were afflicted with the classic conundrum of balancing esteemed qualities of beauty and dignity, including influence from physiognomy, with the need to present a recognisable likeness.

There was significant interest in appearance and identity among highly mobile populations disturbed by war, with frequent emigration to and between colonies, including receipt of banished legal, religious, political or criminal dissidents, where traditional markers like dress and speech did not necessarily correlate with social rank, national identity or free status.[45] Visiting America in 1833, Alexis de Tocqueville

---

[40] Meranze, *Laboratories of Virtue*, 190.

[41] *For the Colony in Virginea Britannia. Lawes Divine, Morall and Martiall, &c.* (London: Walter Burre, 1612), sigs. C2^v, D1^v–D2^r; David Thomas Konig, '"Dale's Laws" and the Non-Common Law Origins of Criminal Justice in Virginia', *American Journal of Legal History*, 26 (1982), 354–75, at 370.

[42] David H. Flaherty (introduction and ed.), *For the Colony in Virginea Britannia, Lawes Divine, Morall and Martiall, etc. Compiled by William Strachey* (Charlottesville, 1969), xx.

[43] Peterson, *Thomas Jefferson*, viii, cited in Peter S. Onuf, *The Mind of Thomas Jefferson* (Charlottesville, 2007), 3; Valsania, *Jefferson's Body*; David Waldstreicher, 'Why Thomas Jefferson and African Americans Wore Their Politics on Their Sleeves: Dress and Mobilization between American Revolutions', in *Beyond the Founders: New Approaches to the Political History of the Early American Republic*, ed. Jeffrey L. Pasley, Andrew W. Robertson and David Waldstreicher (Chapel Hill, 2004), 79–103; G. S. Wilson, *Jefferson on Display: Attire, Etiquette, and the Art of Presentation* (Charlottesville, 2018).

[44] Christopher J. Lukasik, *Discerning Characters: The Culture of Appearance in Early America* (Philadelphia, 2011), 122.

[45] E.g. Gwenda Morgan and Peter Rushton, *Banishment in the Early Atlantic World: Convicts, Rebels and Slaves* (2013); Lukasik, *Discerning Characters*, ch. 2 and *passim*.

commented on the ease with which offenders could move from state to state, avoiding recognition for their crimes in new communities.[46] Identity papers, passes for servants and slaves, hygiene practices, racial science, tattoos and other features were harnessed for the sake of constructing, defining and reading difference between bodies.[47] From the selective outward identification of specific deviant groups and individuals, the development of the passport from the late eighteenth century marked a new interest in a system of identification and surveillance applicable to all citizens.[48] The physiognomical theories of Johann Casper Lavater contributed to scrutiny of character in the face, and Jefferson was himself intrigued by racialised differences (and hierarchies) between bodies, including facial distinctions.[49]

V Bill 64: reducing capital offences

This was the context in which Jefferson presented Bill 64. The initial committee plan of January 1777 did not include specific punishments for disfiguring or maiming, and only stipulated castration for rape, sodomy and bestiality.[50] On 1 November 1778 Jefferson sent the bill to Wythe, asking him to 'scrupulously … examine and correct it', including his notes on the law's sources. In this letter he suggests that he has 'strictly observed the scale of punishments settled by the Committee, without being entirely satisfied with it':

> The lex talionis, altho' a restitution of the Common law, to the simplicity of which we have generally found it so advantageous to return will be revolting to the humanised feelings of modern times. An eye for an eye, and a hand for a hand will exhibit spectacles in execution whose moral effect would be questionable; and even the membrum pro membro of Bracton or the punishment of the offending member, altho' long authorised by our law, for the same offence in a slave, has you know been not long since repealed in conformity with public sentiment. This needs reconsideration.[51]

[46] Simon A. Cole, *Suspect Identities: A History of Fingerprinting and Criminal Identification* (Cambridge, MA, 2001), 17.

[47] Kathleen M. Brown, *Foul Bodies: Cleanliness in Early America* (New Haven, 2009); Nathan Perl-Rosenthal, *Citizen Sailors: Becoming American in the Age of Revolution* (Cambridge, MA, 2015); Craig Robertson, *The Passport in America: The History of a Document* (Oxford, 2010).

[48] Jane Caplan and John Torpey, 'Introduction', in *Documenting Individual Identity: The Development of State Practices in the Modern World*, ed. Jane Caplan and John Torpey (Princeton, 2001), 1–12, at 8.

[49] Lukasik, *Discerning Characters*, 11; Charles A. Miller, *Jefferson and Nature: An Interpretation* (Baltimore, 1988), ch. 3; Jay Fliegelman, *Declaring Independence: Jefferson, Natural Language & the Culture of Performance* (Stanford, 1993), 192–5.

[50] 'I. Plan Agreed upon by the Committee of Revisors at Fredericksburg, [13 January 1777]', *Founders Online*, National Archives, last modified 13 June 2018, http://founders.archives.gov/documents/Jefferson/01-02-02-0132-0002 (original source: *The Papers of Thomas Jefferson*, vol. 2, ed. Boyd, 325–8).

[51] Jefferson to Wythe, 1 November 1778.

Jefferson expressed similar sentiments in his later autobiography, professing 'How ... [the *lex talionis*] came to obtain our approbation I do not remember.'[52] It is also absent from the only surviving record of the committee's meeting – Mason's notes – suggesting that its inclusion was actually all Jefferson.[53] Examining Jefferson's research through his notes, and the legal attitudes toward disfigurement in relevant jurisdictions can help to shed light on this decision.

Bestiality

Jefferson reasoned that bestiality was not 'injurious to society in any great degree' and was therefore outside the rights of criminal law. He also remarked that it 'will ever be properly and severely punished by universal derision', thus revealing his reliance on community shaming efforts.[54] There were very infrequent cases in the Commonwealth, which scholars have interpreted as reluctance among communities to prosecute the action as capital, rather than an accurate indication of the number of occurrences.[55] While we await a full analysis of Jefferson and animal rights, his quasi-vegetarianism and idealism in regard to agriculture and the civilising potential of animal husbandry (especially for Native Americans) are well-established parts of his character.[56]

Suicide

Probably influenced by Beccaria, Jefferson quietly rescinded the forfeiture of property by anyone who committed suicide, considering it not only a useless deterrent to one really 'so weary of his existence here' but one that in practice had only led to fictitious judgements of insanity in order to preserve the inheritance of bereaved families.[57] Terri L. Snyder highlights Jefferson's accordance with wider secularisation in the understanding of suicide, and that local authorities and juries had been reluctant to take action against suicides when it meant forgoing

[52] Jefferson, in *Works of Thomas Jefferson*, ed. Ford, I, 69.

[53] Dubber, '"An Extraordinarily Beautiful Document"'.

[54] Bill 64 Online.

[55] John M. Murrin, '"Things Fearful to Name"': Bestiality in Colonial America', *Pennsylvania History: A Journal of Mid-Atlantic Studies*, 65 (1998), 8–43, at 12; Colleen Glenney Boggs, *Animalia Americana: Animal Representations and Biopolitical Subjectivity* (New York, 2013), 50–1.

[56] Valsania, *Jefferson's Body*, 75; Virginia DeJohn Anderson, *Creatures of Empire: How Domestic Animals Transformed Early America* (Oxford, 2004), 245; M. L. Wilson, 'Thomas Jefferson – Farmer', *Proceedings of the American Philosophical Society*, 87 (1943), 216–22.

[57] Jefferson, in *Works of Thomas Jefferson*, ed. Ford, II, 401, including Beccaria.

the deceased's property to the Crown and forcing local authorities to support their family.[58]

Polygamy

Jefferson added polygamy himself, acknowledging that according to Blackstone it had only been a capital offence in England since 1604, where instead the law was satisfied with its 'nullity'.[59] Polygamy was omitted from the final bill: it therefore remained capital in Virginia until 1819, when it was replaced with up to ten years' incarceration, representing what John Witte judges the 'typical' easing of its punishment across the country.[60] Jefferson might have been influenced as much by Pennsylvania's non-capital punishment as by general liberalism, but his ultimate reluctance to remove the crime speaks to the seriousness with which he judged the offence.

Rape

Jefferson had admitted to Madison in December 1786 that, in contrast to the success of his religious freedom bill, his *lex talionis* measures failed to find much approval in Europe. Utilising 'retaliation' for rape was judged 'indecent and unjustifiable'. He appears to be speaking only of male castration since he goes on to express concern that women will use a false rape charge as an 'instrument of vengeance against an inconstant lover'.[61] The Virginian legislature had severely restricted punitive castration, and in the nineteenth century it was limited to enslaved men convicted of raping a white woman; other jurisdictions like New Jersey and Pennsylvania extended this punishment to Native American and white men, respectively, even if there is no evidence for the latter that the sentence was ever carried out.[62]

Sodomy

Virginia, leading the five southern colonies, had adopted the Tudor definition and capital punishment for sodomy without enacting its own

[58] Terri L. Snyder, 'What Historians Talk about When They Talk about Suicide: The View from Early Modern British North America', *History Compass*, 5 (2007), 658–74, at 663, 668.

[59] Bill 64 Online; William Blackstone, *Commentaries on the Laws of England* (4 vols., Oxford, 1765–9), IV, 164.

[60] John Witte, *The Western Case of Monogamy over Polygamy* (New York, 2015), 400.

[61] Jefferson to Madison, 16 December 1786.

[62] Diane Miller Sommerville, *Rape and Race in the Nineteenth-Century South* (Chapel Hill, 2004), 74–5.

statutes on the matter.[63] Subsequent English cases had established high levels of proof of penetration, the irrelevance of consent, etc., and it remained a rare prosecution; John M. Murrin cites only one confirmed sodomy trial in colonial Virginia.[64] It seems unlikely that women would actually be considered legally capable of sodomy in practice (or similarly, rape), but Jefferson does include this possibility both through the specific punishment, and through including a supporting gloss from Finch that sodomy denoted 'carnal copulation against nature, to wit, of man or woman in the same sex'.[65]

VI Disfigurement as a crime

My search of the limited evidence we have for court decisions in Virginia has failed to unearth any cases offering significant revision of, or prosecution under, laws against inflicting disfiguring injuries.[66] Prior to the Revolution, English statutory and common law was therefore the most relevant corpus available. The first reference for any lawyer of the period was of course Blackstone's *Commentaries*. Blackstone discusses common law mayhem's stress on utility, specifically for battle: thus, 'cutting off [a man's] ear, or nose, or the like, are not held to be mayhems at common law; because they do not weaken but only disfigure him'. Nevertheless, 'striking out his eye or foretooth' *was* classically mayhem, showing the aesthetic component that carried into the common law.[67] In his notes, Jefferson quotes further from *Britton* and *Fleta* on the definition of mayhem as injury affecting capacity for battle.[68] Meanwhile, early modern statutes offered limited protection from crimes against the person not resulting in death.[69] Maliciously

[63] Louis Crompton, 'Homosexuals and the Death Penalty in Colonial America', *Journal of Homosexuality*, 1 (1976), 277–93, at 278. Jefferson cites 25 Henry 8. c. 6.

[64] Murrin, '"Things Fearful to Name"', 12.

[65] Finch in Jefferson, Bill 64 Online; Henry Finch, *Law, or, a discourse thereof* (London, 1759), 219.

[66] Jefferson, *Reports of Cases Determined in the General Court of Virginia. From 1730, to 1740; and From 1768, to 1772* (Charlottesville, 1829); *Virginia Colonial Decisions: the reports by Sir John Randolph and by Edward Barradall of decisions of the general court of Virginia, 1728–1741*, ed. R. T. Barton (Boston, MA, 1909); William W. Hening and William Munford, *Reports of Cases Argued and Determined in the Supreme Court of Appeals of Virginia* (4 vols., Philadelphia, 1801–11); Bushrod Washington, *Reports of Cases Argued and Determined in the Court of Appeals of Virginia* (2 vols., Richmond, 1798–9).

[67] Blackstone, *Commentaries*, IV, 205–6; Patricia Skinner, *Living with Disfigurement in Early Medieval Europe* (New York, 2017), 69.

[68] Edmund Wingate (ed.), *Britton, The Second Edition* (London: John Moore, 1640), sigs. F8ᵛ–G1ᵛ; 'Fleta' and John Selden, *Fleta seu Commentarius Juris Anglicani sic nuncupatus* (London: William Lee and Daniel Pakeman, 1647), sigs. I1ᵛ–I2ʳ.

[69] William Holdsworth, *A History of English Law*, 5th edn (12 vols., 1942), VI, 403.

cutting out the tongue or eyes was felony under 5 Hen. 4. c. 5.[70] This was followed by 37 Hen. 8 c. 6, which targeted malicious cutting of the ears, with a necessary exemption for ears cut 'by authority of law'.[71]

The most important statutory intervention occurred in 1670, and became known as the Coventry Act. This formed the basis of all subsequent colonial disfigurement statutes, including Jefferson's revision. The Act rendered it an unclergyable felony to

> on purpose and of malice forethought and by lyeing in waite ... unlawfully cutt out, or disable the Tongue, putt one out an Eye, slitt the Nose, cutt off a Nose or Lipp, or cutt off, or disable any Limbe or Member of any Subjectt of his Majestie with intention in soe doeing to maime or disfigure in any the manners before mentioned such his Majestyes Subject [or to be one of] their Councellours Ayders and Abetters (knowing of and privy to the Offence as aforesaid)[.][72]

Sir John Coventry had provoked James Scott, 1st Duke of Monmouth, by remarking on Charles II's fondness for actresses in a parliamentary debate. Subsequently, over twenty-five of the duke's men lay in wait and cut Coventry's nose almost clean from his face. Injuries to the nose carried specific symbolic weight, but debates show that Parliament's swift statutory response was as driven by the fact it was an attack on a sitting member as by horror at discovering the wound's legal weakness.[73] The Lords were the most adamant that intention must be explicitly required for felony without benefit of clergy, and that a provision for lying in wait should prevent any 'genuine' fights that happened to result in otherwise actionable injuries from coming under the statute.[74] These requisites would significantly restrict the Act's application. Where they were not met, the defendant was liable for only a fine and imprisonment. The limitations of the Act prompted further legislation to protect officials: 9 Anne c. 16 made it an unclergyable felony to attempt to kill, or strike, assault or wound a privy counsellor in the execution of his office. Like Coventry, this Act was a direct response to a contemporary event, after the Marquis de Guiscard

---

[70] Sir John Gonson, *Sir John Gonson's Three Charges to Several Grand Juries*, 2nd edn (1728), 70.

[71] Joseph Chitty, *A Practical Treatise on the Criminal Law*, 4th edn (3 vols., Springfield, 1841), III, 784; Frank Aydelotte, *Elizabethan Rogues and Vagabonds*, 1913 (Abingdon, 1967), 58.

[72] 'Charles II, 1670 & 1671: An Act to p[re]vent Malitious maiming and wounding', in *Statutes of the Realm: Volume 5, 1628–80*, ed. John Raithby (s.l. 1819), 691–2. British History Online, www.british-history.ac.uk/statutes-realm/vol5/pp691-692 (accessed 13 September 2018).

[73] 'Debates in 1671: January (1st–17th)', in *Grey's Debates of the House of Commons: Volume 1*, ed. Anchitell Grey (1769), 333–53. British History Online, www.british-history.ac.uk/greys-debates/vol1/pp333-353 (accessed 13 September 2018).

[74] 'House of Lords Journal Volume 12: 28 January 1671', in *Journal of the House of Lords: Volume 12, 1666–1675* (1767–1830), 415–16. British History Online, www.british-history.ac.uk/lords-jrnl/vol12/pp415-416 (accessed 13 September 2018).

stabbed the Chancellor of the Exchequer, Robert Harley, in the chest with a penknife in March 1711.[75]

The Virginia General Assembly issued an Act closely following Coventry in 1752. It allowed benefit of clergy, but did not require 'malice' or 'lying in wait'.[76] Another 1772 Act focused on 'gouging, plucking or putting out an eye, biting, kicking, or stamping upon' an individual, which if 'wilful or malicious' should be met with a suit for damages, and the offender whipped if he failed to pay. A suit could also be brought by a third party if the victim failed to act, with damages split between the prosecutor and churchwardens for the support of parish poor.[77] The Privy Council overruled the law for applying a criminal penalty to a civil suit.[78] Elliot J. Gorn noted that the shift of emphasis in this statute reflected concern about the rough fighting popular in the Virginia backcountry, where eye-gouging was a winning blow, but without acknowledging the extent to which statutes enacted in different colonies merely built upon the Coventry Act.[79]

In the absence of Virginian cases, English trials against the Coventry Act can shed significant light on the reception of disfigurement in the period, and legal attitudes to its restitution. In general, the reticence which met application of the Act and its capital punishment are commensurate with Jefferson's rescinding of the death penalty. They also illuminate the vagaries of the Act's application that led to dissatisfaction in the legal profession. Jefferson had informed Pendleton in his plans for the bill of his desire to 'let the judge be a mere machine'.[80] Coventry Act cases had seen them anything but.

Few cases were easily resolved. The very first was a notable exception, in which siblings William, Robert and Mary Dine were indicted for attacking Jane King in 1677. It was a sensational trial, widely reported, and they were executed. But most prosecutions, even if successful, produced worrying questions of law. In the case cited by Blackstone, and widely elsewhere, a lawyer, Arundel Coke (aka Cooke), was found guilty of slitting the nose of his brother-in-law Edward Crispe, with the assistance of John Woodburne, in Suffolk, 1721.[81] The trial became infamous for Coke's attempted defence that he had intended to *murder* Crispe, and therefore did not meet the statute's criteria, and the Lord

---

[75] Blackstone, *Commentaries*, I, 225.

[76] William Waller Hening, *The Statutes at Large; Being a Collection of all the Laws of Virginia, from the First Session of the Legislature, in the Year 1619* (13 vols., Philadelphia, 1809–23), VI, 250.

[77] *Ibid.*, VIII, 520–2.

[78] Preyer, 'Crime', 67.

[79] Gorn, '"Gouge and Bite"', 19.

[80] Jefferson to Pendleton, 26 August 1776.

[81] Blackstone, *Commentaries*, IV, 207; *The Tryal and Condemnation of Arundel Coke alias Cooke Esq; and of John Woodburne Labourer, for Felony, in Slitting the Nose of Edward Crispe Gent.* (1722).

Chief Justice Sir Peter King's rather convoluted ruling on the nature of intent in felony cases to ensure that they did not escape on such a defence. Southwell JP Ralph Heathcote attacked the ruling in a legal treatise that Jefferson owned, stating 'that no true man of the Profession was ever heard to speak with temper upon the Case'. Believing that they did indeed intend to kill rather than disfigure Crispe, Heathcote argued that the Act was wrongfully construed, 'and the same constructive violence, in the interpretation of Laws, might often hang an honest man as well as a knave'.[82] A related standard in English and therefore prior Virginian law made it murder to accidentally kill someone in commission of an unlawful act, regardless of intention; Jefferson's bill explicitly rescinded this equivalence, formalising the need to prove intention for either manslaughter or murder.

In another widely cited case, William Lee was indicted under the Act in 1763 for cutting his sleeping wife Agnis's neck with a razor. Here, the prosecution failed because he did not disfigure her *face*.[83] The Act was invoked in the high-profile case of William, Earl of Devonshire, striking Colonel Culpeper in the palace of Whitehall in 1687, though with quick resolution that the lack of premeditation and significant injury precluded it.[84] The 1765 trial of Barny Carrol and William King included an exchange with the attending surgeon about whether Cranley Thomas Kirby's nose was 'slit' (as per the Act), or 'divided', 'incised', 'cut', 'wounded', etc, which was a recurring course of defence (e.g by Coke/Cooke). They were found guilty, as was Thomas Hand for wounding Joseph Holloway in the arm with a pistol in 1770.[85] In contrast, Samuel Dale failed to have Thomas Brooks's assault on him upgraded to a felony after he lost the sight in his eye, because unable to prove that Brooks had lain in wait with intent.[86]

The actions required to satisfy 'lying in wait' in Britain were substantially expanded by a ruling from Justice Sir James Eyre in the trial of Thomas Mills in April 1783, which held it sufficient 'for a man who has a purpose in his mind to do such kind of mischief, and deliberately watches an opportunity to do it'.[87] It would have little effect, however, as the 1803 revision of the legislation removed the requirement entirely:

[82] Ralph Heathcote, *The Irenarch: or, Justice of the Peace's Manual*, 1771, 3rd edn (1781), 181–3. His remarks on the case were reprinted in *Sylva; or, the Wood* (1786), which Jefferson owned.

[83] Trial of William Lee, *Old Bailey Proceedings: Accounts of Criminal Trials* (hereafter *OBP*), 6 July 1763, LL ref: t17630706-45.

[84] T. B. Howell, *A Complete Collection of State Trials* (21 vols., 1816), XI, 1353–72.

[85] Trial of Barny Carrol and William King, *OBP*, 10 July 1765, LL ref: t17650710-40; Trial of Thomas Hand, *OBP*, 5 December 1770, LL ref: t17701205-10.

[86] Trial of Thomas Brooks, *OBP*, 17 December 1766, LL ref: t17661217-63.

[87] In Thomas Leach, *Cases in Crown Law, Determined by the Twelve Judges*, 3rd edn (2 vols., 1800), I, 297–8.

it remained an unclergyable felony in Lord Ellenborough's Act (43 Geo. III, c. 58 [1803]), before being subsumed by the Offences against the Person Act (1861), which remains in force. Commentators reasoned that by expanding the parameters to 'grievous bodily harm', the statute had more flexibility to incorporate wounds falling short of mayhem, and in places of the body generally covered and thus not 'disfiguring'.[88]

While revisions of Coventry throughout America are beyond the scope of this article, two examples show the diversity of responses. North Carolina still divided the offences according to the principles in the Henrician vs Coventry statutes, and included disfiguring punishment. Their 1791 revision stipulated that anyone who would 'of malice afore-thought, unlawfully cut out or disable the tongue, or put out an eye of any person with intent to murder, maim or disfigure', and their accomplices, will be pilloried, including loss of both ears, and whipped (first offence), then executed for a second offence. For other actions against the nose, lip, ear or 'any limb or member', performed 'on purpose' and 'with intent to murder, or to maim or disfigure' (thus a more cap-acious act than that requiring malice and lying in wait), the punishment was only six months' imprisonment and a fine.[89] New Jersey, in contrast, combined the different actions in 1796 into an offence punishable by fine and/or up to seven years' imprisonment with hard labour.[90] All jurisdic-tions took the offence seriously, and many removed or nuanced the cri-teria for malice and/or lying in wait. The early Virginian revisions had already omitted the waiting requirement, shifting the onus onto the action and its intention. Jefferson noted the lack of restriction to 'wilful and malicious' actions in the older laws, citing further research in Finch, Bracton, Blackstone and others.[91] In the final text sent to the Assembly, the bill omitted the requirement for 'malice forethought', thus further removing the subjective assessment of the accused's mental state from the role of the judiciary and bringing it closer in Jefferson's view to the older laws.[92]

When a revised felony Act was passed on 17 December 1792, it did not include a requirement to 'lie in wait', but stipulated that the eligible disfi-gurements must be inflicted deliberately. It did not preclude benefit of clergy, as the legislature did in the same period for offences like 'buggery, with man or beast', horse stealing and rape.[93] It was not

[88] Phil Handler, 'The Law of Felonious Assault in England, 1803–61', *Journal of Legal History*, 28 (2007), 183–206.

[89] *The Acts of the General Assembly of the State of North Carolina* (Newbern, 1795), ch. VIII.

[90] William Paterson, *Laws of the State of New Jersey* (New Brunswick, 1800), 218.

[91] Bill 64 Online.

[92] Jefferson, in *Works of Thomas Jefferson*, ed. Ford, II, 403.

[93] Samuel Shepherd, *The Statutes at Large of Virginia, [1792–1806] ... Being a Continuation of Hening* (3 vols., Richmond, 1835), I, 112–13, 178.

until 1796 that the Commonwealth abolished benefit of clergy and restricted the death penalty to first-degree murder, facilitated in part by the construction of a new jail (opening in 1800).[94] Inefficiencies in prosecution may have encouraged the reduction of capital offences.[95] Some corporal punishments remained: misbehaviour within the jail could prompt extendable solitary confinement on bread and water and/or 'moderate' whipping/s.[96]

The 1796 provision for disfigurement offered two forms for the offence: in the first, it reintroduced the requirement for 'lying in wait' alongside acting 'on purpose and of malice aforethought'; on the other hand, it removed these requirements for any who 'shall voluntarily, maliciously and of purpose, pull or put out an eye while fighting or otherwise', giving theoretically greater protection against the local eye-gouging brawls, rather than the traditionally symbolic nose. If guilty, the offender and his or her 'aiders, abettors and counsellors' would be jailed for two to ten years, and fined up to $1,000, 'three fourths whereof shall be for the use of the party grieved'.[97] Such compensation rules also removed any need for a separate civil suit by the victim.[98]

This Act was revised again in 1803. In addition to returning hanging to high treason, it was the first to explicitly exclude slaves as defendants from its provisions.[99] A notable case of 1811 held that it could nevertheless protect slaves themselves from malicious disfiguring violence.[100] The revision again rescinded the 'lying in wait' requirement, and created a new two-part offence wherein the key difference was the weapon used: biting, or stabbing or shooting. In each case, the penalty remained the same as in the 1796 Act.[101] The case of John Somerville, charged with maiming John G. Jackson in 1808 (he was ultimately found guilty of misdemeanour assault), still retains reference to 'lying in wait', suggesting it remained an informally aggravating factor even outside of the active statute.[102] Nevertheless, Henry St George Tucker focused on mayhem as permanent injury that 'disabled' the individual from fighting, and

---

[94] *Ibid.*, II, 5, 8.

[95] Preyer, 'Crime', 76.

[96] Shepherd, *Statutes at Large*, II, 13.

[97] *Ibid.*, 7.

[98] Preyer, 'Crime', 63.

[99] Shepherd, *Statutes at Large*, II, 405–6.

[100] Commonwealth v Dolly Chapple. The defence argued that as a slave could not own property s/he could not receive the stipulated damages. The prosecution successfully countered that such logic would exclude *femes covert* from protection, which would be 'monstrous': William Brockenbrough and Hugh Holmes, *A Collection of Cases Decided by the General Court of Virginia [1789–1814]* (Philadelphia, 1815), 184–6.

[101] Shepherd, *Statutes at Large*, II, 405.

[102] Commonwealth v John Somerville, in Brockenbrough and Holmes, *Collection of Cases*, 164–9.

the capacity for the court to increase damages if it thought the jury had
been too lenient.[103]

While obviously a reduction from the death penalty, Jefferson's suggestion that an assailant should be disfigured 'in like manner' was extraordinary. In the bill he cites *Fleta*, *Britton* (which prescribed loss of the
equivalent member for men, but loss of the offending hand for
women) and the law of King Alfred (Ll. Ælfr. 19. 40), rather than
Bracton on *membrum pro membro* as he referenced in his letter to
Wythe.[104] He *omits* Blackstone, who considered the action arcane and
inadequate; however, he may have been influenced by Blackstone's
opinion that one of its drawbacks was inability of repetition, in providing
for retaliation against a part judged equivalent.[105] There are precedents
for this equivalency in English law. Among the provisions for aggravated
cases of affray, for example, anyone convicted for striking another with a
weapon (or drawing with intent to do so) in a church or churchyard
would be excommunicated, and 'have one of his ears cut off; or,
having no ears, be branded with the letter F in his cheek'.[106] It seems
unusual for Jefferson to leave such an open field for the judging of this
equivalency, given his professed intention to remove wiggle room in
courts, but this too carries antecedents in the medieval *wergeld* that
awarded damages for injury based on intricate valuations of body parts.

VII Disfigurement as a punishment

The use of disfiguring punishments was by no means unknown in either
Europe or America, even if Jefferson was a lone voice for the *lex talionis*.
Branding the hand for benefit of clergy remained a key form of both judicial discretion and physical marking employed by British and American
courts, and Arthur Scott demonstrated its frequent use in pre-revolution-
ary Virginia.[107] Acts like Coventry had to specifically preclude benefit of
clergy for felonies. Until 1623 women could not claim benefit of clergy,
and thereafter only for petty thefts; in 1691, clergy was extended to
them as freely as men.[108] Many individuals transported to Virginia

---

[103] Henry St George Tucker, *Commentaries on the Laws of Virginia*, 1826 (2 vols., Winchester,
VA, 1837), II, 53–4.

[104] Valerie Allen, 'When Compensation Costs an Arm and a Leg', in *Capital and Corporal
Punishment in Anglo-Saxon England*, ed. Jay Paul Gates and Nicole Marafioti (Woodbridge,
2014), 17–33; William E. Miller, *An Eye for an Eye* (New York, 2006).

[105] Blackstone, *Commentaries*, IV, 206.

[106] *Ibid.*, 146.

[107] Arthur Scott, *Criminal Law in Colonial Virginia* (Chicago, 1930), 319–21; Jeffrey
K. Sawyer, '"Benefit of Clergy" in Maryland and Virginia', *American Journal of Legal
History*, 34 (1990), 49–68.

[108] J. M. Beattie, *Policing and Punishment in London 1660–1750: Urban Crime and the Limits of
Terror* (Oxford, 2001), 277.

would have carried such marks, such as Sarah Plint, indicted for theft on 16 January 1766 and transported for seven years after previously being branded for marrying five husbands.[109]

Branding offenders also served as an ongoing shaming punishment. To do so in the face, or inflict other permanent injury on the only part of the body almost universally uncovered, was acknowledged as a weighted action. While other facial branding had been used in Britain in the seventeenth century, clergy branding 'in the most visible part of the cheek nearest the nose' only appeared from 1699 to 1706, before it returned to the thumb until abolition in 1779.[110] The introduction formed part of a general harshening of property laws in the 1690s, but local authorities were hesitant.[111] In repealing the sentence, Parliament noted that rather than acting as a deterrent or corrective, 'such offenders, being rendered thereby unfit to be entrusted in any honest and lawful way, become the more desperate', and in the minds of rehabilitative penal reformers like William Eden the use of stigmatising marks impeded reintegration of a reformed individual into society.[112] Later American critics of judicial mutilations similarly emphasised that such practices were antithetical to civil societies, and that they fixed the individual as a permanent member of a criminal class unable to start afresh in another colony.[113] Branding on the cheek for offences like counterfeiting coins did, however, remain on the books.[114] Other facial marks were also inflicted: in London, 1731, Japhet Crook, alias Sir Peter Stranger, had his ears cut, and nostrils slit by the public hangman under an Elizabethan forgery statue.

Facial marking would continue to be used in British colonies against subordinated bodies: from the branding and judicial disfiguring of enslaved individuals in the West Indies, to the use of forehead tattoos known as *godna* detailing criminal status in Indian penal law.[115] Yet, even if corporal punishments such as floggings remained in use in

---

[109] Trial of Sarah Plint, *OBP*, 16 January 1766. LL ref: t17660116-7.

[110] 'William III, 1698: An Act for the better apprehending prosecuting and punishing of Felons that commit Burglary Housebreaking or Robbery in Shops Ware-houses Coach-houses or Stables or that steal Horses. [Chapter XII. Rot. Parl. 10 Gul. III. 3. n. 3.]', in *Statutes of the Realm: Volume 7, 1695–1701*, ed. John Raithby (s.l., 1820), 511–13. *British History Online*, www.british-history.ac.uk/statutes-realm/vol7/pp511-513 (accessed 29 September 2018).

[111] Beattie, *Crime and the Courts in England 1660–1800* (Oxford, 1986), 491; Beattie, *Policing*, 328–34.

[112] 5 Anne c. 6 in William Eden, *Principles of Penal Law*, 2nd edn (1771), 59.

[113] Ayers, *Vengeance and Justice*, 43.

[114] Blackstone, *Commentaries*, IV, 99. In his notes on the crime for Bill 64, Jefferson instead cites Æthelstan's and Cnut's sentence of loss of hand, and common law provisions for it as a capital offence.

[115] Elsa Goveia, *The West Indian Slave Laws of the Eighteenth Century* (Barbados, 1970); Clare Anderson, *Legible Bodies: Race, Criminality and Colonialism in South Asia* (Oxford, 2004).

Britain and its colonial regions, forms of legitimate violence designed to ensure lasting stigmatisation were employed by the independent American authorities against their own citizens much later.[116]

Jefferson observed that some of Bill 64's punishments had precedent in the treatment of slaves. From testimonies, runaway advertisements and other sources, we see slaves marked in a wide variety of ways. Ear-cropping is a recurring one, as is the branding of the master's initials or the letter 'R' for 'runaway' on the face and/or body.[117] A Virginia law of 1699 stipulated that a slave convicted of hog-stealing once would be whipped, and twice would have both ears torn at the pillory.[118] The sentence was extended to any free person in 1748.[119] The threat was also thought a good equivalent to swearing on the Bible in capital trials of slaves: 'Negros, Mulattos, or Indians, not being christians' required to testify were to be informed that if they gave false evidence they would lose both ears at the pillory and be whipped.[120] Formal and informal disfigurements are found throughout British and American slaveholding regions, and were emphasised by anti-slavery writers keen to reveal how 'American taskmasters … notch the ears of men and women, cut pleasant posies in the shrinking flesh, learn to write with pens of red-hot iron on the human face.'[121] Lewis Clark, an escaped slave from Kentucky testifying to abolitionists in 1842, also highlighted that disfigurement outside statute was hardly unexpected: 'The law [of Kentucky] don't allow 'em to brand a slave, or cut off his ear; but if they happen to switch it off with a cow hide, nobody says anything about it.'[122] Early laws based on English vagrancy punishments had marked runaway servants: in 1643 a second-offender's cheek was branded with 'R', before this moved to the shoulder in 1658, and the hair close-cropped for all offenders.[123] But restrictions

[116] On flogging as an increasingly racialised punishment in British colonies, see, e.g., Amanda Nettelbeck, 'Flogging as Judicial Violence: The Colonial Rationale of Corporal Punishment', in *Violence, Colonialism and Empire in the Modern World*, ed. Phillip Dwyer and Amanda Nettelbeck (Cham, 2018), 111–27; David Killingray, 'The "Rod of Empire": The Debate over Corporal Punishment in the British African Colonial Forces, 1888–1946', *Journal of African History*, 35 (1994), 201–16.

[117] John Hope Franklin and Loren Schweininger, *Runaway Slaves: Rebels on the Plantation* (New York, 2000), 217–19; Gwenda Morgan and Peter Rushton, 'Visible Bodies: Power, Subordination and Identity in the Eighteenth-Century Atlantic World', *Journal of Social History*, 39 (2005), 39–64, at 47–8; Philip J. Schwarz, *Twice Condemned: Slaves and the Criminal Laws of Virginia, 1705–1865* (Union, NJ, 1998), 79.

[118] Hening, *Statutes at Large*, III, 179.

[119] *Ibid.*, VI, 121.

[120] *Ibid.*, IV, 127–8.

[121] Charles Dickens, *American Notes for General Circulation* (New York, 1842), 86, 89.

[122] *National Anti-Slavery Standard*, 20–27 October 1842; John W. Blassingame (ed.), *Slave Testimony: Two Centuries of Letters, Speeches, Interviews, and Autobiographies* (Baton Rouge, 1977), 155.

[123] Hening, *Statutes at Large*, I, 254–5, 440, 517–18.

grew, while runaway slaves continued to be branded or dismembered (such as losing toes). Into the nineteenth century, slaves faced capital charges for disfiguring white people in cases where white perpetrators would face only fines, pillory or imprisonment.[124] As Kirsten Fisher notes, the continuation of such practices in the face of increased restraint against white bodies was one way in which racial difference was ingrained.[125]

But despite a significant imbalance in the acceptance, range and frequency of such punishments, corporal punishment including disfigurement was also used on free individuals well into the nineteenth century. Alongside execution, which might be followed by dissection or hanging in chains, public whipping and other forms of judicial mutilation ensured that the body was deeply integrated into 'a public economy of punishment'.[126] Ear-cropping is the most frequent disfigurement meted out as a punishment in colonial America, including Virginia, and carried British precedents.[127] In 1624, the ship captain Robert Cornish (alias Williams) was executed in Virginia for forcibly sodomising one of the ship's boys, William Couse. A number of men linked to the case criticised the execution (on unknown grounds), two of whom were punished by the loss of an ear and either one year of indentured servitude or whipping.[128] North Carolina included ear-cropping among its penalties for perjury: those guilty were fined, ineligible to give further testimony in any court, and pilloried for an hour before their ears were cut off and nailed to the pillory until sunset.[129] New England was the most enthusiastic in its use of branding and other marks, but even Pennsylvania – which Virginia would shortly look to after the success of its new penitentiary – only removed remaining branding, ear cropping, etc., in 1786.[130] The army employed branding well into the nineteenth century after it had left other (white) judicial punishments,

---

[124] See, for example, the case of Abram in Alabama 1847, who successfully appealed a capital conviction for biting off a section of an overseer's ear because (1) part of the ear was not mayhem, and (2) his life was in danger: in Lawrence Friedman, *Crime and Punishment in American History* (New York, 1993), 92 and 491n. The same offence by others – in language closely modelled on Coventry – would be fined and pilloried: John G. Aikin, *A Digest of the Laws of the State of Alabama*, 2nd edn (Tuscaloosa, 1836), 102.

[125] Kirsten Fischer, *Suspect Relations: Sex, Race and Resistance in Colonial North Carolina* (Ithaca, 2002), 180; Anthony S. Parent, Jr, *Foul Means: The Formation of a Slave Society in Virginia, 1660–1740* (Chapel Hill, 2003), 107, 123–7.

[126] Meranze, *Laboratories of Virtue*, 187.

[127] Blackstone, *Commentaries*, IV, 137 (5 Eliz. c. 9: ears nailed to the pillory for perjury), 245 (5. Eliz. c. 14: ears cut and nostrils slit for specific forgery offences).

[128] Murrin, "'Things Fearful to Name'", 12; Crompton, 'Homosexuals'.

[129] *The Acts of the General Assembly of the State of North Carolina* (Newbern, 1795), ch. VI.

[130] *The Statute at Large of Pennsylvania*, Commonwealth of Pennsylvania Legislative Reference Bureau, www.palrb.us/default.php, xii.283; Lawrence Henry Gipson, 'Criminal Codes of Pennsylvania', *Journal of Criminal Law and Criminology*, 6 (1915), 323–44.

especially for desertion. William Chester Minor, a Yale-trained surgeon in the Union army, wrote a traumatised account of being tasked with branding an Irish deserter in 1864.[131] Marking the bodies of criminals was one way in which criminal identity could, in theory, be fixed, but this was never certain: cases of innocent disfigurement resembling the legal practices were recorded in Kentucky courts, so that the individual could be defended against misreadings.[132]

In a rare gap, Jefferson offers no citations for cutting women's noses. His letter to Pendleton shows an early intention to use castration to punish 'rape, buggery, &c.' but makes no mention of nose-cutting, or the use of retaliation for disfigurement.[133] There is a long global tradition of inflicting nasal wounds upon sexual transgressors, with cases stretching from antiquity to the present, across Egypt, Europe and the Middle East, through Southeast Asia and the Pacific islands.[134] Punitive rhinotomy was practised by the Blackfeet in the late nineteenth century, although it is not known how widely or for how long this might have existed in America.[135] It was the status of injuries to the nose as *inhonesta vulnera* – dishonouring wounds – that was in part responsible for the emphatic punishment prescribed by Coventry and related legislation.[136] While male and female noses were protected by his disfigurement law, the distinction between castration and nose-boring for the other offences shows his gendering of official judicial actions against this part of the body.

As with the Hebraic 'eye for eye', there was biblical precedent for rhinotomy as a punishment for female sexual transgression (Ezekiel 23:25). Slitting the nose of adulterous or otherwise sexually transgressive women was a widely known threat in early modern Britain. While King Edgar had used nose-cutting for some thefts, it was Cnut (r. 1016–35) and Archbishop Wulfstan of York (*fl.* 1002–23) who introduced nasal mutilation – along with loss of the ears – for women convicted of adultery.[137] Jefferson does not refer to Cnut here, but does elsewhere. His omission

---

[131] Robert Fantina, *Desertion and the American Soldier, 1776–2006* (New York, 2006), 50; Simon Winchester, *The Surgeon of Crowthorne: A Tale of Murder, Madness, and the* Oxford English Dictionary, 1998 (1999), 54–7.

[132] Ayers, *Vengeance and Justice*, 43.

[133] Jefferson to Pendleton, 26 August 1776.

[134] Jürgen Wasim Frembgen, 'Honour, Shame, and Bodily Mutilation. Cutting off the Nose among Tribal Societies in Pakistan', *Journal of the Royal Asiatic Society of Great Britain & Ireland*, 16 (2006), 245–7; Patricia Skinner, 'The Gendered Nose and Its Lack: "Medieval" Nose-Cutting and Its Modern Manifestations', *Journal of Women's History*, 26 (2014), 45–67, and Skinner, *Living with Disfigurement*, esp. ch. 3.

[135] Adolf Hungry-Wolf, *The Blackfoot Papers*, vol. 4: *Pikunni Biographies* (Skookumchuck, 2006), 1085–6.

[136] Emily Cock, *Rhinoplasty and the Nose in Early Modern British Medicine and Culture* (Manchester University Press, forthcoming 2019).

[137] II Cnut 53; Skinner, 'Gendered Nose', 53.

of Cnut 30.4–5, which carried over Edgar's law of *talion*, is also strange. In the *Report of the Revisors*, the term was altered from 'cutting' to 'boring'. This may have been intended to suggest restraint, but it also more closely echoes established laws in neighbouring jurisdictions, especially boring the tongue in New England. A final clue appears in Jefferson's legal commonplace book. Here, he closely paraphrases a comment from Henry Home, Lord Kames's history of the criminal law that according to Diodorus Siculus, in ancient Egypt, 'he who committed a rape was castrated. A woman committing adultery, lost her nose, that she might not again allure men to wantonness.'[138] Kames holds this an example of Egypt's 'perfection' of the criminal law, since 'revenge is thereby kept within the strictest bounds, and confined to its proper objects'.[139] Diodorus may have overstated the neat equivalency in this case, since adultery was more commonly met with death, but castration and rhinotomy were certainly used elsewhere.[140] While a different crime, the note shows the alignment of rhinotomy with female sexual transgression, their 'allure' to men, and the equivalency with male castration, which evidently had some appeal to Jefferson.

VIII Conclusion

In *Notes on the State of Virginia*, Jefferson presented his revised criminal code in an elegant table, arranged according to punishment: Life, Limb, and Labour. The provisions under question are set out as follows:[141]

II. Crimes whose punishment goes to *Limb*.

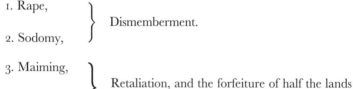

1. Rape,
2. Sodomy,   } Dismemberment.

3. Maiming,
4. Disfiguring   } Retaliation, and the forfeiture of half the lands and goods to the sufferer.

---

[138] Jefferson, *Legal Commonplace Book*, 235; Henry Home, Lord Kames, *Historical Law-Tracts*, 2nd edn (Edinburgh, 1761), 49.

[139] Kames, *Historical Law-Tracts*, 48.

[140] C. J. Eyre, 'Crime and Adultery in Ancient Egypt', *Journal of Egyptian Archaeology*, 70 (1984), 92–105, at 96–7.

[141] Jefferson, in *Works of Thomas Jefferson*, ed. Ford, IV, 59.

There is an element of obfuscation in placing castration behind the broader category of 'dismemberment'. Moreover, these laws had not passed when Jefferson published the book. The summary echoes Jefferson's two ostentatiously careful manuscripts of Bill 64, the notes arranged in columns to mirror legal heroes like Coke.[142] These carefully elucidate the precedents upon which Jefferson was relying to put forward a code he desired to be marked by 'accuracy, brevity and simplicity'.[143] Where Dumas Malone had seen the extensive notes as evidence of Jefferson's interest in the topic, Julian Boyd saw the annotations as Jefferson's 'pedantic ostentation', and Dubber an excuse to 'practice his penmanship'.[144]

Considering the annotations and research alongside the problematic history of the Coventry Act in practice, however, illuminates why the keen lawyer struggled to find an adequate means of revising the provisions against disfigurement – one that even he grew to dislike. When Beccaria's appeal against capital punishment gained traction among reformers, those still in favour of the punishment were compelled to defend it with unprecedented vigour: Vic Gatrell notes that 'elaborate pleading' was newly necessary, 'because older certainties had become uneasy'.[145] Jefferson's exhausting annotations of the corporal punishments hint at similar strain to justify punishments that might seem 'revolting'. Virginia's simplifying of the Coventry Act's requirements of intention and circumstance, for all they fluctuated in different revisions, represented attempts to combat the real problems that the Act had faced in practice in Britain, and criticisms of its application. Replacing the death penalty for this and the other offences with proportional punishments was supposed to increase efficacy, justice and rationality in post-revolutionary Virginian law. I am inclined to agree with Peterson that Jefferson was in a sense 'trapped by a misplaced desire for simplicity', in striving for a code so straightforward, proportional and logical that mercy could never be at 'the eccentric impulses of whimsical capricious designing men'.[146] Neither an out-of-the blue aberration, nor an overlooked hangover from earlier law, Jefferson's *lex talionis* approach to facial disfigurement as both a crime and a punishment drew on precedents from medieval England and closer to home, and reflected the anxious balance of punishment of body and mind at work in eighteenth-century legal reforms.

---

[142] Julian Boyd, Lyman H. Butterfield and Mina R. Bryan (eds.), *The Papers of Thomas Jefferson* (Princeton, 1950), II, 310; Dumas Malone, *Jefferson and His Time: Jefferson the Virginian* (Boston, MA, 1948), 269–70.

[143] Jefferson to Wythe, 1 November 1778.

[144] Malone, *Jefferson and His Time*, 269; Boyd, Butterfield and Bryan (eds.), *Papers of Thomas Jefferson*, II, 505; Dubber, '"An Extraordinarily Beautiful Document"'.

[145] Vic Gatrell, *The Hanging Tree: Execution and the English People 1770–1868* (Oxford, 1994), 263.

[146] Peterson, *Thomas Jefferson*, 127–8; Jefferson to Pendleton, 26 August 1776.

Transactions of the RHS 29 (2019), pp. 153–179 © Royal Historical Society 2019
doi:10.1017/S0080440119000070

MARY WILLIAMSON'S LETTER, OR, SEEING WOMEN AND SISTERS IN THE ARCHIVES OF ATLANTIC SLAVERY*

By Diana Paton

READ 9 FEBRUARY 2018

ABSTRACT. 'I was a few years back a slave on your property of Houton Tower, and as a Brown woman was fancied by a Mr Tumming unto who Mr Thomas James sold me.' Thus begins Mary Williamson's letter, which for decades sat unexamined in an attic in Scotland until a history student became interested in her family's papers, and showed it to Diana Paton. In this article, Paton uses the letter to reflect on the history and historiography of 'Brown' women like Mary Williamson in Jamaica and other Atlantic slave societies. Mary Williamson's letter offers a rare perspective on the sexual encounters between white men and brown women that were pervasive in Atlantic slave societies. Yet its primary focus is on the greater importance of ties of place and family – particularly of relations between sisters – in a context in which the 'severity' of slavery was increasing. Mary Williamson's letter is a single and thus-far not formally archived trace in a broader archive of Atlantic slavery dominated by material left by slaveholders and government officials. Paton asks what the possibilities and limits of such a document may be for generating knowledge about the lives and experiences of those who were born into slavery.

Hanover 26 Oct[r] 1809

Honoured Sir

I was a few years back a slave on your property of Houton Tower, and as a Brown woman was fancied by a Mr Tumming unto who Mr Thomas James sold me; on his leaving the Estate he took me with him to Trelawny, where he died, and left me very well situated. But Mr T. James purswaded me to return to Houton Tower as every relation I have in the world are there, so Sir by his perswasions I returned, and he appointed a place for me to build my house; accordingly I built a house, but finding it too small to contain me and two ~~black~~ Brown sisters I have on the Estate I build

*Revised subsequent to delivery. Many people have helped and supported me in the research and writing of this article. I extend particular thanks to Kate Chedgzoy, Jeanette Corniffe, Camillia Cowling, Nick Draper, Becky Goetz, Catherine Hall, Melissa James, Nicholas James, Tabitha James, Rachel Lang, Andrew Marr, Tracy Robinson, Gemma Romain, Cassia Roth, Matthew Smith, Emily West, Christine Whyte, participants in the Gender History Seminar at the University of Glasgow, and the anonymous reviewer for *Transactions of the Royal Historical Society*. Errors are, of course, my responsibility.

another for my self in particular, and was in all respects very comfortable; Untill Mr James's death. Then Mr Kircady the Overseer turned very severe on the Negroes on the property, and they could find no redress, for on Complaint to Mr Brown the Attorny[1] he punished them the more severely, that the poor critures are harrased out of their lives, many dying; On Mr John H. James coming to the Island he took a look at the Estate, but did not have the Negroes called up in the latter end of August, the Negroes went on a Sunday to Mr James at Green Island, seeking for redress, from there so severe usage for which reason, Mr Brown & Mr Kircady took it into there heads that I had perswaded the Negroes, to aply to Mr James, and early in the morning came and pulled down both my houses, and took away the Timbers; Now Honoured Sir as I was sold of the property free I mought have been disc[ou]raged, as having no property or wright what has my two Sisters and there young children no wright to a house on their Masters Estate, their children are young and left without a shelter.[2] I was a great help to them having a ground and garden with provisions which mought have been given to them, but it pleased your Attorny and Overseer to destroy every thing plowing up the garden and turning the Stocks into the ground or provisions, so that I am not only a sufferer but your poor negroes, are deprived, of the means of subsistence. Honoured Sir this is the truth and nothing but the truth, your negroes are harrased floged, and drove past human strength, with out any redress, to complain to an Uncle against his nephew is needless, it's not my own immediate case that make me address this to you, but my suffering family, who can not go otherwise as I am obliged to do.

Thus Sir I have laid down the state of Estate of Houton Tower, which if not soon redressed you will have no slaves, to work on the Estate. I must beg my Honoured Master, for to give me a little spot somewhere on the Estate, for I do not wish to go from my family, as they want every assistance I can give them; I feel for you Sir as if I was still you slave; and as Mr Kircady says he will make your people sup sorrow by spoonfuls, they really do for he [verifys] his words.

With all respect I am Honoured Master
Your most Obd' Humble Servant
Mary Williamson[3]

In 2016 I was contacted by a student, Tabitha James, who reported that she had been cataloguing 'my family's historical documents which I found in our attic', including material on Jamaica and slavery.[4] A few weeks later she brought me a bundle of around fifty documents including twenty-seven letters written by her relative, Haughton James, between

---

[1] 'Attorney' was the title of the most senior manager of an absentee-owned plantation – the person who held the owner's power of attorney and thus was legally entitled to make decisions on his or her behalf. Some managed multiple estates. On attorneys in Jamaica, see B. W. Higman, *Plantation Jamaica, 1750–1850: Capital and Control in a Colonial Economy* (Kingston, Jamaica, 2008).

[2] The *Oxford English Dictionary* gives 'mought' as a variant of may or might.

[3] Mary Williamson to Haughton James, 26 October 1809, private collection of Nicholas John Rhodes James, Argyll, (hereafter 'James collection') copy in author's possession. Thank you to the James family for lending me the letter and granting permission to quote from it. 'James' in notes refers to Haughton James.

[4] Tabitha James, email to author, 6 July 2016. The documents had been in the possession of Nicholas James since the 1960s, when he acquired them from the new residents of the house of a deceased relative.

1761 and 1812. The collection records James's voice and preoccupations over decades. Among James's many letters was the single letter from Mary Williamson reproduced above, which she in 1809 addressed to James in London.

Mary Williamson's letter brings to mind Carolyn Steedman's description of the archive as a place of social historians' dreams, where we hope and wish that 'ink on parchment can be made to speak'.[5] It gives us Williamson's signature (rather than 'her mark') (Figure 1), her stylish handwriting, her unorthodox spelling, her prose, her account of her life and relationships with others, and her insights into life at Haughton Tower. The dynamics of slave societies and the priorities of centuries of archiving have led, as Marisa Fuentes argues, to the systematic absence of sources 'written by … enslaved person[s] or from their perspective'.[6] In this context, Mary Williamson's letter is extraordinary.

Williamson's letter sheds light on many preoccupations of recent historians of slavery. In particular, it speaks to our understanding of white men's assumed sexual desire for 'brown' women; of the pervasive sexual coercion underpinning Atlantic slave societies; of plantation managers' use of violence; and of enslaved people's tactics in combatting that violence. The letter also suggests an avenue of enquiry that historians have neglected: the significance of connections among adult sisters, and, more generally, siblings. Discussions about the family lives of enslaved people, like those about family history more generally, have focused on parent–child and conjugal relationships. But when we look again at evidence from Jamaica and other slave societies, we see that Mary Williamson's important connections to her sisters were not unusual. This frequently lifelong affiliation, which often outlasted ties to parents, children or spouses, provided critical support and solidarity to many enslaved and freed people. Williamson's connection to a white man was merely one among many human connections, while 'family' meant, primarily, horizontal relationships among sisters. The historiography of the British Empire has increasingly emphasised the significance of extended family links in the organisation of imperial trade, government and culture. Empire families organised themselves through networks of siblings and cousins, parents and children, over large distances and across generations, circulating property and information; the James family is an excellent example.[7] Mary Williamson's letter

---

[5] Carolyn Steedman, *Dust* (Manchester, 2001), 70.

[6] Marisa J. Fuentes, *Dispossessed Lives: Enslaved Women, Violence, and the Archive* (Philadelphia, 2016), 147.

[7] For instance Margot Finn, 'Anglo-Indian Lives in the Later Eighteenth and Early Nineteenth Centuries', *Journal for Eighteenth-Century Studies*, 33 (2010), 49–65, https://doi.org/10.1111/j.1754-0208.2009.00210.x; Emma Rothschild, *The Inner Life of Empires: An*

Figure 1 Mary Williamson's signature on her letter to Haughton James. Reproduced with the permission of Melissa James.

suggests the parallel importance of extended family ties to enslaved and freed people in Jamaica.

Mary Williamson and Haughton James lived through a time of rapid change for Jamaica and its relationship to Britain. We don't know when Williamson was born, but James's life tracked the rise to dominance of Jamaica's sugar industry, as well as the period during which it began to be threatened. James's birth in 1738 took place shortly before the end of the long-standing war between British settlers and the Maroon communities who occupied the Jamaican interior.[8] After the war ended in British–Maroon treaties that provided security for both settlers and Maroons, the land devoted to sugar agriculture rapidly expanded, supplying an apparently limitless demand for the sweetener in Britain and beyond. Planter families like that into which James was born were well placed to take advantage of the boom. Sugar production increased rapidly, as did the importation of enslaved Africans, creating a society intensely dependent on racial slavery. The richest men in the British Empire built their wealth on Jamaican property, and most of all on property in intensely exploited human beings.[9] In 1810 Haughton James

Eighteenth-Century History (Princeton, 2011). For a related argument centred on the Netherlands, see Julia Adams, *The Familial State: Ruling Families and Merchant Capitalism in Early Modern Europe* (Ithaca, 2005).

[8] Hugh Paget, 'The Early History of the Family of James of Jamaica', *Jamaican Historical Review*, 1 (1948), 266.

[9] For recent analyses of Jamaica and its relationship to the British Empire and the wider Caribbean in this period, see Christer Petley, *White Fury: A Jamaican Slaveholder and the Age of Revolution* (Oxford, 2018), esp. 21–5; Trevor G. Burnard, *The Plantation Machine: Atlantic Capitalism in French Saint-Domingue and British Jamaica* (Philadelphia, 2016).

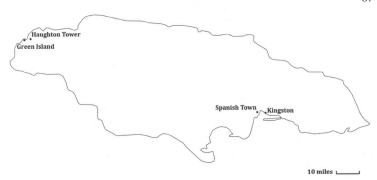

Figure 2 Map of Jamaica, 1804, showing location of Haughton Tower Estate. Map by Kacper Lyskiewicz.

owned 257 people who lived, enslaved, on Haughton Tower estate in the Western Jamaican parish of Hanover (Figure 2).[10]

When Mary Williamson wrote to Haughton James the year before, though, men like him whose wealth depended on Jamaican slavery could no longer feel certain that their power would persist indefinitely. The anti-slavery revolution in next-door Saint-Domingue and the establishment of the independent black republic of Haiti brought home the fact that the profits of sugar-based slavery could only be sustained through enormous levels of repression. Regular plots and rebellions in Jamaica also made this clear. A growing population of free people of colour – people like Mary Williamson – presented a challenge to the equation of whiteness and freedom on which Jamaican slavery was founded. In Britain, the movement against the slave trade had, after two decades of intense campaigning, recently succeeded in getting Parliament to pass the Act for the Abolition of the Slave Trade in 1807. The Act called into question the economic and social model on which Jamaica had been built. That model depended on access to endless supplies of enslaved Africans, often captives in war, who were brought across the Atlantic to take the places of those in Jamaica who died. Without an external source of population or a radical change in the organisation of everyday life, this system was on the verge of becoming unsustainable. Mary Williamson wrote to Haughton James at a time when everyone in Jamaica was responding to these new realities.[11]

---

[10] Jamaica Almanac 1811, cited at 'Haughton Tower Estate', Legacies of British Slave-ownership, www.ucl.ac.uk/lbs/estate/view/3152 (last accessed 23 July 2018) (hereafter LBS HT).

[11] On these developments, see Robin Blackburn, *The Overthrow of Colonial Slavery, 1776–1848* (1988); Brooke N. Newman, *A Dark Inheritance: Blood, Race, and Sex in Colonial Jamaica* (New

James received Williamson's letter as an old man of seventy-one. He had owned Haughton Tower estate since his father's death when he was only two years old.[12] James was born in Jamaica, descending on both sides from some of the earliest English colonists on the island.[13] His father and grandfather were resident planters and merchants. The younger James, though, left Jamaica at the age of seventeen to go to Oxford University, and seems never to have returned.[14] After a period on the 'Grand Tour', he sold his family's Spanish Town home, and settled permanently in Piccadilly.[15] James made the transition to absenteeism that was the goal of many landowning Jamaican families. Like many absentees, he managed his Jamaican property primarily through men to whom he was connected through kinship.[16]

It is unlikely, then, that Mary Williamson ever met Haughton James. Nevertheless, she knew who he was and how to send a letter to him, and thought it worth the trouble of doing so. Her life as a free woman had enabled her to become literate and to understand the conventions of letter writing and posting, but she introduced herself through her status as a former slave.[17] At the end of her letter, in order to drive home her appeal, she wrote that she 'feel[s] for you Sir as if I was still you[r] slave'. Williamson's phrasing drew on a discourse that asserted the ties of dependence and responsibility that allegedly bound master and slave, and infused these bonds with emotional rhetoric, hoping Haughton James would feel obliged to respond.

In contrast to our relatively abundant knowledge of Haughton James, we know little about Mary Williamson. We do not know when she was

Haven, 2018); Katherine Paugh, *The Politics of Reproduction: Race, Medicine, and Fertility in the Age of Abolition* (Oxford, 2017); Sasha Turner, *Contested Bodies: Pregnancy, Childrearing and Slavery in Jamaica, 1770–1834* (Philadelphia, 2017).

[12] Will of Haughton James (senior), 20 May 1737, James collection. Paget, 'Early History', 266.

[13] Haughton James's first name derived from his maternal family name.

[14] Paget, 'Early History'; H. W. Horton to James, 28 March 1760; James to M. James Esq., 15 July 1761 (from Venice). James to 'Dear Sir', 30 May 1765. James's will lists his residence as 'Piccadilly'. Will of Haughton James, 1813, Jamaican Family Search, www.jamaicanfamilysearch.com/Members/JamesWills&Inv.htm, Liber old series 87 folio 188, RGD (accessed 8 January 2018). In 1805 James wrote that he intended to visit Jamaica 'on account of my health'. James to William Rhodes James, 25 June 1805, James collection. I have not located any evidence that he made this visit.

[15] James to unnamed recipient, 30 May 1765, James collection.

[16] For absenteeism as white Jamaicans' aspiration, see Trevor Burnard, 'Passengers Only: The Intent and Significance of Absenteeism in Eighteenth Century Jamaica', *Atlantic Studies*, 1 (2004), 178–95, https://doi.org/10.1080/1478881042000278730. On the management of West Indian property through familial networks, see Hannah Young, 'Gender and Absentee Slave-Ownership in Late Eighteenth- and Early Nineteenth-Century Britain' (Ph.D. thesis, University College London, 2017).

[17] It is unclear when and how Williamson became literate. On Jamaican letters and post, see Higman, *Plantation Jamaica*, 115–26.

Figure 3 Part of Mary Williamson's letter, showing 'black' struck through and replaced with 'Brown'. Reproduced with the permission of Melissa James.

born, how she spent her adolescence and young adulthood, or who her parents were. The only clue to the latter is in her self-description as a 'Brown woman', which reveals that she had European as well as African ancestry. 'Brown' was and is a common Jamaican term for so-called 'mixed' descent. The only correction in Williamson's letter suggests the importance of the status difference between 'black' and 'brown', as well as the permeability of the boundary between them: in referring to her sisters, Williamson first wrote 'black', then crossed this out and instead wrote 'Brown', with an upper case B (Figure 3).

Williamson's birth into slavery means that her mother was certainly enslaved, since that status was transmitted through the maternal line. Her father, grandfather, or perhaps great-grandfather (or more than one of them), must have been a free white man. Perhaps – but this can be no more than speculation – he was the James Williamson who filed Haughton Tower's accounts in 1760 in his role as the estate's bookkeeper.[18] Whoever Mary's white ancestor was, he did not free his mixed-race child. Nor were Mary's 'brown' sisters freed by their white ancestor. This was not unusual. Birth rates of brown or 'coloured' children far exceeded manumission rates.[19] Some white men demonstrated concern for and interest in some of their mixed-race children, leaving them bequests in their wills and sending them to Britain to be educated. Collectively, white men only cared for a small minority of those whom they fathered.[20]

Williamson was not freed by her father, but wrote in 1809 as a free woman. By her own account, she acquired her freedom when she 'was sold of the property free' by the attorney, Thomas James, to Mr Tumming, who 'fancied' her. Two documents confirm this in broad

[18] Accounts Produce, Jamaica Archives 1B/11/4/3 165, cited at LBS HT. Thanks to Nick Draper for drawing this to my attention. A bookkeeper was a low-level estate manager.

[19] Barry Higman, *Slave Population and Economy in Jamaica, 1807–1834* (Kingston, Jamaica, 1995), 141.

[20] Newman, *A Dark Inheritance*, 148. On the minority of mixed-race Jamaicans whose fathers provided for them, see Daniel Livesay, *Children of Uncertain Fortune: Mixed-Race Jamaicans in Britain and the Atlantic Family, 1733–1833* (Chapel Hill, 2018).

outline though not specifics: the will of James Tumming of Hanover, and Mary Williamson's manumission record. According to these documents, Tumming never bought Williamson, who was still owned by Haughton James when Tumming died. In his will, Tumming left £100 sterling to 'Mary Williamson belonging to Haugton [sic] Tower Estate in the parish of Hanover the property of Haughton James'. The money was to be paid to her twelve months after Tumming's death 'for the purpose of purchasing her manumission'.[21]

Using this money, Mary Williamson acquired her legal freedom. Her manumission document, dated 6 November 1802, records Haughton James's declaration that 'I ... have Manumized Enfranchised and forever set [Mary Williamson] free.'[22] Using formulaic language that appears repeatedly in Jamaican manumission records, the deed defines Williamson's freedom as being 'of and from all manner of Slavery Servitude and Bondage to whatsoever which my heirs executors and administrators ... could or might Claim Challenge or Demand'. Williamson's manumission, like all manumissions, had to be recorded to protect her against future claims of ownership by her former owner's family.[23] Despite the document's rhetorical benevolence, from the point of view of Haughton James and his attorney Thomas James this was a commercial transaction, little different to a sale. The Jameses received £140 in Jamaican currency – equal to the £100 sterling that James Tumming had left Williamson – as 'consideration money' for Williamson's freedom.[24] With £140, the Jameses would have been able to replace Williamson with another enslaved person, and probably have money left over. The sum was at the high end of the range of prices for enslaved people in Jamaica in the first decade of the nineteenth

---

[21] Will of James Tumming, proved 14 June 1803, Jamaica General Records Department, Wills, volume 72 folio 22. Thanks to Jeanette Corniffe for locating and transcribing this will.

[22] Manumissions liber 29 f 131, Jamaica Archives, Spanish Town, 1B/11/6. Williamson was manumitted before Tumming's will was proved, suggesting a delay in probate.

[23] On the process of manumission and the formulae used in Jamaican manumission deeds, see David Beck Ryden, 'Manumission in Late Eighteenth-Century Jamaica', *New West Indian Guide / Nieuwe West-Indische Gids*, 92 (2018), 219, https://doi.org/10.1163/22134360-09203054.

[24] Ibid. The money was paid 'on behalf of' Williamson by 'Daniel Burnard', probably Thomas James's nephew Daniel Bernard of Content, St James, to whom James bequeathed three enslaved people. Will of Thomas James, proved 22 January 1805, Liber old series Wills 74 folio 29, Jamaican Family Search, www.jamaicanfamilysearch.com/Members/JamesRichardWills.htm#Thomas (last accessed 23 July 2018). Neither Jamaican Family Search nor Legacies of British Slave-ownership include any Jamaican residents with the last name Burnard. For conversion rates see T. C. Hansard, *Parliamentary Debates*, 27 February 1810, vol. 17 (1812), cols. cccxiv–cccxv. The presence of an intermediary was standard practice in Jamaican manumissions. Ryden, 'Manumission', 220.

century, usually charged for Jamaican-born people aged between twenty and thirty.[25]

I have not located any further information about Tumming, but it is safe to assume that he was white. Mary Williamson's statement that 'as a Brown woman' she was 'fancied by' him, without describing his race, suggests whiteness, in the context of the deeply engrained Jamaican assumption that white men would be attracted to brown women. For her and, she assumes, for Haughton James too, it is self-evident that 'as a Brown woman' she would be 'fancied' by a white man, and that this 'fancying' would lead to her sale to the man in question. Williamson presents this transaction as normal and unremarkable. The absence of racial designation in Tumming's will also suggests that he was white.

The discrepancies between the account in Williamson's letter and in the manumission record and will suggest that Tumming's claims on Williamson during his lifetime were informally negotiated between him and Haughton James, who continued to be her legal owner. Williamson's views on and experience of the situation are hard to discern. However, Tumming's testamentary insistence that she not receive the money to buy her freedom until a year after his death suggests that he wanted to maintain control of her from beyond the grave. Williamson's description of herself as having been 'sold ... free' is thus revealingly descriptive of the in-between status she experienced through her relationship with Tumming, something she shared with people on the path to manumission in many slave societies.[26]

Mary Williamson's life followed a trajectory that is familiar to the point of cliché. By the late eighteenth century and into the nineteenth, the figure of the mixed-race enslaved or freed woman who is sexually

---

[25] Higman, *Slave Population and Economy*, 190–5, 202.

[26] Studies of manumission across slave societies emphasise the fragility and conditionality of freed status, including dependence of the manumitted on those who supported them in acquiring freedom. See, for example, Sue Peabody, *Madeleine's Children: Family, Freedom, Secrets, and Lies in France's Indian Ocean Colonies* (Oxford, 2017); Christine Hünefeldt, *Paying the Price of Freedom: Family and Labor among Lima's Slaves, 1800–1854* (Berkeley, 1994); Douglas Cole Libby and Clotilde Andrade Paiva, 'Manumission Practices in a Late Eighteenth-Century Brazilian Slave Parish: São José d'El Rey in 1795', *Slavery & Abolition* 21 (2000), 96–127, https://doi.org/10.1080/01440390008575297; Sidney Chalhoub, 'The Politics of Ambiguity: Conditional Manumission, Labor Contracts, and Slave Emancipation in Brazil (1850s–1888)', *International Review of Social History*, 60 (2015), 161–91, https://doi.org/10.1017/S0020859015000176; Rosemary Brana-Shute, 'Approaching Freedom: The Manumission of Slaves in Suriname, 1760–1828', *Slavery & Abolition*, 10 (1989), 40–63, https://doi.org/10.1080/01440398908574991; R. Zelnick-Abramovitz, *Not Wholly Free: The Concept of Manumission and the Status of Manumitted Slaves in the Ancient Greek World* (Leiden, 2005), 218–22; Mary C. Karasch, *Slave Life in Rio de Janeiro, 1808–1850* (Princeton, 1987), 335–61.

involved with a white man was everywhere in writing about slave societies. Planter intellectuals like Médéric Louis Élie Moreau de Saint-Méry, Edward Long and Bryan Edwards viewed white men's attraction to mixed-race women as a problem to be solved.[27] Nineteenth-century novels from and about the Caribbean almost without exception included examples of such relationships, often presenting them as romantic but doomed.[28] In visual culture, paintings by Agostino Brunias emphasised the desirability of the mixed-race woman.[29] All of these, and many other fictional, non-fictional and visual representations of Atlantic slave societies, place sex between white men and enslaved or freed mixed-race women at the heart of their depictions of slave society. As Lisa Ze Winters has recently argued, the figure of the 'free(d) mulatta concubine' was 'constitutive of the African diaspora'.[30]

Many of these and other depictions of mixed-race women disavowed what was also known about slave societies: that they were worlds in which women experienced pervasive sexual coercion, from their enslavement in Africa, through the decks and holds of slave ships, and on the plantations and in the towns of the Americas.[31] It was within this culture of assumed

[27] Edward Long, *The History of Jamaica, or General Survey of the Antient and Modern State of That Island: With Reflections on Its Situations, Settlements, Inhabitants, Climate, Products, Commerce, Laws, and Government* (London: T. Lowndes, 1774), II, 326–30; Bryan Edwards, *The History, Civil and Commercial, of the West Indies: With a Continuation to the Present Time* (1819; repr., Cambridge, 2010), II, 25–7; M. L. E. Moreau de Saint-Méry, *Description topographique, physique, civile, politique et historique de la partie française de l'isle Saint-Domingue*, ed. Blanche Maurel and Etienne Taillemite, vol. 1 (1797; repr., Paris, 1984), 106–7.

[28] Several examples have been recently republished. See Anon., *The Woman of Colour*, ed. Lyndon J. Dominique (1808; repr., Peterborough, Ontario, 2007); Anon., *Marly: Or, a Planter's Life in Jamaica*, ed. Karina Williamson (1828; repr., Oxford, 2005); Cynric R. Williams, *Hamel, the Obeah Man*, ed. Candace Ward and Tim Watson (1827; repr., Peterborough, Ontario, 2010); J. W. Orderson, *Creoleana, Or, Social and Domestic Scenes and Incidents in Barbados in Days of Yore: And The Fair Barbadian and Faithful Black, Or, a Cure for the Gout*, ed. John Gilmore (1842; repr., Oxford, 2002); Anon., *Adolphus: A Tale* (1853), and Mary Fanny Wilkins, *The Slave Son* (1854), ed. Lisa Winer (Mona, Jamaica, 2001). For analysis of many of these texts see Sara Salih, *Representing Mixed Race in Jamaica and England from the Abolition Era to the Present* (New York, 2010).

[29] Mia L. Bagneris, *Colouring the Caribbean: Race and the Art of Agostino Brunias* (Manchester, 2018), 136–75; Kay Dian Kriz, *Slavery, Sugar, and the Culture of Refinement: Picturing the British West Indies, 1700–1840* (New Haven, 2008), 37–69.

[30] Lisa Ze Winters, *The Mulatta Concubine: Terror, Intimacy, Freedom, and Desire in the Black Transatlantic* (Athens, GA, 2015), 14. See also Patricia Mohammed, '"But Most of All Mi Love Me Browning": The Emergence in Eighteenth- and Nineteenth-Century Jamaica of the Mulatto Woman as the Desired', *Feminist Review*, 65 (2000), 22–48, https://doi.org/10.1080/014177800406921.

[31] Important works on sexual violence under slavery in the Americas include Angela Davis, 'Reflections on the Black Woman's Role in the Community of Slaves', *The Black Scholar*, 3 (1971), 2–15, https://doi.org/10.1080/00064246.1971.11431201; Darlene Clark Hine, 'Rape and the Inner Lives of Black Women in the Middle West: Preliminary Thoughts on the Culture of Dissemblance', *Signs*, 14 (1989), 912–20; Nell Irvin Painter,

white male sexual entitlement that James Tumming and Mary Williamson became ... well, what did they become? There are no neutral words to describe what Williamson was to Tumming, or he to her. Historians have chosen from among a series of unsatisfactory terms for Williamson's position, including concubine, paramour, mistress, mate, housekeeper, lover, partner or (occasionally and recently) sex slave; and have described the connections and encounters between men and women like Tumming and Williamson as liaisons, relationships, unions, partnerships, affairs, concubinage, interracial sex, marriages, and rapes.[32] The language available tends to fall on one side or the other of a binary division between choice and coercion that fails to convey the complexity of the context and situations that it is used to name. 'Partner' or 'lover' suggests a relative equality that is not attested to by the documents or historical context; 'concubine' and 'paramour' are too easily read as exoticising and Orientalist. 'Housekeeper', the term most widely used in this period in Jamaica, 'served', Brooke Newman points out, 'as a discursive sleight of hand' to disguise 'deeply exploitative relationships between men and women who occupied asymmetrical racial, social, and gender positions'.[33] 'Rape' often accurately describes specific incidents of sex in societies dominated by slavery, but we know too little about Williamson's interactions with Tumming to be confident using it in that context. Historians cannot avoid choosing terms to name the phenomena that we write about, yet our choices inevitably imply conclusions about the extent and significance of inequality, choice and coercion within those contexts. This is so even when we write in order to raise

'Three Southern Women and Freud: A Non-Exceptionalist Approach to Race, Class, and Gender in the Slave South', in *Feminists Revision History*, ed. Ann-Louise Shapiro (New Brunswick, 1994), 195–216. On the slave ship as a space of sexual violence see Sowande' M. Mustakeem, *Slavery at Sea: Terror, Sex, and Sickness in the Middle Passage* (Urbana, 2016), 86–90; Marcus Rediker, *The Slave Ship: A Human History* (New York, 2007), 152, 179.

[32] For these terms, see, among many other sources, Higman, *Slave Population and Economy* (mates, unions, relationships); Livesay, *Children of Uncertain Fortune* (paramour, mistress); Paugh, *The Politics of Reproduction* (liaisons, concubinage, relationships); Philip D. Morgan, 'Interracial Sex in the Chesapeake and the British Atlantic World, c. 1700–1820', in *Sally Hemings & Thomas Jefferson: History, Memory, and Civic Culture*, ed. Peter S. Onuf and Jan Ellis Lewis (Charlottesville, 1999), 52–84 (affair, liaison, mistress, interracial sex, lovers); Christer Petley, '"Legitimacy" and Social Boundaries: Free People of Colour and the Social Order in Jamaican Slave Society', *Social History*, 30 (2005), 481–98, https://doi. org/10.1080/03071020500304627 (concubine, mistress, partner, partnership); Lucille Mathurin Mair, *A Historical Study of Women in Jamaica, 1655–1844* (Mona, Jamaica, 2006) (concubinage, mistress); Trevor Burnard, '"Do Thou in Gentle Phibia Smile": Scenes from an Interracial Marriage, Jamaica, 1754–1786', in *Beyond Bondage: Free Women of Color in the Americas*, ed. David Barry Gaspar and Darlene C. Hine (Urbana, 2004) (marriage); Bagneris, *Colouring the Caribbean* (housekeeper, partner, rape). 'Sex slave' has been used in this context in an unpublished article that I do not have permission to cite.

[33] Newman, *A Dark Inheritance*, 147.

questions about that inequality, choice and coercion. Bearing these points in mind, here I use 'connection' or 'relationship' as the most neutral terms possible, and without prejudging the nature of Mary Williamson and James Tumming's connection and relationship.

The pioneering Jamaican historian Lucille Mathurin Mair presented a common view in describing women like Williamson as 'females slaves' who 'unquestionably benefited from their intimate associations with whites, which facilitated the granting and the purchasing of freedom'.[34] More recent studies have complicated this interpretation, emphasising that, as Sue Peabody puts it, 'one of the master's essential prerogatives' in slave societies across the world 'was sexual access to his female servants and slaves' and that as a result enslaved women never 'consent[ed] as a peer'.[35] More broadly, sexual access to enslaved women was the prerogative of all white men, as long as the women's owners did not object. Even defenders of slavery sometimes admitted this. For instance, a naval officer stationed in Jamaica agreed that it was 'common when an English gentleman visits a planter's estate to have offered to him black girls', although he sought to reintroduce the question of consent by stating that the 'girls' were 'not constrained to come'.[36] Peabody adds that some women could negotiate specific benefits in this context, sometimes including freedom for themselves and (more commonly) their children.[37] Such negotiations constituted a specific form of what Deniz Kandiyoti refers to as 'bargaining with patriarchy' in which women 'strategize within a set of concrete constraints ... to maximize security and optimize life options'.[38]

Whatever term we use to describe it, we cannot know whether Mary Williamson actively sought out her connection with James Tumming, or if, on the other hand, he used, threatened or hinted at the possibility of physical force or other negative consequences to compel her sexual compliance. Or, indeed, whether both these dynamics were in play. Rather, in the power-laden context in which their relationship began, in which he had freedom and financial resources and she was a slave, it makes little

---

[34] Mair, *Historical Study*, 272.

[35] Peabody, *Madeleine's Children*, 47. See also Fuentes, *Dispossessed Lives*, 49.

[36] 'Report from Select Committee on the Extinction of Slavery throughout the British Dominions', PP 1831–32 (721) XX, Evidence of Charles Hamden Williams, p. 288.

[37] Peabody, *Madeleine's Children*, 63. For a similar argument that addresses the complexity of 'sexual–economic exchange' between white men and women of colour in similar Jamaican contexts, see Meleisa Ono-George, '"Washing the Blackamoor White": Interracial Intimacy and Coloured Women's Agency in Jamaica', in *Subverting Empire: Deviance and Disorder in the British Colonial World*, ed. Will Jackson and Emily J. Manktelow (Basingstoke, 2015), 42–60.

[38] Deniz Kandiyoti, 'Bargaining with Patriarchy', *Gender and Society*, 2 (1988), 274, https://doi.org/10.1177/089124388002003004.

sense to frame a sexual relationship between them in terms of the presence or absence of choice or consent, let alone of her sexual desire or satisfaction. As Saidiya Hartman puts it, 'concepts of consent and will' become 'meaningless' in the context of slavery.[39] Moreoever, these are terms that themselves need to be historicised.[40] The irrelevance of a framework focused on choice and consent is clear from the letter, which does not invoke these terms or any related concept in describing Williamson's connection to Tumming. Instead Williamson presents herself as, literally, a commodity: he fancied her, bought her (or bought her freedom), took her with him, and that was that.

Williamson noted that her connection to Mr Tumming, a man who was not her owner, had led to important material consequences. But when their relationship began, her freedom was by no means certain. In making a 'bargain with patriarchy', that is, Williamson had no means of ensuring that the other side of the bargain would be kept. Another contemporary Jamaican example provides a sense of alternative outcomes. In 1800 Annie, an enslaved woman living on Rozelle (also spelled Roselle) estate, St Thomas in the East, was pregnant with her fifth child. Archibald Cameron, the overseer and the children's father, proposed to the estate owners that he pay £360 sterling (around £500 Jamaican currency), much more than the cost of Mary Williamson's manumission, for Annie and her children. Annie's owners initially told him that this was not enough; they asked for a payment equivalent to the cost of a 'prime slave' – around the £100 sterling paid for Williamson – for each individual purchased, of whatever age, plus £10 for Annie's unborn child.[41] This would have totalled £510 sterling, an enormous sum, which Cameron said he could not afford. The next letter that mentions Annie, five years later, states that Mr Cameron 'changed his mind' and did not complete the purchase, and that Annie was in the local workhouse (prison) because she had created a 'very unpleasant situation for some time past' on the estate.[42] The letters provide no details of this 'unpleasant situation', but it is easy to imagine that Annie responded with anger and a sense of betrayal, both at Cameron's refusal or inability to free her and at the

---

[39] Saidiya V. Hartman, *Scenes of Subjection: Terror, Slavery, and Self-Making in Nineteenth-Century America* (New York, 1997), 81.

[40] For a history of 'consent' in the context of marriage, see Emily S. Burrill, *States of Marriage: Gender, Justice, and Rights in Colonial Mali* (Athens, GA, 2015). Thanks to Christine Whyte for this reference.

[41] Adam Ferguson to Hugh Hamilton 12 June 1800, Hamilton of Pinmore Muniments, National Records of Scotland (hereafter HPM), GD 142/35/9. The letter hints at the possibility that Ferguson might have been prepared to accept a lower offer, but it is not clear if this was ever put to Cameron. For another account of these letters see Eric J. Graham, *Burns & the Sugar Plantocracy of Ayrshire* (Ayr, 2009), 56–7.

[42] Adam Ferguson to Hugh Hamilton, 23 June 1805, HPM, GD 142/35/2.

estate's insistence on such a high price. In the context of a historiography that often frames women's involvement in relationships like Annie's with Mr Cameron, or Mary Williamson's with James Tumming, as calculating moves that led to their freedom, it is important to recognise the circumstances in which women did not become free, alongside the precariousness of freedom when it was gained.[43]

The situation of an enslaved woman named Catherine Williams provides further context for understanding the constraints surrounding Mary Williamson's connection to James Tumming. Catherine Williams's circumstances suggest what might have happened should Williamson have refused to be the object of Tumming's 'fancy'. Williams was a member of a missionary congregation in Jamaica in the late 1820s and 1830s. She was flogged and imprisoned because (as a missionary put it) 'the overseer wanted her to live with him in a state of fornication, and ... she would not do it'.[44] Abolitionists publicised the case by framing it in moral terms, suggesting that Catherine Williams refused the overseer because she was a Christian convert. No doubt this was important. But this evidence also suggests the possibility, and the consequences, of not taking the path that Mary Williamson took, and thus the limits both of Williamson's choice and her opportunity. Catherine Williams's story demonstrates that, although being 'fancied' by a white man could lead to free status, an enslaved woman who was the object of a white man's desire had as much choice in what happened next as did an enslaved man instructed to boil sugar. In either case, someone might comply hoping to improve their life; they might gain pleasure or satisfaction from doing so. Another individual in similar circumstances might resist or refuse – and that refusal or resistance would likely have consequences. Like the work of boiling sugar, the affective, intimate and sexual labour of Mary Williamson and women like her was integral to the functioning of Atlantic slave systems.[45]

Like most people in their circumstances, Mary Williamson and James Tumming did not marry. As one observer put it, it was 'not the custom of the country' for brown women to marry white men.[46] This 'custom' of

---

[43] For further examples of situations in which plantation owners 'did not ... follow through' on requests to free enslaved women in sexual relationships with white men, and their children, see Newman, *A Dark Inheritance*, 157–8.

[44] 'Report from Select Committee', PP 1831–32 (721) XX Evidence of William Knibb, p. 251.

[45] For a parallel argument regarding the significance of women's affective labour in the functioning of another colonial context see Durba Ghosh, *Sex and the Family in Colonial India* (Cambridge, 2006).

[46] John Stewart, *A View of the Past and Present State of the Island of Jamaica; with Remarks on the Moral and Physical Condition of the Slaves, and on the Abolition of Slavery in the Colonies* (Edinburgh, 1823), 327.

non-marital relationships made brown women's freedom limited and vulnerable.[47] When Tumming died, Williamson did not inherit sufficient property to become financially secure. The residue of Tumming's estate went to his two sons, Henry and James Tumming. His will does not mention their mother, but it is unlikely that they were Mary Williamson's children. If they had been, they would have been enslaved and Tumming would have needed to provide for their manumission. That they bear his name also suggests that they were the children of marriage to a white woman. Tumming thus followed the widespread white Jamaican inheritance practice made possible by the fact that white–brown relationships did not involve marriage.[48] Married men could not easily disinherit their wives, but men who lived with women without marrying them were not obliged to provide for them in their wills.[49] Mary Williamson's self-description as 'well situated' obscures her relative poverty, which may have been one reason she moved back to Haughton Tower.

For all its resonance with both historians' and popular understandings of slavery, Mary Williamson's connection to James Tumming was only one element of her story, and not even the most important. Her letter emphasises her place within a broader world of human relationships. It demonstrates that the ties that connected her to her family of birth were of the utmost practical and emotional significance. She chose to move back to the site of her own enslavement because of family ties: because 'every relation I have in the world are there'. Especially important was her connection with her two sisters. After Tumming's death they were her community, the people she wanted to be close to. She lacked the resources to free her sisters, but was able to support them materially by ensuring that they had good-quality housing. She notes that she was 'a great help to them having a ground and garden', and that she grew and supplied them with provisions. In Jamaica, enslaved people worked long

[47] Michelle A. McKinley, *Fractional Freedoms: Slavery, Intimacy, and Legal Mobilization in Colonial Lima, 1600–1700* (Cambridge, 2016), explores such 'fractional freedom' in the context of urban colonial Peru.

[48] For analysis of wills that demonstrates this practice, see Petley, '"Legitimacy" and Social Boundaries'. Raymond T. Smith argues that these familial practices provided the foundation for the contemporary Jamaican 'dual marriage system' in which wealthier men marry women of their own class while having long-standing non-marital relationships with women of lower class background and darker skin. *Kinship and Class in the West Indies: A Genealogical Study of Jamaica and Guyana* (Cambridge, 1988), 82–108. It seems likely that Williamson played this role of 'outside' sexual partner in Tumming's life.

[49] In England, James adopted a variant of this inheritance practice. He died, unmarried, in 1813, without acknowledged children. He left Haughton Tower and the bulk of his estate to William Rhodes James IV, his first cousin's grandson. He also left a £250 annuity to 'Miss Sarah Read commonly called Mrs Kingston' of Park Lane, London, and gave one-off sums to several other women. Will of James (n. 14 above).

hours to produce sugar and other staple crops. But they also depended on the subsistence food crops they raised in hours squeezed around the edges of the staple crop working week.[50] In such a context, having a free relative who was not compelled to do plantation labour and who could devote more of her time to growing food could have made a significant difference to Williamson's sisters' quality of life and level of nutrition. An individual woman's connection to a white man could have long-term consequences not just for her, but for her broader network of kin.[51]

Sisterhood has been a powerful metaphor in the study of slavery ever since the abolitionists used the slogan 'am I not a woman and a sister'.[52] But this slogan is generally understood as a metaphor about connections and solidarities, including hierarchical ones, among women who were not literally kin. Mary Williamson's relationship with her sisters directs us to the more literal meaning of sisterhood. It reveals an aspect of enslaved people's family lives that is hard to see in the routine administrative documents of Caribbean slavery. These documents include repetitive lists of slaves, series of names that were created to clarify and facilitate the ownership and management of people.[53] Such lists tell us little about the lives and relationships of the people named. Sometimes they include mother–child relationships, because those who owned enslaved people were interested in understanding the 'increase' of their property. The Haughton Tower document 'Increase of Slaves … from the 1st January 1822 to the 1st January 1823', listing in tabular form the women who had babies with the dates of birth, names and sex of those babies, is typical of the genre (Figure 4). Such documents can enable historians to identify groups of children with the same mother, although not easily: they do not highlight these relationships, certainly not into adulthood. Nor have historians paid much attention to sibling relationships, either in slave societies or elsewhere, perhaps because we also struggle to look beyond the logics of property that led to the creation of the records.[54]

[50] Sidney W. Mintz, 'The Origins of the Jamaican Market System', in *Caribbean Transformations* (Baltimore, 1974); Roderick A. McDonald, *The Economy and Material Culture of Slaves: Goods and Chattels on the Sugar Plantations of Jamaica and Louisiana* (Baton Rouge, 1993).

[51] Thank you to Camillia Cowling for discussion on this point.

[52] For analysis of this metaphor and the abolitionist rhetoric of sisterhood, see Clare Midgley, 'British Abolition and Feminism in Transatlantic Perspective', in *Women's Rights and Transatlantic Antislavery in the Era of Emancipation*, ed. Kathryn Kish Sklar and James Brewer Stewart (New Haven, 2007), 134–5.

[53] On the role of such documents in the broader development of management and accountancy practices, see Caitlin Rosenthal, *Accounting for Slavery: Masters and Management* (Cambridge, MA, 2018).

[54] For exceptions see C. Dallett Hemphill, *Siblings: Brothers and Sisters in American History* (Oxford, 2011); Leonore Davidoff, *Thicker than Water: Siblings and Their Relations, 1780–1920* (Oxford, 2012). Recent scholarship focusing on extended imperial families has begun to

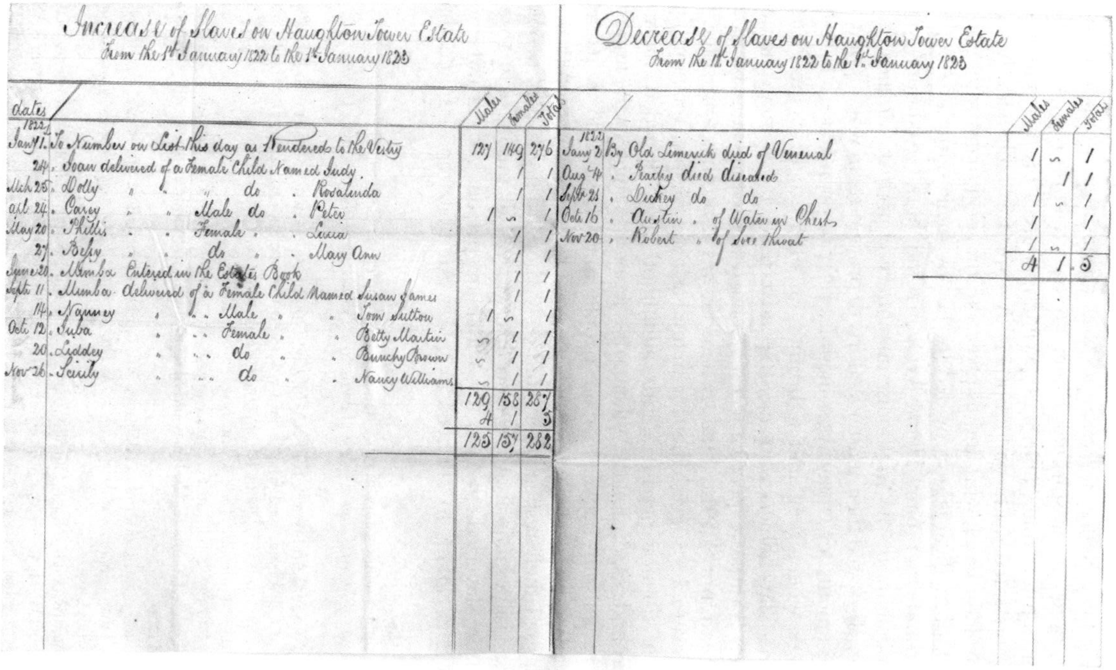

Increase of Slaves on Haughton Tower Estate
From the 1st January 1822 to the 1st January 1823

dates 1822		Males	Females	Total
Jany 1.	To Number on List this day as Rendered to the Vestry	127	149	276
24.	Joan delivered of a Female Child Named Judy		1	1
Mch 25.	Dolly " " " do . Rosalinda		1	1
Apl 24.	Carey " " Male do . Peter	1	"	1
May 20.	Phillis . . Female . . Lucia		1	1
27.	Betsy . . do . . Mary Ann		1	1
June 20.	Mimba Entered in the Estates Book		1	1
Septr 11.	Mimba delivered of a Female Child Named Susan James		1	1
14.	Nanney . . . Male . . Tom Sutton	1	"	1
Octr 12.	Suba . . . Female . . Betty Martin	"	1	1
20.	Liddey . . . do . . Bunchy Brown	"	1	1
Nov 26.	Scicily . . . do . . Nancy Williams	"	1	1
		129	158	287
		4	1	5
		125	157	282

Decrease of Slaves on Haughton Tower Estate
From the 1st January 1822 to the 1st January 1823

1822		Males	Females	Totals
Jany 2	By Old Limerick died of Venereal	1	"	1
Aug 4.	Peachy died diseased		1	1
Septr 25.	Dickey do do	1	"	1
Octr 16.	Austin . of Water in Chest	1		1
Nov 20.	Robert . of Sore Throat	1	"	1
		4	1	5

Figure 4 Increase of Slaves on Haughton Tower Estate from the 1st January 1822 to the 1st January 1823. Reproduced with the permission of Melissa James.

Nevertheless, Mary Williamson's letter is far from unique in high-lighting the significance of sibling bonds. Other documents provide examples of enslaved siblings in Jamaica helping and supporting one another. Jane Henry, for example, was an enslaved woman who in 1831 sought out a spiritual healer to try to cure her sick adult brother.[55] John Nunes and Sarah Williams were a brother and sister who cooperated with one another to care for their elderly sick mother, Tabitha Hewitt, and to protest to the local magistrates about the lack of medical care provided for her by their master.[56] Another brother-and-sister pair, Henry Williams and Sarah Atkinson, were both members of the Methodist missionary church in Jamaica, and together protested their master's efforts to prevent them worshipping.[57] Advertisements for runaways sometimes refer to people as likely to be in places where they had a brother or sister, such as the North Carolina slaveholder who in 1814 advertised for a man named Spencer: 'I rather expect he will make his way for the Catawba river, in the extremity of this State, where he has a brother and sister.'[58] These examples suggest that for many enslaved people, relationships between siblings persisted into adulthood and provided mutual support and responsibility. Williamson's letter also suggests the import-ance of kinship between freed people and those who remained enslaved. While some free people of colour built a community that emphasised their respectability and distinction from enslaved people, the less-visible majority were more like Mary Williamson: only a step away from slavery themselves, and with many personal, social and emo-tional connections to enslaved people.[59] An 1826 report stated that

examine sibling relationships in more depth. For examples see Catherine Hall, *Macaulay and Son: Architects of Imperial Britain* (New Haven, 2012), esp. 113–38; Rothschild, *The Inner Life of Empires*.

[55] The National Archives, UK (TNA) CO 137/209 Sligo to Glenelg No 315, 28 July 1831, available at Caribbean Religious Trials: www.caribbeanreligioustrials.org/Case/Details/ 827. For discussion, see Diana Paton, *The Cultural Politics of Obeah: Religion, Colonialism and Modernity in the Caribbean World* (Cambridge, 2015), 106–8.

[56] TNA CO 137/236 Oldrey to Sir George Grey, 22 June 1838. For discussion, see Diana Paton, 'Gender, Language, Violence and Slavery: Insult in Jamaica, 1800–1838', *Gender and History*, 18 (2006), 246–65.

[57] PP 1830–31 (91) Goderich to Belmore No 9, 9 December 1830, pp. 19–22. For analysis see Mary Turner, *Slaves and Missionaries: The Disintegration of Jamaican Slave Society, 1787–1834* (Urbana, 1982), 134–6.

[58] *The Star* (Raleigh, North Carolina), 26 August 1814, North Carolina Runaway Slave Advertisements, 1750–1840, http://libcdm1.uncg.edu/cdm/singleitem/collection/RAS/ id/2144/rec/6 (last accessed 1 August 2018). Hemphill calculates that at least one-third of runaway advertisements suggested the runaway was heading towards family, of which many (though he doesn't state how many) were siblings. *Siblings*, 192.

[59] On some Jamaican free people of colour's search for respectability see Meleisa Ono-George, '"By Her Unnatural and Despicable Conduct": Motherhood and Concubinage in

more than three-quarters of Jamaican free people of colour were 'absolutely poor'.[60]

In order to be close to her family, then, Mary Williamson moved back to Haughton Tower estate, where she lived as a free woman, in her own house, with access to a provision ground, and in close proximity to her sisters, nieces and nephews. No evidence survives of exactly where on the estate Williamson's house and those of her sisters were located; most likely they were part of a group of houses on a slope leading up from the estate's sugar works, labelled on an early nineteenth-century estate map as 'land occupied by the Negroe houses' (Figure 5). By the time Williamson wrote to Haughton James in late 1809 she had been living near her sisters on Haughton Tower as a free woman for at least five years.[61]

Previously at least partially dependent on Tumming, on her return to Haughton Tower Mary Williamson became dependent on the goodwill of another white man, this time Thomas James, Haughton James's cousin and the estate's attorney.[62] It was he who 'purswaded' her to go back to Haughton Tower, and allowed her to build her house there. When Thomas died in late 1804 or early 1805 his elderly brother, William Rhodes James, became the new attorney and either appointed or reaffirmed William Kirkaldy as overseer. William Rhodes James himself died in 1807; he was replaced by a Mr Brown.[63] Around this time, the situation took a dramatic turn for the worse. As Williamson put it, now 'Mr Kircady the Overseer turned very severe on the Negroes on the property.' Kirkaldy's severity was supported by

the *Watchman and Jamaica Free Press*, 1830–1833', *Slavery & Abolition* 38 (2017), 356–72, https://doi.org/10.1080/0144039X.2017.1317029. On the variety of economic situations of free people of colour, see Petley, '"Legitimacy" and Social Boundaries', 486.

[60] Charles H. Wesley, 'The Emancipation of the Free Colored Population in the British Empire', *The Journal of Negro History*, 19 (1934), 137–70, https://doi.org/10.2307/2714530 citing TNA CO 318/76.

[61] I date the latest point for Williamson's return to Haughton Tower from the fact that her letter states that Thomas James persuaded her to return there, and his will was proved in January 1805. Will of Thomas James (n. 24 above).

[62] Thomas James was Haughton Tower attorney in 1800. Jamaica Accounts Produce, cited at LBS HT.

[63] James to William Rhodes James (II), 30 March 1805, and James to 'Gentlemen', 30 March 1805, James collection. These letters show that Thomas and William Rhodes James were brothers, and cousins of Haughton. William Rhodes James, born in 1733, is listed as attorney, and Kirkaldy as overseer, in Accounts Produce 1807. Kirkcaldy would become attorney for Haughton Tower estate when it was owned by William Rhodes James IV (grandson of William Rhodes James II) after James's death. He filed accounts in that role in 1820 and 1823. LBS HT; 'William Rhodes James II', LBS, www.ucl.ac.uk/lbs/person/view/2146650331 (last accessed 12 November 2018). Will of Haughton James (n. 14 above). For Mr Brown as attorney see, in addition to Williamson's letter, John H. James to [James], 7 September 1809, James collection. Mr Brown may have been the William Brown who served as an executor of Thomas James's will (n. 24 above).

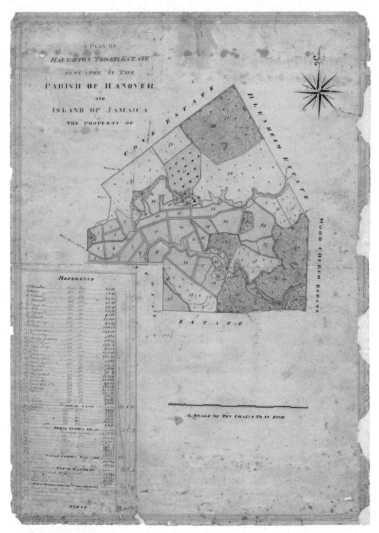

Figure 5 A Plan of Haughton Tower Estate situated in the parish of Hanover, the property of William Rhodes James Esquire. This plan dates from the early nineteenth century. Mary Williamson's house was probably in the steeply sloping area labelled 15, close to the sugar works. The area is described in the legend as 'land occupied by the Negroe houses'. Courtesy of National Library of Jamaica.

Mr Brown, who refused to recognise the Haughton Tower residents' grievances, instead inflicting violence on them ['punishing them'] for complaining. Williamson stated that enslaved people on Haughton Tower were 'harrased floged, and drove past human strength, with out any redress'; and that Mr Kirkaldy threatened to 'make your people sup sorrow by spoonfuls'. Kirkaldy and Brown installed a new regime that relied more openly on terror and violence than before.

This change went beyond variation among management styles. The turn to 'severity' on Haughton Tower took place at the same time as the passage of the British Act for the Abolition of the Slave Trade, which from 1 January 1808 made the importation of new captives from Africa into the British colonies illegal. Advocates of abolition argued that it would lead to the improvement of the conditions of enslaved people, because slaveholders would be forced to provide better living standards once slaves could no longer easily be replaced.[64] On Haughton Tower at least, the consequences seems to have been the opposite. Abolition brought home to managers like Kirkaldy and Brown the fact that they and their allies no longer controlled the political process. The vindictive acts of retribution by Haughton Tower's managers make sense in this context of their own declining power and as a technique to re-establish their control over the estate at a moment when it was contested.

Kirkaldy and Brown could reasonably expect Haughton James's support. At times over the previous decades James had expressed concern for the well-being of the people over whom he claimed owner-ship. In 1787, in the face of abolitionist criticism of the treatment of his slaves, James told his attorney that he would 'rather suffer some loss by my Manager's lenity, than be enrich'd by his severity'.[65] In 1799 he reiterated the point: 'I had much rather suffer in my interest, than that they [enslaved people] should suffer by hard treatment, & ill usage.'[66] But more frequently, and especially in the years immediately before Williamson's letter, James worried about 'heavy outgoings' and empha-sised the need to 'strain every nerve to make' a larger crop.[67] In one of his first letters to William Rhodes James as attorney, Haughton complained about the estate's expenses and emphasised that William should 'drop all thoughts of any fresh purchases' of enslaved people.[68] This decision

---

[64] This argument was made in the 1780s by James Ramsay, and again in a renowned speech by William Pitt in the 1791 parliamentary debate on the slave trade. On Ramsay, see Christopher Leslie Brown, *Moral Capital: Foundations of British Abolitionism* (Chapel Hill, 2006), 326. On Pitt and the broader context of this argument see Paugh, *The Politics of Reproduction*, 46–54.

[65] James to Haughton, 30 December 1787, James collection.

[66] James to Dear Sir, 1 August 1799, James collection.

[67] James to Dear Cousin, 28 May 1803, James collection.

[68] [James] to Dear Cousin, 25 June 1805, James collection.

suggests a lack of concern for the intensity of work that those already on the estate had to do, effectively consigning them to working increasingly hard as the number of available workers decreased.[69] James's repeated complaints about the size of the crop and the lack of labour to produce it suggest the structural reasons that underlay Kirkaldy's 'severity'.

By the time Mary Williamson wrote to Haughton James, the enslaved people of Haughton Tower had sought their own way of challenging the new severe regime. As Williamson explained, they tried to influence the situation by seeking the intercession of another of Haughton's cousins, John H[aughton] James, who had recently arrived in Jamaica. A letter from John confirms Mary's account. He wrote that 'during my stay at Green Island about three weeks since' (that is, in mid-August 1809), 'a vast number of Negroes from your Estate came to complain of the ill treatment which they received from your overseer and head Negro driver and requested me to speak to Mr Brown upon the subject'. John James reported that he had tried to speak to Brown, but had been met with 'violent rage'. Brown accused him of unwarranted inter-ference in the 'management of Haughton Tower Estate'.[70]

In approaching John James, the people of Haughton Tower adopted a common tactic. When managers attempted to worsen conditions on New World plantations, enslaved people frequently responded by complain-ing to another authority figure.[71] Enslaved people often tried to work the complexity of the ownership and management of Caribbean planta-tions to their advantage. The management of large Caribbean estates took place through multiple layers of authority: from the enslaved drivers, to the bookkeeper and overseers who lived on the estate, to the attorneys and relatives who lived elsewhere in the colony, to, in many cases, the absentee plantation owner, in the metropolis. Enslaved people's tactics of playing one authority off against another could lead to the removal of individual overseers and reversion to earlier labour norms. But in this case, the Haughton Tower estate people's application to John James backfired. Brown angrily rejected John James's attempted intervention and then retaliated against those who had complained. For reasons unexplained in the documents, Brown and Kirkaldy perceived Williamson as a leader in this struggle.

[69] For a similar argument in another Jamaican context see Mary Turner, 'Chattel Slaves into Wage Slaves: A Jamaican Case Study', in *From Chattel Slaves to Wage Slaves: The Dynamics of Labour Bargaining in the Americas*, ed. Mary Turner (1995), esp. 40.

[70] John H. James to [James], 7 September 1809, James collection. The town of Green Island is about four miles from Haughton Tower.

[71] For Jamaican examples see Turner, 'Chattel Slaves into Wage Slaves'; Mary Turner, 'Slave Workers, Subsistence and Labour Bargaining: Amity Hall, Jamaica, 1805–1832', *Slavery & Abolition*, 12 (1991), 92–105, https://doi.org/10.1080/01440399108575024.

They destroyed her garden and provision grounds, and pulled down not only her house but also the one that she had built for her sisters.

Williamson drew on legal language in her letter of protest – 'Honoured Sir this is the truth and nothing but the truth' – and framed her concerns within a language of rights. This point in the letter is the only one where her syntax and punctuation breaks down, perhaps suggesting the intensity of Williamson's anger at the turn of events: 'Now Honoured Sir as I was sold of the property free I mought have been disc[ou]raged, as having no property or wright what has my two Sisters and there young children no wright to a house on their Masters Estate, their children are young and left without a shelter.' Williamson's anger at Kirkaldy and Brown's rejection of the obligations of their slaveholding recalls Emilia Viotti da Costa's study of the Demerara slave rebellion of 1823, which argues that 'while masters dreamt of total power and blind obedience, slaves perceived slavery as a system of reciprocal obligations'.[72] It was the breach of these obligations that outraged not only enslaved people but also those, like Williamson, who retained connections with them, despite freedom.

Mary Williamson did not claim to have led or even participated in the slaves' delegation to John James. Perhaps this was because she was writing to complain about damage to her and her sisters' houses and therefore did not want to mention behaviour that James might perceive as justifying Brown and Kirkaldy's attack. But neither did John James mention her. Most likely, Williamson was not prominently involved in the protest, but Brown and Kirkaldy resented her because she was a free person on the estate who was not under their control. Thomas James had allowed her to establish herself as a free woman of colour outside the normal plantation hierarchy – something which, like the abolition of the slave trade, damaged their sense of authority. Their destruction of Williamson's and her sisters' property was probably opportunistic and retributive, taking advantage of a broader dispute to attack someone they had resented for some time.

Indeed, the crux of Williamson's request was to move beyond her dependence on the fluctuating will of the local managers by gaining land of her own. In this she expressed the perennial desire of enslaved and freed people throughout the Americas: for secure access to land.[73] She asked James to provide her with 'a little spot somewhere on the Estate', again stressing the importance of her relationship with her

---

[72] Emilia Viotti da Costa, *Crowns of Glory, Tears of Blood: The Demerara Slave Rebellion of 1823* (New York, 1994), 73.

[73] Jean Besson, *Martha Brae's Two Histories: European Expansion and Caribbean Culture-Building in Jamaica* (Chapel Hill, 2002); Sidney W. Mintz, 'Slavery and the Rise of Peasantries', in *Roots and Branches: Current Directions in Slave Studies*, ed. Michael Craton (Oxford, 1979), 213–42.

sisters: 'I do not wish to go from my family, as they want every assistance I can give them.' But perhaps equally important was the support that they gave to her. If she did not get the land, she would be 'obliged' to leave, she says. Where would she have gone, and what would she have done?

In framing her letter, Mary appealed to Haughton's self-interest: his estate was being so badly mismanaged, she concluded, that if he did not intervene to reduce the severity 'soon … you will have no slaves'. But she also invoked Haughton's familial relationships, half apologising for 'complain[ing] to an Uncle against his nephew'. Williamson's letter acknowledged and tried to use the fact that both slave-owners and enslaved people were deeply enmeshed in family ties extending beyond the conjugal, sexual and parent–child. But these family ties worked to different purposes. James's kinship network allowed him to run his plantation. Williamson's enabled her to mitigate her family members' suffering under slavery.

Mary Williamson's letter affords us a rare glimpse into one formerly enslaved woman's life and the lives of those to whom she was connected. We can learn a great deal from its densely packed five hundred and some words, especially when contextualised with other letters to and from members of the James family. Nevertheless, in reading it we are continually brought up against the limits of what it reveals. It is not as frustratingly sparse as the snippets of information in runaway advertisements or wills out of which scholars like Marisa Fuentes have constructed counter-archival histories.[74] Indeed, the letter seems to challenge Fuentes's pessimism about the possibility of finding the words of enslaved and freed women in the archives of slavery. Still, it remains a fragment, a single sheet of paper from which we may try to rebuild a world. It points to the limits of what even such a powerful source can tell us. Many basic empirical questions remain unanswerable: What was James Tumming's connection to the James family? Did Mary Williamson have children, and if so what happened to them? How old was she when she wrote to Haughton James? How long did each of the phases of her life last: as an enslaved woman; as a woman living in an unstable legal limbo as the sexual partner of the man who (perhaps) had promised to pay for her freedom; as a 'well situated' free woman in Trelawny after Tumming's death; and as a free woman living back on the estate of her likely birth? Even more challenging are more subjective questions such as: what were Mary Williamson's emotions towards James Tumming and his to her? Why did Thomas James want her to return to Haughton Tower? What was Mary's relationship

[74] Fuentes, *Dispossessed Lives*.

with others enslaved on the estate, besides her sisters and their children? How did her sisters understand what was happening?

Such absences are the routine stuff of historical research, perhaps especially in the study of slavery. Saidiya Hartman poses the question, 'How can narrative embody life in words and at the same time respect what we cannot know?' She urges us to resist the temptation to try to 'give voice to the slave', instead allowing ourselves to 'imagine what cannot be verified'.[75] In an article that responds to Hartman's work, Stephanie Smallwood calls for a history that is accountable to the enslaved.[76] I have approached Mary Williamson's letter with these injunctions in mind.

The letter sits aslant, though, to recent scholarly discussions about the nature of archives and 'the archive' (often considered as abstract, singular, metaphorical). Michel-Rolph Trouillot emphasised that 'archives assemble' and 'help select the stories that matter'; Carolyn Steedman writes that, while archives are full of mountains of paper, and historians always anxious about the impossibility of reading everything we want or need within them, 'there isn't, in fact, very much there'.[77] Arlette Farge suggests that historians need to be conscious both of absences and of our own practices of selection in the context of overwhelming quantities of archival paper.[78] Yet these important discussions of archival exclusions rarely consider those traces of the past, like Mary Williamson's letter, that *are* preserved, but outside of any institutional archive, with no official record of their existence. Ann Laura Stoler's attention to 'archiving-as-process rather than archives-as-things' helps to make visible the series of chance events that enable me to raise unanswerable questions about Mary Williamson's letter.[79] Had Tabitha James not become interested in the material in her family's attic, and had she not contacted me (or someone like me), we would not have access to it at all. Yet the preservation of Williamson's letter among a series of other materials produced by and for Haughton James and his descendants powerfully conditions the ways in which we can read it. How might the letter be read if it was preserved alongside the narratives and memories of others who had been enslaved at Haughton Tower estate?

---

[75] Saidiya Hartman, 'Venus in Two Acts', *Small Axe: A Caribbean Journal of Criticism*, 12 (1 June 2008), 3, 10, 12, https://doi.org/10.1215/-12-2-1.

[76] Stephanie E. Smallwood, 'The Politics of the Archive and History's Accountability to the Enslaved', *History of the Present*, 6 (2016), 117–32, doi: 10.5406/historypresent.6.2.0117.

[77] Michel-Rolph Trouillot, *Silencing the Past: Power and the Production of History* (Boston, MA, 1995), 52; Steedman, *Dust*, 68–9.

[78] Arlette Farge, *The Allure of the Archives*, trans. Thomas Scott-Railton (New Haven, 2013).

[79] Ann Laura Stoler, *Along the Archival Grain: Epistemic Anxieties and Colonial Common Sense* (Princeton and Oxford, 2009), 20.

There must be other private collections containing letters like Mary Williamson's, but historians will not have access to them unless their owners realise they are there, and make it possible for others to read them.[80] Privately held papers are at greater risk of damage or loss through lack of preservation than are archival collections. For scholars, it also means that permission to access and quote from them is dependent on the goodwill of the owners. I am grateful to the James family for allowing me extended access to the collection, and for granting permission to quote from it. But even in the light of this, it would be remiss not to draw attention to the fact that one of the legacies of British slave-ownership – to use the phrase coined by the important University College London project – is that this cultural, archival patrimony is owned by relatives of Haughton James, not of Mary Williamson. In today's world of increased public and institutional interest in slavery and in the voices of enslaved people, the uncomfortable truth is that the collection has a potential sale price that is raised by the presence of Williamson's letter. Also uncomfortable is the fact that I have benefited from this maldistribution of the legacies of slave-ownership: I, as a white historian based in Edinburgh, rather than one of my colleagues based in Kingston, was invited to read them. In this article I publish the full text of Mary Williamson's letter, alongside my effort to contextualise it based on further primary evidence and broader scholarship and to 'imagine what cannot be verified'. I do so to ensure that Mary Williamson's words are known, and to enable others to work with them, in the hope that doing so shifts, at least partially, the balance of this maldistribution.

Finally: how does the story end? There is no definitive answer – and of course, stories like this do not really end. I would love to have found a letter from Haughton James in which he agreed that Mary Williamson should have a plot of land on Haughton Tower estate in perpetuity. I would love to imagine a future in which Williamson supported her sisters and their children, and they her, perhaps even living to see her whole family's emancipation in the 1830s. But these are fantasies, deriving from what Smallwood describes as historians', our readers' and students' 'yearning for romance, our desire to hear the subaltern speak, … our search for the subaltern as heroic actor whose agency triumphs over the forces of oppression'.[81] Although the collection includes Haughton James's copies of many outgoing letters, there is no letter to Williamson, or even one that mentions her. Most likely, he did not respond.

---

[80] For consideration of the processes that lead some family letters to end up in archives, see Sarah M. S. Pearsall, *Atlantic Families: Lives and Letters in the Later Eighteenth Century* (Oxford, 2008), 244–6.

[81] Smallwood, 'The Politics of the Archive', 128.

Yet there is a possible clue to Mary Williamson's later life. In 1817, when the colonial government required all slaveholders to register the people over whom they claimed ownership, a Mary Tuming [sic] Williamson of Hanover registered Nelly, a twenty-five-year-old African woman, as her slave.[82] Might this be the same Mary Williamson, who had by this time added Tumming's name to hers, in slightly modified form? By 1820 the same woman, now named as Mary T. Williamson, had acquired two more enslaved women, and by 1823 she had freed one of them, Margaret Williamson, whom the registration documents identify as 'sambo'.[83] Perhaps Margaret was one of Mary's sisters, whom she purchased and then freed.

Or perhaps not. The Mary T. Williamson who freed Margaret signed the document with her 'mark' (an X, routinely used by illiterate people to sign official documents), while Mary Williamson's letter to Haughton James closes with her signature. The similar names may be mere coincidence, the similarity an enticing mirage, part of the seductive fantasy critiqued by Smallwood and others. The uncertainty underscores the challenges of biographical writing about enslaved and freed women who make such fleeting appearances in the archives. The fragmentary archival trace of Mary Williamson's letter to Haughton James can prompt us to revisit a lot of what we know about slavery, especially the significance of sisterhood and siblinghood for enslaved and freed people. It can lead us to confront the possibly ironic consequences for enslaved people in the Caribbean of the 1807 Act for the Abolition of the Slave Trade. It cannot, though, fill the absences at the heart of our knowledge of the experience of slavery.

[82] Slave Registration Returns, Hanover, Jamaica, 1817, TNA T 71/190, f. 736.

[83] Slave Registration Returns, Hanover, Jamaica, 1817, T 71/192, f. 499, TNA. The 1820 return, which would give the name of the other woman, is missing. Thanks to Gemma Romain for research on my behalf in the National Archives. The designation 'sambo' was said to describe a person with one black and one 'mulatto' parent, but could also be used more generally for a dark skinned but visibly mixed-heritage person.

Transactions of the RHS 29 (2019), pp. 181–200 © Royal Historical Society 2019
doi:10.1017/S0080440119000082

DEATH AND THE MODERN EMPIRE:
THE 1918–19 INFLUENZA EPIDEMIC IN INDIA*

By David Arnold

READ 5 OCTOBER 2018
AT STRATHCLYDE UNIVERSITY

ABSTRACT. In India the 1918–19 influenza pandemic cost at least twelve million lives, more than in any other country; it caused widespread suffering and disrupted the economy and infrastructure. Yet, despite this, and in contrast to the growing literature on recovering the 'forgotten' pandemic in other countries, remarkably little was recorded about the epidemic in India at the time or has appeared in the subsequent historiography. An absence of visual evidence is indicative of a more general paucity of contemporary material and first-hand testimony. In seeking to explain this absence, it is argued that, while India was exposed to influenza as a global event and to the effects of its involvement in the Great War, the influenza episode needs to be more fully understood in terms of local conditions. The impact of the disease was overshadowed by the prior encounter with bubonic plague, by military recruitment and the war, and by food shortages and price rises that pushed India to the brink of famine. Subsumed within a dominant narrative of political unrest and economic discontent, the epidemic found scant expression in official documentation, public debate and/or even private correspondence.

The impact of the 1918–19 influenza epidemic on India was devastating. Upwards of twelve million people, and possibly as many as eighteen million, died from influenza or from pneumonia and respiratory complications. This mortality was equivalent to 4 per cent of the population as recorded in the decennial census of 1911.[1] As many people (915,000) died in one Indian province – the Central Provinces – as in the whole of Britain and the United States combined. Unlike bubonic plague,

*The author wishes to thank Margot Finn and the RHS for the invitation to present this lecture and is indebted to the anonymous reviewer and those who attended the talk for their helpful comments and suggestions.
[1] Recent epidemiological studies support a figure of between eleven and fourteen million excess deaths due to influenza: Siddharth Chandra, Goran Kuljanin and Jennifer Wray, 'Mortality from the Influenza Pandemic of 1918–19: The Case of India', *Demography*, 49 (2012), 857–65; Siddharth Chandra and Eva Kassens-Noor, 'The Evolution of Pandemic Influenza: Evidence from India, 1918–19', *BMC Infectious Diseases*, 14 (2014), 510–20; Kenneth Hill, 'Influenza in India: Epicenter of an Epidemic', iuss2009.princeton.edu/papers/93252.

which struck India in 1896 and had caused some twelve million deaths by the late 1920s, mortality from influenza was concentrated in a few short months. It was thought to have begun with the arrival of infected troopships at Bombay and Karachi in May and June 1918. This triggered the milder, first wave of the epidemic, in which old people and children appeared especially at risk, but in which overall mortality rates remained low. In Bombay in late July it was confidently predicted that the epidemic was nearly over.[2] Then a second, far more fatal, wave of influenza swept across India from September to early December 1918.[3] In this second phase, adults between the ages of twenty and forty were thought to be particularly susceptible, with more women than men dying from the disease. In one day alone, 6 October 1918, there were 768 registered deaths from influenza in Bombay city, more deaths than at the height of the plague epidemic in the 1890s and 1900s, while across the Bombay Presidency as a whole more than a million deaths occurred during October and November 1918.[4] N. H. Choksy, an Indian medical officer in Bombay, wrote that 'In its rapidity of spread, the enormous number of its victims and its total fatality …, influenza reached a virulence before which even plague with all its horrors fades into insignificance.'[5]

Across western and central India, the countryside suffered at least as much as the cities. In the Central Provinces, where an estimated 6 to 7 per cent of the population perished, the epidemic spread 'with great rapidity, paralysing towns and decimating villages'.[6] In what was described by the provincial sanitary commissioner, F. G. N. Stokes, as 'incomparably the most violent outbreak of disease of which we have any knowledge', hundreds died in the space of a few days. 'The ravages of the disease were seen at their worst', Stokes wrote, 'in the villages, where the complete helplessness of the people combined with scarcity of food

[2] *Times of India* (Bombay) (hereafter *ToI*), 24 July 1918, 6.

[3] *Annual Report of the Sanitary Commissioner of the Government of India, 1918* (Calcutta, 1920), 56–67. Studies of the epidemic include Mridula Ramanna, 'Coping with the Influenza Pandemic: The Bombay Experience', in *The Spanish Influenza Epidemic of 1918–19: New Perspectives*, ed. Howard Phillips and David Killingray (2003), 86–98; T. V. Sekher, 'Public Health Administration in Princely Mysore: Tackling the Influenza Pandemic of 1918', in *India's Princely States: People, Princes and Colonialism*, ed. Waltraud Ernst and Biswamoy Pati (2007), 194–211. The best demographic study remains I. D. Mills, 'The 1918–1919 Influenza Pandemic: The Indian Experience', *Indian Economic and Social History Review*, 23 (1986), 1–40.

[4] In Bombay Presidency there were 675,222 influenza deaths in October 1918: *Annual Report of the Sanitary Commissioner for the Government of Bombay, 1918* (Bombay, 1919), 23. In Punjab 962,937 deaths were attributed to influenza between 1 October and 31 December 1918: *Report of the Sanitary Administration of the Punjab, 1918* (Lahore, 1919), app. D, xi.

[5] N. H. Choksy, 'Influenza', *Administration Report of the Municipal Commissioner for the City of Bombay, 1918–19* (Bombay, 1919), 79.

[6] *Annual Sanitary Report of the Central Provinces and Berar, 1918* (Nagpur, 1919), 8.

and clothing produced a calamity which baffles description.'[7] Punjab's sanitary commissioner painted an even more apocalyptic picture. At the height of the crisis between mid-October and early November 1918, the scenes, he wrote, were

> such as to render adequate description impossible. The hospitals were choked so that it was impossible to remove the dead quickly enough to make room for the dying: the streets and lanes of the cities were littered with dead and dying people: the postal and telegraph services were completely disorganised; the train service continued, but at all the principal stations dead and dying were being removed from the trains; the burning ghat [cremation site] and burial ground were literally swamped with corpses, whilst an even greater number awaited removal; the depleted medical service, itself sorely stricken by the epidemic, was incapable of dealing with more than a minute fraction of the sickness requiring attention; nearly every household was lamenting a death, and everywhere terror and confusion reigned.[8]

The Ministry of Health in London likewise acknowledged that the 'total mortality in India in the month of October [1918]' was 'without parallel in the history of disease'.[9] And yet after December 1918 the epidemic rapidly lost its destructive impetus and within a few years had sunk to statistical insignificance. Smallpox, cholera, plague, malaria and tuberculosis once again dominated India's public health agenda.[10]

What are we as historians to make of this indisputably catastrophic episode? Clearly, a century on, an event in which twelve million people died (and an unknown number were rendered seriously ill) deserves our close attention and careful scrutiny, but in revisiting the 1918 epidemic what exactly are we seeking to investigate and by what means can we recuperate that 'forgotten' past? In recent years historians, demographers and epidemiologists have had much to say about influenza in India, as elsewhere; but, in concentrating on the epidemic itself they have tended to neglect the wider interpretive issues that surround it. How then should we position India's influenza epidemic in relation to its long-term health and mortality trends and more broadly in relation to Indian society and colonial governance? Was the epidemic a one-off event, which despite the staggering mortality, actually tells us little about India's underlying condition and future trajectory, or was it the exemplification of significant trends and developments? But, in seeking to answer such questions, we should first note an important

---

[7] *Ibid.*

[8] *Report of the Sanitary Administration, Punjab, 1918*, app. D, xi.

[9] S. P. James, 'Australasia and Parts of Africa and Asia', Ministry of Health, *Report on the Pandemic of Influenza, 1918–19* (1920), 383.

[10] From 3,964 registered deaths due to influenza in Bombay city in 1918, the number had fallen to 1,605 in 1920 and 118 in 1924. Deaths from respiratory diseases remained higher for longer. *Administration Report of the Municipal Commissioner for the City of Bombay, 1924–25* (Bombay, 1925), 1.

semantic distinction. In writing about India some authors refer to the influenza *pandemic*, implying that India, though it suffered most, was just one of the many countries ensnared in this global event, a catastrophe whose epidemiological origins lay elsewhere. For others this was in essence an Indian *epidemic*, whose nature and impact, despite its external provenance, were heavily contingent upon India's own material and social conditions. Historians have written of the 'unification of the globe by disease' and cite the 1918–19 pandemic as a prime example of this.[11] But do the events of 1918 more strongly suggest India as a land apart, subject certainly to such global visitations as the influenza pandemic, but otherwise governed rather more by its own preoccupations? How, in this moment of exceptional crisis, do we reconcile the local and the global?

I Situating the Indian epidemic

I would have liked to begin this discussion by turning to visual source material to illustrate the Indian epidemic – photographs of hospital wards crammed with patients or emergency relief centres, pictures of people wearing protective face-masks, piled-up bodies awaiting cremation or burial. Such images are widely available for the pandemic in other parts of the world, such as Britain and the United States, but, so far as I am aware, there are no such images for India. Nor are there many for other Asian societies, apart from Japan: to that extent, the lacuna I am trying to describe was not specific to India alone. That visual absence in 1918–19 is all the more striking in that there are a great number of photographs of the plague epidemic in India in the 1890s and 1900s, showing precisely such scenes from hospitalising the sick to cremating the dead.[12] Why not for 1918–19? Similarly, there are a large number of detailed reports, statistical compendia and commissions of enquiry for the plague epidemic, and the government plague proceedings run to dozens of volumes: there is nothing comparable for influenza. A preliminary report was published early in 1919 by Norman White, the Government of India's sanitary commissioner, but it is brief, appeared before the full impact of the epidemic was known, and was never supplemented by a more comprehensive account. When White wrote his report the mortality was put at no more than six million: five million in British India and one million more in the

---

[11] Notably Emmanuel Le Roy Ladurie, 'A Concept: The Unification of the Globe by Disease', in Ladurie, *The Mind and Method of the Historian* (Brighton, 1981), 28–83. A similar logic informs K. David Patterson and Gerald F. Pyle, 'The Geography and Mortality of the 1918 Influenza Pandemic', *Bulletin of the History of Medicine*, 65 (1991), 4–21.

[12] Such images are available online from the Wellcome Collection, London.

princely states.[13] As we have seen, the provincial sanitary commissioners gave vivid, often detailed, accounts of the epidemic in their annual reports for 1918, but thereafter had virtually nothing to say on the matter, and it was left to the Indian census report of 1921, published in 1923, to provide more comprehensive data on India's missing millions.[14] There was newspaper coverage of the epidemic and the rumours and complaints that swirled around it, but, given how vocal the Indian press could be on other matters, these reports were neither particularly extensive and insightful nor did they greatly embellish the official record.[15] What follows is, then, an attempt to explain such an absence.

In the light of this lacuna, one might agree with the remark made in 2002 by Howard Phillips and David Killingray that the 1918–19 pandemic has 'yielded a relatively poor historiographical harvest', though, given how much new material has appeared since then, that is now questionable. Globally, the pandemic no longer seems to fit the 'forgotten' tag once almost universally applied to it.[16] But it would be hard to accept for India their further view that 'coming in the heyday of the newspaper and the printed word, ... [the pandemic] left behind mountains of written evidence across the world, often in the unlikeliest of places, more so than any pandemic before it'.[17] In India, accounts of cholera and plague over the previous century vastly outweighed the scanty volume of material, personal and public, generated by influenza.[18] Widespread illiteracy is an insufficient explanation for this.[19] Although influenza

---

[13] F. Norman White, *A Preliminary Report on the Influenza Pandemic of 1918 in India* (Simla, 1919), 1.

[14] The true scale of the mortality began to emerge with the first published returns in 1921: 'Indian Census: Influenza Effects', *ToI*, 11 April 1921, 10.

[15] A further contrast can be made with the Indian soldiers' letters from the Western Front intercepted by the censor and used by historians as testimony to their personal experiences: David Omissi, *Indian Voices of the Great War: Soldiers' Letters, 1914–18* (Basingstoke, 1999); Santanu Das, *India, Empire, and First World War Culture* (Cambridge, 2018).

[16] Howard Phillips and David Killingray, 'Introduction', in *Spanish Influenza*, ed. Phillips and Killingray, 2; Alfred W. Crosby, *America's Forgotten Pandemic: The Influenza of 1918* (Cambridge, 1989).

[17] Phillips and Killingray, 'Introduction', 3.

[18] For a similar explanation, see Myron Echenberg, '"The Dog that Did Not Bark": Memory and the 1918 Influenza Epidemic in Senegal', in *Spanish Influenza*, ed. Phillips and Killingray, 230–8.

[19] Some attempt has been made for India, as for Southeast Asia, to tap folklore and oral history: David Hardiman, 'The Influenza Epidemic of 1918 and the *Adivasis* of Western India', *Social History of Medicine*, 25 (2012), 644–64; Kirsty Walker, 'The Influenza Pandemic of 1918 in Southeast Asia', in *Histories of Health in Southeast Asia: Perspectives on the Long Twentieth Century*, ed. Tim Harper and Sunil S. Amrith (Bloomington, 2014), 61–71. But, thus far, this has been less productive than, for example, in recovering the Irish experience: see Ida Milne, *Stacking the Coffins: Influenza, War and Revolution in Ireland, 1918–19* (Manchester, 2018).

claimed most of its victims in India among the poor, they were not the only section of society to observe and experience it. And yet, so far as I am aware, there is remarkably little by way of private correspondence or personal memoirs to shed light on what has been dubbed 'the greatest pandemic in the world's history'.[20] How can twelve million people die, and yet apparently leave so little trace?

One plausible explanation might be that British India was an unmodern society ruled over by an unmodern state, chaotic in form and conduct, unknowing or uncaring about mass mortality or perhaps, after decades of pestilence and famine, impervious to the suffering of its subjects. Appointing enquiry commissions, compiling statistics and reports, applying science to social need – this is surely what modern states do when faced with a crisis of such momentous proportions. Seen thus, India's colonial government in 1918–19 might seem not to have fulfilled its modern responsibilities. This adversarial view would be in keeping with recent, hostile interpretations of the British Raj by Shashi Tharoor and Jon Wilson.[21] Neither of these authors actually discusses the influenza epidemic, but their general line of argument might suggest that it was yet another unnatural disaster attributable to, or greatly accentuated by, imperial misrule. Nobody in government, it might be said, was particularly concerned about the twelve million deaths in 1918–19 because nobody in authority much cared or had the political will, the administrative capacity and the technical resources to do much about it.

In our search for guidance on how to situate the Indian epidemic we could also turn back to an article by Ira Klein published in 1973 which looked at the period 1871 to 1921 and documented the extraordinarily high rates of mortality in India caused by famine and recurrent bouts of cholera, plague, smallpox and malaria (among others), a 'woeful crescendo of death' that culminated with the influenza epidemic of 1918–19.[22] Klein thus appended the epidemic to a long cycle of mass suffering and staggering mortality: its significance lay in reinforcing and carrying to fresh heights a long established pattern of death and disease. Only after 1919, he suggests, did things get better, but not very much. Klein further argues that British attempts to modernize India were themselves partly to blame for this 'woeful' saga: by disrupting natural lines of drainage and creating swamps where none had existed before, irrigation canals and railway embankments facilitated the spread of malaria; British rule, along with railways, the opening of the Suez Canal and the new steamship routes, exposed India to outside epidemics in a

[20] Phillips and Killingray, 'Introduction', 2.

[21] Shashi Tharoor, *Inglorious Empire: What the British Did to India* (2017); Jon Wilson, *India Conquered: Britain's Raj and the Chaos of Empire* (2016).

[22] Ira Klein, 'Death in India, 1871–1921', *Journal of Asian Studies*, 32 (1973), 639.

manner not previously possible; while at the same time the inherent insufficiencies of colonial medicine and public health failed to check or reverse this fatal trend. But in the context of the 1918–19 influenza epidemic is an argument about botched modernisation and 'tatterdemalion' health services sufficient to account for what happened to India and its apparent historical neglect?[23]

II Influenza in context

1918 was not the first time India had been hit by the disease. In common with other regions of Eurasia, epidemic influenza, in a relatively mild form, had struck India in 1890 and lingered on for several years. Interestingly, in the light of 1918, soldiers, both British and Indian, were implicated in this epidemic as transmitting the disease as well as being among its principal victims, though this may simply reflect greater awareness by the sanitary authorities of health in the army than among the civilian population at large.[24] A few medical reports were written about the disease, but, until it recurred with such virulence in 1918, influenza was, one sanitary commissioner confessed, 'regarded with apathy and scepticism by the vast majority of the [medical] profession' in India.[25] By the time influenza had petered out, India was overwhelmed by the monumental impact of bubonic plague, perhaps the greatest epidemic crisis India has ever faced and conceivably the greatest crisis of British rule between the end of the Mutiny/Rebellion in 1858 and the run-up to Independence and Partition in 1947. Unprecedented though it appeared at the time, in retrospect the 1918 influenza can be seen as nestling in the shadow of the earlier plague epidemic.

Historians have written extensively about India's plague episode but some of its salient features deserve to be restated here.[26] Firstly, there was great alarm that by spreading to India in 1896 from Hong Kong

[23] *Ibid.*, 641, 643.

[24] *Annual Report of the Sanitary Commissioner with the Government of India, 1890* (Calcutta, 1892), 26–8, 79; *Annual Report of the Sanitary Commissioner with the Government of India, 1894* (Calcutta, 1896), 67, 102.

[25] *Report of the Sanitary Administration, Punjab, 1918*, app. D, xv; K. C. Bose, 'Influenza as Seen in Calcutta, and Its Treatment', in K. C. Bose, *A Collection of the Medical and Surgical Papers of Rai K. C. Bose* (Calcutta, 1895), 61–73. In Bombay in 1915 there was only one registered death from influenza, and in 1916 six compared to 1,987 from plague and 1,902 from tuberculosis: *Administration Report of the Municipal Commissioner for the City of Bombay, 1916–17* (Bombay 1917), 2, 40.

[26] David Arnold, *Colonizing the Body: State Medicine and Epidemic Disease in Nineteenth-Century India* (Berkeley, 1993), ch. 5; Mark Harrison, *Public Health in British India: Anglo-Indian Preventive Medicine, 1859–1914* (Cambridge, 1994), ch. 6; Raj Chandavarkar, *Imperial Power and Popular Politics: Class, Resistance and the State in India, c. 1850–1950* (Cambridge, 1998), ch. 7.

and potentially moving on to Europe, plague was re-enacting the apoca-lyptic Black Death, with the added fear that India's international trade would be embargoed unless the government took immediate and drastic steps to prevent the onward spread of the disease. Given the imminent threat it seemed to pose to the West, plague generated a vast quantity of scientific research and a coordinated international response in ways that influenza twenty years later conspicuously did not. Secondly, the Government of India and its provincial administra-tions rapidly adopted extraordinarily wide-ranging and draconian mea-sures to try to check the spread of plague. These included body searches of travellers, demolishing infected houses and burning their contents, segregating possible contacts, carrying suspected cases off to hospital, and creating innumerable plague hospitals and evacuation camps. This raft of highly interventionist measures produced such a furious public backlash that within months the government was forced to back-track and, even at the expense of plague's probable spread, was obliged to rely to a far greater degree on Indian intermediaries, on voluntary measures, and even (reluctantly) on practitioners of indigenous medicine. What trumped state intervention in the early plague years was the potent combination of popular discontent (itself a heady mixture of rumour, riot and resistance) and the anger of the middle classes whose lives were pro-foundly disrupted and who felt humiliated and deprived of the leadership status to which they were entitled.

Thirdly, and contrary to the 'chaos' thesis, the state was forced to act in a more overtly scientific manner, agreeing to a specialist plague com-mission and forming a bacteriological department to examine this and other diseases and find urgent solutions to their spread.[27] Plague thus instigated a revolution in colonial medical science and public health. It also created the prospect of a revolution in colonial governance, with sanitary need and the hygienic education of the people spearheading the rationale for a more interventionist state. Some changes did indeed follow, as in the formation of urban improvement trusts in Bombay and Calcutta. But in practice, fearing a recrudescence of popular oppos-ition if it pressed too hard, and mindful of its own security and economic constraints, the state backed away, leaving the exercise of its power more fitful and erratic than ever before. If the government did not intervene more actively in the 1918–19 epidemic it was in part because it had been chastened by its previous experience of plague.[28]

---

[27] Andrew Balfour and Henry Harold Scott, *Health Problems of the Empire: Past, Present and Future* (1924), 131; Pratik Chakrabarti, *Bacteriology in British India: Laboratory Medicine and the Tropics* (Rochester, NY, 2012).

[28] For the relationship between the plague and influenza epidemics, see David Arnold, 'Disease, Rumor, and Panic in India's Plague and Influenza Epidemics, 1896–1919', in

By the outbreak of war in 1914 the medical and public health initiatives generated by the plague epidemic, or contemporaneous with it, were starting to have some effect. Contrary to Klein's argument, there was a growing conviction that the battle for India's public health *was* being won – against plague, smallpox, cholera, malaria, typhoid and all the other diseases to which India had hitherto been prone.[29] And, even if famine had not disappeared entirely, it seemed to be in abeyance. Many issues – malnutrition, infant mortality, women's health, tuberculosis – undoubtedly remained; but, in the principal cities, it was as if a corner had been turned. India, it seemed, was beginning to win its public health war. At the end of 1917 Calcutta's health officer announced that the year had been the healthiest the city had ever known. Deaths from cholera and smallpox, after falling for years, had reached 'phenomenally low' levels. Plague deaths were at their lowest since 1898, having consistently declined since 1905: indeed, plague had 'almost vanished' from the city's vital statistics.[30] India's great eastern metropolis could, it seemed, now anticipate a new age of public health.

Then in 1918, the ink barely dry on the health officer's report, Calcutta was savaged by one of the deadliest epidemics it had ever known, and mortality soared to unprecedented heights. At thirty-five deaths per thousand of the population, the city's death-rate was suddenly back from twenty-three per thousand the previous year to the highest recorded since 1907.[31] No one had been expecting that. As the health officer put it, 'The setback in the progressive decline of the mortality which had been a characteristic feature of the returns since 1913 is to be regretted.'[32] But then, when the influenza crisis had passed by early 1919, it was almost as if it had never happened: deaths from influenza and pneumonia fell rapidly while cholera, plague, malaria and even smallpox re-emerged as the principal challenges to sanitary rule.[33]

Empires of Panic: Epidemics and Colonial Anxieties, ed. Robert Peckham (Hong Kong, 2015), 111–29.

[29] For the downward trend in mortality among Indian and British troops, see *Annual Report of the Sanitary Commissioner with the Government of India, 1913* (Calcutta, 1915), 5–6. Indians troops remained highly susceptible to pneumonia, which accounted for a quarter of their deaths in 1913: *ibid.*, 37; White, *Preliminary Report*, 6.

[30] *Annual Report on the Municipal Administration of Calcutta, 1917–18* (2 vols., Calcutta, 1918), I, 14, 54–7. In Bombay, too, the annual death rate was lower in 1915 than in any year since 1874: *Administration Report of the Municipal Commissioner for the City of Bombay, 1923–24* (Bombay, 1924), 5.

[31] *Annual Report on the Municipal Administration of Calcutta, 1918–19* (2 vols., Calcutta, 1919), I, 81–5.

[32] *Ibid.*, I, 21.

[33] In 1922 Calcutta's health officer recorded only 927 deaths from influenza out of 30,395. He noted continuing mortality from influenza but was more alarmed by the 'terrible epidemic' of smallpox in 1920 which caused 3,000 deaths: *Report on the Municipal Administration of Calcutta, 1921–22* (2 vols., Calcutta, 1923), I, 63–4.

From such a perspective, even in the 1920s, influenza appeared as a temporary aberration, not a regular or indicative feature of the epidemiological landscape.

Moreover, unlike plague, and before it cholera, both of which had erupted from the East to menace the West, in 1918 influenza struck India from the West. It was America and Europe's catastrophe before it was India's, and it was there, in the West, that investigative research and the quest for remedial measures were concentrated. Influenza was a viral disease whose causative agent was impossible to detect at the time even under a microscope: it was not fully identified until 1933. India's expertise in medical science had grown enormously since the 1890s but mostly in parasitology and bacteriology where the enemy was easier to identify and respond to, not in virology. In India, as in the West, laboratory research was misled into believing that influenza had a bacteriological origin. Although an anti-influenza vaccine was prepared in three of India's leading bacteriological laboratories, there was little confidence in its effectiveness.[34] In December 1918 R. H. Malone of the Indian Medical Service (IMS) was appointed to investigate the bacteriology of influenza and find a viable vaccine: his enquiry yielded few results.[35] Compared with recent discoveries in, and treatment of, malaria, plague, typhoid, among other diseases, there was, from the perspective of India's medical experts, nothing about the influenza epidemic to celebrate and memorialise. It was an unhappy episode, not a meaningful encounter. Seen from a global perspective, India was unlikely (again in contrast to plague where India had been fundamental to global research) to provide a key to understanding influenza. Indeed, in the global narrative India was viewed almost as collateral damage, a transit station in the wayward peregrinations of a global disease.[36] Besides, India, the most populous society on the planet, was notorious for its poverty and famines: deaths there, even in their millions, were to many outside observers, unsurprising. To read the medical literature of the period is to feel that India's twelve million dead had rapidly become a mere appendage to a more compelling Western story of disease and public health.

III War fever

If we were to ask: What was the time of influenza? To what temporality did it belong? one answer would be 'the time of war', for it was the Great

[34] Ramanna, 'Coping', 91.

[35] India, Education (Sanitary), no. 17, Dec. 1918, India Office Records (IOR), British Library, London; White, *Preliminary Report*, 13–14.

[36] Ministry of Health, *Report on the Pandemic*, p. xiv.

War that helped give the epidemic its global dynamic and its local character.[37] The war had a massive impact on India and thereby facilitated the epidemic that hurried in its wake. For India engagement in the war began early with soldiers sent in September 1914 to serve on the Western Front, before being relocated to other battlefronts, mostly in the Middle East. In all, close to a million Indian troops served in the war, of whom 53,486 were killed and 64,350 wounded, a heavy loss but one that might seem of relatively little demographic significance compared to the influenza death toll.[38] That British India could mobilise a million men, supply vast quantities of arms, clothing and military materiel, help fund hospitals and troopships, and put its increasingly industrial economy on a war footing itself says something about the modern capabilities of the colonial state. But evident, too, was the enormous strain the Indian economy and its creaking infrastructure were under by 1918.

The impact of the war was apparent from the outset. Troopships from Basra in Iraq were believed to have brought influenza to Bombay and Karachi in May–June 1918 – associating the arrival of the epidemic in India with the protracted and enervating Mesopotamia campaign.[39] Other factors linked influenza with the war and the army. Intensive recruitment for the Indian Army was still actively continuing in the middle months of 1918 when influenza first struck, and the disease quickly impacted on the number of men available or willing to present themselves for enlistment.[40] Once the disease had become established, troop movements and army barracks were central mechanisms in the India-wide dissemination of the disease.[41] Many of India's volunteer soldiers came from agricultural families: this was especially so in Punjab where whole villages were wiped out by the disease and adult males proved particularly vulnerable to influenza and pneumonia. Indeed, officials in Punjab expressed with hindsight their relief that the epidemic had not struck sooner, which would have deprived the army of its principal recruiting ground.[42] India was also a victim of the wartime 'famine

[37] Recent scholarship has increasingly recognised a military connection: see Mark Osborne Humphries, 'Paths of Infection: The First World War and the Origins of the 1918 Influenza Pandemic', *War in History*, 21 (2014), 55–81.

[38] De Witt C. Ellinwood, 'The Indian Soldier, the Indian Army, and Change, 1914–1918', in *India and World War 1*, ed. De Witt C. Ellinwood and S. D. Pradhan (New Delhi, 1978), 184.

[39] *ToI*, 12 July 1918, 9; 16 July 1918, 8.

[40] 'Fortnightly Report on the Internal Political Situation', Madras, for the first half of October 1918, India, Home (Political), no. 23, November 1918, Tamil Nadu Archives, Chennai.

[41] *ToI*, 26 July 1918, 9; 29 July 1918, 8; *Annual Report of the Sanitary Commissioner, United Provinces, 1918*, app. D, 8A.

[42] M. S. Leigh, *The Punjab and the War* (Lahore, 1922), 1–12.

of tonnage', one of the several forms of 'famine' to which India was becoming subject by 1918.[43] Severe shortages and distribution delays, ultimately linked to the stresses and strain of the war itself, affected imports by sea and the capacity to move goods by rail and began to impact on commodity prices which by late 1918 reached record levels for food-grains, cloth, kerosene and other essentials.[44]

In the countryside, famine in a more literal sense stalked several provinces.[45] Although it is frequently argued that the influenza pandemic of 1918–19 was so destructive globally because it attacked some of the healthiest members of the population, whose immune systems went into fatal overdrive, this appears not to adequately explain the situation in India. Certainly, in the deadly second wave of the epidemic it was adults in the twenty to forty age range who were most affected, but the Indian reports almost universally emphasise a strong correlation between poverty, deprivation and debility on the one hand and influenza (and still more tellingly pneumonia) on the other. 'The people who suffer most,' wrote Punjab's sanitary commissioner, 'are the poor and the rural classes, whose housing conditions, medical attendance, food and clothing are in defect.'[46] Even among Indian soldiers, who might otherwise have been regarded as relatively fit and with access to reliable medical attention, fatalities from influenza and pneumonia were remarkably high.[47] Many women in this age group, particularly in the countryside, died because their own health was neglected or, having attended to their sick and dying menfolk, there was no one left to nurse them in turn.[48] As I. D. Mills has remarked, in India in 1918 famine and influenza constituted 'a set of mutually exacerbating catastrophes'.[49] The time of war was also concurrently a time of famine, and almost from the outset influenza was described as 'really a disease of hunger and exhaustion'.[50]

One of the problems India faced was that many officers of the Indian Medical Service (numbering barely 700 even in peacetime) had been drafted into war service overseas: the ultimate rationale for the IMS was as a state-run military medical service, and in an emergency like

[43] *ToI*, 3 January 1918, 2.

[44] 'Statistical Abstract for India, 1917–18 to 1926–27', *Parliamentary Papers*, 1928–9, Cmd. 3291, table 296, on 628.

[45] As in Madras: *Season and Crop Report of the Madras Presidency for the Agricultural Year, 1918–19* (Madras, 1919), 1–3.

[46] *Report on the Sanitary Administration, Punjab, 1918*, app. D, xvi.

[47] On pneumonia deaths among soldiers, see White, *Preliminary Report*, 6.

[48] *Annual Sanitary Report, Central Provinces, 1918*, 3.

[49] Mills, 'Influenza Pandemic', 35.

[50] *ToI*, 16 July 1918, 7; Purshotamdas Thakurdas in Bombay Legislative Council, *ibid.*, 30 September 1918, 6.

the Great War military health took precedence over civilian needs.[51] Some members of this elite medical service had died by 1918, others had yet to revert to their civilian posts. This exposed the underlying fragility of India's medical administration. Doctors had to be drawn in from the Royal Army Medical Corps (RAMC) (whose more normal remit was the care of British troops in India) even for routine hospital work, but they often lacked the local expertise (including basic language skills) to do the job well. Some of the many difficulties faced by medical staff in 1918 are evident from an MD thesis on the Indian epidemic submitted to the University of Edinburgh in 1920 by a Scottish doctor, Thomas Herriot. Herriot had qualified in 1912 with a specialist interest in disease prevention which involved him in intensive laboratory work. He was drafted into the British Army in February 1915 and made a temporary captain in the RAMC a year later. Transferred to the Indian Army in 1918, in the summer of that year he was put in charge of the military hospital at Jullundur in Punjab. The first he knew of 'Spanish influenza' was from reading a newspaper report but this meant little to him until the disease actually arrived in India.[52]

The first wave of the epidemic reached Punjab in August 1918: the second wave in mid-September was far more virulent. With other medical staff off sick with influenza, and himself struggling with recurrent malaria and dysentery, Herriot was burdened with the duties of his invalid colleagues as well as his own.[53] The first cases he was aware of were, characteristically, among Indian soldiers returning from leave. From them influenza spread to Indians in the bazaar, to labourers and domestic servants and hence to Europeans. It was at first assumed that this disease was malaria, already rampant in Punjab in recent years, but analysis in the brigade laboratory failed to reveal either malaria parasites or the plague bacillus. If, Herriot noted, the disease was in fact influenza, 'no information had been received, either from other stations [in India] or from England which would help in diagnosing the disease'.[54] Basically, he was on his own.

Before the epidemic was over there had been a million deaths in Punjab: one in twenty of the entire population. Like Bombay, Punjab had been one of the provinces worst affected by recent famine, plague and malaria, again suggesting that influenza was at its worst among

---

[51] Government of India, *The Army in India and Its Evolution* (Calcutta, 1924), 117–18.

[52] Thomas P. Herriot, 'The Influenza Pandemic, 1918, as Observed in the Punjab, India' (MD thesis, University of Edinburgh, 1920), 1–2.

[53] *Ibid.*, 2. Calcutta's health officer had a similar experience: 'Unfortunately with half my staff down with influenza, very few precise observations were made in the early stages of the epidemic.' *Annual Report on the Municipal Administration, Calcutta, 1918–19*, I, 83.

[54] Herriot, 'Influenza Pandemic', 4.

populations already worn out by disease and hunger.[55] In this specific context, Klein's argument for appending 1918–19 to the earlier history of India's burgeoning mortality since the 1870s seems apposite. In 1918 conditions were exacerbated by the failure of the monsoon and the poor outturn of crops including the fodder – here was yet another 'famine' – needed for cows and buffaloes to produce the milk that medical experts urged Indians to consume as an aid to their recovery. The nights were bitterly cold and many Indians slept indoors, Herriot noted, 'in the little mud huts where there was overcrowding and no ventilation', an environment in which influenza and pneumonia thrived.[56] Victims were wracked with pain; some, delirious with fever, proved hard to control. Their temperature rose to 102 or 103 degrees: they were exhausted but unable to sleep. As their health deteriorated and pneumonia set in, patients' faces turned 'a peculiar violet lavender hue': this, he observed, was a 'grave sign', promising little hope of recovery. For those who did survive, convalescence was painful and slow. Herriot drew some consolation from the fact that of the 214 cases he treated only 21 died: 1 in 10, a relatively low proportion of those hospitalised.[57] Given the bewildering array of symptoms patients presented and continuing medical uncertainty as to the nature of the disease, Herriot would have liked to have examined blood and urine samples for himself, but he lacked the apparatus and the time to do so. His Indian assistant, who helped with laboratory work, was laid up for several weeks with pneumonic influenza: the only authoritative source of information Herriot possessed was articles in *The Lancet*.[58] He struggled to keep track of patients, to record their symptoms, or know how best to deal with their urgent complaints. He could only muddle through: it is not surprising that even before the epidemic was fully over he was invalided out of India and returned, broken in health, to Edinburgh.[59] He died, aged 62, at Berwick-upon-Tweed, in October 1949.

Herriot's personal account of the virtual breakdown of medical services in Jullundur could be taken as indicative of the more general paralysis of modern societies and modern states around the globe in 1918. In this respect India was hardly unique: everywhere during the months when influenza ruled the world, modernity seemingly stood still and medical expertise and public health policy proved of little practical

[55] Leigh, *Punjab*, 11.
[56] Herriot, 'Influenza Pandemic', 6.
[57] *Ibid.*, 8–11, 50.
[58] *Ibid.*, 16, 39.
[59] *Ibid.*, 25.

benefit.[60] But India's medical modernity was fragile, particularly when confronted with an epidemic crisis of such monumental proportions. Workers in the more self-evidently 'modern' sectors of the Indian economy were among those worst hit. Docks, railways, trams, telegraph and postal services came almost to a standstill; productivity in textile factories slumped as half the workforce lay sick and dying or had fled.[61] In the Kolar goldfields in Mysore there were 13,600 cases of influenza (roughly half the workforce) with 960 deaths.[62] The high court in Calcutta was unable to function, as judges, lawyers and jurors were absent sick.[63] The forestry service, among colonial India's largest and proudest state enterprises, ground to a virtual halt as officers and labourers alike fell sick and died.[64] City cremation grounds, which after years of gradual reform had become exemplars of a kind of sanitary modernity, struggled to cope with the sheer numbers of the dead: 22,549 bodies were cremated in Calcutta's half-dozen burning grounds in 1918, more than sixty a day, while in Bombay, amidst wartime shortages, it was hard to find enough wood to consume so many corpses.[65] In the countryside the dead were simply dumped on waste ground or on riverbanks. India's modernity was unable to cope with such a comprehensive onslaught on its war-weary services and fragile infrastructure. This incapacity partly explains the archival absence referred to earlier – the dearth of photographs, the paucity of medical research memoirs, even of private correspondence. Too many people were overworked, sick, or on their deathbeds, to have the time or energy to record what was happening.

IV Influenza and the politics of memorialisation

Influenza received less public attention than it might otherwise have done because for many Indians the epidemic was not the primary issue. It was the symptom, not the underlying cause. Hunger, poverty and soaring prices were what really mattered. Harsh and worsening economic conditions aroused popular anger in ways not seen since the height of the plague years. There were riots across the Madras

[60] Sandra M. Tomkins, 'The Failure of Expertise: Public Health Policy in Britain during the 1918–19 Influenza Epidemic', *Social History of Medicine*, 5 (1992), 435–54.

[61] *Annual Report of the Sanitary Commissioner, United Provinces, 1918*, app. D, 11 A.

[62] *The Times* (London), 11 April 1919, 24. This figure was presumably for deaths from all causes, as elsewhere influenza deaths were reported as 46: C. P. Vinod Kumar, P. G. Revathi and K. T. Rammohan, 'Kolar Gold Mines: An Unfinished Biography of Colonialism', *Economic and Political Weekly*, 33 (1998), 1471.

[63] *ToI*, 17 July 1918, 7.

[64] In the Central Provinces alone 325 forestry workers died: 'Central Provinces Forest Administration Report, 1918–19', *Indian Forester*, 47 (1921), 36.

[65] *ToI*, 13 March 1919, 6.

Presidency in September 1918, not over influenza or any government attempts to control it, but over steep and sudden rises in food prices, exacerbated by shortages, speculation and hoarding.[66] By the same token, sickness and death among the poorer classes partly explain why such protests quickly ebbed away. The collective energy was lacking to sustain them, but wholesale mortality among the poor had the paradoxical effect of creating a labour shortage and so boosted wages and employment.[67]

In the early plague years the popular and middle-class reaction had been against excessive state intervention. In 1918 the complaint was that the government was too lethargic and inactive.[68] Having little to offer in their own defence, medical and sanitary officers were disposed to blame the devastating impact of the epidemic on popular ignorance and the 'absolute helplessness' of the people or on the sudden eruption of a crisis that was beyond the capacity of any state to control. As one official put it, 'no agency can cope with an avalanche'.[69] The inactivity of the state made it the more likely, however, that Indians, especially urban, middle-class Indians, would come forward instead – organising relief committees, visiting the sick, handing out food and medicine, directing the disposal of the dead.[70] In an urban context, colonial claims about the 'absolute helplessness' of the people look thin when measured against the upsurge of middle-class philanthropy. Since the 1890s Indian religious and social welfare organisations like the Arya Samaj, the Ramakrishna Mission, the Seva Samiti and Bombay's Social Service League had gained extensive experience of charitable relief work in times of famine, pestilence and flood: that expertise was now deployed to help those struck down with influenza.[71] The demonstrable inability of Western medicine and public health measures to curb the epidemic or bring relief to sufferers encouraged practitioners of other systems – Ayurveda, Unani, homoeopathy – to offer their

---

[66] David Arnold, 'Looting, Grain Riots and Government Policy in South India, 1918', *Past & Present*, 84 (1979), 111–45.

[67] *Season and Crop Report*, 4.

[68] *Bombay Chronicle*, 16 October 1918, *Report on Indian Papers Published in the Bombay Presidency* (Bombay, 1918), week ending 19 October 1918, 11.

[69] *Annual Sanitary Report, Central Provinces, 1918*, app. C, 1, 5.

[70] *Administration Report of the Municipal Commissioner, Bombay, 1918–19*, 39–40; *Annual Report on the Municipal Administration, Calcutta, 1918–19*, 81–9; *Annual Report of the Sanitary Commissioner, Madras, 1918* (Madras, 1919), 8–9.

[71] Ramanna, 'Coping', 91–6; *ToI*, 30 September 1918, 6; 3 October 1918, 8; *Annual Report of the Sanitary Commissioner of the United Provinces of Agra and Oudh, 1918* (Allahabad, 1919), app. D, 14 A.

services and recommend their own medicines and tonics,[72] leaving IMS officers to rail against such 'questionable remedies'.[73]

The Government of India's sanitary commissioner noted with some condescension: 'Never before, perhaps, in the history of India, have the educated and more fortunately placed members of the community, come forward in such large numbers to help their poorer brethren in time of distress.'[74] He tried to put a positive gloss on the fact that middle-class Indians had mobilised themselves to do what the state had largely failed to. 'History', he declared, 'has shown that unnecessary loss of life through epidemics has been an important factor in awakening a public health conscience.' The 'appalling mortality' of 1918 would not have been in vain 'if it inculcates in the minds of the general public the dire necessity for public health reform, and for taxation to meet essential expenditure'.[75] In reality, though, influenza marked a further stage in the maturing of Indian civil society and the passing of political leadership and social hegemony from colonial officials to the Indian middle classes. In their eyes at least, the response to influenza showed their superior commitment to serving the poor and needy. 'Who', asked one nationalist newspaper, 'are the real well-wishers of the masses?'[76] For any patriotic reader the answer was not seriously in doubt.

Another kind of politics was abroad, too. The war, however physically distant from Indian shores, released in many Indians an impending sense of the apocalypse, a civilisational and existential nightmare of which influenza was only one manifestation. In the popular imagination the mysterious epidemic was not influenza at all but 'war fever'. In September 1918 an Indian identified only as 'B' wrote to the newspapers from Poona claiming that the pandemic had been unleashed by 'vapour from the gas bombs' in France and was now 'spreading all over the globe'.[77] The idea was quickly ridiculed as unscientific and absurd, but that it was published at all and drew such a critical response was a sign that it reflected an underlying collective anxiety.[78] The Government of India's sanitary commissioner insisted that, whatever 'wild rumours' might say, influenza was not a 'war disease'. 'Such wild

---

[72] *Deccan Ryot*, 31 October 1918, *Report on Indian Papers, Bombay*, week ending 2 November 1918, 23; Rajendra Kumar Sen, *A Treatise on Influenza: With Special Reference to the Pandemic of 1918* (North Lakhmipur, 1923), 103.

[73] Glen Liston in *Praja Mitra*, 25 October 1918, *Report on Indian Papers, Bombay*, week ending 26 October 1918, 19.

[74] White, *Preliminary Report*, 12.

[75] *Annual Report, Sanitary Commissioner, India, 1918*, 133.

[76] *Kesari*, 12 November 1918, *Report on Indian Papers, Bombay*, week ending 16 November 1918, 23.

[77] *ToI*, 18 September 1918, 5.

[78] White, *Preliminary Report*, 2.

unfounded rumours', he wrote, 'as those which attributed the pandemic to the extensive use of poison gas on the western front, or to the evil machinations of our unscrupulous enemy [Germany], would scarcely have deserved attention, had they not been so current in India during the months of October and November [1918].'[79] A sense of impending catastrophe was evident nonetheless. Pramanath Nath Bose, a Bengali geologist formerly in state service, joined in the widely shared sense of dismay at the madness of the brutal, mechanised warfare that had seized mankind, threatening societies around the globe and imperilling India. That influenza was a disease everyone with an education knew, but the sickness that underlay it was that of a warped civilisation, modern, mechanical, amoral.[80]

Influenza also connected with the unfolding political crisis as nationalist politicians sought to capitalise on Britain's weakness and India's hardship to win vital concessions. If some of India's leading dissidents, such as Bal Gangadhar Tilak and Annie Besant, were less vocal than they had been in 1917, a new whirlwind force was emerging in Mohandas Gandhi, who in a matter of months switched from recruiting soldiers for the Raj to riding the wave of anti-colonial discontent.[81] Recovering from a protracted illness of his own, he called for non-violent resistance against the repressive Rowlatt Act and so sparked a fresh round of protest and defiance.[82] It might be excessive to argue that agitational politics drove endemic hunger from the newspapers' front pages, or that, imperial violence supplanting epidemic violence, the Amritsar massacre of April 1919, with its nearly 400 deaths, put the twelve million influenza deaths in the shade; but something of that order helps explain why influenza did not command more intense and lasting attention. The Indian middle classes, so vocal over plague, were far more muted over influenza. Though they, too, suffered and died in the epidemic, their minds were elsewhere. As in Ireland in the crucial years 1916–22, influenza in India could be subsumed within a more compelling story

[79] Jim Corbett, *Man-Eaters of Kumaon* (1944), xvi; White, *Preliminary Report*, 1.

[80] Pramatha Nath Bose, *National Education and Modern Progress* (Calcutta, 1921).

[81] Gandhi was involved in army recruitment at Godhra in Gujarat on 14 July 1918 just as 'Bombay influenza' struck the town: *ToI*, 17 July 1918, 7.

[82] I see no reason to doubt Gandhi's own assertion that he was suffering from dysentery and exhaustion and not, as some recent writers claim, from influenza. Nor do I see grounds for arguing that the epidemic 'pushed India closer to independence'. Laura Spinney, *Pale Rider: The Spanish Flu of 1918 and How It Changed the World* (2017), 8, 254–60. On the broad relationship between political unrest and influenza, see Kenneth L. Gillion, *Ahmedabad: A Study in Indian Urban History* (Canberra, 1969), 165; James Masselos, 'Some Aspects of Bombay City Politics in 1919', in *Essays on Gandhian Politics: The Rowlatt Satyagraha of 1919*, ed. R. Kumar (Oxford, 1971), 167; C. A. Bayly, *The Local Roots of Indian Politics: Allahabad, 1880–1920* (Oxford, 1975), 245–6.

of patriotic suffering and aspiring nationhood.[83] Where Klein appended the epidemic to a sustained crisis of mortality dating back to the 1870s, others at the time and since have incorporated influenza into other narratives: hunger, poverty and the subsistence crisis, the political struggle for independence, or, as on the Kolar goldfields, the long history of labour exploitation, industrial accidents and insanitary working conditions.[84]

By the time the full demographic toll from the epidemic had become apparent through the decennial census in 1923, India had moved on to non-cooperation, civil disobedience and a political crisis that threatened the survival of the Raj. By the time *that* crisis was over, India had a new constitution, Gandhi was in jail and influenza mortality had sunk to insignificant levels. The Armistice in November 1918 was duly celebrated in India and the death of Indian soldiers memorialised in monuments from Neuve Chapelle to Basra and New Delhi.[85] But there was no public thanksgiving for the end of the epidemic, no formal commemoration for influenza's twelve million 'fallen'.

Influenza was clearly personal as well as political. It impacted massively on families, communities and individuals across the subcontinent, but the evidence for this is remarkably scarce and fragmentary, not least with respect to women's lives.[86] In one of many obituary notices the 'untimely' death from influenza of Syed Edroos, 'a young man of fine disposition and much promise' and son of a member of the Bombay legislature, was said to have 'caused profound regret and sincere sorrow among all sections of the community'; but we learn little more.[87] In a village in the United Provinces a young widow whose husband and father had both died from influenza returned to an older tradition of honouring the dead by committing sati on her husband's funeral pyre.[88] The poet Nirala recalled how he was summoned home with a telegram informing him his wife was gravely ill with influenza. By the time he arrived at her village his wife had died and the Ganges was swollen with the bodies of the dead. 'This was the strangest time in my life', he wrote, 'my family disappeared in the blink of an eye', as did most of their labourers and sharecroppers.[89] Gandhi wrote a letter in

[83] Milne, *Stacking*, ch. 8.

[84] Kumar *et al.* 'Kolar', 1470–1.

[85] *Neuve Chapelle: India's Memorial in France, 1914–18* (1928); David A. Johnson, 'New Delhi's All-India War Memorial (India Gate): Death, Monumentality and the Lasting Legacy of Empire in India', *Journal of Imperial and Commonwealth History*, 46 (2018), 345–66.

[86] On the need for a more 'feminised' history of the pandemic, see Terence Ranger, 'A Historian's Foreword', in *Spanish Influenza*, ed. Phillips and Killingray, xx.

[87] *ToI*, 19 July 1918, 2.

[88] *ToI*, 10 May 1919, 11.

[89] Suryakant Tripathi Nirala, *A Life Misspent* (New York, 2016), 53–4.

November 1918 to his son Harilal in which he noted that Harilal's family had been badly hit by influenza. But, with what almost seems like indifference, Gandhi added that 'such news is pouring in from everywhere so that now the mind is hardly affected'.[90] In a further letter to his English friend C. F. Andrews, the following January 1919, Gandhi remarked: 'So you have been suffering from influenza,' but he makes no further comment.[91] Such vignettes, however intimate, moving or perturbing in themselves, present us with only a very fragmentary impression of the twelve million lives lost and the millions more whose existence was shattered or destroyed by the epidemic. Instead, influenza is almost always incidental to some other story. In his account of the man-eating tigers of Kumaon, Jim Corbett described how, during the 1918 epidemic, corpses were dumped in the jungle for want of any other means of disposing of them. The bodies were found by leopards who acquired a taste for human flesh and so became man-eaters.[92] An anecdote that begins with human mortality becomes a story of animal predation: leopards, not people, change their behaviour. And even now interest in the 1918 epidemic is often less about recovering the fine-grained materiality of India's past than a means of trying to gauge when and how the next big pandemic will travel the globe and leave millions more dead in its wake.[93]

For all the immensity of lives lost and the enormous suffering it occasioned, India's influenza epidemic did not seem, even to contemporaries, to convey any particular moral or political lesson, to be instructive to state, science or society. It was not, from the perspective of the colonial state and its medical establishment, an episode of which they could be proud or which they could readily incorporate into a narrative of progress. For many Indians, to whatever class they belonged, influenza was part of a more engrossing struggle for survival, subsistence and self-determination. We, as historians, can and should try as far as we can to fill up that apparent void, that seeming absence, in the historiography of the pandemic. But I doubt that for India we will ever quite escape from the characterisation of influenza as a 'forgotten' epidemic.

[90] Gandhi to Harilal Gandhi, 23 November 1918, *Collected Works of Mahatma Gandhi*, vol. 17, 247.

[91] Gandhi to Andrews, 10 January 1919, *ibid.*, 256.

[92] Corbett, *Man-Eaters*, xvi.

[93] Lalit Kant and Randeep Guleria, 'Pandemic Flu, 1918: After Hundred Years, India Is As Vulnerable', *Indian Journal of Medical Research*, 147 (2018), 221–4.

Transactions of the RHS 29 (2019), pp. 201–221 © Royal Historical Society 2019
doi:10.1017/S0080440119000094

THE SELF AND SELF-HELP: WOMEN PURSUING AUTONOMY IN POST-WAR BRITAIN

By Lynn Abrams

READ 11 MAY 2018

ABSTRACT. In the history of post-war womanhood in Britain, women's self-help organisations are credited with little significance save for 'helping mothers to do *their* work more happily'. This paper suggests that the do-it-yourself impetus of the 1960s and 1970s should be regarded as integral to understanding how millions of women negotiated a route towards personal growth and autonomy. Organisations like the National Housewives' Register, the National Childbirth Trust and the Pre-School Playgroups Association emerged from the grass roots in response to the conundrum faced by women who experienced dissatisfaction and frustration in their domestic role. I argue that these organisations offered thousands of women the opportunity for self-development, self-confidence and independence and that far from being insufficiently critical of dominant models of care, women's self-help operating at the level of the everyday was to be one of the foundations of what would become, by the 1970s, the widespread feminist transformation of women's lives.

I Introduction

In 1960 the minutes of an area organisers' meeting of the National Childbirth Trust (NCT), founded four years earlier to promote natural childbirth, announced the birth to 'C. Macdonald (Weston-S-Mare) 3rd, a boy, 9 lbs 4 oz. She had amazed her doctor who had kept exclaiming "Look at that CONTROL! Astonishing!"'[1] Macdonald had subscribed to the methods of the NCT which promoted the philosophy and methods of natural childbirth advocate Grantly Dick-Read via antenatal classes organised by its local branches, countering the medicalisation they experienced in hospital. 'I went to classes, not so much because I had yet become apprehensive about having my child, but because I very much wanted to enjoy the experience as fully as possible, *and to feel in control* of the situation – to have my own child rather than be half-doped and dull while others "had it" for me,' explained Viscountess

---

[1] Wellcome Trust Archives: NCT PP/GDR/F/12: Box 64. Minutes of the area organiser/helpers meeting 1 November 1960, London.

Enfield upon the opening of the London headquarters in 1964.[2] The Trust sought to empower women with the confidence to take ownership of their own birth plans and to consign to history the experience of being treated 'like a machine' in hospital.[3] 'Until the women of this country who have experienced the NCT get up and do something about it,' commented an NCT activist, 'you may be sure nothing will be done and the old fashioned system of castor oil, drugs, forceps and stitches will continue to be the fashion.'[4]

Do-it-yourself women's organisations have so far been largely neglected in the emerging history of post-war womanhood in the United Kingdom and yet they offered millions of women the opportunity for self-development, self-confidence and independence.[5] They were numerous and varied in their objectives. The NCT was one of several so-called self-help organisations founded in the 1950s and 60s, many of them with the help of the *Manchester Guardian* newspaper.[6] The 1960s was, as *Guardian* women's page editor Mary Stott termed it, the 'do-it-yourself decade'.[7] Through giving space to women's issues, the *Guardian* was instrumental in helping to launch a number of other organisations including the National Council for the Single Woman and her Dependants, Mothercare for Children in Hospital and, more significant in respect of longevity, membership numbers and geographical spread, the National Housewives' Register (NHR) and the Pre-School Playgroups Association (PPA).[8] All emerged at a pivotal moment in Britain when women of the so-called 'transition generation' (those who grew to maturity in the post-war decades) began to discover the gap between their expectations and the realities of their lives and took it upon themselves to fill that gap with autonomous activity which met

---

[2] Wellcome Trust Archives: NCT SA/NCT/A/1/1/2: NCT Official Opening of Headquarters 1 December 1964. Opening address by Viscountess Enfield.

[3] Wellcome Trust Archives: NCT SA/NCT/A/1/1/2: Parents' Group Bulletin Vol. 11 no.3 1956.

[4] Wellcome Trust: NCT SA/NCT/A/1/1/2: Handwritten script of a talk or speech (no name or date) to accompany the showing of the film (undated).

[5] These organisations do appear in more popular and journalistic treatments of women in post-war Britain, for instance Mary Ingham, *Now We Are Thirty: Women of the Breakthrough Generation* (1981) and Suzanne Lowry, *The Guilt Cage: Housewives and a Decade of Liberation* (1980). The NCT and PPA have been discussed by Angela Davis in relation to the modern histories of motherhood and childcare: Davis, *Modern Motherhood: Women and the Family in England 1945–2000* (Manchester, 2012) and *Pre-School Childcare in England 1939–2010* (Manchester, 2015). The NHR features in Ali Haggett, *Desperate Housewives, Neuroses and the Domestic Environment 1945–1970* (2012).

[6] Although NCT was launched via the *Times* newspaper.

[7] *Women Talking: An Anthology from the Guardian Women's Page 1922–35, 1957–71*, ed. Mary Stott (1987), 225. Stott edited the page from 1957 to 1972.

[8] *Ibid.*, 225–33.

their needs, rather than looking to existing organisations or the state to act on their behalf.[9] The historiographical neglect of these groups has been symptomatic of a failure of perception. It is in part a hangover from the condescension of those who have regarded such organisations as not being sufficiently critical of gender relations and thus not sufficiently radical to be considered part of the post-war feminist narrative.[10] Self-help initiatives which addressed concerns around childbirth, motherhood, childcare and the isolation of housewives have been seen as reinforcing rather than overturning the subordination of women and thus not integral to dominant contemporary and historical narratives of post-war womanhood and especially of feminism. The result is that organisations that sought to address the tension between women's maternal and domestic roles and self-expression and self-development have, so far, not been integrated into interpretations of post-war change. Rather, the key interpretive frameworks for understanding women's experience in this period are firstly the dual role – the model whereby women engaged in the labour force before marriage and motherhood and then re-entered the workforce when the children were school age or older – and second, the emergence of women's liberation.[11]

In what follows it is argued that these nationwide organisations were a grass-roots response to the post-war reconfiguring of women's life cycles.[12] By conceptualising the self-help organisations in this way we can see how they allowed women to negotiate a route towards personal growth to meet their needs which, in most cases, consisted of conjoining family and motherhood with self-development outside the home. For many, mainly educated women, self-help voluntarist organisations were not merely a stopgap before picking up their career again. Rather, active involvement could be a springboard to a new career

[9] Ingham, *Now We Are Thirty*.

[10] This approach is adopted by Elizabeth Wilson in *Only Halfway to Paradise: Women in Postwar Britain: 1945–68* (1980), and Anna Coote and Beatrix Campbell, *Sweet Freedom: The Struggle for Women's Liberation* (1982).

[11] See Alva Myrdal and Viola Klein, *Women's Two Roles* (1956), and for a recent analysis of the legacy of this interpretive model see Helen McCarthy, 'Social Science and Married Women's Employment in Postwar Britain', *Past & Present*, 233 (2016), 269–305. Organised feminism and women's liberation, whilst still awaiting a comprehensive history, functions as a magnetic pole for analyses of women's position in post-war Britain.

[12] Examples of the former would include Hannah Gavron, *The Captive Wife: Conflicts of Housebound Mothers* (Harmondsworth, 1966); Pearl Jephcott with Nancy Seear and John H. Smith, *Married Women Working* (1962); Viola Klein, *Britain's Married Women Workers* (1965). See McCarthy, 'Social Science'; and Jane Lewis, 'From Equality to Liberation: Contextualizing the Emergence of the Women's Liberation Movement', in *Cultural Revolution? The Challenge of the Arts in the 1960s*, ed. B. Moore-Gilbert and John Seed (1992), 96–117.

and a new identity. This was to be one of the foundations of what would become by the 1970s the widespread feminist transformation of women's lives.

The perception problem at the root of the feminist narrative hitherto has been a mistaken need to distinguish feminist women's organisations of the 'second wave' from non-feminist organisations of the preceding generation. Women's activity of the early 1960s to the late 1970s has been cast as a necessary corrective to earlier initiatives characterised as self-satisfied and uncritical of the structures that framed their dilemmas. Historians of women's voluntary organisations such as the Townswomen's Guild, Women's Citizens' Associations and the National Council of Women have been at pains to portray inter-war women's activism as bridging the gap from first to second wave movements by recasting the work of these groups as 'democratic citizenship'.[13] But early historians of the women's liberation movement have rarely been so generous, contrasting the women's liberation movement's analysis of women's oppression in the home and campaigns such as Wages for Housework with the position of organisations like the PPA which did not question the 'burden of care' and according to one interpretation were 'primarily oriented towards helping mothers to do *their* work more happily'.[14] Others have struck a middle way, arguing that the frustration and disenchantment experienced by so many women in the late 1950s and early 60s was channelled into activity that departed from the positions of feminist social researchers who were obsessed with the issue of the dual role and which developed new organisational models to enable women to achieve a new kind of equality on their own terms.[15] The fact that they did this through organisations that attended to what might be considered 'domestic' concerns – motherhood, childcare, housework and so on – should not detract from the critical interventions they made, both practical and analytical. Indeed, recent contributions have argued that whilst second-wave feminism questioned many post-war assumptions about appropriate models of mothering, women formulated a multitude of individual and collective responses to the challenges posed by the new post-war contract, both practical and

[13] Catriona Beaumont, *Housewives and Citizens. Domesticity and the Women's Movement in England, 1928–64* (Manchester, 2013); Sue Innes, 'Constructing Women's Citizenship in the Inter-war Period: The Edinburgh Women's Citizens' Association', *Women's History Review*, 13 (2004), 621–48.

[14] See Sarah Stoller, 'Forging a Politics of Care: Theorizing Household Work in the British Women's Liberation Movement', *History Workshop Journal*, 85 (2018), 95–119; Wilson, *Only Halfway to Paradise*, 184.

[15] Jane Lewis, 'From Equality to Liberation: Contextualising the Emergence of the Women's Liberation Movement', in *Cultural Revolution?*, ed. Moore-Gilbert and Seed, 96–117.

political.[16] Moreover, at the level of individual women, these organisations were often integral to their retaining or reframing a sense of self and autonomy at a life stage when that self so often became buried and even lost in the identity imposed on them of housewife and mother.

There is also a larger point here about the way we write the history of Western women in the post-war period. In interpretations of change in women's lives, such has been the gravitational pull felt by feminist historians towards the feminist movement and the liberation narrative that historians have tended to ascribe the movement of the 1970s pivotal significance. The wave analogy has been robustly critiqued, but what has begun to take its place is a feminist continuum narrative in which historians have sought to bridge the more distinct phases of feminist activism, or they have identified precursors to or inheritors of particular campaigns and moments.[17] The result is a myopia to other forms of women's actions, an episodic narrative of feminism, and a lack of inclusivity for women who did much to construct the practical, everyday feminism of modern Britain. Rather than bridging the waves, I suggest our scholarship should turn to perceive the causeway through the decades across which women's organisations traversed. Causeways are grounded links; they facilitate movement in both directions through, rather than over, turbulent and shifting waters. This approach might encompass a very wide range of organisations and positions, from the political activism of the Campaign for Nuclear Disarmament to the self-care of keep-fit.[18] Indeed, it might be more profitable to broaden the perspective so that the women's liberation movement is regarded as a minority sport albeit one with significance greater than its size would suggest. Let us start to see the women's liberation movement as one of many social movements and organisations which emerged as a female response to a broad and complex trajectory of social change since the 1940s encompassing women's education and work, increasing rejection of religious morality, decline in family size and control of fertility, social and geographical mobility and the growth of self-therapies and therapeutic

[16] See Carla Pascoe, 'From the Little Wife to the Supermum? Maternographies of Feminism and Mothering in Australia since 1945', *Feminist Studies*, 45 (2019), 100–28; Lynne Marks, '"A Job that should be Respected": Contested Visions of Motherhood and English Canada's Second Wave Women's Movements, 1970–1990', *Women's History Review*, 25 (2016), 771–90; Stoller, 'Forging a Politics of Care'.

[17] See, for example, Beaumont, *Housewives and Citizens*; Beaumont, 'Housewives, Workers and Citizens: Voluntary Women's Organisations and the Campaign for Women's Rights in England and Wales during the Postwar Period', in *NGOs in Contemporary Britain: Non State Actors in Society and Politics since 1945*, ed. N. Crowson *et al.* (Basingstoke, 2009), 59–76; Innes, 'Constructing Women's Citizenship'.

[18] Examples here include Jill Liddington, *The Road to Greenham Common: Feminism and Anti-Militarism in Britain since 1820* (New York, 1991); Eilidh Macrae, *Exercise in the Female Life-Cycle in Britain, 1930–1970* (Basingstoke, 2016).

practices.[19] Within such a picture, what we understand as women's liberation, encompassing the interrogation of personal life as well as advancing interpretations of inequality and working to implement change across a diverse range of issues, might be seen as merely one form of response to the question of how a woman was to live.

The self-help or do-it-yourself women's groups of the 1960s and 70s are the focus here. I argue that these were potentially transformative spaces which enabled women to develop the social relationships, largely with other women, that are integral to the realisation of female autonomy or self-determination. Here the concept of relational autonomy developed by feminist philosophers is helpful. It holds that female selves are inherently social, can only be constituted by social relations and that an autonomous life depends upon healthy relations with others.[20] This is in contrast to the liberal, individualist, rationalistic concept of autonomy associated with free-acting men. However, while historians have written about the self-actualising currents of the 'expressive revolution' of the 1960s when the liberationist movements of that era, including feminism, offered women and men the space to self-fashion, taking in everything from sexual choices to clothing and music, these are generally understood as separate from 'traditional' roles and structures such as the heterosexual family and motherhood and are achieved through oppositional behaviour or self-examination (consciousness-raising, for instance, or psychotherapy).[21] This interpretive framework is too rigid. It does not allow space for self-actualising behaviour, particularly amongst women, alongside marriage and childcare. Whilst this cohort of predominantly middle-class women who lived through the era of near-universal marriage and the opening up

---

[19] Callum G. Brown, *Religion and the Demographic Revolution: Women and Secularisation in Canada, Ireland, UK and USA since the 1960s* (2012); Simon Szreter and Kate Fisher, *Sex before the Sexual Revolution: Intimate Life in England 1918–1963* (Cambridge, 2010). We await a serious study of the 'expressive revolution' as it was experienced by women via therapeutic practice but see Haggett, *Desperate Housewives*, for a discussion of female 'neurosis'.

[20] See M. Freedman, 'Autonomy and Social Relationships: Rethinking the Feminist Critique', in *Feminists Rethink the Self*, ed. D. Teitjens Meyers (Boulder, 1997), 40–61, and C. Mackenzie and N. Stoljar (eds.), *Relational Autonomy: Feminist Perspectives on Autonomy, Agency and the Social Self* (Oxford, 2000).

[21] B. Martin, *A Sociology of Contemporary Cultural Change* (Oxford, 1981). For a discussion of how this impacted on women's narratives of the period see Lynn Abrams, 'Heroes of Their Own Life Stories: Narrating the Female Self in the Feminist Age', *Cultural and Social History* (2019), advance online publication. For an exception to the tendency to see women's autonomy and self-expression as mutually dependent see Dolly Smith Wilson, 'A New Look at the Affluent Worker: The Good Working Mother in Post-War Britain', *Twentieth Century British History*, 17 (2006), 206–29, which argues that working women responded to the denigration of working mothers by demanding part-time work and demonstrating that a woman who worked benefited her family.

of further and higher education and the employment market experienced acute conflicts between the roles expected of them, they nevertheless did find practical ways of pursuing autonomy which intersected with their everyday lives. This was, as often as not, an autonomy that was dependent upon mutually constitutive social connections, especially with other women. And autonomy with these qualities was nurtured by many women in self-help organisations relating to children, education and the home.

II Do-it-yourself

In February 1960 Maureen Nicol, a young mother, had a letter published on *The Guardian*'s 'Mainly for Women' page in which she suggested that 'housebound wives with liberal interests and a desire to remain individuals could form a national register'. Maureen, who had recently moved with her husband to a new area, was responding to an article in the same column by *Guardian* journalist Betty Jerman railing against suburbia and its dulling effects, in the style of Betty Friedan except Jerman challenged women to do something about it. 'They stay here all day. They set the tone. Many of them look back with regret to the days when they worked in an office. Their work kept them alert. Home and child-minding can have a blunting effect on a woman's mind. But only she can sharpen it.'[22] The result of Jerman's goading and Nicol's practical suggestion was the formation of the National Housewives' Register, literally a national register of local groups of women initially run from Maureen's kitchen table. Within ten years there were 8,000 members, and groups in every county. Nicol described the NHR as 'a great groundswell of lively-minded, reasonably educated mothers, torn from family and friends by mobile husbands … largely solving their feelings of mental stagnation and loneliness by getting together and expanding their own lives'.[23] A few months later in 1961 Belle Tutaev, a former teacher with pre-school children in London, wrote to the same woman's page on the subject of 'Do-it-Yourself Nurseries'. Responding to the absence of pre-school provision, Belle started a campaign – the campaign for Nursery Education – but when this failed to have an impact she set up her own playgroup in Marylebone. Her letter was a call to arms to 'mothers and teachers who would like to create their own solutions to their problems'.[24]

---

[22] Betty Jerman, 'Squeezed in like sardines in suburbia', *The Guardian*, 19 February 1960.

[23] Maureen Nicol cited in Betty Jerman, *The Lively-Minded Women. The First Twenty Years of the National Housewives Register* (1981), 29.

[24] *The Guardian*, August 1961.

The National Housewives' Register – originally the Housebound Wives Register, and much later renamed the National Women's Register – occupied a place in British society somewhere between the Women's Institute and Women's Liberation. It was set up in response to the crying need from young mothers for somewhere to engage in 'mental exercise', to 'escape from cabbage syndrome' with like-minded women, many of whom had tertiary or higher education and who were isolated, bored at home and in desperate need of stimulation. In its earliest incarnation the NHR was run from Maureen Nicol's home as she established a 'register' of names of women across the country who wrote in response to her *Guardian* letter. Quickly regional organisers were identified who maintained the register in their area and facilitated meetings of local groups. Meetings took place in members' homes, babies and toddlers were minded on a rota system, 'competitive' baking was not permitted, and most importantly, there was a 'no domestic trivia' rule.[25] What were described as 'mind-stretching chat sessions' characterised most meetings; topics for discussion, often led by a member who had been tasked to do the research in the local library, ranged widely from classical art to eugenics, transcendental meditation to homosexuality. The Worthing, Lancing and Littlehampton group was typical, with topics including comprehensive schools, what to do in the event of a nuclear attack and the pill.[26] 'I feel personally that it will ensure that my brain does not "seize up" during the years I am away from my profession as a teacher,' wrote one member. 'So much one does in the home seems to be of a trivial nature that the effort one makes towards NHR, i.e. Research, preparation of a "speech" and reading, is so refreshing.'[27]

From the start the NHR was determined to distinguish itself and its purpose. 'Intelligent women' not 'cake-icers' summed up the demographic they were seeking to recruit.[28] Advertising in popular women's magazines like *Woman* attracted what were described as 'un-register like' women, a problem overcome in the Lewisham group by the area organiser obtaining the addresses to which her newsagent delivered *The Guardian* and in Northwich where a letter advertising NHR was inserted in copies of *She* and *Nova* magazines in an attempt to attract the 'right kind' of members, not those who merely wished for a

---

[25] Jerman, *Lively-Minded Women*, 10.

[26] Women's Library: NHR Spring Newsletter 1966. (Consulted at the former premises of the Women's Library, London Metropolitan University, where NHR newsletters were available on open shelves.)

[27] Cited in Jerman, *Lively-Minded Women*, 22–3.

[28] The term 'cake-icers' was used by NHR national organiser Lesley Moreland to describe those women who were domestically inclined. Cited in *ibid.*, 35.

mothers and toddlers club.[29] A 1966 survey of NHR members reported that 19 per cent of those who responded were graduates and 50 per cent had a professional training.

> The majority of members are 'bound' in that they are restricted to a routine probably more confining than anything they have hitherto encountered. Intelligent women with small children under school age, who have held interesting, stimulating and responsible jobs, now find their lives centred around the home as never before. They take a pride in their homes and families, accepting the restrictions and responsibilities inherent in their situation, but they find themselves mentally frustrated with the curtailment of their personal freedom.[30]

It is clear, however, that NHR tapped into an existential need of many women to rediscover their identity, their self-confidence and self-respect which was subsumed in the daily round of housework and child-care. Sheila Hunt's *cri de cœur* in the 1966 NHR newsletter spoke for many: 'Organising children, housework etc is surely not the real difficulty. My crying need is for time to be myself, not mother or house-keeper, ten minutes to look at the newspaper when it arrives, instead of in the evening? Must one really give up oneself so much?'[31] The sense that self and the possibilities for self-development were buried within the all-consuming banality of the everyday was acutely summed up by Sheila Partington, NHR national committee member and ex-*Guardian* journalist, in a letter to the NHR national organiser purportedly to discuss some aspect of NHR business: 'Have you read the Feminine Mystique by Betty Friedan that someone mentioned in the newsletter? Oh dear. The gasman long-awaited has appeared: also the baker and the dustmen. Must go.'[32] Women joined NHR to meet like-minded women, to get out of the house once a fortnight, to talk about something other than children and to prove to themselves and to others that 'mother' was not their only identity and that they had not put their 'minds into cold-storage'.[33] 'I seemed to belong and for these evenings at least I was not just Cliff's wife or James' mum. At last I could come to terms with being a housewife because I could still be me as well' was how NHR member Chris White put it.[34] Responses to publicity for a new group in Cardiff in 1966 reflect just these frustrations: 'I

---

[29] *Ibid.*, 67; LSE, Women's Library: NHR Spring Newsletter 1966; Autumn Newsletter 1966.
[30] LSE, Women's Library: 5/NWR/1/16: Survey reports 1966–. Survey published 1967, conducted by University of Manchester Extramural Department.
[31] LSE, Women's Library, NHR Newsletters, Autumn 1966.
[32] LSE, Women's Library, 5/NWR/1/15 Correspondence 1969–1972: Sheila Partington to Lesley Taylor, 1965.
[33] Jerman, *Lively-Minded Women*, 48.
[34] LSE, Women's Library: 5/NWR/5/3: Maureen Nicol. Letter from Chris White, 17 February 1994.

think I'm going round the bend/up the wall/crazy'; 'I'm in such a rut';
'I've been in a steady decline for ages'; 'thank god someone else feels the
same'; 'I never see a soul'; 'I can't seem to meet people'; 'no-one to talk
to'; and so on and so on.[35]

The National Housewives' Register was one conduit for the outpour-
ing of frustration, mainly amongst women who had formerly been
employed in professional and semi-professional roles. It was primarily
a social network, albeit some groups did involve themselves in political
issues and, unlike the Women's Institute, they were not prevented
from discussing religion or politics.[36] In 1966 a third of groups had
taken action on issues such as cervical smear testing, abortion law
reform, primary school overcrowding and pre-school provision.[37] But
the NHR's organisational reticence at adopting a political stance concealed its role as a Petri dish facilitating intellectual and political fermentation. NHR gave women the platform and the permission to question. 'I
wonder how different maternity services would be if run by women –
particularly if they have borne children?' asked a member from
Pevensey in the 1965 Newsletter.[38] 'And would we not allow abortion
to any woman who could not face carrying any particular baby – or
allow her to "put away" an obviously severely defective baby?' The following edition featured an invitation from a member in Cheshire to join
her in contributing to the abortion debate.

> Last night we had a talk on Abortion Law Reform, and the general feeling was that we
> would like to voice our opinion on this subject. The speaker suggested that we write to
> our MP and we later thought that we might write to Lady Phillips. After all, we are an
> articulate, thinking group of women and when we have a strong opinion on some con-
> troversial subject like this, we would like to add our weight to any movement in our
> direction.[39]

Nonetheless, external perceptions of NHR tended to patronise or criti-
cise. With the headline 'Think Tank for Women in the Suburbs', one
regional newspaper described NHR as 'this thriving enterprise which
aims to prove that suburbia can be a "think zone" by arranging mind
stretching chat sessions in members' homes'.[40] An article in the *Sunday
Times* reporting on NHR's weekend gathering in Buxton, by journalist
Moira Keenan, was critical of what she saw as the failure of NHR to
use its collective voice to influence policy. She was perplexed at what

---

[35] LSE, Women's Library: NHR Spring Newsletter 1966 (Cardiff).
[36] See Lowry, *The Guilt Cage*, 86.
[37] LSE, Women's Library: 5/NWR/1/16 Survey reports 1966–.
[38] LSE, Women's Library: NHR Newsletter, October 1965.
[39] LSE, Women's Library: Spring Newsletter 1966.
[40] LSE, Women's Library: NHR 5/NWR/1: unidentified press cutting (Yorkshire newspaper), undated, *c.* 1970.

she had witnessed: 'At the very first conference in seven years their choice of subject for a talk on the second day was not on abortion or birth control, drug addiction, comprehensive schools, under fives or any other subject of concern to young parents – but about the Peak District.' 'This seems like a serious criticism of a large body of intelligent and energetic women.'[41] Yet NHR was unabashed at accusations of lethargy and refused to become a pressure group; and the publicity gave membership a fillip, with more than 1,000 enquiries being received following the article's publication.[42] The insistence on not being a feminist organisation became shriller in the 1980s as NHR increasingly positioned itself in opposition to a stereotypical representation of feminism – 'But don't be put off because your interests are needlework, driving, squash or macramé,' announced one Kent newspaper in 1981. 'You will not be parading a banner, fighting a cause or demanding equal rights.'[43] Yet, at the same time, local groups were making the case for better nursery provision and raising awareness of initiatives to protect women against sexual assault, to name just two campaigning issues.[44] And for individual women NHR provided a space in which they could reconnect with their former selves and an environment in which to think about the future. Kathleen, who had been a draughtswoman before she had children, described her experience thus:

> There was a bit of a black hole in your life if you'd lost your work colleagues, so having sort of, you know, a meeting where you could discuss, I don't know … suicide, or a book group or divorce or any current issue of the day, you know … miners' strikes, um, you know, anything, it was quite interesting actually. And then later on, as NWR progressed, women of my age were then talking about going back to work, you know, further education, that sort of thing.[45]

It was arguably NHR's flexibility, its ability at local level to encompass a range of positions, that was both its weakness and its strength as Keenan had identified. As the organisation grew, its national committee and annual conferences gave some women opportunities to develop new skills or to put to use experience they had gained in the workplace. By the 1970s with a membership in the thousands, running NHR was an operation involving hundreds of women as area organisers or national committee members. And many of them used that knowledge as a

---

[41] *Sunday Times*, 1967. Jerman discusses the article and NHR's response in *Lively-Minded Women*, 62.

[42] LSE, Women's Library: 5/NWR/1/15 Correspondence 1969–1972.

[43] LSE, Women's Library: 5/NWR/4/1 (box 14): *Sheerness Times Guardian*, 28 August 1981.

[44] LSE, Women's Library: 5/NWR/4/1/28 Kent 1970–1992, *Kent and Sussex Courier*, Tunbridge Wells 6 March 1992; 5/NWR/4/1/35 Norfolk 1971–1995, *Norwich Mercury and Advertiser* 7 October 1988.

[45] Interview with Kathleen (pseudonym), conducted by Lynn Abrams, 2011.

stepping stone to further education (especially the Open University) and to careers in the voluntary sector.[46]

The Pre-School Playgroups Association on the other hand, with which many NHR members were also involved, was more multifaceted, providing social contact for mothers and their children but also informal and formal educational and training opportunities for women, and political engagement for some, with education policy, urban planning, social inequality and early years provision.[47] In this sense, PPA straddled the personal and the political in more concrete ways than any of the other self-help organisations of the post-war era. Some of the same frustrations of 'housebound mothers', allied to the absence of pre-school nursery or playschool provision, gave rise to the PPA. There was a gaping hole in any form of pre-school provision for children under five and particularly those under three, exacerbated in some areas – primarily new housing estates in urban areas – by the lack of play provision for the very young.[48] Whilst playgroups, which offered a few hours of supervised play activity, were ostensibly set up to provide pre-school children with social contact and supervised play, it was mothers who arguably gained the most from volunteering as helpers and, in the case of some, becoming more involved as supervisors. In the first issue of *Playgroup News*, a PPA newsletter for parents, Moya Codling who started a playgroup with her neighbours, initially meeting in their own homes in Bracknell new town before moving to a local community hall, expressed the feelings of many women in the same boat:

> You will know how lonely mums can be if you have ever locked the bathroom door and just sobbed. Have you ever rushed out of the house to run anywhere, just to come back again at the end of the garden path? ... Have you ever thrown the sugar bowl at the piano or the nappies out of the kitchen window and two minutes later picked them up and washed them for the nine hundredth and ninety-ninth time?[49]

Whereas in 1967 Brenda Crowe, the PPA's first national organiser, observed that 'it wasn't done to mention mothers' needs', just two years later she noted that supervisors and members were beginning to

---

[46] For examples of this trajectory see Lynn Abrams, 'Liberating the Female Self: Epiphanies, Conflict and Coherence in the Life Stories of Post-War British Women', *Social History*, 39 (2014), 14–35.

[47] PPA's founder Belle Tutaev had helped the NHR Harrow group set up a crèche and helped to edit *New Forum*, produced by NHR members. See Jerman, *Lively-Minded Women*, 151–2.

[48] See Jane Lewis, 'The Failure to Expand Childcare Provision and to Develop a Comprehensive Childcare Policy in Britain during the 1960s and 1970s', *Twentieth Century British History*, 24 (2013), 249–74; Vicky Randall, *The Politics of Child Daycare in Britain* (Oxford, 2000).

[49] UCL, Institute of Education Archive, Pre-School Playgroup Association Collection (hereafter PLA) PPA 16/1–3: Playgroup News, issue 1, 1969.

say, 'I'm sure that I shouldn't be saying it – but I can't help feeling that mothers need playgroups as much as the children do.'[50] Cynthia Robinson, formerly a journalist before she had three children, credited her local playgroup in Norwich with giving her back her confidence:

> In the first three years as a mother it seemed as if I had lost all status and excitement from my life. I slipped into a depressed state and was prescribed the then 'wonder' pill Librium. But here in the playgroup was a new beginning. I was greeted warmly, made to feel I had something to offer the group and then applauded for my usefulness.[51]

Cynthia quickly became a mother helper, was elected to the committee of her local group and went on to take playgroup courses, all the while learning about child development in general and her own boys' needs in particular. For Cynthia, the playgroup movement was the stepping stone to a new career. 'Over the next decade I moved on with confidence through further courses, tutor group, and then to a national PPA committee. At home I watched our sons grow with new enthusiasm and was soon involved with Open University courses in my "spare" time. This led to a Social Services post as Playgroups and Childminding Officer covering a third of Norfolk and then an MA in Social Work.'[52] And an anonymous contributor from Essex who became a playgroup leader wrote in similar terms. 'It has given me confidence ... I forget problems at home ... Since becoming involved my life has changed. I attend courses, talk to parents, counsellors, our MP and leave the family for the weekend to represent my group at the National PPA AGM.'[53]

The sentiment that playgroups were for mothers as much as children was core to the PPA's raison d'être, and from the start playgroups were dependent on an army of parent-helpers, not only those who supported children's play but those who made the hall bookings, undertook fund-raising, dealt with local authorities and all the other day-to-day requirements of running a community organisation. In a national survey conducted in the 1980s, the vast majority of the 459 mothers who responded said the playgroup helped them get on with their child better and they 'gained confidence in themselves as mothers and individuals'.[54] This had been the mantra of Brenda Crowe who had a background in Froebel nurseries. She acknowledged the various needs of mothers, from distraction from the monotony of everyday routine at

[50] PLA/PPA 1/1: Comparison Report, 1967–9, p. 1
[51] PLA/PPA 6/1 (3): Memories of Playgroups: Cynthia Robinson.
[52] *Ibid.*
[53] PLA/PPA 6/1: Memories (Anon Essex).
[54] M. Gray and L. McMahon, *Families in Playgroups. A Study of the Effect of Playgroup Experience on Families* (Reading, 1982) cited in L. McMahon, 'The Significance of Play for Children and Adults', in *Insights from the Playgroup Movement: Equality and Autonomy in a Voluntary Organisation*, ed. A. Henderson (Stoke-on-Trent, 2011), 30.

home to the opportunity to share their frustration and guilt for those who found it 'more difficult to adapt to a maternal role'.[55] Linnet McMahon, a parent co-founder of a village playgroup in 1968 who went on to become a playgroup course tutor, concurred: 'What mothers were doing was, like their children, learning through play, in the sense that they were able to try things out – or try new ways of being – in an emotionally facilitating environment where it felt safe, where it was alright to make mistakes. In the process they created something new or became someone different. They were developing a sense of autonomy and identity.'[56] And they were doing this *in relation to* other women. While attempts to include and involve fathers were regularly made, PPA was a women-centred and woman-led organisation.

In contrast to the National Housewives' Register, which largely retained its original format and purpose as a social network for women at home and which explicitly stated its separation from women's liberation, the PPA quickly expanded in size and purpose, from do-it-yourself and home-based playgroups to a national network with funding from local and national government and a structured training regime for those who wished to qualify as playgroup leaders and early years educators. And it is this expansion of PPA which took it beyond its initial constituency of mainly middle-class parents and children. Whereas NHR had always been somewhat picky about its members – identifying its constituency as 'lively-minded' and distinguishing itself from the 'Tupperware scene'[57] – the PPA early on, and perhaps acknowledging that it had 'got stuck with the middle class tag', engaged with working-class communities in urban areas where the need for pre-school facilities of all kinds, from playgroups to nurseries, was more acute.[58] PPA was conscious that its mode of operation, which required time, money (to hire halls and buy equipment) and connections, could not be easily replicated in 'deprived' areas; they also acknowledged that playgroups were not the only solution for mothers and children in such areas. On a visit to Birmingham in 1968, Brenda Crowe observed that 'playgroups can't be a solution' in deprived areas where mothers possessed less social capital and where many were in part-time employment.[59] Working mothers needed day care where they could leave the children.

The difficulty of the do-it-yourself approach when it left the leafy suburbs was highlighted in Glasgow where thousands of city inhabitants

[55] PLA/PPA/4/6: Brenda Crowe, 'Parent Involvement', in *Parents in Playgroups* (*c*.1971).
[56] McMahon, 'The Significance of Play', 32–3.
[57] LSE, Women's Library: 5/NWR/4/21/33 Merseyside 1968–1990: *The Reporter*, 19 April 1985 St Helens.
[58] PLA/PPA 5/4: *Contact* magazine 1964.
[59] PLA PPA 1–4: Crowe area report, Birmingham February 1968.

had been rehoused in new council housing estates and high flats in the 1960s and 70s and where there was a shortage of suitable accommodation for a playgroup or indeed a lack of any appropriate indoor or outdoor space for pre-school children to play safely. New estates had been built quickly and plans for play parks were rarely implemented.[60] The Scottish PPA's suggestion of building a 'simple hutted structure on the rooftop of a multi-storey block' was presumably not taken seriously.[61] Here too mothers' part-time working was an issue. The PPA had established a playgroup in a high flat in the city with a paid supervisor for just one term in acknowledgement of the inability of local mothers to manage it on their own. But once the supervisor was withdrawn, Brenda Crowe recognised this playgroup had no future, echoing the contemporaneous observations of social researcher Pearl Jephcott who, in the 1960s, was undertaking a major study of the city's high flats and who had a particular interest in the provision for children's play. Her research team worked with local women in one of the study areas, Royston, to establish a playgroup but soon understood that without support the playgroup would not be sustained.[62] The women there just did not have the capacity to maintain it given their own challenging circumstances. While the spokesperson for the Scottish Playgroups Association wrote of 'the seeming apathy and indifference on the part of the mothers' in some playgroups and their 'unreliability' for the rota of helpers, she also acknowledged that 'the needs of mothers to talk about their problems and their lives seem equal to their children's need to play'.[63] When the Scottish PPA undertook a study of playgroups in areas of need in 1977 they discovered that the majority had been initiated by outside agencies, usually social workers, and were grant aided; not surprising given the poor circumstances in which many families were living: in poor-quality housing, poor economic circumstances and often unsupported by other family members. In these conditions the PPA's philosophy of the centrality of voluntary parental involvement (in practice this meant mothers) was seriously challenged. In the early days of these groups the mothers were reluctant to get involved, preferring to treat the playgroup as a safe space for their

---

[60] V. Wright, A. Kearns, L. Abrams and B. Hazley, 'Planning for Play: Seventy Years of Ineffective Public Policy? The Example of Glasgow, Scotland', *Planning Perspectives*, 34 (2019), 243–63.

[61] PLA/PPA 2/9: Scottish PPA to Scottish Education Department, 1965.

[62] B. Hazley, V. Wright, L. Abrams and A. Kearns, '"People and their homes rather than housing in the usual sense"? Locating the Tenant's Voice in Homes in High Flats', *Women's History Review*, 29 (2019), 728–45.

[63] PLA/PPA 2/28: Scottish Pre-School Playgroups Association, *Playgroups in Areas of Need* (1977), 13.

children to play. It took time for mothers to participate. 'Some families have sunk so low in their self esteem that they cannot compete with the neighbours who can cope, and who despise them,' observed the report. 'They need to come together first and gain in dignity before venturing into the wider playgroup context where the more efficient mums can easily overwhelm them.'[64]

It is not easy to see how the women discussed in this report, and else-where in the PPA's work with 'deprived' communities, could achieve the growth and confidence through involvement with playgroups so com-monly reported by more affluent women. The autonomy achieved by middle-class women through the many relationships PPA facilitated was not easily transferable to working-class women in areas of depriv-ation. Many women were bringing up children in conditions of material and cultural poverty in the 1960s and 70s, and isolation in high-rise flats compounded their problems. It was unlikely that involvement in a play-group once a week would lift them out of their position, although it might have alleviated their isolation somewhat.[65] Women's liberation groups recognised this, preferring to argue for twenty-four-hour nurseries and childcare provision over playgroups which would enable women to take on paid work. The PPA, on the other hand, emphasised the need of the child for its mother in the first three years of life, but, as the author of an article in the *Times Educational Supplement* on playgroups for working mothers astutely remarked: 'the logical conclusion seems to be that no mother with a child under 5 can work. Many clearly do. So where are all their children? And can it be that all the children who are excluded from playgroups – those deprived of their mothers all day – are precisely the group who need them the most?'[66] This writer was part of a wider debate about playgroups within the context of government provision of childcare and early years education which acknowledged that playgroups were not the solution their advocates claimed. The voluntary principle of PPA which underpinned parental involvement was difficult to implement in working-class areas, which meant that playgroups soon folded without outside support.[67] More

---

[64] *Ibid.*

[65] See L. Abrams, L. Fleming, B. Hazley, V. Wright and A. Kearns, 'Isolated and Dependent: Women and Children in High-Rise Social Housing in Post-War Glasgow', *Women's History Review*, 29 (2019), 794–813.

[66] PLA/PPA FAW: 'Playgroups for Non-Working Mothers', *Times Educational Supplement* (1971).

[67] See *Playgroups in Areas of Need* and Janet Finch, 'The Deceit of Self Help: Preschool Playgroups and Working-Class Mothers', *Journal of Social Policy*, 13 (1984), 1–20. The PPA was not blind to the problem. On a visit to Birmingham in 1968 Brenda Crowe was con-fronted with the realities of a 'deprived' area where mothers required nurseries and

fundamentally some were concerned that the playgroup model of provision merely entrenched the existing advantages of middle-class children and presumably the mothers too.[68]

The PPA, whilst making serious efforts to expand provision to working-class areas and acknowledging that mothers' needs were often as urgent as those of their children, maintained its stance on voluntarism and the benefits to mothers of active participation. Some of its activists were more evangelical than others. Barbara Keeley, one of the founders of the movement, was outspoken in her belief that involvement with playgroups was 'an introduction to a career-like sequence of development'.[69] Indeed she suggested that women would not have realised the same potential if they had 'returned to the subordinate paid employment that they would have been expected to take', and dubbed voluntary work as 'employment-like'.[70] For Keeley, child-rearing and care was equal in value to paid work – not in economic terms but in terms of personal satisfaction and growth. She cites the example of 'Carol' who left school at sixteen, found employment as a dental nurse and then married and had three children which precipitated a period of depression. Becoming a parent volunteer at the playgroup led to her becoming secretary of her local PPA, a tutor for playgroup courses followed by work in a private nursery and then as a home visitor for a local authority-run nursery school. Carol said, 'Without the playgroup and tutoring experience I wouldn't have stood a chance – but then I wouldn't have had the confidence to apply anyhow!'[71] Clearly PPA had done wonders for Carol's sense of self, but what Keeley failed to consider sufficiently was the economic ramifications of a woman choosing to undertake voluntary work with a playgroup as opposed to paid work. And the PPA never engaged with the kind of thinking that made a case for valuing childcare in macro-economic terms.

One might regard playgroups as the quintessential middle-class organisation run by middle-class women for themselves and their children who in turn benefited in respect of improved social contacts, access to training and, for some, a track to a career in early years care and education.[72] This might suggest that the relational autonomy model yields benefits

---

nursery schools with trained staff rather than playgroups. PLA/PPA 1–4, Area Report, Birmingham February 1968.

[68] PLA/PPA FAW: 'Social Gap and Playschools', *The Guardian* 1971.

[69] PLA/PPA 4/46: Barbara Keeley, 'The Effect of Pre-School Provision on the Mothers of Young Children' (M.Sc. thesis, Cranfield Institute of Technology, 1980), 70.

[70] *Ibid.*, 76.

[71] *Ibid.*, 72–3.

[72] Finch, 'The Deceit of Self Help'; Janet Finch, 'A First-Class Environment? Working-Class Playgroups as Pre-School Experience', *British Educational Research Journal*, 10 (1984), 3–17.

for those who have the economic and cultural capital in the first place. Yet the picture is more nuanced. Davis's oral history research on motherhood in Oxfordshire indicates that working-class women did benefit socially from the playgroups, and contemporary studies in areas of need in Southwark in London and in Scotland demonstrate that mothers were willing to participate as organisers and helpers although they were not usually the initiators of groups.[73] In Scotland a study of eleven playgroups by the Scottish PPA identified that mothers in deprived areas were unlikely to initiate playgroups on account of the difficulties they faced with housing, poverty, family problems and the environment in which they lived. 'The difficulties these women face are enormous,' noted the study authors, 'and all … face them alone inasmuch as their families are usually unable or unwilling to provide any support and the husbands or co-habitees feel little or no obligation to the children.'[74] The mothers needed the playgroup for social chat and sharing of anxieties as much as the children needed it for play. 'The mothers' desperate needs override those of the children,' remarked one playleader. 'The mothers have a need to come and be calmed down.' Some worked part time, some were 'unreliable' and others were reluctant to become involved, regarding the group as a social work department initiative. The study authors remained optimistic however, recommending that more emphasis in these playgroups needed to be on mothers learning alongside their children and in workshops and meetings in order to bolster the mothers' confidence. 'Through learning there is growth of confidence in one's abilities, and this can then be used to take both learning and experience further.'[75] Although there is little evidence to support that optimism in the short term, the Scottish PPA report did lead to the Stepping Stones project which explicitly recognised the challenges faced by families in areas of deprivation and began to question the commitment hitherto to being a voluntary, parent-led, self-help organisation and recognised the need for paid workers as facilitators.

III Conclusions

Women's self-help groups in this period were spaces for reconstituting female autonomy and rediscovery of the self. They facilitated a set of social relationships that were freely chosen rather than imposed and which enabled some women to pursue new directions in education, training and work. In addition, these organisations facilitated new and

---

[73] Davis, *Modern Motherhood*, 38–9.
[74] PLA/PPA/2/28: *Playgroups in Areas of Need*, 7.
[75] *Ibid.*, 15.

necessary forms of social relations in the absence, often, of extended family or community support, that enabled women to free themselves and their thinking from patriarchal frameworks. None of the self-help organisations of this era described themselves as feminist but each played a role in expanding women's horizons and expertise, in turn underpinning women's active engagement with social policy and social expectations. This is most evident in the case of the NCT which supported women to challenge medical professionals and to educate and train themselves to take control of the birth process. The network of NCT groups, area organisers, trainers and helpers provided support for pregnant women and new mothers but in itself constituted a set of often long-term social relationships for the women who became part of the organisation.[76] Likewise, the National Housewives' Register and Pre-School Playgroups Association created local and national social networks which provided a structure for women to develop their knowledge, skills and confidence, whether it was via organising a conference, acting as treasurer or secretary for a local branch or embarking on training courses.[77] 'PPA enabled me to grow, regain confidence in myself as a learner, to make long and lasting friendships and be an active member of the community,' recorded a Bedfordshire woman who graduated from being a 'Mum help' to a governor at an LEA nursery.[78] And in 1966, in an article in *The Guardian* entitled 'The sultanas of surburbia', Betty Jerman summed up the significance of NHR:

> I came to regard suburban life as a heavy rice pudding with a few well-met sultanas here and there. Women have immense capacity. Most of it is unused. Enough women with confidence to chair a meeting, sit on a committee, organise action and we should not be moaning about bad schools, poor maternity services, too few nursery schools. We should be battling for our daughters' education if we want marriage to be a partnership. We should learn to distinguish between a home and a house that looks as though a staff of servants maintain it. But mostly we can break down the tiny family units by helping each other to get out of the house to develop new or old interests simply by taking over each other's children now and again.[79]

Here the social activity engendered by NHR is critical to change on a personal level. In the case of the PPA, involvement, according to one of its key activists, 'did not just equip its beneficiaries with a few quick tips on laying out a playroom or writing a letter to the head of social services; it made them into different people'. 'I have found myself again as a

---

[76] See Davis, *Modern Motherhood*, 36–7.

[77] The PPA at national level regarded itself as a network rather than a hierarchy, 'mutually supportive and independent'. *Insights*, ed. Henderson, xvii.

[78] PLA/PPA 16/1: Memories (Anonymous Dunstable).

[79] *The Guardian*, 16 February 1966.

person in my own right,' remarked one activist. A Scottish volunteer put it more pithily.[80] 'See me! I used to be deid.'[81]

The organisations discussed here have been subject to some critical comment by those who regard them as insufficiently challenging of the gender and social relations that underpinned women's inequality. More benignly some have accepted their value to women who suffered isolation but note that such organisations worked within the system, rarely challenging patriarchal structures and ideologies and ignoring social inequalities.[82] In essence it is suggested they recognised the roots of women's subordination lay in the home and in their prime responsibility for childcare, but in their actions they replicated gender inequalities through their organisations. Yet, these were mass organisations involving thousands of women at every level. Testimonies from those who participated elicit life-changing narratives in which self-help organisations play a pivotal role. As historians we need to take these testimonies seriously. Feminist philosophers have argued that women's sense of self is 'enmeshed in relationality'.[83] This study of three women's self-help organisations of the 1960s supports the view that women lean towards the social in order to shore up their sense of self as opposed to pursuing the path of differentiation and detachment from others. The women who engaged in do-it-yourself, primarily although not exclusively educated women of the middle classes, recognised the value of voluntaristic relational responsibilities as a means of meeting their own needs and those of others, primarily their children. They understood how cooperation and collective effort could benefit them and they believed this model could be made to work more generally. Women could assume multiple roles within these complex social networks and could use them to grow in confidence and ability. Those with the economic and social capital to do so, used the domain of the self-help organisation with its many levels and opportunities to pursue autonomy.

Do-it-yourself women's organisations were a practical response to a conundrum. That conundrum – how to maintain some semblance of autonomy and self-respect whilst 'lost in the exhausting daily round' of family and childcare– spurred women into action, armed with the economic and intellectual capital many had accrued prior to marriage. These organisations should not be regarded as the poor sisters of women's liberation or even a forerunner to the critical thinking and activism that avowedly feminist organisations came to espouse. Rather,

---

[80] *Insights*, ed. Henderson, xv.

[81] PLA/PPA 1/3: Text of speeches given at PPA conference, June 1972. Max Paterson 'Parents Matter Most', 21.

[82] Wilson, *Only Halfway to Paradise*; Lowry, *The Guilt Cage*, 82.

[83] Chodorow cited in Friedman, 'Autonomy and Social Relationships', 43.

women's collective voluntarism should be understood as a practical and grass-roots response to fundamental changes in women's lives in the post-war decades which endeavoured to meet both the needs of women for practical support and social and intellectual engagement and the same desires of those women to fulfil their roles as mothers and partners. Self-help organisations allowed women to be in control.

Transactions of the RHS 29 (2019), pp. 223–251 © Royal Historical Society 2019
doi:10.1017/S0080440119000100

THE POLITICS OF TIME AND STATE IDENTITY IN THE GERMAN DEMOCRATIC REPUBLIC*

By Marcus Colla

Alexander Prize Winner

ABSTRACT. The communist regimes of Eastern Europe carried a particular set of assumptions about the way past, present and future related to one another. In the case of the German Democratic Republic (the GDR), these assumptions manifested themselves in official language and propaganda as a defence of the regime's dynamic and forward-looking historicity against the 'ahistorical' and 'nostalgic' modes of understanding that supposedly typified the historical consciousness of its West German adversary. By this view, the German Federal Republic – and the capitalist West more generally – lacked both a meaningful past and a meaningful future. This article investigates how the East German regime articulated its historicity as a direct expression of its state identity. In particular, it examines how it sought to rationalise newly emerging historical and cultural practices in the GDR within the framework of a modern and progressive socialist historicity, and how it deployed these as an argument against the 'nostalgic' practices of the Federal Republic.

I

In his seminal 1976 essay on the character of historical time, Reinhart Koselleck narrates the following 'political joke' from the Soviet Union:

'Communism is already visible on the horizon,' declared Khrushchev in a speech.
Question from the floor: 'Comrade Khrushchev, what is a "horizon"?'
'Look it up in a dictionary,' replied Nikita Sergeevich.
At home the inquisitive questioner found the following explanation in a reference work:
'Horizon, an apparent line separating the sky from the earth which moves away when one approaches it'.[1]

---

*This article has gone through many versions and has been presented at several conferences and workshops along the way. I would like to thank everybody who has made suggestions and comments on the piece, and in particular the following: John Arnold, Tobias Becker, Giulia Bellato, Nora Berend, Matthew Champion, Chris Clark, Allegra Fryxell, Caroline Goodson, Oliver Haardt, Olivier Higgins, Charlotte Johann, Rhys Jones, Eirik Røsvik, Anika Seemann, Mark Smith, Daniel Spinks, Auriane Terki-Mignot, Emiliano Travieso and Roseanna Webster. In addition, I would like to thank Andrew Spicer and the anonymous reviewers from this journal.

[1] Reinhart Koselleck, 'Space of Experience and Horizon of Expectation: Two Historical Categories', in Reinhart Koselleck, *Futures Past: On the Semantics of Historical Time*, trans. Keith Tribe (New York, 2004), 273.

As this joke suggests, the language of 'lived socialism' was temporally charged. And its temporal content was filled by a clear understanding of how past, present and future were meant to interact. In other words, communist language was explicitly geared towards calibrating the relationship between what Koselleck terms the 'space of experience' and the 'horizon of expectation', holding them in a meaningful relationship to one another by reference to a specific, communist future. The absurdity of the joke derives from the evident disjuncture between official language and lived reality in post-war Eastern Europe.

The communist project begun in 1917 was the most ambitious, forceful and explicit attempt in human history to master time through the medium of politics – and politics through the medium of time. As an emphatically modern project, communism represented a re-enchantment of the world in a secular age, promising a vision of terrestrial paradise as the inevitable denouement of history.[2] The telos of communist time structured the metanarrative of History and imbued daily toil and struggle with a transcendent purpose. As Koselleck puts it, so radically future-oriented was this vision that 'expectation' came to 'swallow up experience' completely.[3] But by the era of 'late socialism' in the 1970s and 1980s, these polarities had been reversed: the accumulated experience of political stagnation, resource shortages and unfulfilled promises had consumed most of what remained of communism's futurist optimism. The socialist states of Eastern Europe found themselves trapped in a crisis of time. This article explores the unfolding of this crisis in the German Democratic Republic (the GDR) – a state in which time assumed a particular significance as a marker of identity against its capitalist West German adversary.

Of particular value in evaluating 'crises of time' is the notion of 'historicity', defined by the historian François Hartog as the way 'individuals or groups situate themselves and develop in time'; that is to say, their collective 'assumptions about the relationship between past, present and future'.[4] Hartog's work belongs to a growing body of recent literature that has demonstrated how belief in a progressive, linear, modern conception of time began to fragment across Europe from the early

---

[2] See Stephen E. Hanson, *Time and Revolution: Marxism and the Design of Soviet Institutions* (Chapel Hill and London, 1997); Stefan Plaggenborg, *Experiment Moderne. Der sowjetische Weg* (Frankfurt am Main and New York, 2006), 81ff.

[3] Reinhart Koselleck 'Geschichte, Historie', in *Geschichtliche Grundbegriffe. Historisches Lexikon zur politisch-sozialen Sprache in Deutschland*, ed. Reinhart Koselleck (8 vols., Stuttgart, 1975), II, 705.

[4] François Hartog, *Regimes of Historicity: Presentism and Experiences of Time*, trans. Saskia Brown (New York, 2015), xv; Christopher Clark, *Von Zeit und Macht. Herrschaft und Geschichtsbild vom Großen Kurfürsten bis zu den Nationalsozialisten*, trans. Norbert Juraschitz (Munich, 2018), 9.

1970s.[5] These studies have documented the way that the future ceased to be 'an open horizon' of political and social possibilities and instead assumed something of an ominous quality.[6] This declining faith in future hopes manifested itself in an aversion to the radically new, and a yearning for the comforts of the past. Modernist visions – already tainted by authoritarian associations – rapidly fell from favour. Intellectually, too, the rise of postmodernism captured the dead-ends into which the modernist paradigm had led, while post-colonialism began to decentre modern European temporal assumptions, in turn revealing their deeply constructed character. In the public and cultural spheres, these fears and desires were amply nourished by a burgeoning 'heritage industry' equipped to commodify and propagate nostalgia in all its many guises.[7]

Hartog diagnoses this era as subsisting in a 'regime of presentism', in which societies lack both meaningful pasts and meaningful futures. In our contemporary order of time, Hartog argues, the accelerating pace of social change ensures that the past bears ever less relevance for the present, while the future is too unimaginable – or too threatening – to provide a coherent vision worth striving for. As a result, the past becomes a nostalgic source of comfort rather than a meaningful guide for present-day action. The 'regime of presentism' thus stands in contrast to the 'modern' regime of historicity that structured the temporal assumptions of states like the GDR. This was a linear and progressive regime of time that resolutely sought to draw meaning for the present by situating it on a historical trajectory between a specific past and a specific future: the claim that the past and the future could be *known* was never rejected. Seen from the East German perspective, then, a Hartogian 'regime of presentism', in which past and future were collapsed into a static and all-encompassing present, could be seen as nothing other than a threat.

This article is an effort to show how extending the exemplary scope of Hartog's analytical paradigm 'beyond' the Iron Curtain can help to reintegrate the history of communist Eastern Europe into a more transnational European story. It seeks to demonstrate how the crisis of time

[5] Lutz Raphael and Anselm Döring-Manteuffel, *Nach dem Boom* (Göttingen, 2012); Aleida Assmann, *Ist die Zeit aus den Fugen? Aufstieg und Fall des Zeitregimes der Moderne* (Munich, 2013); Marc Abélès, 'European Construction, Democracy and Historicity', *Vingtième siècle. Revue d'histoire*, 117 (2013), 57–68; Hartog, *Regimes of Historicity*; *Zeitenwandel. Transformationen geschichtlicher Zeitlichkeit nach dem Boom*, ed. Fernando Esposito (Göttingen, 2017).

[6] Hans Ulrich Gumbrecht, *Our Broad Present: Time and Contemporary Culture* (New York, 2011), xiii.

[7] David Lowenthal, *The Past Is a Foreign Country* (Cambridge, 1985); Robert Hewison, *The Heritage Industry: Britain in a Climate of Decline* (London, 1987); Svetlana Boym, *The Future of Nostalgia* (New York, 2001).

that the GDR began to experience in the 1970s in many ways resembled the concurrent rise of 'presentism' in Western Europe. In this way, the article argues that a number of shifts in the historical culture of the GDR during this era actually drifted on the currents of a pan-European cultural change, in which an increasing depletion of the future as a depository for collective hopes led to an irruption of the past into the present. In East Germany, this decade witnessed a dramatic shift in attitudes to history at both the popular and elite-political levels. The regime began incorporating traditional regional and local histories into its new concept of a 'socialist homeland (*Heimat*)'.[8] Conservation activities proliferated in all East German towns and cities. 'Neo-historicism' became fashionable in architectural circles. Countless radio and television programmes dedicated themselves to the lives and deeds of historical figures. 'Popular history' books and historical novels became bestsellers. And most strikingly of all, non-proletarian historical icons like Martin Luther and Frederick the Great were fully 'rehabilitated' into East German culture. This transformation in the historical consciousness of the East German state was exemplified by the triumphant return of Christian Daniel Rauch's equestrian statue of Frederick the Great to the historic centre of East Berlin in 1980 and the extravagant festivities granted in tribute to Martin Luther on his 500th birthday in 1983. The effect of the shift was dramatic: even if Frederick the Great had always maintained a latent presence in East German historical memory, official narratives had rarely portrayed the eighteenth-century Prussian king as anything other than a militarist and a servile instrument of his reactionary nobility. Luther, meanwhile, had traditionally been vilified in GDR histories as the reactionary nemesis of Thomas Müntzer, whose 1525 Peasants' Uprising occupied a seminal position in official narratives as the radical and popular fulfilment of the revolution triggered by the Reformation in 1517.[9] The transfigured historical culture of the GDR was underwritten by the development of a new concept of *Erbe* ('inheritance' or 'heritage') that sought to capture and incorporate the *totality* of German history, not simply those aspects that anticipated the emergence of a 'workers' and peasants' state'.[10]

Because its historical culture was so deeply implicated in and receptive to historical and cultural discourses from both sides of the Iron Curtain,

---

[8] Jan Palmowski, *Inventing a Socialist Nation: Heimat and the Politics of Everyday Life in the GDR, 1945–1990* (Cambridge, 2009).

[9] See Martin Roy, *Luther in der DDR. Zum Wandel des Lutherbildes in der DDR-Geschichtsschreibung. Mit einer dokumentarischen Reproduktion* (Bochum, 2000); Laurenz Müller, *Diktatur und Revolution. Reformation und Bauernkrieg in der Geschichtsschreibung des 'Dritten Reiches' und der DDR* (Stuttgart, 2004), 167ff.

[10] Jan Herman Brinks, *Die DDR-Geschichtswissenschaft auf dem Weg zur deutschen Einheit. Luther, Friedrich II und Bismarck als Paradigmen politischen Wandels* (Frankfurt am Main and New York, 1992).

the GDR is an instructive starting point in expanding study of this subject eastward. We do not necessarily have to accept Hartog's theory that a 'regime of presentism' emerged in this era in order to situate GDR cultural history within this wider European story. What matters more is that his theory of 'presentism' enables us to perceive at once the fundamental similarities of cross-border cultural trends while at the same time realising how differently they could manifest themselves under distinct political regimes. This article accordingly poses the question of how damaging 'presentism' proved for a regime predicated on a hermetic vision of linear, progressive history. Did the palpable changes in historical understanding evident in the GDR from the 1970s amount to a renunciation of the stable futurities on which regime legitimacy rested? The question here is not whether the changes in historical self-understanding that took place in the GDR throughout the 1970s and 1980s actually led inevitably to the state's collapse in 1989. This would be a crude and reductive conclusion, and one that risks mistaking the symptom for the cause. What the article argues instead is that the loss of historical direction experienced by the GDR in this era was demonstrative (*not* causative) of a deepening disorientation in the political culture of the East German leadership during its twilight years of power. It both reflected and reaffirmed the disjuncture that was opening up between a regime that could countenance no alternative to the progressive, supersessionist narrative that it itself adumbrated and disseminated, and a culture that was media-saturated, attentive to the complexities of the past and – most consequentially – increasingly apprehensive of what the future might hold.

II

Each of the socialist states of Eastern Europe was governed under the auspices of an idealised 'temporal order' that aimed to assimilate all competing temporalities to the time-rhythms of the regime. Since the fall of communism in Europe, a handful of historians have tackled the question of how the ruling parties sought to fashion their states in their own temporal image, configuring work patterns, economic and technological development and, above all, historical consciousness into their all-embracing orders of time. Katherine Verdery and Roman Krakovsky have documented the 'etatization' of time in Romania and Czechoslovakia respectively, charting the attempts and failures of party officials to coordinate new social relationships to space and time.[11] As

---

[11] Katherine Verdery, *What Was Socialism and What Comes Next?* (Princeton, 1996), 39–57; Roman Krakovsky, *Réinventer le monde. L'espace et le temps en Tchécoslovaquie communiste* (Paris, 2014). Deema Kaneff has also studied socialist temporalities at the village level in

they show, it certainly inhered in the logic of socialist rule that the state itself would be the sole container of temporal energies: nothing outside it could be permitted to mobilise revolutionary momentum. But by promoting a textured understanding of how the state's centralising, 'rational' ambitions to transform social relationships to time were forced to encounter and navigate a multitude of temporalities engrained in local customs and traditional historicities, studies like those of Verdery and Krakovsky help illuminate the limits of the 'totalitarian' paradigm. The interstice between state time and private time, they demonstrate, could be a fertile zone of resistance.

In regard to the GDR, Rainer Gries and Martin Sabrow have analysed the manner in which the state's political language was marked by a series of 'virtual time horizons', in which the promise of socialism's consummation was continuously postponed by ever-lengthening stretches of time, until talk of the 'victory of socialism' ceased to possess any temporal content whatsoever.[12] Nevertheless, right up until its demise in 1990, signs of a rigid order of time remained ubiquitous in the life of the East German state. All social, economic and cultural activity was subjected to the tyranny of the 'Plan'. All commemorative and festive activity gravitated around officially designated anniversaries bearing ordinal numbers, imposing a stark linearity onto the cyclical character of the western calendar. Sabrow therefore speaks justifiably of the 'radical linearity' of the GDR's temporal order: from the perspective of the ruling Socialist Unity Party (SED), time was irreversible and quantifiable, while the present constituted but a 'moment in the historical process'.[13]

Regime language in the GDR also evoked an order of time that aimed at synchronising the plurality of temporalities that subsisted within East German society. The logic of this temporal vision meant that even the basic everyday needs of individuals were enchanted with a metahistorical significance. Witness for instance a 1963 report produced by the SED's

Bulgaria: Deema Kaneff, *Who Owns the Past? The Politics of Time in a 'Model' Bulgarian Village* (New York and Oxford, 2004).

[12] Rainer Gries, 'Virtuelle Zeithorizonte. Deutsch-deutsche Geschichtsbilder und Zukunftsvisionen Ende der fünfziger Jahre', in *'Die Heimat hat sich schön gemacht…': 1959. Fallstudien zur deutsch-deutschen Propagandageschichte*, ed. Monika Gibas and Dirk Schindelbeck (Leipzig, 1994), 9–28; Rainer Gries, '"…und der Zukunft zugewandt". Oder: Wie der DDR das Jahr 2000 abhanden kam', in Enno Bünz, Rainer Gries and Frank Möller, *Der Tag X in der Geschichte. Erwartungen und Enttäuschungen seit tausend Jahren* (Stuttgart, 1997), 309–33.

[13] Martin Sabrow, 'Time and Legitimacy: Comparative Reflections on the Sense of Time in the Two German Dictatorships', *Totalitarian Movements and Political Religions*, 6 (2005), 361. The quotation is from Joachim Streisand, 'Die Geschichte im geistig-kulturellen Leben der DDR', in 'Volksmassen und Fortschritt in der Geschichte. Ausgewählte Materialien des VI. Historiker-Kongresses der DDR (Berlin, 6. – 9. Dezember 1977)', ed. Büro des Präsidiums der Historiker-Gesellschaft der DDR, *Wissenschaftliche Mitteilungen*, 1–3 (1978), 136–54.

'Institute for Social Sciences' which argued that the most common medium-term desires of those it had surveyed – 'peace, development opportunities at work and a happy family life' – were not merely the banalities of twentieth-century industrial society, but in fact expressions of 'a developed understanding of true conditions and knowledge about our path of the struggle for peace and social progress through the construction of socialism'.[14] Although East Germany – like any society – was inhabited by a multitude of temporalities, it was central to the very logic of the regime's temporal order that these would be drowned out or repatterned to its own melody.[15] Its intolerance to competing temporal rhythms derived from the secure belief of the communist leaders that *only* their specific form of political regime could 'master' historical time itself. In this way, the GDR's temporal order – and specifically the historicity it exemplified – was also essential to the state's political identity. Because of the exceptional conditions of German division, this may have been a quality unique to the GDR within the Soviet bloc. And as a result, the historicity of the East German state was explicitly invoked – time and again – within regime propaganda to demarcate the identity of the GDR from that of its capitalist West German adversary.

The recognition that there was an emphatically temporal aspect to the GDR's political identity in turn demands a reassessment of previous notions of East German identity construction. The convention in GDR scholarship has been to ascribe the new set of historical practices that emerged in the 1970s primarily to shifts in the wider political environment. By this view, popular engagement with, for instance, the dynastic histories of Prussia and Saxony derived from an expressly political need on the part of the SED to strengthen emotional bonds to the East German state at a time when *Ostpolitik* and the GDR's entry into the United Nations were demanding a cultural 'demarcation' (*Abgrenzung*) from the Federal Republic. Figures like Martin Luther, Frederick the Great, Otto von Bismarck and August the Strong of Saxony were called upon to populate the historical stocks of the new, separate 'East German nation' that the SED's new leader Erich Honecker pronounced as coming into being at the Eighth Party Conference in 1971. Now, Honecker affirmed, Germany was no longer one indivisible nation provisionally partitioned into two separate states, but had in fact evolved into 'two nations' distinct from one another.

It has now been twenty years since Mary Fulbrook outlined her pointed criticism of this 'functionalist' identity narrative, in which she

---

[14] Fred Staufenbiel, *Sozialismus und Kultur. ABC des Marxismus-Leninismus. Institut für Gesellschaftswissenschaften beim Zentralkomitee der SED* (Berlin 1963), 11.
[15] On 'regime temporalities' see Clark, *Von Zeit und Macht.*

questioned whether the mere 'coincidence' of the GDR's new attitudes to history with 'wider political trends' actually sufficed to explain them.[16] But few alternatives have since come to take this narrative's place. In what follows, I seek to tie together the cultural and political aspects of the GDR's 'historical turn' in the 1970s by identifying both as manifestations of a slower, less immediately perceptible shift in historicity. The new identity that East German cultural and political leaders sought to establish in this decade, I argue, also reflected the specific historicity of their state. And defending this mode of historicity against that of the Federal Republic became a central feature of GDR propaganda, revealing in turn the underlying importance for the regime's stability of its own unique sense of how the past related to the present and the future.

The SED's relentless compulsion to distinguish its state from the Federal Republic manifested itself in a wholesale repudiation of what history there *meant*. A fully developed socialist 'historical consciousness' could be juxtaposed with the 'ahistorical' and 'nostalgic' forms of historical understanding prominent in the 'late capitalist' West.[17] Furthermore, the bourgeois assumption that historical interpretation ideally derived from an objective, elevated standpoint was contrasted critically with the GDR's own notion of 'partisan objectivity', according to which the historian was obliged by the laws of historical progress to side unapologetically with the 'progressive classes'. As the 'History of the German Workers' Movement' put it in the early 1970s, any 'historiography that is concerned with historical truth must take the part of the working class and its scientific politics'.[18] Viewed from within the logic of East German historiography, then, the consequence of abandoning 'genuine' (i.e. 'partisan') objectivity meant that the Federal Republic was marked by a total 'absence of history'.[19] There, the utter deficiency of any lawlike explanatory structure had the effect of fissuring the past into so many dispersed components: 'the searching eye does not meet history, but only scattered facts that do not coalesce into one image'.[20] Bourgeois and 'imperialist' modes of conceiving history were

---

[16] Mary Fulbrook, *German National Identity after the Holocaust* (Cambridge, 1999), 134.

[17] Rolf Döhring, 'Forschungsbericht zur Analyse des Standes und zu einigen Problemen der Entwicklung einiger Elemente des sozialistischen Geschichtsbewußtseins bei Jugendlichen unter den Bedingungen der Entfaltung des entwickelten gesellschaftlichen Systems des Sozialismus in der DDR' (unpublished dissertation, Institut für Gesellschaftswissenschaften beim Zentralkomitee der Sozialistischen Einheitspartei Deutschlands, Berlin, 1971), 50.

[18] Quoted in Andreas Dorpalen, 'The Role of History in the DDR', *East Central Europe*, 3 (1976), 61.

[19] 'Genuine objectivity' is from the *Sachwörterbuch der deutschen Geschichte*, quoted in Andreas Dorpalen, *German History in Marxist Perspective: The East German Approach* (London, 1985), 56.

[20] Hans Meier, 'Die Abwesenheit der Geschichte', *Geschichte in Wissenschaft und Unterricht*, 3 (1960), 265, 272.

fragmentary and non-dynamic, reflecting the crisis of a society in which 'history can no longer play a role in explaining the present and the future'.[21] By contrast, historical consciousness in the GDR was predicated on a unified, encompassing, progressive and ultimately *meaningful* view.

From the late 1960s, an argumentative mode of distinguishing between these two historicities assumed increasing importance within the GDR's propaganda organs. In 1969, it was taken up by the television programme *Der schwarze Kanal*, in which excerpts from West German broadcasts were replayed and cynically dissected by the presenter, Karl-Eduard von Schnitzler. The episode of 18 July was entitled 'The Good Old Days', and lambasted an entertainment series that depicted Germany's imperial era in nostalgic tones, as well as West German television coverage of the weddings and goings-on of the descendants of Germany's abolished royal families.[22] As von Schnitzler put it: 'Is this blather about the "good old days", this praise of the most reactionary phenomena, this evocation of a society from yesterday and before yesterday – is that actually only "entertainment …"?'[23]

In a similar way, the arguments most prominently employed as a defence of the GDR's 'rediscovery' of Frederick the Great and Martin Luther against sceptical Western critics explicitly framed East German practices as antithetical to those of the West. In 1980, functionaries within the Central Committee's 'Culture Department' drafted a series of responses for Erich Honecker to questions put by the British publisher Robert Maxwell on the GDR's apparent transformation in historical attitudes.[24] Developed expressly with an international audience in mind, these defended the activities of the SED by making explicit a distinction between East and West German modes of historical practice: 'the forms of heritage preservation in our socialist society have nothing in common with the forms of heritage preservation officially practised in the FRG'.[25] The lead-up to a controversial 1981 West Berlin exhibition on Prussian history likewise witnessed an eruption of polemics in

[21] Döhring, 'Forschungsbericht', 50. See also Rolf Döhring and Helmut Meier, 'Sozialistisches Geschichtsbewußtsein – sozialistisches Geschichtsbild und Geschichtsunterricht', *Geschichtsunterricht und Staatsbürgerkunde*, 3 (1971), 205–14.

[22] Deutsches Rundfunkarchiv (hereafter DRA), E001-00-01/0002/030, 'Der schwarze Kanal: Die gute alte Zeit', 18 July 1969.

[23] *Ibid.*

[24] This interview formed part of a broader 'autobiography' project of Erich Honecker which had an international audience in mind. On its development see Martin Sabrow, *Erich Honecker. Das Leben davor. 1912–1945* (Munich, 2016), 475–87.

[25] Stiftung Archiv der Parteien und Massenorganisationen der DDR im Bundesarchiv (hereafter SAPMO BArch) DY 30/IV B2/9.06/87, Horst Laude, 'Die Antworten auf drei Fragen für ein Interview mit Genossen Erich Honecker', 30 June 1980.

the East German press contrasting the two distinctive historicities, with the progressive spirit of East German dialectical materialism confidently contrasted to the 'nostalgic' impetus of the Federal Republic's own 'Prussia-Wave'.

The idea that West German historicity floundered helplessly in a sea of timelessness was contrasted explicitly to the 'certainty of the future' furnished by the uncompromising laws of dialectical materialism.[26] This contrast was expounded at length in 1970 by Joachim Siebelt, an East German theorist of 'socialist consciousness'. In the 'movement' from the social formation of capitalism to that of socialism, Siebelt wrote, the study of the past in the GDR provided

> vast materials for general, scientifically-justified foreknowledge of the future and a scientific awareness of one's historical perspective (*Perspektivbewußtsein*). The socialist awareness of one's historical perspective is here understood as the *future-oriented side of socialist consciousness*.[27]

Siebelt boasted that the absence of such future certainties in the Federal Republic was indicative of that state's chronic existential weakness. He quoted the West German historian Felix Messerschmid's complaints that the FRG lacked a sense of nationhood precisely because it was unable to position itself in a lawlike relationship between past, present and future: 'Though communism lives off it, we still haven't articulated such an awareness of the future,' Messerschmid had written. 'For many of us, the future essentially means a perennial present'.[28] Siebelt concluded from this that the West German 'imperialist' mode of historical understanding was 'incapable of becoming the foundation for genuine visions of the future'.[29]

From the middle of the 1970s, 'nostalgia' became the central polemical term in distinguishing the allegedly 'dynamic' mode of East German historicity from that of the West. As Tobias Becker has shown, a 'semantic shift' in the commonly understood meaning of 'nostalgia' from a spatial to a temporal yearning had been completed sometime in the 1960s and

---

[26] Martin Sabrow, 'Sozialismus als Sinnwelt. Diktatorische Herrschaft in kulturhistorischer Perspektive', *Potsdamer Bulletin für Zeithistorische Studien*, 40/41 (2007), 20.

[27] Joachim Siebelt, 'Die Rolle des sozialistischen Geschichtsbewußtseins bei der Herausbildung des sozialistischen Perspektivbewußtseins', in *Geschichtsbewußtsein und sozialistische Gesellschaft. Beiträge zur Rolle der Geschichtswissenschaft, des Geschichtsunterrichts und der Geschichtspropaganda bei der Entwicklung des sozialistischen Bewußtseins*, ed. Helmut Meier and Walter Schmidt (Berlin, 1970), 191 (emphasis in original).

[28] Felix Messerschmid, 'Die Nation in der politischen Bildung', *Geschichte in Wissenschaft und Unterricht*, 17 (1966), 663.

[29] Siebelt, 'Die Rolle des sozialistischen Geschichtsbewußtseins', 195.

stimulated an explosion of usage of the word in the Western media.[30] In the East, the term 'nostalgia' likewise began to appear in official publications with any regularity only from the mid-1970s. But here its use principally remained limited to the field of propaganda. In a context where history was inherently progressive, nostalgia represented, as Paul Betts puts it, 'crass capitalist decadence and ideological cowardice in the face of the iron laws of Marxist historical progress'.[31] As a result, East German polemicists hurled the accusation over the Iron Curtain with increasing intensity. The contrast, naturally, was the Marxist-Leninist theory of history, which could not and would not permit itself to be sunk in an all-encompassing present.

However, in the historical discourses of the GDR, the apparent danger posed by 'nostalgia' was not limited to the 'reactionary' tendencies it purportedly awakened and legitimised in the West. Closer to home, GDR cultural authorities were attuned to the problems it posed to the Marxist-Leninist conception of history itself. The impetus behind the attacks on 'nostalgia' was that it was exclusively a capitalist malady. Writing in *Neues Deutschland* in 1975, for example, the cultural theorist and future Central Committee member Hans Koch confidently asserted that 'socialism's certainty of the future excludes nostalgia'.[32] The previous year, in an article pointedly entitled 'History or Nostalgia?', Harald Wessel, the propaganda chief of that same newspaper, had made a programmatic case for the profoundly distinct characters of historical understanding between the two German states:

> The Marxist-Leninist worldview by its very nature encompasses past, present and future equally. It connects the demands of the day with the lessons of history and [a] forward-looking perspective. In this respect our cultivation of tradition differs fundamentally from that historical sentimentality that imperialist opinion makers today play up as a 'Nostalgia Wave' … The 'Nostalgia Wave' impels a homesickness for a hazy yesterday. It impels an escape from the aggravations of the crisis-filled capitalist present and also an escape from the clear lessons of history. 'Nostalgia' is the historically cloaked escape into the private, the escape from social responsibility and the sentimentally veiled surrender before the tasks of the present and future.[33]

Not only was it the case that nostalgia did not exist in the East: by the reasoning of Koch and Wessel, it most assuredly *could* not. Even more

---

[30] Tobias Becker, 'Rückkehr der Geschichte? Die "Nostalgie-Welle" in den 1970er und 1980er Jahren', in *Zeitenwandel*, ed. Esposito, 96–9. See also Tobias Becker, 'The Meanings of Nostalgia: Genealogy and Critique', *History and Theory*, 57 (2018), 234–50.

[31] Paul Betts, 'Remembrance of Things Past: Nostalgia in West and East Germany, 1980–2000', in *Pain and Prosperity: Reconsidering Twentieth-Century German History*, ed. Paul Betts and Greg Eghigian (Stanford, 2003), 181.

[32] Hans Koch, 'Unsere Kultur erschließt alle progressiven Werte', *Neues Deutschland*, 1 March 1975.

[33] Harald Wessel, 'Geschichte oder Nostalgie?', *Neues Deutschland*, 7 December 1974.

explicitly, the GDR's chief ideologue Kurt Hager stated in a 1975 speech that:

> While we carry out with revolutionary verve … a fundamental socialist renewal of society, while we change the world, everything in the FRG and the other capitalist countries remains the same. Indeed, the maladies of capitalism are being accentuated ever more acutely, its general crisis is becoming ever deeper, its contradictions – especially the contradiction between capital and labour – are intensifying ever more. In view of this situation, nostalgia – the 'yearning for the old days' – has propagated itself in the capitalist world.

Capitalism, then, had estranged West Germans from the present. But what is especially interesting about the critical nostalgia discourses in the East is the way in which they prompted a number of conscious reflections on socialist historicity and the fundamental challenges with which it was being confronted during the 1970s. In the same article, Hager turned to the real ideological challenge posed by the GDR's transformation in historical ethos:

> It is said that also some of *us* are infected by nostalgia. Of course, it is not a question of whether, say, someone loves old kerosene lamps and old chairs or likes listening to classic hits. That is left up to each for themselves. It is rather a question of where we see our ideals.[34]

Hager's underlying concern was that evidence of 'nostalgic' practices in the East would signify disenchantment with the socialist project itself. And the new popular forms of history being cultivated in the East certainly risked conveying that impression. As a result, it was imperative that new historical practices be embedded in a consistent socialist rationale. In other words, the amateur restoration of dilapidated buildings, the exploration of local histories, the accumulation of historical artefacts, the consumption of historical novels and dramas, the preference for the urban schemes and architectural styles of the 'old city', and the surge in regional museums, local heritage initiatives and interest in folkloric customs were not to be viewed as symptoms of fatigue with the modern world, but were in fact practices explicitly engaged in the forging of a socialist 'historical consciousness'. They did not undermine, but *reinforced*, socialist historicity.

III

This German–German confrontation over historical meaning was not simply a propaganda operation carried out by the SED. In practice as well as in theory, there were a number of real differences between the historical cultures of the two German states that reflected both their

---

[34] Kurt Hager, 'Unsere Partei verläßt sich fest auf ihre Kampfreserve', *Neues Deutschland*, 14 July 1975 (emphasis added).

political values and their competing senses of historical continuity. In an obvious sense, the comparative freedoms afforded in the Federal Republic for public debate on historical subjects necessarily gave conceptions of history there a more subjective and contested colour. In respect to historical practices, moreover, an even more striking point of contrast between East and West lay in the emergence of a new form of memory culture in the Federal Republic throughout the 1970s and especially the 1980s on subjects such as the Second World War, Nazism and the Holocaust. In the GDR, there could be no talk of anything like the public reckoning that the subsequent 'memory boom' helped stimulate in the pluralistic cultures of Western Europe. Because the East German regime saw itself as the guarantor of socialist historicity, its privileged hold over historical interpretation – however ambiguous in practice – secured its position as the GDR's sole arbiter of memory as well. The force of the arguments advanced by its historical practitioners in defence of socialist historicity therefore depended entirely on the unchallengeable powers of the state over history to successfully guard against any incursions of alternative memory that might challenge official narratives or the stable, linear vision of history by which these narratives were structured.

In the GDR, history as conceived through the lens of 'memory' was a political threat as much as it was an intellectual and cultural challenge, and this was amply reflected in the language that East German theorists and historians used in their polemical attacks against West German historicity. Their chief problem was not so much the risk that recovered memory of the twentieth-century past posed to the GDR's foundational myth of 'anti-fascism' – though this was certainly far from unimportant. Rather, their anxiety stemmed from the more general threat that 'memory' and its attendant popular practices posed to the rigidities and forward-moving thrust of modern, socialist historicity. With its need to disturb the abstract, homogeneous chronologies on which 'traditional' history is constructed, memory collapses linearity and with it the idea that differences exist 'between periods and qualities of time': it is for this reason that Oriane Calligaro argues that memory is indeed the 'privileged modality' of history within a Hartogian 'regime of presentism'.[35] As a result, the distinction between 'memory' and 'history' so important to Western historical debates in the 1980s was entirely unarticulated

---

[35] Amos Funkenstein, 'Collective Memory and Historical Consciousness', *History and Memory*, 1 (1989), 9; Oriane Calligaro, 'Legitimation through Remembrance? The Changing Regimes of Historicity of European Integration', *Journal of Contemporary European Studies*, 23 (2015), 331.

within the GDR itself,[36] where even as monumental a work as Pierre Nora's *Les lieux de mémoire* attracted next to no attention in official academic and public organs.[37] The history that had stood at the core of East German political identity since the state's foundation in 1949 had always been contorted and instrumentalised for 'presentist' political and ideological purposes, but it had nevertheless served to situate the communist state on a precise historical trajectory between past and future. Whatever its failings, this was history as progressive narrative, not history as memory. And as Andreas Huyssen argues, whereas '[h]istory as a narrative of emancipation and liberation always points to some future ... history as memory and remembrance is always a narrative concerned with a past'.[38]

Huyssen's observation reinforces the central argument of this article that a sense of forward-moving, modern historicity was not only a distinguishing feature of East European historical culture during the Cold War era, but was in fact of existential significance to the very legitimacy of communist rule itself. So it was of no minor consequence that the cultural and political authorities of the GDR had begun, through theoretical vehicles like *Erbe*, to authorise forms of history that bore at least some superficial similarities to the personalised and localised historical practices associated with the West European 'memory boom', at least insofar as they were emptied of their 'emancipatory' content. At the same time that 'memory' became the totemic term of historical and historiographical discourses in much of Western Europe, the GDR was also dealing with a transformation in public historical consciousness that summoned the attractions of heritage and locality as vectors to a vanished past.

The GDR's new concept of *Erbe* therefore demands closer analysis. By the start of the 1980s, East German historians and theorists had come to distinguish *Erbe* from 'tradition'. According to this conceptual distinction, 'tradition' referred to the progressive qualities of history that inhered in the socialist identity of the German Democratic Republic, while *Erbe* encompassed the *entirety* of German history 'in all its contradictions'.[39] 'Tradition' and *Erbe*, in other words, partitioned the German past into its dynamic and non-dynamic components. When contrasted to the progressive spirit of 'tradition', *Erbe* was a concept synonymous with the

---

[36] Martin Sabrow, 'Einleitung: Geschichtsdiskurs und Doktringesellschaft', in *Geschichte als Herrschaftsdiskurs. Der Umgang mit der Vergangenheit in der DDR*, ed. Martin Sabrow (Cologne, Weimar and Vienna, 2000), 27.

[37] Pierre Nora (ed.), *Les lieux de mémoire* (3 vols., Paris, 1992).

[38] Andreas Huyssen, *Twilight Memories: Marking Time in a Culture of Amnesia* (London, 1995), 87.

[39] Horst Bartel, 'Erbe und Tradition in Geschichtsbild und Geschichtsforschung der DDR', *Zeitschrift für Geschichtswissenschaft*, 29 (1981), 389.

ever-present. It drew the past into the present without any sense of a developmental logic. It represented a sense of history that was not dynamic, but static and suspended in time. The GDR radio journalist Heinz Winter expressed it thus in November 1980: '"historical *Erbe*" is for us a fact, it is simply there. We cannot seek it out or undo it when it doesn't suit us.'[40] Similarly, the architect Isolde Andrä affirmed that '*Erbe* is not restricted to certain time-horizons – it encompasses all historical epochs.'[41] In its new manifestation, *Erbe* therefore placed at the heart of the GDR's identity a flattened, timeless approach to understanding the past.

This leads us in turn to question what relationship initiatives like the *Erbe–Tradition* distinction and the 'socialist *Heimat*' bore to the new historical conditions of Western Europe. Should their striking contemporaneousness be seen only as a correspondence or coincidence? Or should the SED's new enterprises in historical management during the 1970s rather be interpreted as a distinctive political response to a cultural shift that was in fact much more widespread and fundamental? The GDR's concepts of *Erbe* and the 'socialist *Heimat*', of course, were not *explicitly* designed to reflect, imitate or respond to the memorial discourses gaining currency in Western European history: to the contrary, they were cast as means of authorising an engagement with non-proletarian and non-progressive history in a way that remained conducive to the forward thrust of socialist historicity. But the effect was in any event the opposite of the party's intention: in reality, *Erbe* and the 'socialist *Heimat*' legitimised historical practices that in many people's view were socialist in name only, or that indeed were reinscribed by GDR citizens with something of an *anti*-socialist impulse.[42] In 1991, the former GDR historian Helga Schultz reflected that the *Erbe–Tradition* distinction signalled nothing less than a 'conservative turn in the GDR's concept of history'.[43] In her view, the SED's new theory of *Erbe* had emptied the socialist mission of its progressive content while seeking to root socialist identity in the soil of eternity. No dialectic could overcome this sense of history as permanence.

In light of these concerns, some professional historians articulated a fear that the GDR's new attitudes and practices risked liberating historical consciousness from the state's official historical master-narrative.

---

[40] Reproduced in Klaus Kühnel, '"Grosser Friedrich, steig hernieder …". Wie die DDR Preussen entdeckte', *Wortspiel* radio programme, 22 February 2001.

[41] Isolde Andrä, 'Tradition und Fortschritt – Erkenntnisse und Erfahrungen im Städtebauprozeß', *Architektur der DDR*, 34 (1985), 461.

[42] Palmowski, *Inventing a Socialist Nation*.

[43] Helga Schultz, 'Was bleibt von der Geschichtswissenschaft der DDR?' *Österreichische Zeitschrift für Geschichtswissenschaften*, 2 (1991), 31.

Upon discovering in 1982 that a Potsdam brewery had produced a series of beers packaged in labels depicting symbols and icons from the militarist Prussian past, for instance, the historian Gustav Seeber wrote with some alarm to the brewery in the hope of warning them, from a position of professional authority, that the dissemination of thousands of such bottles daily among the population could give the impression of 'drawing or at least supporting an idea of Prussian history that is historically false and politically damaging'.[44] As he reflected a few years later with reference to the episode, this was an example of the problems that could arise when the 'cultivation of heritage' (*Erbepflege*) became unconstrained by the professional oversight of historians.[45] While academic historical research in the GDR was much more sophisticated than would be suggested by the caricature of historians as mere party instruments, professional historians nevertheless remained indispensable agents through whom the SED could retain its unchallengeable prerogative over the East German interpretation of history.[46] One of their fundamental roles within the greater political-cultural apparatus of East German society was to uphold a distinctive vision of socialist history by synchronising and synthesising historical understandings into the regime's formal, linear and progressive metanarrative.

IV

The flow of non-proletarian and non-progressive history into the bloodstream of the GDR's politics and culture from the 1970s reflected more than a shift in historicity: it also signalled the reanimation of *spatial* categories of identity at the expense of the temporal.[47] This was apparent both at the local level, with the emergence of the new language and practices of *Heimat* and regional history, and on the national stage, through Honecker's doctrine of the 'two nations'. At the level of official identity, the German Democratic Republic now existed in a separate time and space from its West German rival. This spatial distinction was also encompassed by the new concept of *Erbe*, as the histories of the core territories of Brandenburg-Prussia and Saxony assumed a heightened importance simply in virtue of their geographical correspondence with

[44] Archiv der Berlin-Brandenburgischen Akademie der Wissenschaften (hereafter ABBAW), Nachlass Gustav Seeber 26, letter from Seeber to VEB Brauerei Potsdam, 22 February 1982.

[45] ABBAW Nachlass Gustav Seeber 26, notes for 'Erbe und Tradition' conference.

[46] Sabrow, 'Einleitung', 18.

[47] On the manner in which the SED employed both temporal and geographical markers of collective identity, see Ralph Jessen, 'Einschließen und Ausgrenzen. Propaganda, Sprache und die symbolische Integration der DDR-Gesellschaft', in *Politische Wechsel, sprachliche Umbrüche*, ed. Bettina Bock, Ulla Fix and Steffen Pappert (Berlin, 2011), 135–52.

the GDR. The permanence of spatial categories of identity – much like the permanence of all that constituted *Erbe* – was purposely contrasted to the progressive vitality of 'tradition'.

While geography was one dimension of identity that could offer stability in place of flux, the cultural and political authorities of the GDR held steadfast to the idea that it could be accommodated to and synthesised with the ever-moving, future-oriented spirit of socialist identity: indeed, this was the very essence of the 'socialist *Heimat*' idea. But a much more dangerous variant of the 'stable' identity narrative was nationalism. In contrast to the rigid progressivism of Marxist-Leninist histories, as Katherine Verdery points out, nationalist histories accentuate continuities at the expense of breaks, ruptures and changes. In their pursuit of enduring ethnic origins, they wrench events from their contexts, 'flattening' time and rendering history 'motionless'.[48] Hence, from the East German perspective, nationalist histories threatened to undermine – perhaps fatally – the very dynamism by which Marxist-Leninist historicity had sought to distinguish itself from the 'nostalgic' histories of the capitalist West.

This was not simply an abstract problem. In actuality, the threat posed by competing or antagonistic modes of history and historicity was acutely perceived by the East German cultural authorities, who were attuned to the risk that a more popular and 'differentiated' approach to history could ultimately legitimise a counter-productive form of nationalism.[49] In 1980, officials in the Central Committee's Department of Culture reported with some alarm on the phenomenon of 'protochronism' unfolding in Nicolae Ceauşescu's Romania, in which nationalist intellectuals thrust themselves into the pursuit of 'discovering' specifically Romanian antecedents for intellectual currents and cultural movements that would later come to prominence in Europe more generally. Through protochronism, the East Germans noted, a raw form of nationalism was percolating into ever more published works and cultural artefacts.[50] While 'national pride' and 'historical consciousness' could, they conceded, be cautiously employed in the service of a socialist identity

---

[48] Katherine Verdery, *National Ideology under Socialism: Ideology and Cultural Politics in Ceauşescu's Romania* (Berkeley, Los Angeles and Oxford, 1991), 249.

[49] As Denis Koslov has demonstrated in the Soviet case, the reasons for the 'historical turn' from the 1960s onwards were far more multifaceted than a simple reduction to nationalism would suggest. But the perception that it was a risk was nevertheless real; Denis Koslov, 'The Historical Turn in Late Soviet Culture: Retrospectivism, Factography, Doubt, 1953–91', *Kritika* 2 (2000), 577–600.

[50] SAPMO BArch DY 30/IV B 2/9.06/20, Abteilung Kultur, Sektor internationale kulturelle Arbeit, '7. Information 1980', April 1980.

(as had been the case in the GDR itself during the 1950s),[51] a nationalist historiography that neglected the 'internationalist aspect' and the 'class character of culture and art' constituted a potent threat to the entire temporal order of socialist society.[52]

The awareness of this risk prompted restraint on the part of those theorists and ideologues entrusted with rationalising and publicly defending the GDR's new historical practices. One such figure was Ernst Diehl, president of the Council of Historical Scholarship and thus the SED's chief guardian of Marxist-Leninist orthodoxy among the East German historical profession. Addressing his Council of Historical Sciences in January 1979, Diehl noted a 'corresponding interest' in past epochs within neighbouring socialist countries, drawing attention to the great popularity and international resonance met by a recent exhibition on the fourteenth-century Holy Roman Emperor Charles IV in Prague, the reconstruction of the Royal Palace in Warsaw and a Budapest exhibit of the crown of St Stephen, Hungary's first king (see below). Collectively, Diehl concluded, these instances 'drew a picture' and demonstrated the need for a 'long-term perspective' in historical propaganda.[53] For the time being, though, he urged caution, 'restrictions' and 'further deliberations' before following these countries' leads: 'We also have to consider here how that will also be noticed by our enemies and there be expressed in a series of activities that we will have to take into account.'[54] The caution that Diehl and his colleagues in the Department of Culture exercised in questions of nationalist representation reflected the unique political conditions faced by the GDR within Eastern Europe. In an environment where the invocation of national histories potentially bore geopolitical as well as ideological consequences, the pursuit of 'flattened' histories carried a great number of political dangers.

The international instances to which Diehl pointed could be interpreted as cultural manifestations of the 'more independent, "nationalist" course' pursued by the ruling parties of many bloc countries in the 1970s.[55] But they also reflect the more recursive modes of historicity that began to permeate the political cultures of Eastern Europe's communist states throughout the 'late socialist' era. Diehl's comments

---

[51] On national histories in communist Eastern Europe see Stefan Berger, *The Past as History: National Identity and Historical Consciousness in Modern Europe* (2015), 290–7.

[52] SAPMO BArch DY 30/IV B 2/9.06/20, Abteilung Kultur, Sektor internationale kulturelle Arbeit, '7. Information 1980', April 1980.

[53] SAPMO BArch DY 30/36157, Ernst Diehl, report on meeting of Council for Social Sciences, 31 January 1979.

[54] *Ibid.*

[55] Stephen A. Smith, 'Introduction', in *Science, Religion and Communism in Cold War Europe*, ed. Paul Betts and Stephen A. Smith (2016), 31.

therefore prompt a number of reflections on the transnational dimension of the GDR's historical turn. Not only do they demonstrate that East German cultural leaders were closely attuned to shifts in the historical practices of neighbouring states, and that they factored in these shifts when preparing their own exhibitions and propaganda offensives – Diehl's remarks also expose the unique set of problems posed by these shifting sentiments for the one bloc state that could not easily afford to indulge in nationalist sentiments. The following discussion will therefore concern itself with situating the GDR within a more general Eastern European context, comparing and contrasting the character of its histor-ical turn to those of other bloc states.

Because of its multi-ethnic make-up, the Soviet Union in particular found itself confronted with a number of theoretical difficulties on national questions, especially in relation to Russian nationalism, which would come to play such a central role in the Union's dissolution from the mid-1980s. 'Progressive' traditions, of course, had always been valorised in the state's political language and propaganda, forming the central pillars of Soviet socialism's historical culture. But early Soviet rulers cultivated an equivocal relationship to their historical inheritance, fetishising the new while at the same time adopting a sophisticated approach to its management of imperial and Russian national heritage. In the 1930s, meanwhile, Stalin's purges of revolutionary heroes impelled a revision of the USSR's historical master-narrative, drawing it away from the abstractions of the class struggle and towards the emotional sanctuaries of 'monarchs, dates and battles'.[56] The state's professional historians populated this new historical landscape with narratives, myths and symbols extracted from the previously suppressed domains of 'religion, ethnicity, and the state'.[57] Even the Romanov dynasty could find its unwilling place in this history in virtue of its creation and consolidation of the core territory on which the Soviet Union now stood.[58] These tendencies were magnified during the darkest days of the Great Patriotic War, as Stalin – who had previously served as Lenin's 'People's Commissar for Nationalities' – came to invoke the lan-guage and symbolism of Mother Russia and the Orthodox Church in an urgent appeal to the traditional historical consciousness of many Soviet citizens.

---

[56] Geoffrey Hosking, *Rulers and Victims: The Russians in the Soviet Union* (Cambridge, MA, 2006), 155.

[57] *Ibid.*, 156.

[58] *Ibid.*, 155. Though arguably more important than the Romanovs in this respect was Ivan IV ('Ivan the Terrible'); see Kevin M. F. Platt, *Terror and Greatness: Ivan and Peter as Russian Myths* (Ithaca and London, 2011), 176–252; Maureen Perry, *The Cult of Ivan the Terrible in Stalin's Russia* (London and New York, 2001).

In the long run, however, Stalin's efforts to mobilise Russians' primal strength of feeling for the 'Motherland' was not without consequence for the stabilising futurities of communist time; rather, the penetration of Russian nationalism into Soviet political culture only aggravated 'the problem of interruption versus continuity' in the writing of 'patriotic history'.[59] It ruptured the clean, unidirectional historical trajectory on which socialist consciousness was predicated. And when the Russian victory itself was later cemented as the central legitimating myth of the Brezhnev era, this only served to deepen the period's sense of cultural and political stagnation.[60] Nevertheless, the differences between the Soviets' often ambivalent relationship to the pre-1917 Russian past and what transpired in the GDR during the 1970s are perhaps of greater importance than the similarities: the Soviet narrative was after all a triumphant one, focused on the forging of patriotic unity through military glory. Further, it had evolved from the complex matrix of ethnic groups unique to that state in a particularly tense geopolitical atmosphere. Indeed, it is notable that East German historians and cultural officials did not invoke any Soviet precedent – either privately or publicly – in their rationalisations for their new theory of *Erbe*.

Better international comparisons with the GDR's historical turn are perhaps to be found in other 'satellite states', and particularly those also forced to reckon both with difficult wartime legacies and the reality that their communist governments had been imposed by the Soviets. The problem was especially acute in Romania, the major bloc state possessing perhaps the weakest historical attachment to communism of all.[61] Here, national history had propped up the regime since the Soviet troop withdrawal of 1958, appealing, as Dragoş Petrescu puts it, to a historical sense of 'independence and territorial integrity'

[59] Gennady Bordyugov, 'War and Peace: Stalin's Regime and Russian Nationalism', *History Today*, 45 (1998), 31. See also E. A. Rees, 'Stalin and Russian Nationalism', in *Russian Nationalism Past and Present*, ed. Geoffrey Hosking and Robert Service (New York, 1998), 77–106.

[60] See Geoffrey A. Hosking, 'Memory in a Totalitarian Society: The Case of the Soviet Union', in *Memory: History, Culture and the Mind*, ed. Thomas Butler (Oxford, 1989), 117; Koslov, 'The Historical Turn'; Katerina Clark, 'Changing Historical Paradigms in Soviet Culture', in *Late Soviet Culture: From Perestroika to Novostroika*, ed. Thomas Lahusen and Gene Kuperman (Durham, NC, and London, 1993), 289–306; Catriona Kelly, 'The Shock of the Old: Architectural Preservation in Soviet Russia', *Nations and Nationalism*, 24 (2018), 99ff. Pavel Kolář argues that the shift to a more reformist and less radical utopian vision characterised the distinctive *Sinnwelt* of 'post-Stalinism'; Pavel Kolář, *Der Poststalinismus. Ideologie und Utopie einer Epoche* (Cologne, Weimar and Vienna, 2016).

[61] Dragoş Petrescu, 'Communist Legacies in the "New Europe": History, Ethnicity, and the Creation of a "Socialist" Nation in Romania, 1945–1989', in *Conflicted Memories. Europeanizing Contemporary Histories*, ed. Konrad H. Jarausch and Thomas Lindenberger (New York, 2007), 38.

pervasive among Romanians.[62] The political employment of nationalist histories intensified following Nicolae Ceauşescu's ascent to power in 1965 and his affirmation of full Romanian independence at that year's Ninth Party Congress.[63] The phenomenon of 'protochronism' encountered above was one manifestation of this shift, and was accordingly adopted with vigour by a regime increasingly looking to anchor the legitimacy of its rule in the unique qualities of Romanian history.[64] Throughout his long reign, Ceauşescu continued to invoke the mythic imagery of Romania's medieval and ancient past to buttress his country's drift from Moscow's orbit.[65] The result, from the mid-1970s onwards, was the phenomenon of 'Dacomania', in which the historical culture of Romania became saturated by the imagery and symbols of the ancient Dacians, to whom Ceauşescu and his cultural apparatchiks wished to ascribe the ethnogenesis of the Romanian people. Ceauşescu could be confident of his strategy's popularity: at the same time, the historical films of director Sergiu Florin Nicolaescu were attracting mass audiences. His 1967 *Dacii* ('The Dacians') and 1971 *Mihai Viteazul* ('Michael the Brave') – both among the most-watched Romanian films in history – rendered with great artistic sophistication and style the narrative that the history of the Romanian nation consisted of an ancient and continuous struggle for independence and unity.[66]

In Bulgaria, meanwhile, an intellectual circle tied to Lyudmilla Zhivkova – Politburo member and daughter of the long-standing Bulgarian communist leader Todor Zhivkov – actively sought in the 1970s to animate a historical sense of Bulgarian national identity so as to help overcome what Ivanka Nedeva Atanasova terms 'the complex of shame of being Bulgarian'.[67] Their principal historical motifs consisted of the ancient Thracians (a group that encompassed the Dacians), the ninth-century saints Cyril and Methodius, and Bulgaria's two medieval empires. The campaigns were accompanied by a series of popular exhibitions, publications and commemorations both within Bulgaria and abroad.[68] The year 1981 witnessed a series of international festivities to celebrate the 1300th anniversary of the First Bulgarian Empire.

---

[62] *Ibid.*, 40. See also Verdery, *National Ideology under Socialism*.

[63] Kenneth Jowitt, 'The Romanian Communist Party and the World Socialist System: A Redefinition of Unity', *World Politics*, 23 (1970), 38–60.

[64] Verdery, *National Ideology under Socialism*, 167ff.

[65] See Lucian Boia, *History and Myth in Romanian Consciousness* (Budapest, 2001), 73ff.

[66] Dragoş Petrescu, 'Legitimacy, Nation-Building, and Closure: Meanings and Consequences of the Romanian August of 1968', in *The Prague Spring and the Warsaw Pact Invasion of Czechoslovakia, 1968: Forty Years Later*, ed. M. Mark Stolarik (Mundelein, 2010), 252.

[67] Ivanka Nedeva Atanasova, 'Ljudmila Zhivkova and the Paradox of Ideology and Identity in Communist Bulgaria', *East European Politics and Societies*, 18 (2004), 298.

[68] *Ibid.*, 299.

In Hungary, the cult of the King St Stephen was dramatically revitalised at precisely the same moment that Frederick the Great physically and spiritually re-emerged at the centre of East German cultural life.[69] The historian György Györffy's immensely popular biography of Stephen was published in 1977,[70] the same year in which the Hungarian government began negotiations with the Carter administration to retrieve the king's crown from the United States.[71] More spectacular still was the success of Levente Szörényi's and János Bródy's 1983 rock opera *István, a király* ('Stephen, the King'), which portrayed Hungary's patron saint in his struggle to become the first king of Hungary at the turn of the eleventh century.[72] The culmination of socialist Hungary's reinvigoration of the cult of St Stephen was a nationwide ceremonial tour of the king's right hand – 'the country's most holy relic'.[73]

Of course, even comparing Romania, Bulgaria and Hungary to the GDR risks oversimplification in view of the wider geopolitical context of the 1970s and 1980s. Since distancing itself from Moscow, Romania had become one of the poorest and most ruthless of Eastern Europe's dictatorships, while Hungary, at least in Western eyes, was widely recognised as the 'least unattractive', boasting comparatively lax restrictions on foreign media and communications and offering its citizens a relatively high standard of living.[74] In addition, the reasons why these countries' political elites – to say nothing of their populations – chose to invoke ancient icons in a new nationalist spirit could also be traced to domestic idiosyncrasies, touching on those states' specific religious and ethnic compositions in addition to the failures of alternative, ideological sources of identity. Nevertheless, the basic point remains; namely, that political elites in all of these countries could rely on a high degree of

---

[69] As C. M. Mann points out, not only had the Hungarian communist leadership suppressed commemoration of Stephen during the previous decades, but he also had not featured as a symbol for the opposition; C. M. Mann, 'Socialism and King Stephen's Right Hand', *Religion in Communist Lands*, 18 (1990), 12.

[70] György Györffy, *István király és műve* (Budapest, 1977). A much-condensed translation appeared in English in 1994 as *King St. Stephen of Hungary*.

[71] It was returned on 6 January 1978. See Jimmy Carter's letter to President Pal Losonczi at www.jimmycarterlibrary.gov/digital_library/sso/148878/57/SSO_148878_057_01.pdf. On the story of the crown see Anthony Endrey, *The Holy Crown of Hungary* (Melbourne, 1978), 85–105.

[72] Zoltán Falvy, 'Stephan, der König: eine ungarische Rock-Oper', in *Mittelalter-Rezeption III. Gesammelte Vorträge des 3. Salzburger Symposions: Mittelalter, Massenmedien, Neue Mythen*, ed. Jürgen Kühnel, Hans-Dieter Mück, Ursula Müller and Ulrich Müller (Göppingen, 1988), 85–91. On the anti-Soviet thrust of Hungarian folk traditions, see the remarks in Tamás Hofer, 'Construction of the "Folk Cultural Heritage" in Hungary and Rival Versions of National Identity', *Ethnologia Europaea*, 21 (1991), 165.

[73] Mann, 'Socialism and King Stephen's Right Hand', 15.

[74] Ian Kershaw, *Roller-Coaster: Europe 1950–2017* (2018), 129.

popularity when drawing on historical events, figures and conventions that were not generally understood to belong to the armoury of progressive traditions. And in the end, in all of these cases the guarantee of popularity overrode whatever theoretical reservations they may have harboured.

In light of these international examples, one can see why cultural and political officials in the GDR kept a close but critical eye on the history-politics of their 'brotherlands' – they were acutely aware of the fact that their own efforts to recalibrate East German historical practices to the demands of socialist historicity reflected an international trend towards embracing a deeper and non-proletarian past as a legitimate component of socialist national identity. But at the same time, they were also aware that the nationalist thrust of these trends carried particular dangers in the unique political circumstances of the GDR – not only because of the ever-present problem posed by a national history shared with a competitor capitalist state, but also because the resuscitation of national traditions could so easily be read as a statement of independence from Moscow.[75] Caught on the horns of this dilemma, the GDR's cultural leaders were especially careful to develop strategies and theories – like *Erbe* and the 'socialist *Heimat*' – that appropriated the new cultural energies for the purpose of deepening their specific, forward-moving sense of historicity.

Around Eastern Europe at the same time, however, one can detect a number of subtler examples of shifts in historical attitudes that collectively pointed to something much more fundamentally troubling to socialist structures of time. In this respect, a better clue to the pan-European character of these cultural shifts is perhaps provided by a controversial aesthetic counterpart to Hungary's historical turn of the 1970s. In the so-called 'Tulip Debate' of that decade, a series of predominantly younger architects derived artistic inspiration for a series of prefab housing developments from the traditions of regional and national folk-art.[76] The striking results of these proposals appeared in the workers' village at the Pécs nuclear power plant in the country's south. Yet the designers were forced to confront accusations of 'antimodernism' by some of the Hungarian architectural establishment's more dogmatic members, who even compared the young architects' practices to those of the interwar fascists.[77]

[75] Virág Molnár, *Building the State: Architecture, Politics, and State Formation in Post-War Central Europe* (Milton Park, 2013), 105.

[76] Daniel Kiss, 'From the Hungarian Tulip Dispute to a Post-Socialist Kulturkampf', in *Re-Framing Identities: Architecture's Turn to History*, ed. Ákos Moravánszky and Torsten Lange (Basel and Berlin, 2016), 108.

[77] *Ibid.*; Jeffrey Cook, *Seeking Structure from Nature: The Organic Architecture of Hungary* (Basel, Bern and Boston, 1996), 25.

The use of language here is crucial. The new designs offered by the young Hungarian architects, as Virág Molnár points out, abounded with 'ornamentation, vernacular traditions, historicism, and cultural identity', rendering them convergent with the principal tenets of the 'postmodern turn' in architecture concurrently taking place in the West.[78] What's more, the purposes of the designs 'grappled with similar challenges to modernism' to those that had begun to stimulate postmodern ideas in the architectural circles of Western Europe.[79] To all intents and purposes, then, this was evidence that postmodernist ideas were taking root in Eastern as well as Western Europe in the early 1970s, and were being inspired in both halves of the continent by a sense of discontent not only with the aesthetic soullessness of modernism in practice, but also with its increasingly evident incapacity to reshape society along the lines its practitioners had promised. The problem, however, was that the language of postmodernism – and especially the term itself – was utterly taboo within the cultural discourses of Eastern Europe's communist states, whose inherent devotion to a modern vision of progress was incapable of accommodating anything that smacked of 'a critical appraisal of modernity', let alone *post*-modernity.[80] In the GDR, planners spoke of 'neo-historicism' instead of 'postmodernism', despite the obvious aesthetic similarity between the two.[81] As with the 'memorial turn' in history and literature, then, the 'postmodern turn' in architecture was not something that could be subscribed to in the same language as that used in the West.[82]

In this sense, the 'Tulip Debate' provides an intriguing parallel to the GDR's own turn to the 'old city' and urban environments that displayed 'visible traces of history' during the 1970s and 1980s, including projects such as the reconstruction of the *Gendarmenmarkt* in East Berlin, the *Semperoper* in Dresden and the 'Dutch Quarter' in Potsdam.[83] What is interesting about these design projects are their clear parallels to contemporaneous developments in Western Europe. Florian Urban has argued

[78] Molnár, *Building the State*, 106.

[79] *Ibid.*; Kiss, 'From the Hungarian Tulip Dispute to a Post-Socialist Kulturkampf', 105–18. On preservation activities in Hungary during the late 1960s and 1970s, see Miklós Horler, 'Architectural Heritage and European Culture: New Dimensions in the Preservation of Monuments in Hungary', *New Hungarian Quarterly*, 26 (1985), 205–10.

[80] Stefan Guth, 'One Future Only: The Soviet Union in the Age of the Scientific-Technical Revolution', *Journal of Modern European History*, 13 (2015), 366.

[81] Manfred Ackermann, 'Veränderungen in Architektur und Städtebau der DDR', in *Tradition und Fortschritt in der DDR. Neunzehnte Tagung zum Stand der DDR-Forschung in der BRD* (Cologne, 1986), 162.

[82] In the context of the Soviet Union, Stefan Guth makes a similar point in regard to the term 'post-industrial'; see Guth, 'One Future Only', 370.

[83] Florian Urban, *Neo-Historical East Berlin: Architecture and Urban Design in the German Democratic Republic 1970–1990* (Burlington, 2009), 234.

that this turn in East German architectural practice 'grew from an intellectual field that reached beyond the borders of the German Democratic Republic and included both capitalist and socialist countries'.[84] While it is true that East German planners and architects accessed and discussed Western journals,[85] this was arguably less important than the simple fact that societies in both halves of Europe faced similar sets of problems. The reality was that architects east of the Iron Curtain were often searching for 'responses to the social and economical change of the 1960s and 1970s' in much the same way as their Western counterparts.[86] The 'old city' in East Germany, much like the vernacular designs developed by the Hungarian architects at Pécs, was a product of the failings of 'urban modernism'. Where events differed in the East was in the 'shortsightedness of [their] government officials'.[87]

As GDR historians had done in questions of historiography and memory, East German architectural theorists also insisted on a fundamental difference between trends in their field and ostensibly similar phenomena in the capitalist world. And – also like their historian compatriots – they sought to distinguish their own language and practices by accusing their Western counterparts of capitulating to the temptations of 'nostalgia'. In 1982, for instance, the GDR architectural theorist Christian Schädlich attacked postmodernism's 'nostalgic reproduction of the pre-industrial architectural environment'.[88] It was imperative, wrote his colleague Hermann Wirth, that each historical citation employed in an architectural work 'be accompanied by an examination of that being cited which is concerned not merely with its form, but with its content'. In other words, architects were to 'make intelligible' what they were seeking to achieve: 'Otherwise the impression of formal trickery emerges, of "nostalgia" or frivolous haphazardness, of a need for history without a historical consciousness'.[89] A historical turn in architecture, then, could only be justified through reference to the master-narrative of progressive, materialist history. Anything else was mere indulgence.

[84] *Ibid.*

[85] Ákos Moravánszky, 'Piercing the Wall: East–West Encounters in Architecture, 1970–1990', in *Re-Framing Identities*, ed. Moravánszky and Lange, 27–43.

[86] Urban, *Neo-Historical East Berlin*.

[87] Annemarie Sammartino, 'Mass Housing, Late Modernism, and the Forging of Community in New York City and East Berlin, 1965–1989', *American Historical Review*, 121 (2016), 495.

[88] Christian Schädlich, 'Der Postmodernismus – eine alternative Architektur?', *Architektur der DDR*, 6 (1982), 346.

[89] Hermann Wirth, 'Historische Werte im gegenwärtigen Architekturschaffen', *Architektur der DDR*, 31 (1982), 347.

In highlighting the transnational dimension of the changing relationship to history that Europe experienced in the 1970s, it is necessary to emphasise how the fundamental similarities between corresponding phenomena like Eastern 'neo-historicism' and Western 'postmodernism' are much more significant than the differences in how they were expressed and explained. The correlation is not only significant because both 'neo-historicism' and 'postmodernism' gave new forms of aesthetic expression to the past, but also because the recursive temporality they betrayed was understood as a very conscious reaction to the sense of sterility that had come to be attached to the futurist orientation of modernist styles. In this respect, the parallel between 'neo-historicism' and 'postmodernism' is symptomatic of a much more general disillusionment with the future promises of a previous era that set in during the 1970s on both sides of the Iron Curtain, and that had great consequences in recasting relationships to heritage, commemoration and identity.[90]

So how to explain this apparent synchronicity between East and West in shifting cultural attitudes to the past? At an international level, this was an era of comparative cooperation between the two Cold War blocs, and particularly across the Cold War's German front line. The early 1970s saw the GDR more completely integrated into the international political order, at a time in which this order was turning its attention to conservation and heritage in the most visible ways possible. Under the refrain 'a future for the past', the inaugural European Heritage Year was held in 1975, three years after UNESCO adopted its convention for the preservation of 'World Cultural and Natural Heritage'.[91] Furthermore, events like the 1973 oil crisis drew attention to the finitude of global resources, among which were soon counted 'cultural and natural heritages'.[92] The GDR was far from hermetically sealed from this world. As Mary Fulbrook puts it, with the explosion of the 'heritage industry' in the West,

> engagement with the past was opening up to popular consumption in ways that could not be ignored even in the GDR. History was sufficiently central to communist politics that parts of it could not be written out of the political script; and the themes which would attract attention and popular significance in the West could not, in a time of more porous borders and enhanced communications (not least through television), be ignored.[93]

Perhaps more significant, however, was an increasing acknowledgement that the value of the future had been depleted as a political resource both in Western Europe's liberal democracies and in Eastern Europe's

---

[90] Hartog, *Regimes of Historicity*, 119.

[91] J. Düwel *et al.*, 'Epilogue: Postwar Continuities', in *A Blessing in Disguise: War and Town Planning in Europe, 1940–1945*, ed. J. Düwel and N. Gutschow (Berlin, 2013), 387–9.

[92] *Ibid.*, 387.

[93] Fulbrook, *German National Identity*, 90.

socialist states. In the West, new major challenges to social cohesion, job security and the welfare state were met with a wealth of diagnoses that 'pinned their hopes on the present, and nothing but the present', while the vast expansion of a middle-class consumer culture helped forge a new set of social values focused exclusively on the immediate obtainment of material reward.[94] In the East, the very grandness of socialism's own ambitions left it especially vulnerable to disenchantment, as regime language drifted ever further from empirical reality. SED First Secretary Walter Ulbricht's 1958 promise that the GDR would 'overtake' West Germany in per capita consumption within three years constituted a microcosmic German counterpart to Khrushchev's reckless 1961 vow to deliver communism to the Soviet Union by the year 1980. In the short term, reality's frustrating tendency to invalidate these forecasts openly revealed the many structural shortcomings of socialist economic planning. But in the long term, the chief problem turned out to be less the hollow idealism of regime language than the utter exhaustion of the future as a viable instrument of political legitimacy.

The socialist regimes' efforts to replenish the depleting power of their future visions with the possibilities of technology and cybernetics also proved illusory.[95] As the 1970s unfolded, faith rapidly collapsed in the idea that technological advancement could be an ally of political progress. From the middle of the decade, a number of critics in the GDR began to recognise the dangerous directions in which the failures of the regime's 'Scientific-Technical Revolution' from the 1960s and early 1970s could lead, with a number even echoing the post-materialist and post-growth discourses of the West European Left.[96] Meanwhile, in the early 1980s, functionaries in the Ministry of Culture were increasingly drawn to a disquieting new wave of literature that expressed – in their words – 'uncertainty about the future'.[97] It was with good reason, then, that the West German political scientist Gert-Joachim Glaeßner observed that it could prove 'fatal' when a socialist system, having already discarded its old shibboleths of a global socialist future and a

---

[94] Hartog, *Regimes of Historicity*, 112–13.

[95] Elke Seefried and Dierk Hoffmann, 'Einführung', in *Plan und Planung. Deutsch-deutsche Vorgriffe auf die Zukunft*, ed. Elke Seefried and Dierk Hoffmann (Berlin, 2018), 10–15.

[96] Alexander Amberger, *Bahro – Harich – Havemann. Marxistische Systemkritik und politische Utopie in der DDR* (Paderborn, 2014). On the contested futurities of the Scientific-Technical Revolution in the Soviet Union see Guth, 'One Future Only', 355–76.

[97] Bundesarchiv Lichterfelde (BArch) DR 1/13077, 'Zur Verwirklichung der vom X. Parteitag beschlossenen Kulturpolitik auf dem Gebiet der DDR-Literatur', 10 January 1983.

belief in real socialism's superior economic capabilities, began to acknowledge the downsides of progress.[98]

But even amidst this collapse of faith in a bounteous socialist future, it remained essential to the very identity of the East German state – and by extension to its rulers' claims to political legitimacy – that its mode of understanding history be insulated and distinguished from that of the capitalist West. In the GDR's dying days, this was a theme that continued to occupy the playwright and poet Heiner Müller – one of the state's most perceptive critics of the way it had dealt with its historical inheritance. Even in 1988, the Berlin Wall continued to represent for him a partition between two contrasting regimes of historicity. In the East, he wrote, there was 'still a past, or memories, and there is still a future, expectations'. In the West, by contrast, there was 'no past, no memory, no expectations: only the present'.[99]

V

The tumultuous events that would befall Europe over the following two years, of course, were as unthinkable for Müller as they were for anybody else. But his reflections nevertheless reveal the profundity of the 'temporal anxiety' that played as ominous background music to the GDR's sclerosis and decline in the 1970s and 1980s: for the socialist dream to remain alive, the historicity of the East *had* to be distinct from that of the West. It had to invest *meaning* into the past, orienting the present to the inevitable unfolding of a glorious, classless future. But, as the historical practices of the East German state seemed to converge with those of its Western antagonist – assuming new, popular forms and concerning themselves ever more with the legacies of long-vanished dynasties and their material traces – the dynamism furnished by the GDR's progressive and modern sense of historicity could no longer marshal the powers of national identity, let alone legitimate the state's very existence. Instead, there arose a sense that history – if not time itself – could no longer be mastered.

The point of this article has not been that the GDR – or indeed any of the socialist states of Eastern Europe more generally – 'discovered' or 'rediscovered' their histories during the 1970s and 1980s: the significance of the past, it should be clear, had *always* been fundamental to socialist life. What was distinctive about the late socialist period was the

---

[98] Gert-Joachim Glaeßner, 'Wissenschaftlich-technische Revolution – Intelligenz – Politik in der DDR. Soziale und ideologische Differenzierungsprozesse und ihre Folgen für das politisch-gesellschaftliche System', in *Tradition und Fortschritt in der DDR*, 26.

[99] Heiner Müller, 'Für ein Theater, das an Geschichte glaubt. Gespräch mit Flavia Foradini', in *Heiner Müller, Gesammelte Irrtümer 2. Interviews und Gespräche*, ed. Gregor Edelmann and Renate Ziemer (3 vols., Frankfurt am Main, 1990), 130.

emergence of a new *historical culture*, in which the ideal of the seamless integration of past, present and future was ruptured by new, popular forms of historical recognition that in turn prompted a conscious and determined effort by the GDR's political elites to reinforce and defend their Marxist-Leninist historical citadel. The surge of the past into East German historical culture – and the exhaustion of the future it reflected – was a sobering reality for the GDR's leaders, whose ironclad commitment to a specific temporal order was predicated on a belief that their form of regime could make a unique claim to have mastered historical time by embodying the inner logic of its motion. Since 1949, they had drawn energy from the awesome mission they were fulfilling, and legitimacy from their privileged knowledge of its methods. The temporal essence of their ideology conferred both meaning and hope upon their project. But as new political and economic realities began to bite, their once-fervid conviction shrivelled into a hollow and derisible doctrine. Disoriented and devoid of ideas, history itself seemed to have abandoned them.

Transactions of the RHS 29 (2019), pp. 253–272 © Royal Historical Society 2019
doi:10.1017/S0080440119000112

TIME AND DISTANCE: REFLECTIONS ON LOCAL AND GLOBAL HISTORY FROM EAST AFRICA

By Richard Reid

READ 23 JUNE 2018
AT THE UNIVERSITY OF OXFORD

ABSTRACT. This paper is concerned with East Africans' perceptions of the intersection between their own, highly charged and contested, local histories, and the global past, as well as their place in it. The two case studies on which the paper is based – Eritrea and Uganda – have much in common in terms of recent history, not least in their experience of prolonged violence, and thus taken together they elucidate distinctive characteristics. Yet they also illustrate broader phenomena. On one level, particular interpretations of local history – both the deeper, precolonial past and the more recent, twentieth-century past – are utilised to *critique* the flow of global history, as well as the impositions of globalisation, and to emphasise the bitter experience of marginality and lack of agency. At the same time, the global past – conceptualised as the evolution of an intrusive, imperialist, hypocritical global order imposed by foreigners, usually Western in provenance – is seen as omnipresent and pervasive, and thus the arguments made around marginality serve to remind us, paradoxically, how *central* these communities are (or should be) to the framing of global history.

I Introduction: the global(ising) history of Africa

This article is concerned with the intersection between the local and the global. The central issue under examination is local perceptions of global history, and specifically the intersection between East Africans' own highly contested local histories and the global past, as well as their place in it. But it is also the case that in both Uganda and Eritrea – the case studies on which the article is primarily based – 'global history' is often synonymous with 'globalisation', a conscious or subconscious equivalence to which the researcher needs to be alert. Eritrea and Uganda have much in common in terms of recent history, not least in their experience of prolonged violence, and thus taken together they elucidate distinctive characteristics. Yet they also illustrate broader phenomena. On one level, particular interpretations of local history – both the deeper, precolonial past and the more recent, twentieth-century past – are utilised to *critique* the flow of global history, as well as the impositions of globalisation, and to emphasise the bitter experience of

marginality and lack of agency. At the same time, the global past –
conceptualised as the evolution of an intrusive, imperialist, hypocritical
global order imposed by foreigners, usually Western in provenance –
is seen as omnipresent and pervasive, and thus the arguments made
around marginality serve to remind us, paradoxically, how *central* these
communities are (or should be) to the framing of global history.

Be that as it may, as will be evident from what follows, the dominant
perspective of local informants is that global history is the history of the
world as shaped by those with power on a global stage – chiefly the
European empires, the United States, China. Everyone else is marginal
within such a model. The tyranny of the word limit prevents a full eluci-
dation of how this is far from being the only possible reading of what con-
stitutes the practice of researching and writing global history; suffice to
note that we find ourselves at a moment of reflection as to the trajectory
and potential of the field.[1] But local actors are far removed from current
scholarly debates, although their concerns – the marginalising forces of
historic globalisation; ideas about the role of 'tradition' in the face of
modernity; the increasingly urgent need to protect and nurture local historical production – should certainly be made relevant to those debates.
An older scholarship dealing with the tense interactions between the
local and the global, dating back to the 1990s, remains germane in this
respect.[2]

Nevertheless, the Africanist academy has not been immune from the
seemingly inexorable rise of global history – far from it – and certainly
not from the debates around globalisation.[3] In some ways, of course, historians of Africa have always been global historians, by the very nature of
their work. Arguably, they have had cause to think about global and certainly transnational connections in ways that other, more mainstream
'area studies' scholars – including historians of Western Europe – have
not. Core to the study of Africa's past has been the impact of imperialism
and colonialism, or the transcontinental slave trades, themselves global
historical phenomena. Yet in some respects the shift into global history

---

[1] See, for example, Jeremy Adelman, 'What Is Global History Now?', *Aeon*, 2 March 2017;
Richard Drayton and David Motadel, 'Discussion: The Futures of Global History', *Journal
of Global History*, 13 (2018), 1–21; *Global History, Globally: Research and Practice around the World*,
ed. Sven Beckert and Dominic Sachsenmaier (2018).

[2] Stuart Hall, 'The Local and the Global: Globalization and Ethnicity', in *Dangerous
Liaisons: Gender, Nation and Postcolonial Perspectives*, ed. Anne McClintock, Aamir Mufti and
Ella Shohat (Minneapolis, 1997); *Global History: Interactions between the Universal and the Local*,
ed. A. G. Hopkins (Basingstoke, 2006).

[3] Frederick Cooper, 'What Is the Concept of Globalization Good for? An African
Historian's Perspective', *African Affairs*, 100 (2001), 189–213; John Lonsdale, 'Globalization,
Ethnicity and Democracy: A View from "the Hopeless Continent"', in *Globalization in World
History*, ed. A. G. Hopkins (2002).

on the part of African historians looks like something of a matriculation, or an elevation: I am thinking here of Tony Hopkins, Frederick Cooper, Crawford Young and Patrick Manning, for example.[4] The area-specialist research of their earlier careers – often dealing with the political and economic impacts of British or French colonialism – pushed their work toward an exploration of empire as a global phenomenon. Others considered the roots and meanings of Creole identity, transnationalism or cosmopolitanism, or the multiple, reciprocal dynamics underpinning oceanic communities.[5] More generally, however, it is true that Africanist scholars occupy a peculiar place in the discipline. While Richard Evans could point toward the outward-looking community of British Europeanists compared to the relative insularity of their continental colleagues,[6] Africanists in the UK constitute a very small share of the 'market': we do (or at least represent) the 'wider world' in our academic departments, but our relevance to the field of global history is debatable given that we only represent a very small proportion of all historians in Britain – part of the 13 per cent of historians who work on Africa, Asia, the Middle East and Latin America.[7]

Still, it remains the case that increasing numbers of us think about the framing of African history in a global context. In so doing, however, we are confronted with the problem of how to relate the global to the lived experience of local actors, and the ways *they* think about the past. Central to that struggle is the need to get to grips with the contested nature of historical memory itself, as well as with *dehistoricising* trends in certain quarters, not least in political circles. As foreign historians doing 'fieldwork' in our chosen areas, we are the agents of an intellectual globalism whether we like it or not, and perhaps unconsciously our frame is unavoidably global. The position of the historian is not, therefore, unproblematic, especially when conducting oral interviews, as in my own case. At the local level, there is an overwhelming concern for *local* history in a particular form, and historians from the West find that their own postmodernist parameters – whether these are subliminal or

---

[4] Jane Burbank and Frederick Cooper, *Empires in World History: Power and the Politics of Difference* (Princeton, 2010); *Globalization in World History*, ed. Hopkins; P. Manning, 'African and World Historiography', *Journal of African History*, 54 (2013), 319–30; Crawford Young, *The African Colonial State in Comparative Perspective* (New Haven, 1994).

[5] John Thornton, *Africa and Africans in the Making of the Atlantic World, 1400–1800* (Cambridge, 1992, 1998); Pier Larson, *Ocean of Letters: Language and Creolization in an Indian Ocean Diaspora* (Cambridge, 2009); 'Special Feature: Africa and the Indian Ocean', *Journal of African History*, 55 (2014). See also the path-breaking work by Paul Gilroy, *The Black Atlantic: Modernity and Double Consciousness* (1993).

[6] Richard J. Evans, *Cosmopolitan Islanders: British Historians and the European Continent* (Cambridge, 2009).

[7] 'The Long View: Scholars Assess the State of History', *Times Higher Education*, February 2018.

more overtly embraced – are alien to the concerns of local interlocutors: in Uganda, the desire to forge an explicitly *national* history, for example, and to carefully demarcate a Ugandan identity, in both spatial and temporal terms; and in Eritrea, the emphasis on the identity and ethos arising from lonely, violent struggle against a backdrop of perceived global neglect, giving rise to a solipsistic, militant territorialism. Even so, those concerns are linked to exogenous dynamics and, whether consciously or otherwise, local actors do indeed reflect on the global past, and articulate ideas about how the local context intersects with the larger flow of history beyond it.

My two case studies have deep global historical heritage: Eritrea, or at least its highland plateau and adjacent coast, as part of Axum and the Red Sea world, with direct links to the Eurasian core of antiquity; Uganda as the fulcrum of slow but seismic and globally significant population movements, those of the Bantu-speakers in the course of the first millennium CE, which were among the most dramatic in human history.[8] And yet both cases highlight local struggles with the global modernity of which they are a product. In both cases, there is an at least tacit – and, sometimes, explicit – focus on the profound rupture imagined in the moment of imperial contact, and on the violence of globalising colonial rule which is subsequently imposed upon them. Existential and epistemological challenges abound in an era of increased globalism, and of heightened identity politics which are frequently resistant to that globalism – although identity politics forged around the clash between local and global, while they have mutated over time, are not in themselves novel.

II History wars: Uganda

When he was at school in the early 1960s, in the final days of British rule, Yoweri Museveni – now president of Uganda – had a deep interest in history, which he studied as an A-level subject. But it was not Africa's past that interested him. Rather, he was enthused by the study of European history: specifically, the French Revolution and the fundamental political and social change thus effected; and the unification of Germany and Italy, and the creation of conditions conducive to rapid economic, particularly industrial, growth.[9] These were lessons that

[8] David W. Phillipson, *Ancient Ethiopia. Aksum: Its Antecedents and Successors* (1998); David Schoenbrun, *A Green Place, A Good Place: Agrarian Change, Gender, and Social Identity in the Great Lakes Region to the 15th Century* (Portsmouth, NH, 1998); Christopher Ehret, 'Bantu Expansions: Re-envisioning a Central Problem of Early African History', *International Journal of African Historical Studies*, 34 (2001), 5–41.

[9] Yoweri Kaguta Museveni, *Sowing the Mustard Seed: The Struggle for Freedom and Democracy in Uganda* (Oxford, 1997), 14.

stayed with him. In the meantime, however, he developed a clear sense of Africa's place in global history – and his was not a positivist vision. While Europe was achieving remarkable economic development, underpinned by robust markets and political unity, Africa was in the grip of mindless tribalism; this, according to Museveni, was the continent's enduring 'problem', a theme to which he has returned repeatedly over the last thirty years.[10]

It might reasonably be assumed that the time has long since passed when African historians had to bitterly but unavoidably set up that musti-est of straw men, Lord Dacre, Professor Hugh Trevor-Roper, who in his capacity as Regius Professor of Modern History at Oxford had famously dismissed the study of the African past as a complete waste of time.[11] There was a time when it was de rigueur to do so.[12] Dacre himself was drawing on a well-established trope, first articulated by Georg Wilhelm Friedrich Hegel in 1822 when he described the continent, in essence, as lying outside of global history – a curiously ahistorical place, mired in its own terrible solipsism. It was 'the land of childhood ... enveloped in the dark mantle of Night', as he famously put it. 'It is no historical part of the World ... it has no movement or development to exhibit.'[13] But the ghosts of Hegel and Dacre pop up in unexpected places. Museveni appeared to be broadly in agreement with the basic idea, as he sought to rebuild a nation ravaged by political catastrophe and economic collapse. He reflected a conviction widely held within the National Resistance Movement (NRM), Uganda's governing party since 1986, that the supposed accomplishments of the precolonial past, highlighted by Africanist scholars, had been greatly exaggerated. How could this *not* be the case, said Museveni, when all the evidence pointed to the inescapable fact that Africa was *backward*? To some extent Africa was undone by colonial rule, true; but even when one cast one's eye further back, all that could be beheld was perhaps the occasional note-worthy material achievement (an impressive earthwork here, a stylish vase there) but otherwise what looked very much like the unrewarding gyrations of barbaric tribes which had haunted Trevor-Roper's vivid imagination. This view constituted a distinctive strand of the new developmentalism which underpinned the political and economic projects of the late twentieth and early twenty-first centuries, eschewing

[10] For example, see Yoweri K. Museveni, *What is Africa's Problem?* (Minneapolis, 2000), 163–4.
[11] Hugh Trevor-Roper, *The Rise of Christian Europe* (1965), 9–11.
[12] A. G. Hopkins, *An Economic History of West Africa* (1973), 32; see also Finn Fuglestad, 'The Trevor-Roper Trap or the Imperialism of History: An Essay', *History in Africa*, 19 (1992), 309–26.
[13] G. W. F. Hegel, quoted in *Archives of Empire*, vol. II: *The Scramble for Africa*, ed. Barbara Harlow and Mia Carter (Durham, NC, 2003), 21, 28.

the study of the past in favour of building the future, as though the two could and *should* be uncoupled.

Museveni's thinking represented just the latest stage in successive generations of Ugandans' imaginings about their role in the flow of global history. In the late nineteenth and early twentieth centuries, at the outset of British colonial rule, the people of Buganda – the kingdom at the core of the British colonial order and after which the protectorate was named – were regarded as bright, outward-looking and worthy of British benevolence; they were receptive to change, and embraced the British imperial project with its distinctive historical trajectory.[14] The Ganda certainly saw themselves in those terms: this was a melding of histories, encapsulated to some extent in the writings of Apolo Kagwa and Hamu Mukasa, and represented by their large-scale conversion to Christianity and their willingness to grow cotton, Britain's cash crop of choice in the area.[15] Buganda, in other words, had entered the world, and become a part of global history.

A generation later, in the 1920s and 1930s, Ganda royalists worried about the loss of 'traditional culture' as younger Ugandans clamoured to look and sound like foreigners. *Kabaka* (King) Daudi Chwa's short treatise on the subject, produced in 1935, extolled the virtues of precolonial tradition and the importance of understanding local history.[16] (With hindsight, the sentiment was ironic, given that his own son, Edward Mutesa – *kabaka* from 1939 to 1966 – was privately educated, commissioned as an officer in the British army, and spoke with the same received pronunciation as his English peers.) On this reading, foreign influence and the excessive zeal for buying into an exogenous vision of the global past was something to be feared, and resented. Indeed, it was a struggle which intensified at the very heart of the Buganda kingdom over the ensuing decades, and especially as independence approached in the course of the 1950s. While many Ugandan nationalists embraced a unitary, modernist vision of the independent nation – one freed from the cloying anachronism of monarchy and 'tribe', and drawing on more global histories of socialism or pan-Africanism for succour and

[14] Michael Twaddle, 'The Ganda Receptivity to Change', *Journal of African History*, 15 (1974), 303–15; for a contemporary assessment of Buganda's supposed capacity for progress, given the correct tutelage, see A. M. Mackay (ed. by his sister), *A. M. Mackay, Pioneer Missionary of the Church Missionary Society to Uganda* (1890).

[15] Apolo Kagwa, *The Kings of Buganda*, ed. and trans. M. S. M. Kiwanuka (Nairobi, 1971; 1st edn, 1902); Hamu Mukasa, *Uganda's Katikiro in England*, ed. Simon Gikandi (Manchester, 1998; 1st edn, 1904); Cyril Ehrlich, 'The Uganda Economy, 1903–1945', in *History of East Africa*, vol II, ed. V. Harlow and E. M. Chilver (Oxford, 1965).

[16] 'Education, Civilisation, and "Foreignization". The *Kabaka*'s Pamphlet, 1935', in *The Mind of Buganda: Documents of the Modern History of an African Kingdom*, ed. D. A. Low (London, 1971).

inspiration – others, notably in Buganda, were anxious at the prospect of their own history becoming subsumed within a larger entity. Ganda neo-traditionalists responded by forming the *Kabaka Yekka* (KY) movement – the Luganda term means 'the king alone' – which argued for autonomy, even outright secession, from a future independent Uganda, and which eschewed the globalism implied by the ostensibly more progressive politics of the Uganda People's Congress (UPC) or the Democratic Party.[17] Importantly, these were not simply, or not only, presentist debates about future status, reflecting a divided nationalist politics. They were also arguments over the nature of history itself, and reflected a growing chasm between those who embraced a global historical order (manifest in the British imperial project) in their pursuit of political legitimacy, and those who expounded the virtues of 'tradition' and ethnicity as the defining principles of socio-political organisation, and who feared the disappearance of those principles in a unitary future.[18] Ironically, there were many in Buganda – the bedrock of the colonial order, and the supposed agent of global modernity half a century earlier – who now felt that the kingdom had most to lose from the latter.

They were right to be afraid, as it turned out; by the late 1960s, after a brief strategic alliance between KY and Milton Obote's UPC government, Buganda and the other kingdoms had been abolished as Obote embarked on a programme of socialist modernisation.[19] But the struggle, the central dichotomy – between a local and a global past – was perennial, and in evidence elsewhere. It was captured in the work of Acholi poet and playwright Okot p'Bitek: the epic poem *Song of Lawino*, first published in 1966, is performed in the first person by Lawino, who laments – in alternately trenchant, sorrowful, comical and bitter terms – the fact that her husband (Ocol) has abandoned African culture and tradition, dresses and behaves like a European and seemingly aspires to be white, and has taken up with Clementine, an African woman who has likewise adopted European ways. p'Bitek gave Ocol a scathing reply, in *Song of Ocol*.[20] Taken together, the poems – in which the lead characters pile insults on one another – encapsulate the global/local conundrum, with implicitly or explicitly historical strains. In the political realm, as Obote's authoritarianism hardened, the opposition Democratic Party under the leadership of Benedicto Kiwanuka sought self-consciously to

---

[17] I. R. Hancock, 'Patriotism and Neo-traditionalism in Buganda: The Kabaka Yekka ('the King Alone') Movement, 1961–62', *Journal of African History*, 11 (1970), 419–34.

[18] 'Annexure to the Appeal by *Kabaka* Mutesa II to the Secretary-General of the United Nations, 11 March 1966', in *Mind of Buganda*, ed. Low, 222.

[19] D. A. Low, *Buganda in Modern History* (1971), 245–6.

[20] Both poems are in Okot p'Bitek, *Song of Lawino & Song of Ocol* (Johannesburg, 1984). They were first published in 1966 and 1967 respectively.

evoke the language of global human rights and democracy, and joined their vision of the nation to a Whiggish interpretation of global history. They drew parallels, for example, with the American Revolution and the liberal ideals which thereafter seemed to undergird a global political narrative.[21] It was no coincidence that Kiwanuka himself was a Roman Catholic Muganda – Catholics had long felt marginalised by the royalist establishment in Buganda – and belonged to a group of Ganda who eschewed the narrow, traditionalist monarchism of *Kabaka Yekka* and embraced a much more global vision of nationalist politics and political freedoms. This central cleavage in Ganda politics – whether to be open to the world, or culturally protectionist – could be traced to the turbulent nineteenth century, when the world itself first intruded on Ugandan societies.[22]

Since the catastrophes of Idi Amin in the 1970s and the violence of the early 1980s, these history wars have persisted and, if anything, have intensified. But this is not simply the preserve of political elites, concerned with various versions of national history. Ordinary citizens have likewise developed locally rooted historical narratives which are used to critique both global history and historic globalisation – again, frequently interchangeable concepts. It is important to stress that these 'external forces' are conceptualised on multiple levels. Firstly, and most obviously, they are explicitly *historical* – most dramatically manifest in the arrival of long-distance commerce and, ultimately, British imperialism and colonial rule in the late nineteenth and early twentieth centuries. Secondly, however, they are evident in foreign cultural influences which are often framed in negative terms: bad music, sexually promiscuous women or depraved homosexual men are frequently understood as the products of 'foreign influence'. And thirdly, the government itself is seen as the agent, and is emblematic, of a brutal political and economic globalism – manifest in authoritarian developmentalism and neoliberal economics which produces a political elite linked to overseas investors from China, India or the Gulf States; an elite which extols the virtues of an ahistorical patriotism in ordinary Ugandans but which in reality acts with criminal neglect toward its own citizens. Visions of the local versus ideas about the global past need to be understood in this context. Extensive interviewing of a range of Ugandan informants in recent years reveals something of an entrenchment of the view that the forces of global modernity have disrupted Uganda in unpleasant ways. This no doubt reflects disillusion with both the perceived predations of globalisation and with the agent of those predations, a stubborn and

---

[21] Ben Kiwanuka's preface in *Forward to Freedom, Being the Manifesto of the Democratic Party* (Kampala, 1960).

[22] See, for example, H. M. Stanley, *Through the Dark Continent* (1899; 1st edn, 1878), vol I.

increasingly authoritarian regime which has sought to 'modernise' Uganda and which projects negative visions of local history. Localised histories have come to the fore, and the deeper, precolonial past – histories of neatly quarantined, pristine tradition before the irruption of external forces – is romanticised as a means of critiquing the perceived tyranny of global historical forces which have pushed people to the economic and political margins.[23]

Notably, informants frequently emphasised the pristine nature of local history at some point in the past being 'passed down' in moral and instructive terms – a strikingly Orientalist trope familiar to anyone with a passing acquaintance with ideas about supposed 'primitive wisdom', and perhaps self-consciously reclaimed by modern informants. In this scenario, we have the imparting of knowledge, the confirmation of origins, the exhortation to cultural purity and convention – often expressed through riddles, proverbs and stories; the lessons of time presented in the abstract.[24] Informants stressed how the deeper past – what might once have been called 'traditional history', or more recently, perhaps, 'ethno-history'[25] – occupied a central place in the temporal imaginary of a bygone age. Elders sat around the flickering flames and imparted cultural wisdoms, offering a vision of both serenity and stability. It was a simpler time. This romantic, emotional process of reconstruction served many purposes, no doubt, but it certainly spoke to the rupture and violence and discontent of the modern age. 'In the evenings,' said one informant, 'older relatives would gather around fireplaces and educate their children and grandchildren about … past experiences, i.e. how man came into existence, where they came from …' Acquaintance with the past instilled ideas about proper, decorous behaviour, notably in terms of sexual chastity and propriety. (This particular informant referenced the anti-homosexuality bill then advancing through the Ugandan parliament as the product of those enduring

---

[23] This formed part of a Leverhulme Trust-funded project between 2012 and 2015 concerned with historical culture and consciousness in Uganda since the mid-nineteenth century. In their interviews, conducted in selected communities across the country in the attempt to achieve geographical spread, the research team aimed for a cross section in terms of age, gender and occupation. Informants included teachers, priests, farmers, shopkeepers and traders. They were asked – in a mixture of English and vernacular languages – about the importance of 'national history', and of history as a subject more broadly, including as taught at school. What follows is a modest sample of those interviews, which are anonymised to protect informants.

[24] Interview, Bugobero, farmer, *c.* forty-three years old, 25 January 2014.

[25] There is a wider literature exploring these issues: see for example *History and Ethnicity*, ed. Elizabeth Tonkin, Maryon McDonald and Malcolm Chapman (London and New York, 1989); *Recasting the Past: History Writing and Political Work in Modern Africa*, ed. Derek R. Peterson and Giacomo Macola (Athens, OH, 2009).

conservative values.)[26] Homosexuality, the subject of angry debate in contemporary Uganda, is for some the product of a creeping, nefarious, global culture which first intrudes upon Ugandan communities in the late nineteenth century.[27] The 'precolonial past' represented political charters of local origin and settlement. Narratives demonstrated provenance and the rightful occupation of land, for example.[28] History was about space protected from outsiders – whether aggressive immigrants, greedy governments, or, more recently, Chinese or Indian investors – but it was also consistently linked with morality and 'values'. The past was thus a cultural and psychological realm as well as a physical arena.[29] For others, against a backdrop of spiralling living costs and the ravages of neoliberalism, the precolonial past offered ample evidence of economic coping mechanisms – the gathering of food during famine, for example – and was salutary in terms of what it revealed about 'the high level discipline in society', and the positive outcomes of communal living.[30] For some, knowledge of 'history' – by which was frequently meant 'traditional custom' – enabled one to avoid 'bad behaviour', thanks to the taboos laid down by ancestors.[31] Yet of course there was a degree of careful selection among informants and interviewees – and this could come out in interesting, sometimes paradoxical, ways. So, while one informant, for example, recalled as a boy listening to elders talk about 'tribal wars' – an early memory of how history 'mattered' in his community – he was clear that the precolonial past provided lessons in 'love' and 'unity'.[32] For one farmer from the Mbale area, history inculcated a sense of 'good values', respect for customs, upright behaviour, and respect between people – despite the fact that much of the history he remembered at school involved migrations and, again, 'tribal wars'.[33]

For some, the precolonial past had been the time of true democracy, and the lessons were there for the learning; but this 'has been eroded by selfish politicians who have not picked a leaf from history', asserted one informant. The incumbent NRM regime had learnt nothing from this deeper well of experience and wisdom: 'The current government's

---

[26] Interview, Bugobero, teacher, *c.* thirty-five years old, 26 September 2013.

[27] See, for example, Apolo Kagwa, cited in Sylvia Antonia Nannyonga-Tamusuza, *Baakisimba: Gender in the Music and Dance of the Baganda People of Uganda* (New York, 2005), 212.

[28] Interviews in Bubutu, unemployed, *c.* forty years old, 15 January 2014; Bugobero, teacher, *c.* thirty-five years old, 26 September 2013; Mbale, teacher, *c.* twenty-eight years old, 26 January 2014.

[29] Interview, Mbale, teacher, *c.* twenty-eight years old, 26 January 2014.

[30] Interview, Bugobero, teacher, *c.* thirty-five years old, 26 September 2013.

[31] Interview, Mbale, teacher, *c.* twenty-eight years old, 26 January 2014.

[32] Interview, Mbale, teacher, *c.* fifty years old, 1 February 2014.

[33] Interview, Mbale, farmer, *c.* sixty years old, 24 January 2014.

attitudes [toward] history [are] oblique, being overshadowed by generations of modernity and Western influence.'[34] The implication is clear enough: that the intrusion of Western history and political culture into Uganda had produced grasping, authoritarian regimes whose behaviours were contrary to ancient indigenous practice. 'Modern civilisation', indeed, in a wonderfully simple summation of much of the argument underpinning this paper, 'tends to outdate our historical past.'[35] Moreover the absorption of Ugandan communities into a unitary nation, the most dramatic legacy bequeathed by global imperialism, was scarcely a matter for celebration. 'Uganda has [a] distorted history of the various ethnic groups that populate it,' suggested one Gisu informant. 'Uganda's national history is that of political crooks who mainly misinform the public instead of genuinely mobilising them for development. Uganda has no national history or culture to talk about. It is a dysfunctional society that is only getting worse.'[36] For others, national history might be traced to the 'coming of colonialists', but even then it was mostly 'tribal history', rather than a discernible national past.[37] Informants were keen to point to the fact that the current regime, like those before it, was essentially disinterested in history because it supposedly undermined its modernist credentials and compromised its globalising outlook: 'Governments tend not care so much about history. They tend to adopt Western ways of life management ... [and] pay more attention to science from Western cultures.'[38] The government evidently believed that 'the values of long ago are outdated', and as a result, despite the current government's own putative agenda to eradicate division, this had bred disunity and sectarianism.[39]

On the other hand, belief in a rather more depressing continuity emerged when informants were asked to survey the behaviour of 'government' over *la longue durée* – a continuity which also highlighted a certain paradox in this affective, idealised vision of the deeper past. 'Politics today favours only the rich,' intoned one informant. 'Even in precolonial days, leadership was for the wealthy families and even hereditary. It has changed only with the introduction of democracy ...' There was no substantive difference between past and present: 'The recent Ugandan governments were dictators and murderers. They used their powers and authority to oppress and exploit their subjects

---

[34] Interview, Bugobero, teacher, *c.* thirty-five years old, 26 September 2013.

[35] Interviews in Bugobero, farmer, *c.* forty-three years old, 25 January 2014; Mbale, teacher, *c.* twenty-eight years old, 26 January 2014.

[36] Interview, Mukono, agricultural consultant, *c.* forty years old, 22 January 2014.

[37] Interviews in Mbale, teacher, *c.* twenty-eight years old, 26 January 2014; Kitindya, priest, *c.* fifty years old, 6 February 2014.

[38] Interview, Mbale, teacher, *c.* twenty-eight years old, 26 January 2014.

[39] Interview, Mbale, teacher, *c.* fifty years old, 1 February 2014.

as was the case in the precolonial times as leaders made decisions without considering the fate of their subjects.'[40] But here again, the political past is mobilised to condemn the modern state: *they are all the same, political leaders, and they always have been.*[41] And history, at least, equipped those willing to accept its lessons to gather such insights, for it instilled 'the power of reasoning', according to one informant.[42]

More broadly, a fixation with 'the modern' had blinded Ugandans to the lessons of the past. In particular, a supposedly universalist, modernising education system had depleted the values of the precolonial, and as a result young people had no regard for this kind of history and thought only of their career prospects. They only studied, and valued, the kinds of things that would facilitate this – naturally enough.[43] Others went further. When asked whether young Ugandans prized the study of history, one informant asserted baldly: 'Largely, they do not. They would rather act ... more European than the Europeans themselves. They hate their own identity because throughout history we seem as a people to have failed to make significant progress ... In time they will implode and then find themselves without reference [points].'[44] It was a common perception.[45] Children needed to learn history as a foundation for their becoming 'good citizens'.[46]

But the young were ever the source of anxiety. 'Today our youth have a different lifestyle – their needs are pinned to the Western world ... They think the past belongs to the older generation.'[47] For another informant, 'broader society considers the precolonial past irrelevant. Most of them, especially the youth, are concentrating on copying foreign culture ... Young people don't think much about history because they are taken up with foreign culture ... [T]he problem is they no longer stay in our traditional setting.'[48] Damned modernity, for tradition is set to flight: 'The problem', asserted one informant with evident distaste, 'is that most of our children don't read serious things and their role models are Chameleon,[49] Bobi Wine,[50] Beyoncé, etc.' Here, interestingly, our informant emphasised that for his

[40] Interview, Bubutu, unemployed, *c.* forty years old, 15 January 2014.

[41] Interviews in Mukono, agricultural consultant, *c.* forty years old, 22 January 2014; Mbale, teacher, *c.* twenty-eight years old, 26 January 2014.

[42] Interview, Bubutu, unemployed, *c.* forty years old, 15 January 2014.

[43] Interview, Bugobero, teacher, *c.* thirty-five years old, 26 September 2013.

[44] Interview, Mukono, agricultural consultant, *c.* forty years old, 22 January 2014.

[45] Interview, Kitindya, priest, *c.* fifty years old, 6 February 2014.

[46] Interview, Mbale, farmer, *c.* sixty years old, 24 January 2014.

[47] Interview, Hoima, priest, *c.* sixty years old, 17 January 2013.

[48] Interview, Hoima, priest, *c.* sixty years old, 17 January 2013.

[49] Chameleon, or Chameleone, is a Ugandan Afrobeat singer, born Joseph Mayanja.

[50] Born Robert Kyagulanyi, Bobi Wine is a popular musician who made international headlines briefly in 2014 when he was denied a UK visa on account of his virulently

generation, global history offered important reference points and inspirational icons: 'For us who were born earlier our role models were Socrates, Gamal Nasser, Kwame Nkrumah, Napoleon, Machiavelli, Sadat, Senghor and their likes. We like to learn more. Youth now only want money not knowledge and worse still historical knowledge which they find so distant and seemingly irrelevant because of their shallowness.'[51] Harsh, but hardly novel, with echoes of the anxieties expressed by Daudi Chwa in the 1930s. It is, unquestionably, a perennial gripe: the inevitable complaints on the part of the old about feckless, callow youth.

The cost of not knowing history was high: it left people feeling 'confused and empty', according to one informant.[52] 'You may avoid being eaten by a lion if you listen to elders who know where it hides,' as one interviewee expressed it.[53] History was a living, curative entity; a pool of sagacity; oracular and didactic. History was a guide to the future, full of lessons for those willing to learn them, and even more specifically, as a means to unity, for all Ugandans can learn about one another and join forces, asserted another informant.[54] It is a significance attached to the past often heard, in a manner a world away from the contested, revisionist, postmodernist debates of the professional academy of the global North. Ultimately, precolonial history, claimed one informant, 'is the true history of our people before it was adulterated by the colonial powers through their forms of education and religion. It is therefore important if we want to understand our real selves and what shaped or influenced attitudes, perceptions, culture and other aspects of our society.'[55] The notion of 'the true history of our people' is revealing, and hugely significant: it encapsulates the idea that there is a temporal cut-off point – the moment of imperial contact, colonial rule, globalisation – at which history becomes less 'real', less authentic, certainly less believable. History is a journey; it is a form of therapy, and a source of knowledge and wisdom. It is 'empowering', said one informant. 'Precolonial history is particularly important because today when we lose our way, we try to look back and try to see where we came from and discover where we have gone wrong.'[56]

Yoweri Museveni's evident despair over the history of the nation, then, is shared by many Ugandans, but for very different reasons. For

---

homophobic lyrics. He is now a political activist and an increasingly vocal and influential critic of Museveni.

[51] Interview, Bulucheke, trader, c. forty-five years old, 20 February 2014.

[52] Interview, Mukono, agricultural consultant, c. forty years old, 22 January 2014.

[53] Interview, Bulucheke, trader, c. forty-five years old, 20 February 2014.

[54] Interview, Manafwa, local councillor, c. sixty-seven years old, 20 October 2013.

[55] Interview, Bulucheke, trader, c. forty-five years old, 20 February 2014.

[56] Interview, Hoima, priest, c. sixty years old, 17 January 2013.

Museveni, the nation had failed – or come mightily close to it – because of the local, 'sectarian' interests which characterise Uganda's precolonial past; but for many Ugandans, those interests are all that matter in the face of a brutal, detached state which is the product of global historical forces over which they have little control.

III Lonely planet: Eritrea

Although the two have much in common in many ways, Eritrea offers a somewhat different case study from Uganda. There is comparatively little of the kind of source material from the earlier twentieth century which we have in abundance for Uganda, and so our analysis is inevitably centred in the more recent past – or more specifically, the popular consensus around that recent past, which is presented below.[57] Further, as in Uganda, local interlocutors often conflate *globalisation* and *global history*; but in Eritrea, the sense of explicitly *historical* trajectory is much more prominent in national psychology and self-image, and is readily articulated by both the leadership and ordinary citizens. Moreover, while Uganda is an increasingly authoritarian state, Eritrea is in a league of its own in this respect: its political space is much more tightly controlled, and therefore formal interviewing is difficult. Much of the following is based on more or less informal 'interviews' and conversations around historical memory and lived narrative, mostly gathered at a particularly traumatic moment in Eritrea's modern history – namely the years immediately before, during and after the recent war with Ethiopia.[58] Nonetheless, the central theme emerging from these is that Eritrea has long been excluded from the mainstream of global history, and that cycles of violence are at least partly the outcome of such marginalisation.

At Eritrea's annual independence celebrations, President Isaias Afeworki is wont to offer comments on the country's troubled past. It has become a ritual in the national calendar, and a desperately monotonous one for many citizens, but one which is dutifully broadcast on state television.[59] The underlying message is supposed to be uplifting – how

---

[57] For an exception, and one which hopefully marks the beginning of a new field of research, see James de Lorenzi, *Guardians of the Tradition: Historians and Historical Writing in Ethiopia and Eritrea* (Rochester, NY, 2015).

[58] Formal citations are therefore unavoidably truncated. The vast majority of informants were either former guerrilla fighters from the liberation war of the 1970s and 1980s, many of whom were now government officials; or current national service recruits, who made up a substantial proportion of Eritrea's youth. Some of this material has been written up in Richard Reid, *Shallow Graves: A Memoir of the Eritrean–Ethiopian War* (forthcoming).

[59] See, for example, www.youtube.com/watch?v=NmqFDo-_oN8&t=1150s; and www.eriswiss.com/president-isaias-afewerkis-speech-on-the-occasion-of-the-26th-independence-day-celebrations/.

the young nation has made progress, how it remains resilient in the face of various challenges, and so on – but it is in fact a grim trawl through the trials and tribulations of Eritrean history: its subjugation as a colonial possession, its betrayal at the hands of a brutal international order, its ongoing abuse and/or neglect by the international community. It is an exercise in the reification of Eritrea's national history in the context of a malign global past: Eritrea's place in that past is that of an ill-treated corner of the world, compelling its people, through seemingly endless struggle and sacrifice, to transform itself into an independent state. But this is not just the idiosyncratic view of a seemingly immovable president. The core idea – a history of isolation and neglect – resonates with Eritreans, even if many of them blame him and his movement, the Eritrean People's Liberation Front (EPLF), for bringing this situation about, or at least exacerbating it.

It is a narrative which in some ways has its roots in 1962, when Ethiopia annexed Eritrea in violation of a federal arrangement put in place a decade earlier and supposedly guaranteed by the UN Security Council.[60] The UN did nothing at that moment, and the armed struggle which had begun the year before in the country's western lowlands escalated dramatically in the course of the 1960s. But nationalist guerrillas would also point to the events preceding the annexation as evidence of the country's neglected status, and as reinforcing the idea of lonely, violent liberation as the nation's destiny. In the late 1940s, the future of Eritrea – a former Italian colony and now under temporary British administration – was discussed first by a commission of the main wartime allies, and then by the UN itself in one of the first such cases for the newly formed organisation. There were local consultations with a select group of Eritreans who were asked whether they preferred full independence, or union with Ethiopia, which laid claim to the territory on cultural and historical grounds. The outcome of those consultations was inconclusive – there was vocal support for both options – but in the meantime the US had quietly decided that an independent Eritrea was emphatically not in American interests. An agreement was reached between the Truman administration and Haile Selassie's government involving US support for Eritrea being 'federated' with Ethiopia – though it was to have its own assembly, and considerable autonomy – in exchange for a major US military base on the outskirts of the capital, Asmara. (For a number of years Kagnew station in Asmara was the largest such US base in the world.) The British pulled out in 1952 – not before dismantling and selling off much of the territory's infrastructure, another key grievance in the nationalist memory – and the

---

[60] Ruth Iyob, *The Eritrean Struggle for Independence: Domination, Resistance, Nationalism 1941–1993* (Cambridge, 1995), ch. 5.

federation came into being. But for much of the next decade, Ethiopia systematically undermined Eritrean autonomy – removing the flag, banning the languages of government (Tigrinya and Arabic), and steadily closing down the political space – until finally abolishing the Eritrean assembly in 1962.[61]

The period between the late 1940s and the early 1960s was thus a seminal moment, in the view of later nationalists. This was the moment in which it was made clear that Eritreans were irrelevant in the Cold War global order: the cash-strapped British had barely managed the territory, and then asset-stripped it before scurrying off; the Americans had betrayed the country with shocking disregard for local concerns (John Foster Dulles had famously declared that while he had some sympathy with their desire for independence, there were greater issues at stake in a volatile region[62]); and the grasping and backward Ethiopians had proceeded to brutalise and oppress Eritreans with impunity. All of this was framed in historical terms, and convinced a cohort of nationalists – schoolchildren in the 1950s, guerrillas in the 1960s – that the history of British imperialism was that of larceny and perfidy; that the supposed history of American liberalism was an artifice which disguised an imperialism no less avaricious or mendacious than that of Britain; that a global order centred on the UN had evolved which took no account of the oppressed peoples of the world and which was in any case controlled by an oligopoly of major powers. The forces of global history, in other words, were fundamentally hostile to Eritrea, which was thus going to have to find its own way in the world to carve its own path; and Frantz Fanon, whose exhortation to anti-colonial struggle in the Algerian context served as a global rallying call, offered inspiration.[63]

Ironically enough, it was Eritrea's earlier incarnation as an Italian colony – between the 1890s and 1941 – which reinforced the nationalist notion of essential difference from Ethiopia. Indeed, for at least some Eritreans in the 1940s and 1950s, the fact that they had been governed by a putatively 'advanced' foreign power justified their demands for independence from Ethiopia, which was feudal, regressive, undeveloped. Eritrea, by contrast, had experienced 'development', of a kind, and had experienced at least some of the accoutrements of supposed modernity. Even Eritrean unionists – those who feared a return of European imperialism, and who believed that union with Ethiopia would best serve Eritrean interests and was in effect an exercise in

---

[61] See, for example, G. K. N. Trevaskis, *Eritrea, a Colony in Transition* (1960); Roy Pateman, *Eritrea: Even the Stones Are Burning* (Lawrenceville, NJ, 1998).

[62] Okbazghi Yohannes, *Eritrea: A Pawn in World Politics* (Gainesville, FL, 1991), 103.

[63] Frantz Fanon, *The Wretched of the Earth* (1967).

African nationalism – privately or otherwise believed Ethiopia to be a somewhat backward country, and Eritreans (or at least Eritrean Tigrinya) to be really rather superior.[64] It was a curious reworking of Italian colonialism, with its record of under-educating Eritreans, of racial segregation and of frequently ill-conceived development projects. But the overriding point was that, however harsh the experience, governance by a foreign power had raised Eritrea to a status which meant that incorporation into feudal Abyssinia could have no legitimacy. In a strikingly teleological argument, imperialism was the *sine qua non* of the nationalist cause.[65] There was an additional irony in that Eritrea was not actually supposed to exist, in this form anyway: Italy had originally occupied the plateau as a launching pad for its invasion and occupation of Ethiopia, a project which unravelled spectacularly with Italy's defeat by Emperor Menelik's army at the battle of Adwa in 1896. Eritrea was, then, the product of imperial failure.

In the 1960s and 1970s, as the violence of the liberation struggle engulfed Eritrea, the wonderful examples of Art Deco architecture in Asmara – arguably Italy's most enduring legacy – became curious anachronisms, reminders of a distant epoch. The EPLF, the dominant liberation front from the early 1970s, honed its political vision in the northern mountains, a political vision underscored by a distinctive conceptualisation of the territory's global past. The isolation of the struggle, and the militant solipsism it engendered, compounded the vision. There was little external support – a key shibboleth of the EPLF's war – and as a result a culture of complete material and military self-reliance evolved, which was quickly extended into the realms of ontology, politics and history. The EPLF would operate according to its own temporality, its own sense of mission and special destiny: Western liberal time was rejected, just as Soviet-inspired Marxism was eschewed as simply another form of foreign hegemony.[66]

After independence in 1991, achieved through military victory and the collapse of the Ethiopian socialist regime, the Eritrean government under Isaias Afeworki and the leadership of the EPLF sought to recreate the visions of the armed struggle in wider society, with mixed results. But when war with Ethiopia re-erupted in 1998, it seemed that the isolation that had been framed as a virtue was now a dangerous burden.

---

[64] Interview with former member of the Unionist Party, Asmara, 31 August 2006.

[65] For an overview of the Italian period, see Redie Bereketeab, *Eritrea: The Making of a Nation, 1890–1991* (Trenton, NJ, 2007), ch. 4.

[66] For EPLF visions, and supportive assessments of those visions, see *Behind the War in Eritrea*, ed. Basil Davidson, Lionel Cliffe and Bereket Habte Selassie (Nottingham, 1980); James Firebrace, with Stuart Holland MP, *Never Kneel Down: Drought, Development and Liberation in Eritrea* (Trenton, NJ, 1985); *The Long Struggle of Eritrea for Independence and Constructive Peace*, ed. Lionel Cliffe and Basil Davidson (Trenton NJ, 1988).

Compared to Ethiopia's long-standing place in the international order, which it occupied with ease, underpinned by a deep historical relationship with that order, Eritrea came across as angry, trenchant and laconic; ill-at-ease in diplomatic circles; convinced of the righteousness of its own position without necessarily having to justify itself to external powers undeserving of detailed explanations. This was not merely political inexperience, although for sure there was some of that. It was the outcome of an explicitly historical lens through which the nation and its place in the world was viewed. During the war itself, as yet another lonely, bitter cycle of violence ravaged yet another generation of young men and women, Eritreans bemoaned in private the dreadful trajectory which had led them to this position, and reflected on the nature of their history. They reflected, in particular, on the waves of imperialism and domination which seemed to characterise Eritrea's experience of the global past, and which had apparently necessitated the kinds of violence which had ultimately led to the young nation's partial quarantine from the world. There was increasing criticism – again, in private – of the EPLF and of Isaias, and despair at the direction the nation was taking; but when the president spoke of the gruesome past, and the seclusion which had characterised that past, people had no reason to doubt it. They were living it.[67]

In the years after the war, time itself weighed heavily on those millions of Eritreans trapped in a system of indefinite national service, but the government continued to exhort them to be vigilant, and to sacrifice themselves in defence of a nation beleaguered, and surrounded by enemies. The national calendar was peppered with events – Independence Day, Martyrs' Day, 1 September (marking the start of the armed struggle in 1961), festivals celebrating Eritrean heroism and achievement at Sawa, the national military training centre – which were opportunities for the president to remind an increasingly exhausted population of the lessons of global history. And for good measure, there would be performances to act out that history – often involving rubber dragons (representing the forces of colonialism and imperialism) being slain by heroic fighters.[68]

There was one last twist in the tale – to date. Eritrean identity had long been remarkably diasporic. Since the first activists went into exile in the 1950s, and the refugee community in Italy, Sweden, Germany, the US, Australia, and elsewhere, swelled in the 1970s and 1980s, Eritrean citizenship and nationality became entwined with new, more global identities,

---

[67] Author's field notes and informal interviews, Eritrea, between May 1998 and September 2002.

[68] Author's field notes and informal interviews, Eritrea, between December 2002 and August 2008. See also Richard Reid, 'Mourning and Glory: Toward Affective Histories of Violence in Africa over *la longue durée*', *Emotions: History, Culture, Society*, 1 (2017), 113–36.

and Eritreans joined their own turbulent histories with those of their host nations. Now, from the early 2000s, they were complemented by a new cohort, as increasing numbers of Eritreans fled the country through Ethiopia or Sudan to escape interminable military service and economic hardship. The unfortunate ones died on the journey, or were trafficked across the Sahara, or were trapped in holding centres in third countries, or drowned in the Mediterranean.[69] The 'lucky' ones reached Calais, desperate to enter the UK, long seen as a haven and a place where lives could be rebuilt, and where education and employment were possible.[70] It represented a veritable movement of Time itself: the mass rejection of EPLF Time and the desire to rediscover a different, more global kind of Time, one which perhaps moved a little more briskly and in which there were rather greater opportunities for self-expression and self-realisation. The desperation to reach Britain was also a curious kind of global historical feedback: few Britons were probably even aware of Britain's role in Eritrea in the 1940s and 1950s, a seminal moment in the histories of both countries, but public discourse in the UK was increasingly dominated by the need to control immigration, the perils of admitting asylum-seekers, and – in the wake of the EU referendum – the amorphous visions of an imperial past in which Britain was great and globally dominant.[71] A swathe of the British political class – and many British people themselves – seemed to hanker after a particular vision of the global past; many Eritreans, likewise, aspired to a version of global history which was not rooted in visions of cyclical violence, militarised isolation, and unending personal sacrifice. It was a curious intersection of historical aspirations.

IV Conclusions: the world from below

How best do we go about conceptualising 'global history' while doing justice to the views of the local? This is a challenge for all historians from the global North who are themselves agents of a scholarly globalism on which their local interlocutors often have, at the very least, a rather different perspective. In some respects, this is a gulf which has, if anything, widened in recent decades, and represents a methodological, epistemological and pedagogical struggle between the global and the local with which all historians of Africa must eventually engage. Ultimately, what does our area-specific history mean in a global world? How do

[69] Council on Foreign Relations, 'Authoritarianism in Eritrea and the Migrant Crisis', 16 September 2016, www.cfr.org/backgrounder/authoritarianism-eritrea-and-migrant-crisis.

[70] Author's conversations with asylum-seekers in London, since c. 2002.

[71] Sally Tomlinson and Danny Dorling, 'Brexit has its roots in the British Empire – so how do we explain it to the young?', *New Statesman*, 9 May 2016; Julianne Schulz, 'Why the dream of Empire 2.0 is still "cobblers"', *The Guardian*, 11 February 2018.

we make our research relevant and legible? In an age of epistemological uncertainty, and indeed anxiety, an exploration of the connection between the local and the global seems critically important.

The issue is given further urgency by the fact that, increasingly, our students have roots in the very regions on which we do our research, with distinctive perspectives on the scholarship we bring before them. If we discover – as in Uganda and Eritrea – particular visions of 'the global' in the regions themselves, we also find a student body which demands much more in the way of global perspectives because of their own multiple and overlapping identities, and thus their own politics, than might once have been the case in the university. It is no coincidence that these young people are frequently in the vanguard of the 'decolonis-ing the curriculum' movement.[72] In class, I have certainly found myself facilitating, or at least moderating, the expression of a particular form of global historical consciousness. To a considerable extent, decolonising the curriculum therefore means globalising it, while in the process de- (or re-)centring the world itself – including taking into account how dia-sporas think about the local to which they have familial and cultural links. But in other ways, it also means *localising* it, and certainly getting to grips with how local actors perceive and interact with the global.

It is vital that the views of Ugandans and Eritreans as briefly surveyed here are brought into the larger debates referenced at the beginning of this paper. For sure, their distinctive visions of the global past are indica-tive of the desire – the *need*, even – for stable, usable, *national* and *local* his-tories; school and university curricula in turn are often conceived around a nationally or locally bounded temporality, in ways that would seem 'outdated' to Western eyes. In many ways, global, or transnational, his-tories offer little in the way of succour to the local actors whose views underpin this paper. And yet, almost everyone – excepting, perhaps, jeal-ously self-interested political elites, as in Eritrea – might find that locating their histories in a multi-sited global past offers rich and interesting rewards. That is a project for the future. Suffice to conclude with the observation that my own approach to global history as a field has been profoundly influenced by the voices I have encountered over a number of years in Uganda and Eritrea, and elsewhere in the region. It has never been more important to provide a more robust, supportive environment for the expression and exploration of the *local* – wherever that takes place – which is where the global begins, and, perhaps, where it ends, too. At least it seems so for millions of Ugandans and Eritreans, and their perspectives are overlooked at enormous risk to the integrity of our research and teaching.

---

[72] For example, Priyamvada Gopal, 'Yes, we must decolonize: our teaching has to go beyond elite white men', *The Guardian*, 27 October 2017.

Transactions of the RHS 29 (2019), pp. 273–292 © Royal Historical Society 2019
doi:10.1017/S0080440119000124

POLITICISING CHERNOBYL: WALES AND NUCLEAR POWER DURING THE 1980s

By Seán Aeron Martin and Mari Elin Wiliam

READ 14 APRIL 2018
AT THE UNIVERSITY OF SOUTH WALES, CARDIFF

ABSTRACT. The Chernobyl disaster of 1986 had international repercussions, as nuclear fallout, and accompanying fear, traversed well beyond the borders of the Soviet Union. In Britain, raised radioactivity levels caused some upland regions, such as north-west Wales, to become subject to restrictions on the sale of livestock, which created upheaval for the agricultural community, leading to an uncharacteristic outburst of protest from farmers who were unhappy with the government's response to the crisis. Concurrently, nuclear sceptics in Wales attempted to politicise the tragedy in the Ukraine to underline the dangers of nuclear power, dovetailing the accident with the looming perils of Wales's domestic nuclear industry. In exploring these issues, this paper contributes to a growing body of work on 'British nuclear cultures', moving away from its generally urban focus by examining a Welsh rural case study. This approach also circumvents the well-trodden historiographical narrative surrounding the politics of nuclear warfare by highlighting debates arising from civil nuclear power. Crucially, the work demonstrates how looking at the modern Welsh past through the prism of a transnational nuclear event such as the Chernobyl catastrophe shows that the history of twentieth-century Wales is enriched by moving beyond the stereotypically 'Welsh' industrial shibboleths of the south Wales coalfield and the slate mines of north Wales.

CRYNODEB. Roedd oblygiadau rhyngwladol i drychineb Chernobyl ym 1986, wrth i lwch ymbelydrol, ac ofnau cysylltiedig, deithio ymhell y tu hwnt i ffiniau'r Undeb Sofietaidd. Ym Mhrydain, achosodd lefelau ymbelydredd uwch i rai ucheldiroedd, megis yng ngogledd-orllewin Cymru, ddod o dan gyfyngiadau ar werthu da byw, gan arwain at ansicrwydd i'r gymuned amaethyddol, ynghyd â ffrwydrad o brotest gan ffermwyr oedd yn anhapus gydag ymateb y llywodraeth i'r argyfwng. Yn gydamserol, ceisiodd sgeptigiaid niwclear yng Nghymru wleidyddoli'r ddamwain yn yr Wcrain i danlinellu natur fygythiol ynni niwclear, gan blethu'r drychineb gyda pheryglon y diwydiant niwclear yng Nghymru. Trwy archwilio'r materion hyn cyfranna'r papur at gronfa gynyddol o waith ar 'ddiwylliannau niwclear Prydeinig', gan wthio heibio ei ffocws dinesig arferol trwy ganolbwyntio ar astudiaeth achos yn seiliedig ar gefn gwlad Cymru. Mae'r dull hwn hefyd yn dargyfeirio o'r naratif hanesyddiaethol traddodiadol am wleidyddiaeth rhyfel niwclear trwy amlygu trafodaethau a ddeilliai o gynlluniau ynni niwclear sifil. Yn hanfodol, dengys y gwaith y modd y gall edrych ar y gorffennol modern trwy brism digwyddiad niwclear trawsgenedlaethol, megis Chernobyl, gyfoethogi hanes Cymru'r ugeinfed-ganrif, gan symud y tu hwnt i sibolethau diwydiannol ystrydebol 'Gymreig' maes glo de Cymru a chwareli gogledd Cymru.

I Introduction

The Chernobyl catastrophe on 26 April 1986 in the Ukraine coincided with a decade of heightened Cold War tensions, leading to renewed nuclear scepticism, echoing concerns first seen during the birth of the 'atomic age' in the 1950s.[1] In Britain, this involved a resurgence in the Campaign for Nuclear Disarmament (CND) along with the development of grassroots anti-nuclear agitation, which in Wales included local authorities declaring the country the first European 'nuclear (weapons) free zone' in 1982.[2] However, as this example attests, the common spectre in the 1980s British nuclear debate was the cataclysm of nuclear warfare more than the perils of a nuclear accident.[3] This resonates in nuclear historiography, which has tended to pursue the politics of the nuclear deterrent and the threat of global annihilation, thereby overlooking more prosaic fields involving civil nuclear power and atomic stations.[4] Wales's own nuclear historiography, moreover, follows a similar – if considerably sparser – trajectory to its British counterpart, with historians' pursuit of distinctively 'Welsh' industries such as coal and slate pushing the nuclear presence in Wales, most strikingly the power stations at Trawsfynydd and Wylfa in north-west Wales, to the margins, leading to a predictable emphasis on nuclear warfare discourse and its interaction with Welsh national identity.[5] This neglectful attitude towards civil nuclear power extends to the Chernobyl accident, which only makes very limited incursions into academic historical scholarship

---

[1] Jonathan Hogg, 'Cultures of Nuclear Resistance in 1980s Liverpool', *Urban History*, 42 (2015), 1–19; Mark Phythian, 'CND's Cold War', *Contemporary British History*, 15 (2001), 133–56; Martin Johnes, 'Wales and the Cold War', *Llafur*, 10 (2011), 5–15.

[2] Christoph Laucht and Martin Johnes, 'Resist and Survive: Welsh Protests and the British Nuclear State in the 1980s', *Contemporary British History*, 33 (2019), 226–45.

[3] The 'immediate threat of nuclear war' suffuses an infamous civil defence campaign of the 1980s: Central Office of Information, *Protect and Survive* (1980).

[4] This is often blatant, e.g. Frank Barnaby and Douglas Holdstock, *The British Nuclear Weapons Programme, 1952–2002* (Abingdon, 2003), but also central to more socio-cultural works, e.g. John Baylis and Kristan Stoddart, *The British Nuclear Experience: The Roles of Beliefs, Culture and Identity* (Oxford, 2014).

[5] Rare engagement includes a *Llafur* special Cold War edition in 2011; Christopher R. Hill, 'Nations of Peace: Nuclear Disarmament and the Making of National Identity in Scotland and Wales', *Twentieth Century British History*, 27 (2016), 26–50; and most recently and comprehensively, Laucht and Johnes, 'Resist and Survive', and John Baylis, *Wales and the Bomb* (Cardiff, 2019). Historical emphasis on the civil nuclear industry in Wales is virtually non-existent. For a comprehensive overview of historical writing on modern Wales see Martin Johnes, 'For Class and Nation: Dominant Trends in the Historiography of Twentieth-Century Wales', *History Compass*, 8 (2010), 1257–74.

in the UK, let alone Wales, being conveyed as a tragic, overseas, Soviet-era accident, rather than an event with any deep repercussions on the British Isles, even though, as this paper contends, it accentuated the debate on the relationship between nuclear power and rural communities.[6]

A significant departure in recent historiography is the growing emphasis by scholars such as Jonathan Hogg and Christoph Laucht on exploring 'British nuclear culture', moving away from the 'official narrative' of nuclear high-politics.[7] This fresh approach involves examining the varying responses of everyday people to different nuclear technologies through concentrating on more 'unofficial narratives', thus bolstering Jeff Hughes's argument that such is the phrase's pluralism, hybridity and openness to geographical particularisms that it should be recognised instead as 'British nuclear *cultures*'.[8] This article will consider a different aspect of nuclear cultures in Britain by focusing on rural, Welsh responses to the risks of civil nuclear power, diversifying from the dominant regional case studies, which are mainly urban, English and based on rhetoric relating to atomic warfare.[9] Inherent in the examination of more 'unofficial' narratives is a challenge to the dominance of the nation-state in nuclear discourse. Chernobyl demonstrated, as the fallout from the accident spread far and wide, that nuclear power, in any guise, does not respect or recognise traditional borders of nations, and what in other circumstances would have been seen as a national problem, or easily dismissed in the West due to its occurrence behind the 'Iron Curtain', was very quickly acknowledged, in the words of Ursula K. Heise, as a European-wide, 'transnational risk scenario'.[10] This blurs national lines, and suggests the potential for innovative

---

[6] Examples of recent popular historical scholarship include Serhii Plokhy, *Chernobyl: A History of a Tragedy* (2018); Adam Higginbotham, *Midnight in Chernobyl: The Untold Story of the World's Greatest Nuclear Disaster* (2019). The recent release of UK government documents could change this; see Alan W. Robertson, 'Chernobyl: The Response in Northern Ireland', *History Ireland*, 24 (2016), 46–8.

[7] Key works include a 2012 special edition of the *British Journal for the History of Science* (*BJHS*), esp. Jonathan Hogg and Christoph Laucht, 'Introduction: British Nuclear Culture', *BJHS*, 45 (2012), 479–93; Jonathan Hogg, *British Nuclear Culture: Official and Unofficial Narratives in the Long Twentieth Century* (2016).

[8] Jeff Hughes, 'What Is British Nuclear Culture? Understanding *Uranium 235*', *BJHS*, 45 (2012), 495–518; Gabrielle Hecht, *The Radiance of France: Nuclear Power and National Identity after World War II* (Boston, MA, 2009).

[9] Hogg's *British Nuclear Culture* makes only three short mentions of Chernobyl on 133, 144, 164. See special edition of *Urban History*, esp. Matthew Farish and David Monteyne, 'Introduction: Histories of Cold War Cities', *Urban History*, 42 (2015), 543–6.

[10] Ursula K. Heise, *Sense of Place and Sense of Planet: The Environmental Imagination of the Global* (Oxford, 2008), 177. For a transnational approach to nuclear culture see Christoph Laucht, 'Transnational Professional Activism and the Prevention of Nuclear War in Britain', *Journal of Social History*, 52 (2017), 1–29.

subnational approaches, as demonstrated in this article, to assess the Chernobyl disaster's effect on the political debate over nuclear power in the mid-1980s.

One of the first signs that the Chernobyl fallout had arrived in north Wales was radiation alarms going off in the region's two nuclear power stations, as workers clocked in and triggered the alarms due to high readings on their clothing.[11] This transnational coalescing of nuclear sites in Wales with a spatially distant nuclear catastrophe is representative of two key ways Chernobyl shaped political discourse in Wales, which will be examined in this paper. Firstly, radioactive dust from the accident penetrated the uplands of north-west Wales, creating disruption for the food chain and farmers' incomes, which consequently led to a rare period of political discontent in the agricultural sector. This paper will demonstrate how a distant nuclear accident was concurrently viewed as a threat to one of the most mythologised crucibles of Welshness, rural Wales, and as an uncertain risk to public health.[12] Secondly, the catastrophe was harnessed by more conventional nuclear agitators involved in environmental politics in Wales to highlight the dangers of producing nuclear energy, heightening fears over the safety ramifications of nuclear power stations and seemingly justifying the apocalyptic historical scenarios painted by activists since the 1950s. As research suggests, their narrative was shaped by casting doubt over the radiation's ownership: did it really all stem from Chernobyl, or was there more sinister 'domestic' radiation at work, particularly emanating from Trawsfynydd, the only inland nuclear power station in the UK, which was also based in a post-Chernobyl radiation hotspot? By deploying a range of rarely utilised bilingual source materials – from collections including the Welsh Office, CND Cymru and oral history – this paper will explore political expressions of nuclear scepticism from a Welsh, rural and civil perspective, underlining the plurality of 'British nuclear cultures', as well as shedding new light on the particularisms of the contemporary Welsh past.[13]

II Fallout: fear, farmers and the Welsh Office

Whilst the Chernobyl 'cloud' that reached Britain at the beginning of May swathed many parts of the country, the topography of some regions meant that radioactive fallout was retained in the ground, and

---

[11] Authors' interview with Tom Jones, Anglesey, 16 August 2016.

[12] Wil Griffith, 'Saving the Soul of the Nation: Essentialist Nationalism and Interwar Rural Wales', *Rural History*, 21 (2010), 177–94; Gareth Hughes, Peter Midmore and Anne-Marie Sherwood, 'The Welsh Language and Agricultural Communities in the Twentieth Century', in *Let's Do Our Best for the Ancient Tongue*, ed. Geraint H. Jenkins and Mari A. Williams (Cardiff, 2000), 551–76.

[13] All source translations from Welsh to English provided by the authors.

thus the food chain, for a longer period of time. Some of the uplands of north-west Wales – especially in parts of Snowdonia such as Meirionnydd, bordering on Trawsfynydd nuclear power station, towards the Denbigh Moors and briefly Anglesey – were particularly hospitable to this radioactivity due to the climate, soil type and drainage factors, meaning that the contamination, and the need for countermeasures, lingered for years.[14] However, despite these easily known facts, the initial reaction from the British government was one of calm, describing the contamination level as 'very low' and posing 'no health risk to the public'.[15]

Nevertheless, these reassurances failed to assuage the anxieties of the public, who, when looking at the wider international reaction, were frustrated by the reticence of Margaret Thatcher's Conservative government on a matter that evidently had deeper repercussions than previously thought: visitors recently returned from 'contaminated' Eastern Europe were being told to report to their local police stations for 'help'; serious rumours were circulating about the safety of staples such as meat, milk and vegetables; and governmental telephone lines were 'jammed' by concerned members of the public.[16] As time passed, monitoring of areas and foodstuffs affected by the fallout continued to display high levels of radioactivity, seemingly confirming such fears, and it became obvious to government ministers that they had gravely underestimated the problem: action was urgently needed in order to counter the public outcry that had already started to ferment around the country. Therefore, on 20 June 1986, seven weeks after the accident, Michael Jopling, the secretary of state for agriculture, announced that livestock with radiation levels over 1,000 Bq/kg would be prevented from entering the food chain, and introduced a prohibition on the movement and slaughter of sheep in regions that were registering a cluster of high measurements, such as south-west Cumbria, north Wales and parts of Scotland. Portraying it as a short-term problem, Jopling initially placed these restrictions for just twenty-one days, which would be 'reduced as soon as the monitoring results ... confirm the expected fall in levels'.[17]

[14] The National Archives, Kew (TNA), Welsh Office (WO), BD 119/32, Chernobyl Incident, Memorandum 26 September 1986.

[15] *The Guardian*, 3 May 1986.

[16] House of Commons Agriculture Committee, Second Report, *Chernobyl: The Government's Reaction*, Vol. 1, Section III (1988).

[17] Hansard, *House of Commons Debate (HC Deb)*, 20 June 1986, vol. 99 cc 1333–8. The becquerel (Bq) is the unit of radioactivity, 1 Bq being defined as the activity of a quantity of radioactive material in which one atom decays per second. Thus, 1000 Bq/kg means for every second in every kilogram of lamb.

The initial groundswell of public anxiety due to Chernobyl was in no small part linked to the government's prevarication over firstly admitting there was a problem with radiation levels, and secondly identifying how to deal with it. Arguably, Jopling's hurried pronouncement on a Friday – breaking Parliamentary convention, Friday usually being a quiet day when MPs returned to their constituencies – cast a further shadow of uncertainty. In addition, due to this delay in enacting restrictions, speculation flourished on the potential contamination of meat that had already been on sale for over a month, which propagated the panic, the very element that the government wanted to arrest in the first place. According to one Welsh-language weekly paper, *Y Cymro*, this miscalculation was reprehensible, with an editorial in the newspaper stating in uncompromising, Cold War semiotics, 'If there is no full explanation … then Michael Jopling and his ministers will be as guilty of concealing the truth as the Kremlin itself.'[18]

The Welsh Office was in an understandably conflicted position. On the one hand, it was responsible for implementing the restrictions on animals out of a public health rationale. However, these measures were equally aimed at retaining and restoring market confidence in British agriculture, and officials therefore needed to minimise fears about the impact of the Chernobyl fallout on the food chain. This tightrope act was, almost inevitably, calamitous, with a press release in September 1986 announcing that there was 'no hazard to the health of sheep and cattle grazing the most heavily contaminated pastures in the UK', whilst simultaneously confirming the continuation of controls over tracts of Welsh land.[19] Although farmers understood the justification for the restrictions due to safety concerns, this contradictory language caused some bewilderment, for if lamb was apparently safe to eat, the fundamental question was why there was a ban on it in the first place.[20] Indeed, the regular insistence by officials in Cardiff that the 1,000 Bq/kg level was a 'conservative figure', 'which incorporates a substantial safety margin', would no doubt have caused further consternation to the agricultural communities affected, who could find little solace in statements which were clearly designed to reassure consumers.[21] Furthermore, in a debate in Parliament on the matter, Dafydd Wigley, Plaid Cymru MP for Caernarfonshire, chastised the government for its

---

[18] *Y Cymro*, 25 June 1986, 6.
[19] TNA, WO, BD 119/32, *Welsh Office News*, 26 September 1986.
[20] National Library of Wales, Aberystwyth (NLW), Keith Best Papers (KB), KB 21, Chernobyl Radioactivity Lamb, G. Moss Jones, Cymdeithas Defaid Mynydd Cymreig to Keith Best, 7 July 1986.
[21] TNA, WO, BD 119/32, Briefing note 'The Ban on the Movement and Slaughter of Sheep in North Wales', 26 September 1986.

'haphazard' and 'chaotic' introduction of the ban, which many believed had unwittingly amplified the panic, ultimately doing more harm than good when it came to the public's perception of the safety of Welsh lamb.[22]

The impression of the Welsh Office in the midst of the Chernobyl crisis is of a department on the back foot, scantily prepared for a predicament of this nature and unsure of its remit. In one 'Emergency Planning' meeting in the autumn of 1986, officials expressed doubt as to whether they should be in charge of a civil nuclear emergency at all, and seemed to want to delegate responsibility back to Westminster. There was also bickering over who in the Welsh Office should be doing what, to the extent that the normally staid tone of the minutes was broken by a comment in parentheses '(Heated discussion followed!).'[23] Keith Best, the Conservative MP for Anglesey, brusquely conveyed his constituents' scathing critique of the Welsh Office to the secretary of state for Wales, Nicholas Edwards, declaring that there were 'grave misgivings' about whether officials appreciated the seriousness of the situation for the agriculture industry, and that they were 'deeply aggrieved' that no minister had visited the area, since this was emerging as 'a most damaging and critical situation' for his government.[24] However, as strong an advocate as Best was for the island's farmers, as a Conservative MP he was also tainted by the Thatcher government's perceived silence over the central issue of compensation. In between the announcement of controls on 20 June and early July, nothing seemed to have been done to assuage the financial concerns of the agricultural sector. This led to the Anglesey Conservative Association writing to Nicholas Edwards and senior Tory Norman Tebbit to express concern about the potential 'adverse political effects' on Best and the constituency, unless the government took swift action over the lamb compensation issue since Plaid Cymru, the Welsh nationalist party, was already trying to 'blacken his reputation'.[25] A Conservative peer from Anglesey described the Ministry of Agriculture's handling of the crisis as 'ghastly', even acidly commenting that the government was clearly intent on provoking farmers to 'break the law and vote Plaid'.[26] The Welsh Countryside Landowners' Association drew up a highly critical report on the Welsh Office's handling of the compensation issue, and

[22] *HC Deb*, 24 July 1986, vol. 102, cc 736–56.
[23] TNA, WO, BD 119/32, 'Emergency Planning Meeting', September 1986.
[24] TNA, WO, BD 119/31, Chernobyl Incident Welsh Office, 'Sheepmeat restrictions, note of conference held on Monday 23 June 1986'; NLW, KB 21, Keith Best to Nicholas Edwards, 1 July 1986.
[25] NLW, KB 21, M. H. Norris to Nicholas Edwards, 1 July 1986.
[26] NLW, KB 21, 'Tom', Lord Stanley of Alderley, Amlwch to Keith Best, 17 September 1986.

it was clearly a matter that percolated through the agricultural industry from the landed elite to the marginal hill farmer.[27] Indeed, criticism was not limited to political point-scoring or farmers with a vested interest in the issue. Professor Glyn O. Phillips, founder and editor of Welsh language science journal *Y Gwyddonydd* (The Scientist), claimed that there was 'complete befuddlement' in the response of political leaders to Chernobyl, with no one delivering an answer as to why there was such a difference in radiation levels between the uplands of Wales and the lowlands of England, and that clearly nobody in Britain had an idea how they would deal with a similar accident in Britain, least still a nuclear war.[28] These concerns were echoed in the political sphere by Dafydd Elis-Thomas, Plaid MP for Meirionnydd Nant Conwy, who believed that the British government and Welsh Office's response in the aftermath of the Chernobyl disaster was a 'moral failure':

> If we have a nuclear industry, we have a moral responsibility to cope with the effects of the industry. If we have a defence policy that is based upon a nuclear deterrent, we have a moral obligation to ensure that the basic industry of society is not damaged as a result of any prospect of nuclear fission. We have failed in that moral responsibility.[29]

However, financial compensation for losses due to 'Chernobyl-lambs' was the paramount issue for farmers, some of whom were 'disgusted' that they appeared to have to persuade the government of the severity of their situation.[30] This was intermixed with some obscurity over whose government should shoulder the responsibility. Beata Brookes, the Conservative MEP for North Wales, resorted to writing to Soviet leader Mikhail Gorbachev, claiming that the Kremlin should pay for all the losses shouldered by the agricultural community in her constituency, since their livelihoods had been 'devastated by the radiation'.[31] There is no record of his response, but in trying to deflect blame away from her own government, she at least appeared to validate the concerns of farmers. Previously she had expressed concern that there was an attempt by officials to avoid paying compensation to the sheep industry in north Wales.[32] Simultaneously, some cursory efforts were made to draw compensation from the European Economic Community (EEC), although, ultimately, the agricultural challenges thrown up by this

---

[27] 'Chernobyl: Our Hills are Hot', *Farmers' Weekly*, 4 March 1988.

[28] Glyn O. Phillips, 'Golygyddol', *Y Gwyddonydd*, Summer 1986, 4.

[29] *HC Deb*, 24 July 1986, vol. 102, cc 736–56.

[30] NLW, KB 21, Keith Best to Nicholas Edwards, 1 July 1986.

[31] NLW, Beata Brookes Papers 72, Letter from Beata Brookes, *Daily Post*, 24 June 1986.

[32] NLW, KB 21, Beata Brookes to Nicholas Edwards, cc Keith Best, 3 July 1986.

international emergency were viewed by the sector itself as ones to be tackled domestically by the national government.[33]

Much to the chagrin of the farmers affected, a decisive response by the British government on the financial issue remained unforthcoming throughout the summer of 1986. The secretary of the Meirionnydd branch of the National Farmers' Union (NFU) wrote in early July that the lack of clarity over compensation was of 'grave concern', and that not only was compensation a necessity, but also an investment in a major drive to rehabilitate confidence in the safety of Welsh lamb, which through cruel irony had just been at the centre of a three-year promotional campaign, at a cost of £500,000 to the union.[34] Meanwhile, according to the Farmers' Union of Wales (FUW) even an official assurance of eventual compensation would have sufficed as 'considerable relief' to many, and yet the attitude of the government, in the words of FUW president Huw Hughes, had been to 'let the farmers stew', leaving simmering tensions to increase throughout the summer.[35] A reply in early August by leading Welsh Office civil servant Martin Bevan warned that his office had no idea how much the 'price blight' of livestock held back from market would be, and that the level of compensation that would have to be paid by the Treasury was 'unknowable', especially since 'the Farmers' Unions were drumming up an ever-mounting bill for consequential losses (food, vet bills ...)'.[36] The tone of his comments is indicative of the hostility between Welsh farmers and the Welsh Office, particularly in complaints from north Wales that the secretary of state had yet to visit the afflicted area 'first hand', sending in his place Welsh Office minister Wyn Roberts.[37] Edwards's insistence that meeting some of them at the Royal Welsh Show in Builth Wells was sufficient demonstrated to many that their grievances were still being ignored.[38] The situation deteriorated to such an extent that in early September two hundred Welsh sheep farmers, angry at the lack of action regarding compensation, 'rushed' a meeting in Llanrwst, Conwy, and prevented two officials from the Welsh Office from leaving, in what was described in *The Guardian* as a 'hostage' situation.[39] In equally passionate language, leaders of the farmers' unions stated that the farmers were at 'boiling point', and at risk of flouting regulations,

[33] NLW, Dafydd Elis-Thomas Papers (DET), E2/4, Dafydd Elis-Thomas to F. H. J. Andriessen, vice president, European Communities Commission, 3 July 1986.

[34] NLW, KB 21, NFU Memorandum, 3 July 1986.

[35] *Y Cymro*, 23 July 1986, 3.

[36] TNA, WO, BD 119/32, 'Chernobyl: Compensation', 7 August 1986.

[37] *Ibid.*

[38] NLW, KB 21, 'Parliamentary Question for Answer on Friday 25th July 1986'.

[39] *The Guardian*, 5 September 1986.

since they expected the government 'to do its duty'.[40] While the language does perhaps exaggerate the severity of the event – the so-called 'block-ade' was lifted after two hours – it nevertheless shows the frustration felt by the farmers at not being taken seriously. It also interestingly displays a level of militancy and political engagement which is uncharacteristic of the farming community, who are usually portrayed as a quiet, reserved group, and associated with small-c conservatism.[41]

This long-standing reputation stood the farmers in good stead, as far from ostracising them to the fringes of political influence, this unusual burst of radicalism brought them almost immediate gains. Following the Llanrwst meeting, Edwards met representatives of the farming unions in Cardiff, leading to the swift announcement of a compensation package worth around £5 million for the agricultural sector.[42] This fluid acquiescence demonstrates that farmers in 1980s Britain were not such a marginalised sector. Unlike the miners, they did not have a long list of grievances against Thatcher's Conservative administrations (nor vice versa), while most enjoyed relative economic prosperity and were gener-ally satisfied with the status quo. These sentiments were reflected in our 2016 interview with Tom Jones, vice-president of the FUW during the Chernobyl crisis, who said he held no political or personal animosity towards the secretary of state for Wales, who he felt was generally sym-pathetic and supportive on the issue of compensation. He also empathised with the position of the British government at the time, saying that it was evidently not to blame for the radiation. However, he did reserve some ire for Welsh Office civil servants, recalling that it was the derogatory attitudes of senior officials such as Martin Bevan which had aggravated farmers, evoking a clash not so much based on political tribalism as founded in the chasm between grassroots rurality and metropolitan Cardiff-based elites.[43] Indeed, it was a clash that seemed to be defused by the offer of financial remuneration, exposing its essence as a single-issue protest. In a letter to Dafydd Elis-Thomas, for example, the county secretary of the Meirionnydd NFU commended the compensation arrangements, saying that they had worked effectively for those willing to engage with them.[44] The Parliamentary Agriculture

[40] NLW, DET E2/4, FUW Press Release, 'Llanrwst Meeting on Restriction Regulations', 2 September 1986.

[41] Chris Butler, 'The Conservative Party in Wales: Remoulding a Radical Tradition', in John Osmond, *The National Question Again* (Llandysul, 1985), 155–68; Michael Woods, 'Deconstructing Rural Protest: The Emergence of a New Social Movement', *Journal of Rural Studies*, 19 (2003), 309–25.

[42] *The Guardian*, 6 September 1986.

[43] *Ibid.*, 5 September 1986; interview with Tom Jones, 16 August 2016.

[44] NLW, DET, E2/4, David James Jones, NFU to Dafydd Elis-Thomas, 3 November 1986.

Committee's Chernobyl Report of 1988 echoed these sentiments, commenting that 'The Government got it right for nearly everybody.'[45]

Nonetheless, this accomplishment did not mark the end of the issue, and although restrictions were lifted in many areas by late summer, in parts of Meirionnydd it was clear that Chernobyl countermeasures were going to become a protracted affair as radiation levels showed 'no sign of falling'.[46] In fact, not only was the dissipation of radioactive fallout in north Wales a long-drawn-out issue, it was also an oscillating one, with fluctuating radioactivity levels leading to temporary derestriction, only for the controls to be reapplied later on in the year, making a mockery of the Ministry of Agriculture's initial short-term '21-day ban'.[47] Farmers still felt they were being kept in the dark about the radiation levels and the predicted longevity of the controls, leading to an aggrieved letter from Gwynedd County Council to Peter Walker, the new secretary of state for Wales in the summer of 1987, declaring that they were 'most put out' at having to find out about the newly imposed restrictions from the front page of the *Daily Post*, rather than from the Welsh Office, leading to more needless disruption for the farmers affected.[48] Moreover, the continuing restrictions on certain areas reopened the debate on compensatory measures, which, when compounded by apparently 'unacceptable delays' in meeting claims, led to further agitation from farmers, culminating in a mass picket outside the Welsh Office in London in late September 1987 to show their continuing dissatisfaction at the government's response.[49] By this time a Welsh Office Chernobyl Review meeting was wondering 'Do we come clean with the farmers?', since there was 'no early end in sight', admitting that for nearly eighteen months they had coped with the event on an 'ad hoc basis' which had undermined morale within Welsh agriculture.[50]

In the grand narrative and debates on class, society and the state in 1980s Britain, farming communities are not traditionally depicted as being 'on the margins'. Indeed, following the country's accession to the European Economic Community in 1973, and the introduction of grants under the Common Agricultural Policy,[51] there is a tendency to view their social position at this time as relatively privileged and prosperous. Nevertheless, following the prolonged agricultural crisis caused by

[45] House of Commons Agriculture Committee, Second Report, *Chernobyl: The Government's Reaction*, Vol. I, Section III (1988).

[46] *The Guardian*, 29 September 1987.

[47] See copies of *Welsh Office News*, June 1986–August 1987, in NLW, DET, E2/4.

[48] NLW, DET, E2/4, Ioan Bowen Rees to Peter Walker, cc Dafydd Elis-Thomas, August 1987.

[49] *The Guardian*, 29 September 1987.

[50] TNA, WO, BD 119/34, Chernobyl Review Meeting Notes, *c.* September 1987.

[51] Martin Johnes, *Wales since 1939* (Manchester, 2012), 399–400.

the Chernobyl radiation fallout, this normally conservative and moderate social group suddenly found themselves at risk of being sidelined in a political debate in which they believed they were the main aggrieved parties. This shock to the system resulted in the use of uncharacteristic rhetoric and methods by a sector not known for rocking the boat, and a significant amount of political antagonism towards a government that in ideological terms was otherwise their natural ally, adding an intriguing new layer to Hughes's concept of 'British nuclear cultures'. In fact, the discourse over Chernobyl led to some rather unusual alliances, with environmentalists and farmers finding some common ground in the wake of the disaster. Both groupings were, to quote a Welsh Anti-Nuclear Alliance (WANA) document, concerned about the 'paucity of fallout information', the lack of 'leadership' and the 'disarray' in the Welsh sheep industry.[52] Elisabeth Rowlands-Hughes, a CND Cymru activist, observed from her experiences at the Royal Welsh Show the 'noticeable … changed response of the farmers. I tested this out with the Civil Defence … leaflets, and they not only accepted them gracefully but in quite a few cases were prepared to open up and give a few strongly worded opinions on the whole sorry saga.'[53] In another example of the merging of public concerns and heightening of nuclear scepticism, Dafydd Elis-Thomas saw Chernobyl as an event that had 'imprinted on the agricultural community generally the dangers of the nuclear industry'.[54] Furthermore, former FUW vice-president Tom Jones recollected sharing platforms in public meetings with environmentalists, as the 'token farmer'. Although he felt he was often talking in the abstract, about a lifestyle that was incomprehensible to many in the audience, he also saw an unfamiliar coalescing in their interests, as both wanted to protect their interpretation of the natural environment.[55]

III 'Lies, cover-ups, … and misinformation': perceptions of the nuclear industry in Wales

Following the Chernobyl disaster, while some British farmers feared for their livelihoods, environmental activists turned their critical gaze on the country's own civil nuclear programme. The positioning of the accident in the Ukraine vis-à-vis the nuclear industry in Britain was certainly fruitful ground for accusations of cover-ups and conspiracies. A National and Local Government Officers' Association magazine accused the government and the National Radiological Protection Board of collaborating

[52] NLW, CND Cymru Archive (CND), D/31, WANA Memorandum, 29 June 1986.
[53] NLW, DET, E2/4, Elisabeth Rowlands Hughes to Dafydd Elis-Thomas, 24 July 1986.
[54] NLW, DET, E2/4, Dafydd Elis-Thomas to Alun Hughes, 1 July 1986.
[55] Interview with Tom Jones.

to mislead the public by minimising the health risks from Chernobyl in an attempt to save the British nuclear industry: an industry that had a 'great future behind it', but now had its 'back to the wall'.[56] A similar charge was made by Dafydd Elis-Thomas, who believed that Michael Jopling had delayed making a statement 'until the last minute' in the hope that radiation levels would drop, thus avoiding negative publicity for nuclear power.[57]

Fears over the effect of this undesirable exposure were particularly acute in north Wales: concern had been growing in the 1980s about the economic and social impact of closing both nuclear power stations, Trawsfynydd in Meirionnydd and Wylfa on Anglesey, opened in 1965 and 1971 respectively, following the fast-approaching fulfilment of their operational lives. This escalated in the wake of the post-Chernobyl safety fears, with the chief executive of Gwynedd County Council warning that the closures would be a 'tragedy', using language that perhaps could have been reserved for the nuclear disaster itself.[58] Indeed, the accident in the Soviet Union happened at a particularly inopportune time for Trawsfynydd: the Central Electricity Generating Board (CEGB) had been planning a highly publicised twenty-first birth-day for the plant which now had to be curtailed; these planned celebra-tions also ironically coincided with an overdue twenty-year safety check; and there was intense speculation regarding the potential expansion of the site.[59] However, for the plethora of environmental groups who had long been hostile to and suspicious of the presence of nuclear power generation in Wales, Chernobyl had unmasked the true 'tragedy' of the dangers of the nuclear industry, encompassing not only nuclear weapons but also nuclear power stations.[60]

In fact, in a rather perverse sense, Chernobyl presented a golden pol-itical opportunity for the environmentalists, which they grasped enthusi-astically. In response to the accident, CND Cymru produced a document entitled 'Chernobyl: The Silent Catastrophe', claiming that the impact of the incident in Britain had been 'surrounded, as is always the case with nuclear power, by lies, cover-ups, secrecy and misinformation'. It alleged that children and babies around Wylfa were as susceptible to the effects of radiation as those in Hiroshima, tainting north Wales's nuclear

[56] TNA, WO, BD 119/32, Copy of 'Chernobyl Fallout: How We Were Deceived and Why', *The Steward Magazine*, 5 September 1986.

[57] *Y Cymro*, 25 June 1986, 1.

[58] NLW, Beata Brookes Papers 107, copy of Pamela M. Lewis, Institute of Economic Research, UCNW Bangor, 'The Economic Impact of the Closure, without replacement, of Trawsfynydd Power Station', May 1985; *Daily Post*, 17 June 1986.

[59] *The Guardian*, 7 May 1986.

[60] Christopher R. Hill, 'Nations of Peace: Nuclear Disarmament and the Making of National Identity in Scotland and Wales', *Twentieth Century British History*, 27 (2016), 26–50.

industry not only with the Chernobyl disaster, but also with the toxic legacy of international atomic warfare.[61] Moreover, Chernobyl was deployed by WANA as a key rationale to oppose the expansions discussed at Trawsfynydd and, due to its proximity to the Welsh border, the nuclear facility at Hinkley Point in Somerset. WANA also questioned the suppression of a Meteorological Office report which purportedly showed that only 40 per cent of the Chernobyl plume over the UK 'fell out'. This was a minuscule amount in scientific terms, but still led to widespread problems with radioactive contamination.[62] Meanwhile, others noted the coincidence that high levels of radiation from Chernobyl were being registered in areas that housed nuclear power stations. This exhibited not only a genuine fear of a 'British' Chernobyl, but also demonstrated how the opponents of nuclear power employed the catastrophe to hammer home both the known and unknown dangers of such a nuclear accident.[63]

The conflation of Trawsfynydd and Chernobyl was made explicit in the 'Trawsfynydd Seminar', held in November 1986 by opponents of nuclear power in Wales. One speaker ridiculed the CEGB's assurance that Chernobyl 'could never happen here' by arguing that 'the poisonous finger of [Chernobyl's] radioactivity spread to the UK, it contaminated our crops, our livestock and our people, so in this respect Chernobyl has happened here'.[64] This rhetoric inferred Trawsfynydd's potential as a site for an international calamity that would rival such disasters as Windscale, the American SL-1, Three Mile Island, and Chernobyl, polemically linking these historical nuclear accidents with the dangers posed by Wales's own nuclear industry.[65] In response to these enhanced fears, Elis-Thomas promised to oppose the building of a new pressurised water reactor at Trawsfynydd – a move that could revitalise the site – due to safety concerns.[66] There was also a suggestion in the light of Chernobyl that the inquiry into commissioning a second reactor at the Sizewell nuclear complex in Suffolk – Sizewell B – was obsolete in light of the magnitude of effects from the Chernobyl fallout. The fermentation of public nuclear anxiety in the aftermath of Chernobyl was thus undoubtedly a useful tool for nuclear resistors.

This agitation was far from simply a case of political opportunism on the part of the environmental groups: Chernobyl exposed a severe lack of

[61] NLW, CND, F/5, 'Chernobyl: The Silent Catastrophe'.

[62] NLW, Wales Green Party Papers (WGP), 5, Report from the Welsh Anti-Nuclear Alliance Meeting, 6 December 1987.

[63] NLW, CND, D/31, *News/ Newyddion WANA/ CWNC*, Summer 1986.

[64] NLW, DET, C40, Trawsfynydd Seminar – R. Ross Mackay, 'Trawsfynydd – An Alternative Strategy', 19 November 1986.

[65] *Y Cymro*, 25 June 1986.

[66] *Western Mail*, 25 September 1987.

preparedness in dealing with potential nuclear crises in north Wales. Dr J. A. V. Pritchard, a scientific adviser at the Welsh Office, wrote to civil servants that pre-Chernobyl he had been under the impression that the CEGB had whole-body radiation counters at both Trawsfynydd and Wylfa. This had proved to be inaccurate, and since none were available at the regional hospital, Ysbyty Gwynedd, either, there were clearly insufficient monitoring preparations in place in the event of a comparable emergency at either of the north Wales nuclear power stations.[67] Similar concerns were expressed about lack of decontamination facilities in north Wales, and the Welsh Office also had to admit after Chernobyl that a major nuclear accident had not been incorporated into any of its emergency planning. This led it to look towards developing two separate plans, 'one for "Welsh" incidents and one for international incidents affecting Wales'.[68] An article in WANA's newsletter in the winter of 1986/7 reported on a public open day at Trawsfynydd power station, which left the reporter aghast at the CEGB's over-confidence and 'half-lies' that no further safety measures were required at the reactor.[69] This prompted one nuclear opponent to announce that he was going on a hunger strike 'to warn the nation of the risks involved in the nuclear programme'.[70] Such remonstrations were not confined to partisan campaigners: leading nuclear engineers also attacked the CEGB's emergency plans for handling a nuclear accident at Trawsfynydd 'post-Chernobyl' as 'inadequate', and ridiculed the board's claims of a 1.5-mile affected radius as 'incredible'.[71] These allusions to 'pre-' and 'post-'Chernobyl eras demonstrate the accident's place as a watershed moment in British nuclear politics. Moreover, before long, public fears about the immediate consequences of a potential nuclear accident became suffused with longer-term health concerns. By 1988, newspapers carried numerous items on north Wales cancer levels, some of them based on reports in the Welsh Office *Environmental Digest for Wales*, that young children in north Wales may have been exposed to much higher doses of radiation than normal in the wake of Chernobyl. The malignancy rates in the Bala & Penllyn area – which incorporated both the locale of Trawsfynydd nuclear power station and the area hit hardest by Chernobyl fallout – were reported as

[67] TNA, WO, BD 119/32, Circular from Dr J. A. V Pritchard, Scientific Adviser WO on 'Medical Physics North Wales: Post Chernobyl', August 1986.

[68] TNA, WO, BD 119/32, J. P. Williams, General Administration Gwynedd Health Authority, to M. L. Lloyd, Welsh Office, 11 July 1986; 'Note of meeting held on 6 June 1986 to review Chernobyl nuclear incident'.

[69] NLW, CND, D/31, *Newyddion/ News WANA/ CWNC*, Winter 1986/87.

[70] NLW, CND, D/31, *News/ Newyddion WANA/ CWNC*, Summer 1986.

[71] *The Guardian*, 14 October 1986.

being much higher than the Welsh average.[72] Again, however, these issues were shrouded in uncertainty: was Chernobyl to blame, or the dosage of radiation emanating from Trawsfynydd?

The Welsh Office made convenient use of the existing radioactivity levels in north Wales, ironically in an attempt to mollify fears over elevated readings from the Chernobyl 'cloud'. On 7 August 1986 a Welsh Office memorandum was sent to Nicholas Edwards, informing him that one brown trout caught in Trawsfynydd Lake had been measured with over the Ministry of Agriculture's 'trigger level' of 1,000 Bq/kg of radiation in its flesh. This sent civil servants into an initial frenzy, but one that was immediately ameliorated by the finding that radiation levels over 1,000 Bq/kg 'are nothing new in this lake and are not connected to the Chernobyl disaster', meaning that 'There is no risk to anglers or the public.'[73] In 1977, for example, brown trout in Trawsfynydd Lake had averaged 2,300 Bq/kg, and perch even higher at 3,700 Bq/kg. In fact, the Welsh Office was keen to highlight that the only reason the reading was flagged up in the summer of 1986 was the introduction of the 'generous' 1,000 Bq/kg post-Chernobyl safety margin. As one civil servant, G. R. Waters, divulged, 'Even in normal times, the level in Lake Trawsfynydd is likely to be of the order of 300 Bq because of the discharges into the lake from the nuclear power station … there is no cause for concern.'[74] The Welsh Office attempted to engage directly with the public over this matter, with R. A. Page from its environmental protection unit writing an article that he hoped would clarify the structure of radiological protection in Wales, but also 'dispel' many of the anxiety-driven conspiracies surrounding the dangers of nuclear. In this he stated that 87 per cent of UK radiation had 'natural' origins, with only 0.1 per cent from nuclear waste, and, at 0.5 per cent of the total, that televisions and watches emitted more radiation than the nuclear industry.[75]

However, although this diluted the risk factors stemming directly from Chernobyl itself, it nonetheless had the unwelcome effect of bringing the nation's own nuclear programme into sharp focus. Some people wondered why this 'trigger level', regardless of its 'conservative' nature, had not been brought to bear on Britain's own nuclear industry earlier. Indeed, for anti-nuclear campaigners, this type of evidence signified the long-standing health perils that had been oozing from the two nuclear power stations in north Wales for decades, posing the

---

[72] *Western Mail*, 20 July 1988; *Daily Post*, 11 March 1988.

[73] TNA, WO, BD 119/32, 'Contamination of Lake Trawsfynydd Fishery', 12 August 1986.

[74] TNA, WO, BD 119/32, Memorandum by G. R. Waters, 7 August 1986.

[75] R. A. Page, 'Ymbelydredd yng Nghymru', *Y Gwyddonydd*, Summer 1986, 10–14.

question of whose radiation was being scattered in north Wales during the mid-1980s. The Wales Green Party expressed its doubts in June 1986 about the long-term accuracy of historical radioactivity data, stating that 'most of what had been collected was being withheld from the public'.[76] In a letter to Peter Walker, Dafydd Elis-Thomas expressed his concern following the results of 'Whole Body Monitoring for Radioactivity in Gwynedd' which had been conducted in the autumn of 1987, asking if there was any possibility of distinguishing between discharges emanating from the Chernobyl fallout and any 'untoward discharge from Trawsfynydd during an operational fault', an issue his fellow Plaid MP Dafydd Wigley deemed worthy of an 'urgent' investigation.[77] Similarly, in October 1987, nearby Bala town council requested that the Welsh Office conduct two independent surveys, one into radiation levels in the Gwynedd population, and the other into working practices at Trawsfynydd nuclear power station.[78] Clearly Chernobyl had tapped into local concerns, even validating them, helping to move nuclear health fears from the realm of conspiracy into the mainstream. As late as 1994, in a pamphlet entitled 'Cymru: Land of Radiation', CND Cymru were linking Trawsfynydd – which allegedly hosted 'the most radioactive lake in the world' – with the Chernobyl fallout, leaving 337 farms in Wales 'still radioactive', and concluding with a missive that 'Radiation knows no boundaries.'[79] A similar narrative was at play in Cumbria, with the *Farmers' Weekly* reporting that the spectre of Sellafield nuclear power station – also adjacent to Chernobyl restriction zones – made local inhabitants equally 'suspicious of the nuclear power industry and the government's willingness to deal honestly with its problems'.[80]

Inevitably, a transnational event of Chernobyl's magnitude would see a shared experience of public health fears, anger and nuclear resistance across national borders,[81] but regional particularisms also played a role in shaping political responses. In Wales, a certain anti-nuclear Welsh pride had been established by the mid-1980s, institutionalised by the existence of a decentralised Green Party in Wales, a CND Cymru, and WANA, as well as the anti-nuclear credentials of several Welsh Labour politicians, and by a left-leaning, environmentalist surge in

[76] NLW, WGP, 4, Minutes 7 June 1986.
[77] TNA, WO, BD 119/34, Dafydd Elis-Thomas to Peter Walker, 21 December 1987; *Western Mail*, 30 September 1987.
[78] TNA, WO, BD 119/34, Bala Town Council to Welsh Office, 17 October 1987.
[79] NLW, CND, A1/92, 'Radiation in Wales'.
[80] *Farmers' Weekly*, 11 March 1988.
[81] Heise, *Sense of Place*, 177–81.

Plaid Cymru.[82] However, two flagship events reinforced this impression: firstly, the well-documented role of Welsh women in the peace protests at Greenham Common, and secondly, the campaign for Wales to become the first European country to declare itself 'nuclear-free', a goal reached in 1982.[83] This was, according to CND Cymru, achieved in a spirit of local anti-nuclear activism, which gave a 'moral lead to ... the World'.[84] Of course, one could question the validity of such a declaration whilst the country continued to accommodate two nuclear power stations – and an atomic weapons component factory outside Cardiff – within its borders.[85] Nonetheless, its significance was arguably symbolic, signifying a broader Cold War context, by linking Wales with the global 'nuclear-free zone' movement, where local authorities in Britain, and throughout the world, responded to the heightened tensions between the great powers and the accompanying nuclear fear by refusing to have nuclear weapons positioned in their jurisdictions. In this respect, the next natural step for Wales to become a 'nuclear-free zone' in the eyes of the world was to reject not only nuclear weapons, but also civil nuclear power. As a post-Chernobyl Green Party Wales local authority election leaflet declared, the accident's fallout had 'blighted' a large part of north Wales, so the onus was now on to 'phase out ... these deadly nuclear power stations before the next century'.[86]

Jonathan Hogg has delineated the 1980s as a period of 'Extreme Realism' for those catastrophising a nuclear apocalypse.[87] However, his discussion is predominantly based on debates surrounding nuclear war: a travesty that ultimately remained in the realms of the imagination. By contrast, Chernobyl was a real, measurable nuclear event, which patently showed that the elongated entrails of nuclear fallout need not originate from an atomic bomb to create devastation. This was capitalised upon by Welsh anti-nuclear campaigners, who enmeshed the Chernobyl accident with localised and historical concerns about the nuclear industry in Wales, particularly in Trawsfynydd, consciously merging the radioactivity from both locations into one transnational concern. This narrative was made more compelling by the fact that

[82] Johnes, *Wales since 1939*, 304–6; Richard Wyn Jones, *Rhoi Cymru'n Gyntaf: Syniadaeth Plaid Cymru* (Caerdydd, 2007), 202–60.

[83] Avril Rolph, 'Greenham and its Legacy: The Women's Peace Movement in Wales in the 1980s', in *The Idiom of Dissent: Protest and Propaganda in Wales*, ed. T. Robin Champan (Llandysul, 2006), 97–122.

[84] NLW, CND, A1/68 File 2, *YNNI*, CND Cymru newsletter, March/April 1982; Clwyd Declaration, 23 February 1982.

[85] For more on this see Laucht and Johnes, 'Resist and Survive', esp. 234–5.

[86] NLW, Ian and Thalia Campbell Papers, 9/2/1, Toby Hodd Election Leaflet, Cardiganshire District Council Elections, 1982–89.

[87] Hogg, *British Nuclear Culture*, 133.

the disaster had not only revealed the flaws of the government in dealing with a major international accident, but also exposed dire shortcomings in dealing with emergencies at Welsh nuclear plants. In this respect, a transnational, Welsh and localised discourse over Chernobyl was carved out by nuclear sceptics, demonstrating that nuclear cultures could paradoxically perpetuate national borders out of a seemingly 'borderless' event.

IV Conclusion

The legacy of Chernobyl in Wales lasted well-beyond the hotspots of 1986–7. Regular 'Cofio Chernobyl' (Remember Chernobyl) rallies were held in the country, and many campaigners became involved in the Chernobyl Children's Project, where Welsh communities hosted, and raised money for, the victims of the tragedy. A letter written by Jill Stallard, the general secretary of CND Cymru, in 1994, 'to the Children of Chernobyl', stated that the radioactive connection between the Ukraine and Wales would last 'forever', in what can be seen as an attempt to create a lasting transnational link between these two geographically disparate regions.[88] Long-term health concerns regarding the disaster also retained a powerful hold on some Welsh rural communities. In 2004 the *Western Mail* carried the headline 'Chernobyl "to blame" for Bala cancers', although the article still showed some prevarication over ultimate responsibility: it could either be 'Chernobyl', 'Trawsfynydd', or even social deprivation and unhealthy lifestyles.[89] This further demonstrates how the disaster in Ukraine muddied the waters between 'foreign' and 'domestic' contamination, contributing to the nation's ongoing engagement with international nuclear anxiety. Crucially, the restrictions put on sheep farming in north Wales, initially thought to be a short-term measure, were in fact not lifted entirely until 2012, a staggering twenty-six years after the disaster, ensuring that Chernobyl would live long in the memory of the Welsh agricultural sector.

Of course, the significance of this catastrophe in changing the narrative on nuclear culture should not be overstated. There was no grand shift away from the 'nuclear deterrent' policy, and the 'fall' of the British nuclear industry in the 1990s owed as much to the economic realities of the private sector as to the agitation over health and safety fears.[90] Moreover, with the ending of the Cold War in the early 1990s and the

---

[88] NLW, CND, F/6 1994/95, 'From the Children of Cynghordy to the Children of Chernobyl'.

[89] *Western Mail*, 22 June 2004.

[90] Simon Taylor, *The Fall and Rise of Nuclear Power in Britain: A History* (Cambridge, 2016).

thawing of enmities between the great powers, anxieties over nuclear power gradually receded as a salient issue for the British public. Nevertheless, Chernobyl arguably opened the eyes of the public to the potential dangers of civil nuclear power generation, while also exposing the serious shortcomings of the British government in dealing with both an international nuclear disaster and a potential home-grown catastrophe, forcing administrations throughout Europe to effectively rewrite the rulebook on large-scale nuclear emergencies. In this sense then, it seems that the green surge that accompanied the Chernobyl crises may not have been such a temporary aberration, as the 'unofficial' narrative of the 1980s, over time, came to the forefront of global politics. This change in attitudes can even be seen in the Welsh Office, which, despite initially perpetuating the chaos in the aftermath of the nuclear fallout crisis, did seem to make the concerns of the activists more mainstream, affirming that the disaster had drawn attention to 'the importance of nuclear safety', spawning a concern amongst the public 'for the natural environment in which they live'.[91]

German sociologist Ulrich Beck identified during this period the emergence of a 'risk society', where the perils of technological modernisation became far more prominent in public debate.[92] Arguably, this article demonstrates how this 'risk society', far from being exclusively an 'urban' phenomenon, could permeate the least expected of spaces, namely a small region of rural Wales. In contrast to much of the existing scholarship around nuclear discourse, it breaks down the nation-state centricity of nuclear historiography, allowing an alternative depiction to emerge of British nuclear cultures. Furthermore, it demonstrates not only the salience of exploring a more rural angle to nuclear politics, but also displays how this novel approach can broaden the understanding of the historical shibboleth that is 'rural Wales',[93] while at the same time opening a hitherto largely unexplored avenue of historical research: 'nuclear Wales'.

[91] NLW, DET, E2/4, *Welsh Office News*, 24 July 1986.
[92] English version in Ulrich Beck, *Risk Society: Towards a New Modernity* (London, 1992).
[93] Moving away from the traditional socio-economic story conveyed in works such as Richard Moore-Colyer, *Farming in Wales 1936–2011* (Talybont, 2011).

Transactions of the RHS 29 (2019), pp. 293–311 © Royal Historical Society 2019
doi:10.1017/S0080440119000136

HOW NATURAL IS NATURAL? HISTORICAL PERSPECTIVES ON WILDLIFE AND THE ENVIRONMENT IN BRITAIN

Colin Matthew Memorial Lecture

By Tom Williamson

READ 17 OCTOBER 2018

ABSTRACT. This article explores some of the ways in which historians can, and should, engage with current debates about the environment. What we often think of as 'natural' habitats in Britain – heaths, ancient woodland, meadows and the like – are largely anthropogenic in character, and much of our most familiar wildlife, from rabbits to poppies, are alien introductions. The environments we cherish are neither natural nor timeless, but are enmeshed in human histories: even the kinds of tree most commonly found in the countryside are the consequence of human choice. The ways in which the environment was shaped by past management systems – to produce fuel, as much as food – are briefly explored; and the rise of 'rewilding' as a fashionable approach to nature conservation is examined, including its practical and philosophical limitations and its potential impacts on the conservation of cultural landscapes.

There are many reasons why we study history, but perhaps the most important is that it helps us to understand our present situation, and how the things we think of as 'normal' developed out of very different pasts. Only by appreciating how present 'reality' came into existence, came to be constituted, can we decide how to act in the present: what we need to do to maintain things as they are, or to change them in the future. In the case of the environment – an area of pressing concern in both the popular and the political spheres – it has mainly been environmental historians like Paul Warde who have used the past to throw light on both the present and the future.[1] But other forms of history can also make a contribution. This article looks at the natural environment in England from the perspective of landscape history. It does not examine, in the way that Keith Thomas has so ably done, changes in social attitudes to and perceptions of 'the natural'. It focuses instead

[1] P. Warde, *Energy Consumption in England and Wales 1560–2000* (Naples, 2006).

on the extent and character of human interventions in the natural environment in Britain over the centuries, and in so doing highlights how little was really 'natural' about it.[2]

Landscape history as a subject was first developed in the 1950s by social and economic historians like Maurice Beresford and, in particular, W. G. Hoskins.[3] These pioneers sought to explain aspects of the physical environment – the layout of villages, the shapes of fields, the varying chronologies of vernacular buildings in different areas – in terms of historical processes. But they also sought to use the physical environment to contribute to wider debates in history, especially social and economic history. Such things as field patterns and settlement morphologies could be regarded as a kind of continuous above-ground archaeology. In Hoskins's words, the landscape was itself 'the richest historical record we possess'.[4] The subject developed through the later twentieth century in new ways. Firstly, real field archaeologists began to be involved, people like the great Christopher Taylor. The earthworks of abandoned sections of villages were now interpreted alongside their surviving, upstanding portions; aerial photography and other non-invasive forms of archaeological investigation were embraced wholesale.[5] Beresford and Hoskins had indeed used these approaches, but there was a new emphasis and rigour, and a new – longer – timescale, with many now suggesting that the 'making of the English landscape' had begun well before the Roman Conquest, rather than in Saxon times, as Hoskins had mainly believed. In addition, the late 1970s and 80s saw the increasing involvement of historical ecologists in the subject, most notably the late Oliver Rackham.[6] Again, an interest in ecology was not entirely new. Max Hooper's work on how hedges could supposedly be dated by counting the number of species they contain (since comprehensively refuted) had been used by Hoskins.[7] But landscape history now expanded to embrace the study of a whole range of 'semi-natural habitats' – woods, heaths, moors, meadows and the like.

Within such areas, particular forms of management, practised over long periods of time, created particular suites of species. Meadows, for example, were areas of low-lying grassland managed to produce a hay crop – vital as winter feed for livestock – and were accordingly closed

[2] K. Thomas, *Man and the Natural World: Changing Attitudes in England 1500–1800* (1983).

[3] M. Beresford, *History on the Ground: Six Studies in Maps and Landscapes* (1971); W. G. Hoskins, *The Making of the English Landscape* (1955); W. G. Hoskins, *Fieldwork in Local History* (1967).

[4] Hoskins, *Making of the English Landscape*, 14.

[5] C. Taylor, *Fieldwork in Medieval Archaeology* (1974); *Village and Farmstead: A History of Rural Settlement in England* (1983).

[6] O. Rackham, *Trees and Woodland in the British Landscape* (1976); *Ancient Woodland* (1980); *The History of the Countryside* (1986).

[7] E. Pollard, M. D. Hooper and N. Moore, *Hedges* (1974).

to sheep and cattle during the spring and early summer. As a result, plants intolerant of grazing and trampling could flourish, flower and set seed without disturbance, many of them tall, bulky species like meadowsweet, globeflower or ox-eye daisy. Over the centuries, a particular kind of management thus created a distinctive, rather beautiful, biologically diverse – but essentially unnatural environment.[8]

Heathland is another example. Heaths are largely treeless environments associated with poor, acid soils overlying porous sands and gravels. Their vegetation features a distinctive range of dwarf shrubs, principally heather or ling, gorse or furze, and broom, together with characteristic grasses such as sheep's fescue and common bent.[9] Such environments sustain particular kinds of fauna – reptiles like the adder, birds like the Dartford warbler. Like meadows, heaths are essentially artificial environments. Most if not all examples developed from woodland, often in remote antiquity but sometimes as late as the sixteenth century.[10] As trees died of old age, were barked by livestock or were cut down for timber and wood, regeneration was prevented by grazing and by further exploitation for fuel, with gorse, broom, heather now being harvested for domestic and industrial firing. Indeed, the importance of heaths as a fuel source in the pre-industrial period is often underestimated by historians. In the early seventeenth century Thomas Blenerhasset memorably described how Horsford Heath in Norfolk was 'to Norwich and the Countrye heare as Newcastle coales are to London'.[11] Conversely, most heaths which escaped enclosure and 'improvement' in the eighteenth and nineteenth centuries, or the attentions of the Forestry Commission in the twentieth, have become colonised by secondary woodland during the last century or so, as the intensity of management has declined.

Mousehold Heath, also near Norwich, is a good example of all this. In the eighteenth century this was a huge tract of open heather, an iconic landscape painted by John Sell Cotman and other members of the Norwich School of painters. But its name incorporates the Old English term *holt*, 'a wood', and as late as the thirteenth century it was largely tree-covered. Local people exercised rights to graze livestock and

[8] G. Peterken, *Meadows* (2013).

[9] N. *Webb, Heathlands* (1986); N. Webb, 'The Traditional Management of European Heathlands', *Journal of Applied Ecology*, 35 (1998), 987–90.

[10] J. A. Groves, M. P. Waller, M. J. Grant and J. E. Schofield, 'Long Term Development of a Cultural Landscape: The Origins and Dynamics of Lowland Heathland in Southern England', *Vegetation History and Archaeobotany*, 21 (2012), 453–70; G. Barnes, P. Dallas, H. Thompson, N. Whyte and T. Williamson, 'Heathland and Wood Pasture in Norfolk: Ecology and Landscape History', *British Wildlife*, 18 (2007), 395–403.

[11] T. Barrett Lennard, 'Two Hundred Years of Estate Management at Horsford during the 17th and 18th Centuries', *Norfolk Archaeology*, 20 (1921), 57–139.

gather fuel, and by the sixteenth century the whole 6,000 acres was largely treeless.[12] Those parts of the heath lying close to Norwich survived enclosure and reclamation in the nineteenth century but, as management declined, they were rapidly colonised by birch, oak and sycamore. When conservation bodies attempt to clear some of this woodland, to restore areas of heath, they often face stiff opposition from local people exercised by this attack on 'nature'.

Ancient woodland is another important 'semi-natural habitat'. By the thirteenth century 'coppice with standards' woodland was common in Britain. In such woods, most of the trees and shrubs were cut down to a point at or near ground level on a rotation, usually of between eight and fifteen years, to produce a regular crop of 'poles' useful for fencing, tools, fuel and a host of domestic uses.[13] Relatively small numbers of trees were allowed to grow as 'standards', for timber, and these were usually felled before they were sixty or seventy years of age.[14] Because the regenerating coppice would be damaged by grazing, livestock was generally excluded by banks and fences for all or most of the time (unlike most heaths, medieval woods were enclosed land, part of the manorial demesne). The exclusion of stock, coupled with the recurrent cycles of light and shade resulting from coppicing, encouraged the development of a distinctive ground flora, characterised by wood anemone and other so-called 'ancient woodland indicators'.[15] Conversely, as intensive management has declined in the course of the last century, and as browsing by wild deer has increased, this distinctive flora has, in many cases, suffered a marked decline.[16]

Ancient woods are often thought of as the most natural of our habitats, fragments of the original forests which once covered the country – islands of preservation. But they are, perhaps, better considered as factories for the production of wood and timber which have, for the most part, become derelict. Their flora and fauna have been shaped in critical ways by this history. Survey after survey from medieval and post-medieval times shows that woods were overwhelmingly dominated by standards of oak. In contrast, the primeval woods of lowland England, before the advent of farming, had been dominated by small-leafed lime (*Tilia cordata*), now rather a rare species.[17] Oak was widely planted

[12] Rackham, *History of the Countryside*, 299–303.

[13] Rackham, *Ancient Woodland*; G. Barnes and T. Williamson, *Rethinking Ancient Woodland* (Hatfield, 2015).

[14] T. Williamson, G. Barnes and T. Pillatt, *Trees in England: Management and Disease since 1600* (Hatfield, 2017), 81–2.

[15] Barnes *et al.*, *Rethinking Ancient Woodland*, 6–11, 122–30.

[16] P. Doman, R. Fuller, R. Gill, D. Hooton and R. Tabor, 'Escalating Ecological Impact of Deer in Lowland Woodland', *British Wildlife*, 21 (2010), 242–54.

[17] O. Rackham, *Woodlands* (2011), 82–90; Williamson *et al.*, *Trees in England*, 122.

or encouraged in managed woods because it provided the best structural timber. The coppiced understorey was, and is, variously constituted but likewise does not simply represent a managed version of the 'natural' vegetation. Numerous documentary references show that coppices were often weeded of unwanted shrub species or even extensively replanted with useful ones like ash, hazel or hornbeam. A lease for South Haw wood in Wood Dalling in Norfolk, drawn up in 1612, bound the lessee to plant sallows in cleared spaces following felling; the tithe files of 1836 describe how there were thirty-five acres of coppice wood in Buckenham in the same county, 'part of which has been newly planted with hazel'; while Lowe, writing about Nottinghamshire woods in 1794, described how 'vacancies are usually filled up with ash', and reported how, on one estate, the hazel and thorns were regularly stubbed up after the coppice was cut and 'and young ashes planted in their stead. By which mode ... these woods have been very considerably improved.'[18] Vancouver in 1810 noted how, in Hampshire, some of the best ash shoots were retained when the coppice was felled, and plashed 'in the vacant spaces' to form new plants; a similar practice is recorded in Surrey woods in 1809.[19] Boys in 1805 suggested that many of the coppices in Kent were regularly supplemented with new plants simply because 'wood, like everything else, decays and produces fewer poles every fall, unless they are replenished'.[20] One Herefordshire landowner described in 1852 how 'the wood after successive fallages deteriorates as numbers of the old stools die and unless there is a considerable amount laid out in filling up the vacant places with young wood, ditching, etc a quantity of useless stuff such as birch, orl [alder?] and brambles grow up and consequently reduces the value of the wood'.[21] Some important coppice species seem to have been relatively rare in woods before the high Middle Ages, most notably hornbeam.[22]

Indeed, so unnatural are woods – and all the other 'semi-natural habitats' found in Britain – that natural scientists, archaeologists and others now argue about what form, precisely, the landscape took before the adoption of farming from the fourth millennium BC. Until recently it was assumed that most of north-west Europe was originally covered with dense forest, but this idea has been challenged by Frans Vera and others, who suggest that grazing by wild cattle, deer and other herbivores

[18] Norfolk Record Office BUL 2/3, 604X7; IR 29/5816; estate survey, 1752, Boughton House archives, no catalogue number. R. Lowe, *General View of the Agriculture of the County of Nottingham* (London, 1794), 34, 114.

[19] C. Vancouver, *General View of the Agriculture of Hampshire* (London, 1810), 297; W. Stevenson, *General View of the Agriculture of the County of Surrey* (London, 1809), 127.

[20] J. Boys, *General View of the Agriculture of the County of Kent* (London, 1805), 144.

[21] Herefordshire Archives and Records, A63/111/56/12.

[22] Williamson *et al.*, *Trees in England*, 128–30.

maintained a much more open landscape of grazed woodland, perhaps resembling savannah in places.[23] The arguments marshalled in support of, and in opposition to, this view need not concern us here. Suffice it to say that much of the evidence presented by Vera has been contested, or subject to different interpretations; while there are doubts about whether herbivore numbers would indeed have been enough to prevent substantial woodland regeneration, given the presence of significant hunter-gatherer populations.[24] What is important is that the debate itself demonstrates how far we are removed from any truly 'natural' environment, unaffected by human agency.

This is true in other important ways. A surprising number of familiar plants and animals are introductions, made since late prehistory. We agonise about recent ones, invasive species like Japanese knotweed, Himalayan balsam, muntjac, Chinese water deer, grey squirrel, sika deer, or mink. Others, longer established, are not unreasonably accepted as part of our native flora and fauna.[25] An extraordinary range of familiar species are non-native: sycamore, sweet chestnut, the poppy (and most weeds of cereal crops), the snowdrop; even the lovely snake's-head fritillary may be an early garden escapee.[26] The house mouse arrived in later prehistory, the black rat in Roman times and the brown rat in the 1720s (in 1777 Gilbert White considered a black rat killed at Shalden in Hampshire something of a rarity: 'the Norway rats destroy all the indigenous ones').[27] A number of alien animals were intentional introductions, including carp, fallow deer and the rabbit, made by the feudal elite in the Middle Ages as quarry, or as a food reserved for the privileged.[28] The rabbit was initially so domesticated that it was kept in specially constructed mounds, complete with ready-made burrows.

[23] F. Vera, *Grazing Ecology and Forest History* (Wallingford, 2002).

[24] See, in particular, K. H. Hodder, P. C. Buckland, K. J. Kirby and J. M. Bullock, 'Can the Pre-Neolithic Provide Suitable Models for Rewilding the Landscape in Britain?', *British Wildlife*, 20, 5, 4–14; and the essays in I. Rotherham, *Trees, Forested Landscape and Grazing Animals* (2013).

[25] *Invasive and Introduced Plants and Animals: Human Perceptions, Attitudes and Approaches to Management*, ed. I. D. Rotherham and R. A. Lambert (2011).

[26] R. Mabey, *Flora Britannica* (1998), 138–40; P. Oswald, 'The Fritillary in Britain: A Historical Perspective', *British Wildlife*, 3 (1992), 200–10; D. A. Webb, 'What Are the Criteria for Presuming Native Status?', *Watsonia*, 15 (1985), 231–6; S. Thomas and T. Dines, 'Non-Native Invasive Plants in Britain: A Real, Not Imagined, Problem', *British Wildlife*, 21 (2010), 177–83.

[27] D. Yalden, *The History of British Mammals* (1999); D. J. Rackham, 'The Introduction of the Black Rat into Britain', *Antiquity*, 53 (1979), 112–20; W. Johnson (ed.), *Gilbert White's Journal* (1931), 46.

[28] C. Currie, 'The Early History of Carp and Its Economic Significance in England', *Agricultural History Review*, 39 (1991), 97–107; R. Liddiard, *The Medieval Deer Park: New Perspectives* (Macclesfield, 2007); J. Sheail, *Rabbits and Their History* (1971).

Rabbits had an important social significance now largely forgotten. Manorial lords holding a grant of free warren could, by law, establish warrens on common land regardless of the opposition of their tenants. Rabbits depleted the herbage rapidly, and soon spread more widely, damaging the crops growing in the neighbouring fields.[29] Not surprisingly, warrens were regarded with particular hostility by peasant communities, and were frequently targeted by rebels and rioters. During the Peasants' Revolt of 1381 the rebels in St Albans placed one of the abbot's rabbits, liberated from one of his many warrens, in the town pillory.[30] So important were warrens as symbols of status that they were, before the eighteenth century, sometimes incorporated (like fish ponds and dovecotes) into the gardens and designed landscapes laid out around the homes of the wealthy.[31] Only gradually did the rabbit spread into the wider countryside, in the course of the eighteenth and nineteenth centuries; and over the same period the importance of commercial warrens declined. The rabbit's semi-domesticated status, and symbolic significance, is largely lost to us. Our joint history was forgotten as the species became part of our 'wildlife'.

A related problem is that we often think of the countryside as 'timeless', and its various constituent elements as being older and more stable than they actually are. In reality they have a history, because they are as much a part of the human world – the world studied by social, economic and agricultural historians – as they are of the 'natural'. That history is, in some cases, a relatively short one. Introductions aside, indigenous species have changed their habits and habitats, and their numbers, quite dramatically over recent centuries. The Act for the Preservation of Grain of 1597 allowed churchwardens to pay individuals for killing a range of specified birds and animals considered to be a threat to agriculture: the records of payments rendered are an important source, used to great effect by Roger Lovegrove in his book *Silent Fields: The Long Decline of a Nation's Wildlife*.[32] The wood pigeon, somewhat surprisingly given its modern status as a major agricultural pest, was not on the list of species which churchwardens could pay people for killing. This is because it was still rare, and still largely confined to woods. Its numbers rose steadily from the later seventeenth century, for it feasted on the leaves of turnips and other 'roots', and to some extent on clover, now growing in the winter fields. Gilbert White, writing about the Selbourne area in 1780, attributed its recent

[29] T. Williamson, *Rabbits, Warrens and Archaeology* (Stroud, 2007).
[30] C. Omans, *The Great Revolt of 1381* (Oxford, 1906), 462–3.
[31] C. Currie, 'Fish Ponds As Garden Features', *Garden History* 18 (1990), 22–33; Williamson, *Rabbits, Warrens and Archaeology*, 164–75.
[32] R. Lovegrove, *Silent Fields: The Long Decline of a Nation's Wildlife* (Oxford, 2002).

success to 'the vast increase in turnips', something which also explains, in part, the expansion of the rabbit in the wild.[33]

We have thus developed a bad habit of thinking of habitats, and their associated species, as being more timeless and more 'natural' – more divorced from human agency and human history – than they really are. But there is nothing new in this. The tendency to conflate 'nature', and the rural, developed in England and elsewhere in western Europe from the late seventeenth century, amongst a social elite whose lifestyle was increasingly focused on urban life, and divorced from the realities of agricultural production and the practicalities of land management. 'God made the country, man made the town' – William Cowper's famous adage – would make little sense to the farmer at work in the fields, still less to the agricultural labourer.[34] In reality, both countryside and town were equally shaped by human agency. Indeed, the popular assumption that nature is found in the countryside, and not in towns and cities, is itself wrong or at least over-simple. Urban environments have their own distinct ecologies, critically shaped, as Owen Gilbert has demonstrated, by the individual histories of particular towns and cities.[35] Our less intensively built-up developments, at least, may score well in terms of the opportunities afforded to wildlife. A study begun in the 1970s, by Jennifer Owen, of a small suburban garden in Leicester recorded – over a thirty-year period – no less than 2,673 species of flora and fauna, including 54 per cent of Britain's lady-bird species, 23 per cent of its bees and 48 per cent of its harvestmen. And this was not a garden specially designed for wildlife.[36] There are good reasons for resisting the ongoing conversion of farmland to housing – issues of food security among them – but the maintenance of biodiversity may not always be the most important.

Since the start of the twentieth century, most conservationists have agreed that the best way of sustaining nature in Britain is to maintain as much as possible of the 'traditional' framework of the countryside, and to perpetuate the old, traditional methods of management of the kinds of key 'semi-natural environments' just discussed. But woods, heaths, meadows – even hedges – have been in retreat for over two centuries. Enclosure; the new forms of husbandry of the agricultural revolution; industrialisation and 'high farming'; the mechanisation of farming; have

[33] G. White, *The Natural History and Antiquities of Selbourne in the County of Southampton* (London, 1813), 113.

[34] W. Cowper, *The Task* (London, 1785), bk I, 37.

[35] O. Gilbert, *The Flowering of the Cities: The Natural Flora of 'Urban Commons'* (Peterborough, 1982); O. Gilbert, 'The Ecology of an Urban River', *British Wildlife*, 3 (1992), 129–36; O. Gilbert, *The Ecology of Urban Habitats* (1989).

[36] J. Owen, *Wildlife of a Garden: A Thirty Year Study* (Peterborough, 2010).

all rendered most of them rare, redundant or both. Those examples that have survived are always in danger of losing their distinctive characteristics through neglect. Woods, no longer coppiced, grow shady and species-poor; heaths and other areas of common land and rough grazing, no longer used for producing livestock, revert to secondary woodland. With practical and economic considerations no longer guaranteeing their survival, such environments can only be maintained through targeted subsidies to farmers and landowners, or by their acquisition and appropriate management as 'nature reserves' by wildlife trusts and other conservation bodies.

Recently, however, such approaches have been challenged by the rise of 'rewilding', that is, the idea of creating tracts of land in which human influence is minimised or removed altogether. This approach first emerged in the United States but has become highly influential, in a variety of forms, in Europe and the UK over recent decades.[37] It has begun to be put into practice at Oostvaardersplassen in the Netherlands, and at Ennerdale in Cumbria and on the Knepp Castle estate in Sussex. It has reached a wide audience through a number of books, most notably George Monbiot's *Feral*.[38] Rewilding represents a very different approach to nature conservation. Rather than maintaining 'traditional' practices, human intervention is removed, key predators like the lynx or even the wolf are reintroduced, and nature is allowed to reassert itself, in the form of the grazed savannahs and wood-pastures envisaged by Frans Vera. The long, shared history of humankind and other species is thus effectively denied and the two, in a spatial sense, are separated. And in one important way, as should by now be clear, such a stance has a certain persuasive logic, for most if not all 'traditional environments' are essentially arbitrary artefacts. If pre-industrial communities had exploited them in radically different ways, they would have had a different appearance and species composition.

There are, it should be noted, other ideas currently circulating about how to ensure a future for wildlife in Britain, including 'land sharing' – the concept of effectively 'zoning' the landscape to ensure that conservation is prioritised in some areas and abandoned altogether in others, to allow the intensive production of food.[39] But in most versions, this

---

[37] D. Foreman, *Rewilding North America: A Vision for Conservation in the 21st Century* (Washington, DC, 2004); P. Jepson, 'A Rewilding Agenda for Europe: Creating a Network of Experimental Reserves', *Ecography*, 36 (2015), 1–8; M. Soulé and R. Noss, 'Rewilding and Biodiversity: Complementary Goals for Continental Conservation', *Wild Earth*, 8 (1998), 19–28; J. D. Linnell, P. Kaczensky, U. Wotschikowsky, N. Lescureux and L. Boitani, 'Framing the Relationship between People and Nature in the Context of European Conservation', *Conservation Biology*, 29 (2015), 978–85.

[38] G. Monbiot, *Feral: Searching for Enchantment on the Frontiers of Rewilding* (2015).

[39] H. von Wehrden, D. J. Abson, M. Beckmann, A. Cord and S. Klotz, 'Realigning the Land-Sharing/Land-Sparing Debate to Match Conservation Needs: Considering Diversity

approach effectively shades into the concept of 'rewilding', and the latter remains, in philosophical terms, the principal alternative to 'traditional' modes of conservation. Such debates about the place of nature in the modern world reflect the perceived crisis in conservation in the UK, with many key species currently undergoing catastrophic declines, as a consequence of large-scale urbanisation, intensive farming, globalisation and, perhaps, ongoing climate change.[40] Historians can usefully contribute to such discussions in a number of ways, beyond merely repeating the rather obvious observation that what we often think of as the natural world is arbitrary and contingent, and that humans and other organisms have shared a long history.

For example, teasing out the real character of environmental change over the last few centuries can allow us to see the current state of the environment in perspective, and in context, and thus help us to make more informed policy decisions. It is thus widely assumed that woodland cover in England has massively declined over the last century: that thousands of hectares of woodland have given way to urban development, quarries or intensive agriculture. But in reality, government surveys leave no doubt that the area of woodland has, in fact, roughly *doubled* in England since 1895, from around 5 to around 10 per cent of the land area.[41] Some of this new woodland comprises conifer plantations, mainly established by the Forestry Commission in the period since 1922. But rather more represents secondary woodland which has regenerated naturally over abandoned heaths and other common land, or over derelict industrial land, in the course of the twentieth century.[42] We can legitimately debate the ecological value of these various forms of woodland – which, in some cases at least, is unquestionably high – but it is useful to establish some basic, essentially historical, facts before we start. Dead wood is perhaps a more straightforward example. This is a really important resource, especially for forms of fungi and invertebrates. Ecologists understandably worry when land managers clear away fallen trees and branches. But there was unquestionably much less of this material in the past, when it was gathered on a massive scale as fuel by the local poor, who were regularly prosecuted for stealing it even from hedges.

Scales and Landuse History', *Landscape Ecology*, 29, 941–8; E. A. Law and K. A. Wilson, 'Providing Context for the Land-Sharing and Land-Sparing Debate', *Conservation Letters*, 8 (2015), 404–13.

[40] For a recent audit, see the 'State of Nature 2016' report: www.rspb.org.uk/our-work/stateofnature2016/.

[41] Board of Agriculture Returns, 1896, 36; Forestry Commission, *Forestry Statistics 2016* (Edinburgh, 2016).

[42] Williamson *et al.*, *Trees in England*, 172–82.

An historical perspective is particularly useful when we consider the mounting concern about threats to tree health in Britain. Dutch elm disease first arrived in the UK in the 1920s, but a more virulent strain appeared in the late 1960s, and within a decade had effectively wiped out elm as a tree.[43] A series of epidemics has followed, including *Phytophthora ramorum*, leaf minor and canker in horse chestnut and, more recently, ash chalara (*Hymenoscyphus fraxineus*). All are caused by invasive organisms – fungi, bacteria or insects – and have thus been seen as a consequence of globalisation, of the long-distance transport of timber and live plant materials, perhaps compounded by climate change. In addition, there are worries that tree health in Britain is suffering a more general deterioration, with recognition of such complex and diffuse conditions as 'oak decline', manifested in progressive thinning of the crown and general ill-health, leading to gradual death. Many of our hedgerow trees simply look ill.[44]

Systematic examination of the surviving documentary evidence leaves little doubt that, in this case, history provides no immediate solace. It is certainly true that before the start of the twentieth century trees often fell ill – sometimes in large numbers – and that we may have unrealistic expectations about tree health. The terms used to categorise trees in a survey of Staverton in Northamptonshire in 1835, for example, included 'decayed', 'damaged', 'small and very bad', 'very bad', 'decayed very bad' and 'dead', while at Mundford, Norfolk, in 1805 the surveyor was 'disappointed in the quantity of trees in the Square Plantation, finding such a quantity of dead ones'.[45] Felling and sales records often refer to dead trees. The categories of trees sold from the Evan-Lomb estate in Norfolk in 1835, for example, comprised 'Spruce, Hornbeam, dead ash, and elms'.[46] All this said, large-scale epidemics, embracing the whole country, do not seem to have occurred before the twentieth century, nor is there any clear earlier evidence for the long-distance movement of pathogens.

[43] C. M. Brasier, 'Ophiostoma novo-ulmi sp. nov., Causative Agent of Current Dutch Elm Disease Pandemics', *Mycopathologia*, 115 (1991), 151–61.
[44] C. M. Brasier, 'The Biosecurity Threat to the UK and Global Environment from International Trade in Plants', *Plant Pathology*, 57 (2008), 792–808; R. Cheffings and C. M. Lawrence, *Chalara. A Summary of the Impacts of Ash Dieback on UK Biodiversity, Including the Potential for Long Term Monitoring and Future Research on Management Scenarios*, JNCC (Joint Nature Conservation Committee) Report No. 501 (Peterborough, 2014); S. Denman and J. F. Webber, 'Oak Declines – New Definitions and New Episodes in Britain', *Quarterly Journal of Forestry*, 103 (2009), 285–90.
[45] Northamptonshire Record Office, ZB 887; Norfolk Record Office, MS 13751, 40E3.
[46] Norfolk Record Office, HNR 465/3/1.

The first arrival was oak mildew, caused by the fungus *Erysiphe alphitoides*, probably of Asian origin, in 1908.[47] Dutch elm disease, caused by the fungus *Ophiostoma ulmi*, disseminated by the elm bark beetle *Scolytus*, came next, in the 1920s. It may have infected tree populations in Britain in earlier periods, although many supposed examples of previous outbreaks were probably caused by infestations of the beetle alone. It is noteworthy that European diseases were, at around the same time, spreading to other parts of the world. Beech bark disease, common in Europe, arrived in Nova Scotia in 1890; a European *phytopthera* appeared in Maine in 1930.[48] This chronology suggests that the long-distance movement of wood and timber was not in itself the reason for the wide dispersion of pathogens (it had, indeed, been continuing for centuries), but rather the increasing *speed* of movement. By 1870 a number of inventions, including the screw propeller, the compound engine and the triple-expansion engine, made the shipping of bulk cargoes (as opposed to passengers) by steam, rather than wind, economically feasible, and goods thus travelled much faster.[49]

In addition, it is useful to consider ways in which the changing character of British tree populations, over time, may have increased their vulnerability to disease. Maps, correspondence and timber surveys from the period after *c.*1600 reveal clearly that the lowland landscape has, at least since the sixteenth century, been overwhelmingly dominated by just three species: oak, ash and elm. But just as the kinds of tree and coppice found in woods were the consequence of selection and management, rather than being 'natural', the same was true of trees found in hedges and growing in pasture fields. Most were deliberately planted, others were self-seeding or suckering but, rather than being laid or coppiced with the other shrubs in the hedge, were preserved so that they could grow into trees. Blagrave urged the raising 'upon each Lordship or Pasture, Fuell and Firewood sufficient to maintain many Families, besides the Timber which may be raised in the Hedge-rows, if here and there in every Pearch be but planted an Ash, Oak, Elm ...'[50] Mortimer in 1707 thought that 'The best way of raising Trees in Hedges, is to plant them with the Quick' but he also gave advice on

---

[47] A. Mougou, C. Dutech and M. L. Desprez-Loustau, 'New Insights into the Identity and Origins of the Causal Agent of Oak Powdery Mildew in Europe', *Forest Pathology*, 38 (2014), 275–87.

[48] J. Ehrlich, 'The Occurrence in the United States of *Cryptococcus fagi (Baer) Dougl*, the Insect Factor in a Menacing Disease of Beech', *Quarterly Journal of Forestry*, 13 (1932), 73–80; K. P. Chester, 'The Phtopthora Disease of the Culla in America', *Quarterly Journal of Forestry*, 11 (1930), 169–71.

[49] J. Carlton, *Marine Propellors and Propulsion* (2012).

[50] J. Blagrave, *The Epitome of the Art of Husbandry* (London, 1675), 114.

how to establish them 'wheare Hedges are planted already, and Trees are wanting'.[51]

Oak, ash and elm were favoured by land managers because they were catholic in their habits, grew reasonably quickly and, above all, because their wood and timber supplied most of the requirements of a pre-industrial economy. This said, in most regions they were accompanied by a small minority of other species, growing in hedges and pastures, which usually accounted for between 5 and 20 per cent of the total population. In different regions, trees like hornbeam, maple, black poplar or aspen were found alongside the three key species. But only in restricted districts did such alternatives rival or outnumber oak, ash and elm: examples include parts of the 'champion', open-field landscapes of the Midlands, where large numbers of willows on the meadows contrasted with sparser quantities of oak, ash and especially elm scattered through the open fields; the Vale of Aylesbury, noted for its black poplars; and parts of the west Midlands and the Chilterns, where fruit trees often featured prominently in hedges.[52]

Another striking feature of the landscape was that, until the nineteenth century, there were generally very high densities of trees, in enclosed districts at least: commonly upwards of twenty-five per hectare. Moreover, a very high proportion of these (usually over 80 per cent in southern Britain) were managed as pollards, or aerial coppices, mainly to provide fuel (as also were the hedges in which they grew). Economic necessity ensured that hedgerow trees were tolerated in large numbers even though this reduced the yield of crops in adjacent fields: 'Corn never ripens so kindly, being under the Shade and Droppings of Trees; the Roots likewise of the Trees spreading to some distance from the Hedges, do rob the Earth of what should nourish the Grain.'[53] Individual pollarded trees were, in many cases, replaced after two centuries or so of cropping because their vitality declined and, as in woods, timber trees were generally felled before they were sixty years old. For centuries the countryside was thus characterised by very dense populations of young and regenerating trees, mainly of just three species.

From the end of the eighteenth century, improvements in transport infrastructure led to the spread of coal use, and pollarding rapidly declined. Pollards were removed wholesale so that hedges lost a high proportion of their trees. Timber trees remained, but their average age increased as the development of industrial saw mills (and the improvement of transport links to them) made it possible to process larger trunks. By the end of the nineteenth century, in many contexts, farmland

[51] J. Mortimer, *The Whole Art of Husbandry* (London, 1707), 309.
[52] Williamson *et al.*, *Trees in England*, 119–22.
[53] T. Nourse, *Campania Felix* (London, 1699), 27.

trees were becoming less intensively managed, as landowners concentrated their forestry activities in woods and plantations and as a new attitude to trees in the wider countryside developed, with a more general upsurge of conservationist enthusiasm. By the end of the nineteenth century the felling of prominent timber was being seen by many as a desecration of nature's beauties, rather than as good husbandry. Raymond Unwin famously boasted that only a single tree had been felled during the construction of Letchworth Garden City in north Hertfordshire in the first decades of the twentieth century.

All this means that, by the second half of the twentieth century, the countryside contained far more ageing trees than in previous periods, and it is possible that some tree 'illnesses' may not really be diseases at all. 'Oak decline', in particular, only affects middle-aged or old trees. Few of these existed in the period before the mid-twentieth century. Moreover, when farmland trees were intensively managed they were usually taken down quickly if they fell ill, and sold for timber before they lost value. In 1676 Moses Cook described what we would today call 'oak decline', and advised on how the woodsman should deal with it:

> When a Tree is at its full Growth, there are several signs of its decay, which give you warning to fell it before it can be quite decay'd; as in an Oak, when the top boughs begin to die ... but before it decays much, down with it, and hinder not your self.[54]

Today diseased trees are more likely to be left standing, either through neglect or to provide dead wood for wildlife, probably aiding the spread of infections. The intensively managed tree populations of the past were thus probably healthier than those of today, largely left to their own devices. None of this, of course, can have any relevance to diseases like ash chalara, which mainly affect younger trees. But here, too, an historical perspective is informative. The species composition of our rural tree populations has little to do with nature – it was shaped by human choices, made for practical and economic reasons. We can now make different choices, for different reasons, and one obvious one would be to diversify our planting to reduce vulnerability; to increase the proportion of the 'minority' trees, like hornbeam or wild service or small-leafed lime, to ensure a greater degree of resilience in the face of future epidemics.

In innumerable other ways an historical perspective can help us to understand key aspects of the rural environment, and how these were shaped by past practice, allowing us to make meaningful decisions about future management. Knowledge of this kind allows us to understand, in particular, the complexity and diversity of past management systems, the intricate and varied ways in which 'semi-natural habitats'

---

[54] M. Cook, *On the Manner of Raising, Ordering and Improving Forest-Trees* (London, 1676), 171.

were exploited. I noted earlier how heaths were maintained by grazing and fuel cutting, but there was much variation in the balance between these two uses, and there were several other ways in which such environments were exploited. The precise combination of uses varied from place to place, and from period to period, because heaths were integrated into local economies and farming systems, so that not all 'heaths' were the same.[55] The ecologist Paul Dolman and colleagues recently carried out a 'biodiversity audit' of the area called Breckland in East Anglia, still known for its heathland. They noted that a number of important species of plant and invertebrate, largely restricted to this region, had declined significantly over recent decades. Most of the surviving heaths in the area are maintained by continuous, light grazing by sheep, a prescription intended to ensure a reasonably high growth of heather. But many of the characteristic Breckland species in fact depend on the juxtaposition of areas of stable heather, and areas of regular *disturbance*.[56] From an historical perspective this is unsurprising – until the nineteenth century the region was characterised by extensive rabbit farms, characterised by much disturbed ground, and large areas of heath were sporadically cultivated as outfield 'brecks'.[57] It was thus a region in which, for centuries, stable heathland indeed existed beside areas of disturbance. 'Traditional' management needs to be historically informed: we need to know precisely how distinctive habitats were managed and thus shaped in the past if we are to manage them effectively into the future. Yet at the same time, understanding past management systems and what, precisely, they achieved in terms of biodiversity may have another purpose. It may allow us to design, in some circumstances, entirely new forms of management that mimic – perhaps in new combinations – their principal features. Historical research can also highlight some more general, shared characteristics of past management systems, including variation in character over short distances, repeated disturbance, and constant nutrient and biomass depletion.[58]

[55] R. J. Fuller, T. Williamson, G. Barnes and P. Dolman, 'Human Activities and Biodiversity Opportunities in Pre-Industrial Cultural Landscapes: Relevance to Conservation', *Journal of Applied Ecology*, 54 (2017), 459–69.

[56] P. M. Dolman, C. Panter and H. L. Mossman, *Securing Biodiversity in Breckland: Guidance for Conservation and Research. First Report of the Breckland Biodiversity Audit* (Norwich, 2010); P. M. Dolman, C. Panter and H. L. Mossman, 'The Biodiversity Audit Approach Challenges Regional Priorities and Identifies a Mismatch in Conservation', *Journal of Applied Ecology*, 49 (2012), 986–97.

[57] J. Belcher, '"The Greatest Wealth of Our Country": The Fold Course in East Anglia' (Ph.D. thesis, University of East Anglia, 2016); M. Bailey, *A Marginal Economy? East Anglian Breckland in the Later Middle Ages* (Cambridge, 1989).

[58] Fuller *et al.*, 'Human Activities and Biodiversity Opportunities', 468–9.

Traditional management, characterised by repeated and intensive interventions by humans, represents a clear antithesis to 'rewilding'. But it is important to emphasise that little research has been carried out to demonstrate the superiority of either approach in terms of wildlife conservation. Indeed, much of the enthusiasm for 'rewilding' has been based more on *emotion* – the 'call of the wild' – than on any careful assessment of what it actually achieves. In fact, it is arguable that the conversion of the 'natural' landscape – whatever its precise character – to farmland *increased* rather than lessened biodiversity, and that agricultural landscapes, at least those managed on 'traditional' lines, provide a greater diversity of habitats and niches, at a range of spatial scales, than would be afforded by the secondary grazed woodland of rewilded reserves.[59] They certainly sustain the particular species which we now think of as part of our common 'natural' inheritance, and which have become culturally important to us. Many of these, like the flowers characteristic of meadows, were probably rare in the pre-agricultural landscape. The highest levels of species diversity are to be found in fine-grained habitat mosaics, with an abundance of edges and juxtapositions, each endlessly disturbed and never reaching equilibrium: the kinds of habitats generated by traditional management systems. This is a particularly important consideration, perhaps, across the more populous areas of Europe, where land is in short supply and the competing demands made on it increasing. In such circumstances, 'rewilded' reserves, complete with reintroduced alpha-predators, would tend of necessity to be placed in more marginal areas, agriculturally and spatially. While 'rewilding' should, and will, have an important place in future conservation policies, most people will always experience nature in more domestic settings – in the countryside or on the urban fringe – and this is where a significant proportion of our conservation energy should continue to be concentrated. The more we accept the 'rewilding' approach, the more we may be encouraging a situation – developing across much of the globe anyway for economic and technological reasons – in which the landscape comprises three sharply contrasting types of habitat: densely settled urban areas; intensively farmed countryside; and 'wilderness', often by definition remote from human habitation (the policy of 'land sharing' is problematic for similar reasons).

Perhaps more importantly from the historian's point of view, we need to emphasise that 'rewilded' landscapes can never closely resemble the natural landscape, in the sense of the grazed woodlands which existed in remote prehistory, before the advent of farming. To use George Peterken's terms, 'future nature' would of necessity be radically different

[59] *Ibid.*

from 'past nature'.[60] 'Rewilded' reserves would contain a range of animals which were not naturally present in this country, including (as we have seen) both species of rat, the rabbit, the grey squirrel, fallow deer, muntjac, sika deer and Chinese water deer. They would boast a flora featuring an even greater range of naturalised species, such as syca-more and rhododendron – especially the latter, given that many areas targeted for large-scale 'rewilding' are in upland districts, where this plant has become seriously invasive.[61] Indeed, in an important sense 'rewilded' reserves would still be *cultural* landscapes, for the motley array of plants and creatures living within them would represent a dim memory of specifically human actions and desires, ranging from medi-eval hunting fashions to Victorian gardening fads. They would still have a history. But this in turn raises the more profound question of how far even the landscapes of the Mesolithic period – post-glacial, but pre-farming – were really 'natural', in the sense of being unshaped by human activities, given the sheer scale of the impact made by hunter-gatherers on the environment, together with the accumulating evidence for such an impact in Britain itself.[62] Since the ice retreated, this country may always have had an ecology which was extensively, fun-damentally, shaped by man.

One of the most worrying aspects of 'rewilding' is what it implies about the past. The creation of extensive 'rewilded' reserves must inevitably involve the wholesale disappearance of many elements of the historic landscape: hedges, traditionally managed woodland, field patterns, land-scape parks. What, one wonders, would W. G. Hoskins have made of it all? Rural landscapes embody values other than those relating to the natural world. They have important cultural and historical associations. They can, in the hands of great landscape designers like Lancelot 'Capability' Brown, in themselves be a form of art. While few advocates

[60] G. F. Peterken, *Natural Woodland: Ecology and Conservation in Northern Temperate Regions* (Cambridge, 1996), 13.

[61] I. D. Rotherham, 'Rhododendron Gone Wild: Conservation Implications of *Rhododendron ponticum* in Britain', *Biologist*, 48 (2001), 7–11.

[62] A. G. Brown, 'Clearances and Clearings: Deforestation in Mesolithic/Neolithic Britain', *Oxford Journal of Archaeology*, 16 (1997), 133–46; C. Caseldine and J. Hatton, 'The Development of High Moorland on Dartmoor: Fire and the Influence of Mesolithic Activity on Vegetation Change', in *Climate Change and Human Impact on the Landscape*, ed. F. M. Chambers (1993), 119–31; J. B. Innes and I. G. Simmons, 'Mid-Holocene Charcoal Stratigraphy, Fire History and Palaeoecology at North Gill, North York Moors, UK', *Palaeogeography, Palaeoclimatology, Palaeoecology*, 164 (2000), 151–65; H. T. Lewis, 'Fire Technology and Resource Management in Aboriginal North America and Australia', in *Resource Managers: North American and Australian Hunter-Gatherers*, ed. N. M. Williams and E. S. Hunn (Boulder, 1982), 45–67; S. K. Lyons, F. A. Smith and J. H. Brown, 'Of Mice, Mastodons and Men: Human-Mediated Extinctions on Four Continents', *Evolutionary Ecology Research*, 6 (2004), 339–58.

of rewilding would perhaps wish to allow grazed woodland to return to the bleak Howarth Moors, inspiration for Emily Brontë's *Wuthering Heights*, or to Dedham Vale, the subject of so many of John Constable's paintings, in many other contexts the erasure of all signs of the human past appears to be actively welcomed, precisely *because* it serves to foster the 'experience' of wilderness. All this marks a significant and worrying shift in the relationship between ecology and history, for in the twentieth century a succession of conservationists and historical ecologists, most notably Oliver Rackham, saw the landscape as something which embodies both natural *and* human history, the two connected in complex ways.

Perhaps the most interesting question of all is why this is happening now. Why, at this particular point in history, should so many people wish to adopt approaches to conservation based on a sharp separation of man and nature? 'Rewilding' represents, to some extent, a rational response to the fact that in western Europe most habitats are arbitrary and anthropogenic and can only be maintained by continuing management practices which have been rendered redundant by economic and technological change. Connected with this is a realisation that some of these habitats, while long-established and to an extent culturally valued, are not in fact very biodiverse, and that some of the land they occupy might be better used. There are more than 45,000 square kilometres of upland moor in Britain, for example, much of it species-poor. Allowing a proportion to regenerate to grazed woodland would increase biodiversity and also bring additional benefits, in terms of reducing run-off after rains and thus reducing the risk of flooding in the surrounding areas of lower ground. But the popularity of 'rewilding' probably owes less to scientific argument, and more to shifts in popular attitudes towards the environment. The overwhelming majority of the population in Britain, as elsewhere in western Europe, is now urban. Many people have little experience of or affinity with the countryside, and few now work on the land. Some have little connection with any specific place, in our socially mobile and culturally complex world: in Goodhart's terms, they are 'anywhere' rather than 'somewhere' people.[63] Much of rural Britain is today mainly occupied by middle-class incomers, and large tracts of the countryside have effectively been suburbanised, in social terms at least. All this has perhaps encouraged a belief that nature can only really be experienced in raw and dramatic form, as spectacle, and in places remote from humans, rather than in 'the countryside', even on nature reserves. Such an experience can already be supplied by the Knepp estate, with its organised 'safari' tours of the

---

[63] D. Goodhart, *The Road to Somewhere: The Populist Revolt and the Future of Politics* (2017).

'wilderness' which is gradually regenerating over abandoned farmland a short drive from central London. But whatever the precise explanations for the rise of 'rewilding', at this time of environmental crisis historians need to make their own distinctive contribution to debates about the future of nature, in Britain and beyond.

Transactions of the RHS 29 (2019), pp. 27–63 © Royal Historical Society 2019
doi:10.1017/S0080440119000021

COLOURING OUTSIDE THE LINES: METHODS FOR A GLOBAL HISTORY OF EASTERN EURASIA 600–1350*

By Naomi Standen

READ 21 SEPTEMBER 2018

ABSTRACT. We are still working out how to do global history, especially for pre-modern periods. How do we achieve the necessary shift in scale without falling back on standard definitions of categories like states, ethnicity, religion, urbanisation, when these are increasingly challenged at the specialist level? This article sets out an approach that could help pre-modern historians 'going global' to challenge claims that 'there is no alternative' to modern frameworks such as neoliberal economics, and especially the nation-state. Useful alternative techniques include thinking in layers rather than blocks, not seeking narrative arcs, and not using words like 'China'. These methods are illustrated with analysis of three Liao dynasty (907–1125) cities and three comparators from neighbouring states to the north, south and east of the Liao. The intention is to disrupt the re-emergence in the new venue of global history of essentially national narratives, using the opportunities presented by pre-modern worlds before nation-states to free us from teleological concepts. This article argues that there is indeed an alternative to the putative precursors of modern nation-states, and offers a framework for doing without them.

*Thanks to the two audiences who heard earlier versions of this paper and asked helpful questions, at the Royal Historical Society and at a workshop on 'Cities in the Eurasian Steppe 10–14th Century', Bonn University, December 2018, organised by Jan Bemmann and Susanne Reichert; to Bob Moore and Chris Wickham; to Conrad Leyser for pinpoint suggestions at a crucial stage; and to my colleagues on the KLASH (Kitan Liao Archaeological Survey and History) project, who patiently tolerate the strange things a historian does with archaeological evidence: Gwen Bennett and Josh Wright, and our Ph.D. students Lance Pursey and Callan Ross-Shepard.

Research takes time, and I am grateful to all those who have given me some. The work and thinking for this paper benefited from an AHRC fellowship (2010–11) and a research network (2012–14). Field observations and discussions with archaeologists about city forms, functions and landscapes were enabled by an Insight Grant from the Social Science and Humanities Research Council of Canada (2013–16, PI Gwen Bennett). The writing was done during parts of a visiting research fellowship at Jesus College, Oxford (2017–18) and a fellowship at the International Institute for Asian Studies, Leiden (2018–19). I offer deep thanks to both institutions for providing ideal circumstances in which to work effectively and recover the pleasures of academic research and community. Finally, the invitation from the RHS provided a valuable stimulus to pull together this aspect of my wider project.

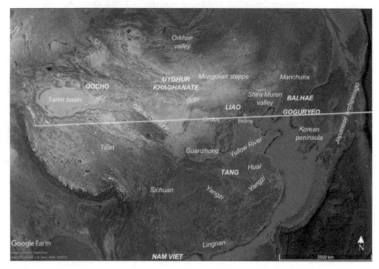

Figure 1 Map of eastern Eurasia showing selected regimes and regions named in the text; the former did not all coexist and the latter are convenient geographical descriptions derived from different historical periods. Image: Standen, based on Google Earth.

I am currently writing a global history of eastern Eurasia between 600 and 1350, without using the word 'China' (Figure 1).[1] This paper explains why and how, illustrated with a worked example. The thinking here feeds my broader search for methodologies for identifying distinctive characteristics and elements of the global medieval or pre-modern,[2] to help to challenge claims that 'there is no alternative' to teleological modernities such as neoliberal economics, and especially the nation-state. My habitual starting place is a critique of historians' standard categories, enmeshed as they are in modernity; there are more productive ways of approaching pre-modern histories. Historical writing is always a product of its own time, and as I write, in 2019, there is also an increasing urgency to offer new understandings of the past that speak against the worst instincts of human beings and the ideologies that support those

---

[1] 'A Global History of Eastern Eurasia, 600–1350', in *A History of the World*, ed. Jürgen Osterhammel and Akira Iriye, vol. 2: *Multiple Medieval Worlds 600–1350* (Munich and Cambridge, MA), in preparation. Since this is an essay on methodology, 'China' will unavoidably come up occasionally, always in scare quotes.

[2] A better term – and its accompanying concept – would be preferable, but pending their emergence, either of these suffices.

impulses in the present day.[3] Once freed from standard concepts, pre-modern global histories – worlds before nation-states – are well placed to generate such understandings. Here I argue that there is indeed an alternative to the putative precursors of modern nation-states, and offer a framework for doing without them.

I The problem of modern categories in pre-modern contexts

Global history may be usefully distinguished from World History:[4] standard categories of World History analysis are inadequate for studying pre-modern global histories. Top-down analyses of economics, power, monotheistic religion, identity and above all the nation-state carry assumptions that valorise the pursuit of profit, competition, secularism, ethnicity – and by extension modernity and the West. These categories and assumptions pay little respect to social relations, gender, localities, anything on a human scale, or to the majority of the world. Much World History continues to be variations on the 'rise of the West', focused on the implicit inevitability of the rise of modern nation-states from anticipatory versions, traced over the last 500 years.[5] Challenges have focused on matters such as amending the eurocentricity, periodisation or regional focus of the analysis, and developing more sophisticated comparisons, but have not changed the basic socio-economic or 'national' frameworks.[6]

Global history starts from a different place and follows different priorities, seeking connections and patterns in any and all aspects of planetary life, society and environment, encouraging attention to different scales of analysis, from overview to localities or even individuals, and exploring the connections across different scales.[7] Most importantly, global

---

[3] For historians troubled by the origins of their discipline as the handmaiden of nationalism, it is essential to write actively against the dangerous resurgence of nationalistic sentiment, action and policies around the world. The nineteenth-century concept of the nation-state has proved persistently powerful, but any positive aspects visible in the liberation movements that countered colonialism in the long twentieth century have long been overshadowed by the oppressions of powerful state actors wielding the same idea in – once again – increasingly pernicious ways.

[4] I am indebted to the succinct and cogent distinctions made by Pamela Crossley, *What is Global History?* (Cambridge, 2008).

[5] This approach is rooted in World Systems Analysis, starting with Immanuel Wallerstein, *The Modern World-System* (2 vols., New York, 1974). The term 'global' may also be rejected on exactly the same grounds (R. I. Moore, personal communication); the point, of course, is not the label but the definition.

[6] Most notably, Kenneth Pomeranz, *The Great Divergence: China, Europe, and the Making of the Modern World Economy* (Princeton, 2000).

[7] Ken Pomeranz also drew attention to the question of scale in his 2013 presidential address to the American Historical Association: 'Histories for a Less National Age',

approaches resist teleology to focus on the historical present, exploring worlds where the future was still unknown, rather than seeking links to modernity.[8]

It is from this perspective that I eschew the word 'China'. Adopting this as a formal restriction has proved to be highly effective in forcing me to confront habits and shortcuts that I share with many others, and it makes a substantive contribution by forcing a rethink of basics such as the terminology for regions, groups and periods, which in turn requires contemplation of what these labels really mean: what are the specific referents implied by a name that seems solid until we try to define it? The answers to that question are more precisely delineated entities that require further consideration of how to structure the relationships between them, which has generated a layered approach.[9] In what follows I shall briefly discuss terminology, then explain the framework I am adopting, and illustrate it with a comparative discussion of some Liao 遼 dynasty (907–1125) cities. I hope to persuade you that other ways are possible: that we can discuss premodern history without the misleading shorthand of 'national' terminology, and that this offers opportunities for fresh insights and lines of enquiry.

Terminology

The first problem is what to call the groups who may be identified in this segment of history. 'The Chinese' or 'the Koreans' refer to the people claimed by (and indeed claiming) modern states,[10] and use of these terms by present-day historians for pre-modern contexts implies primordial national status (in the technical sense) for these groups in ways that are denied to, for instance, 'the Uyghurs' or 'the Tibetans', whose premodern states and empires have transmuted into 'minority ethnic' status

---

American Historical Review, 119 (2014), 1–22, https://academic.oup.com/ahr/article/119/1/1/20264 (accessed 11 January 2019).

[8] For further comment in this vein see Catherine Holmes and Naomi Standen, 'Introduction: Towards a Global Middle Ages', in *The Global Middle Ages*, Past & Present, Supplement 13, ed. Catherine Holmes and Naomi Standen (Oxford, 2018), 1–44.

[9] Braudel's environment–*longue durée–événement* division was not a direct influence on this framework, although it is entirely likely that my brain made subconscious connections. Braudel's schema concerned speeds of change over time, and mine seeks to reconfigure the lineaments of human praxis and the (largely material) worlds they inhabit. Fernand Braudel, *The Mediterranean and the Mediterranean World in the Age of Philip II*, trans. Sian Reynolds (2 vols., Berkeley, 1995).

[10] 'The Chinese' – or 'the Han Chinese' – is particularly problematical, and has latterly become subject to conceptual analysis: *Critical Han Studies: The History, Representation, and Identity of China's Majority*, ed. Thomas S. Mullaney, James Patrick Leibold, Stephane Gros and Eric Armand Vanden Bussche (Berkeley, 2012).